D0297889

Transactions of the Royal Historical Society

SIXTH SERIES

XVIII

CAMBRIDGE
UNIVERSITY PRESS

Published by the Press Syndicate of the University of Cambridge
The Edinburgh Building, Cambridge CB2 8RU, United Kingdom
32 Avenue of the Americas, New York, NY 10013–2473, USA
477 Williamstown Road, Port Melbourne, VIC 3207 Australia
Ruiz de Alarcón 13, 28014 Madrid, Spain

A catalogue record for this book is available from the British Library

First published 2008

ISBN 9780 521 429658 hardback

SUBSCRIPTIONS. The serial publications of the Royal Historical Society, *Royal Historical Society Transactions* (ISSN 0080–4401) and Camden Fifth Series (ISSN 0960–1163) volumes may be purchased together on annual subscription. The 2008 subscription price (which includes print and electronic access) is £101 (US$166 in the USA, Canada and Mexico) and includes Camden Fifth Series, volumes 32 and 33 (published in July and December) and Transactions Sixth Series, volume 18 (published in December). Japanese prices are available from Kinokuniya Company Ltd, PO Box 55, Chitose, Tokyo 156, Japan. EU subscribers (outside the UK) who are not registered for VAT should add VAT at their country's rate. VAT registered subscribers should provide their VAT registration number.

Subscription orders, which must be accompanied by payment, may be sent to a bookseller, subscription agent or direct to the publisher: Cambridge University Press, The Edinburgh Building, Shaftesbury Road, Cambridge CB2 8RU, UK; or in the USA, Canada and Mexico; Cambridge University Press, Journals Fulfillment Department, 100 Brook Hill Drive, West Nyack, New York 10994–2133, USA. Prices include delivery by air.

SINGLE VOLUMES AND BACK VOLUMES. A list of Royal Historical Society volumes available from Cambridge University Press may be obtained from the Humanities Marketing Department at the address above.

Printed and bound in the United Kingdom at the University Press, Cambridge

CONTENTS

PAGE

Presidential Address: Britain and Globalisation since 1850: III.
Creating the World of Bretton Woods, 1939–1958   1
Martin Daunton

High and Low: Ties of Dependence in the Frankish Kingdoms
(*The Alexander Prize Essay*)   43
Alice Rio

Text, Visualisation and Politics: London, 1150–1250   69
Derek Keene

Centre and Periphery in the European Book World   101
Andrew Pettegree

A Tale of Two Episcopal Surveys: The Strange Fates of Edmund
Grindal and Cuthbert Mayne Revisited
(*The Prothero Lecture*)   129
Peter Lake

The Language and Symbolism of Conquest in Ireland, *c.* 1790–1850   165
Jacqueline Hill

Writing War: Autobiography, Modernity and Wartime Narrative in
Nationalist China, 1937–1946   187
Rana Mitter

The Death of a Consumer Society   211
Matthew Hilton

Report of Council for 2007–2008   237

Transactions of the RHS 18 (2008), pp. 1–42 © 2008 Royal Historical Society
doi:10.1017/S0080440108000649   Printed in the United Kingdom

TRANSACTIONS OF THE

ROYAL HISTORICAL SOCIETY

PRESIDENTIAL ADDRESS

By Martin Daunton

BRITAIN AND GLOBALISATION SINCE 1850: III. CREATING THE WORLD OF BRETTON WOODS, 1939–1958

READ 23 NOVEMBER 2007

ABSTRACT. During the Second World War, attention turned to reconstructing the world economy by moving away from competitive devaluations, protectionism and economic nationalism that had marred the 1930s. The Americans had considerable economic and political power, and they wished to restore multilateral trade, fixed exchanges and convertibility of currencies. The British government was in a difficult position, for it faced a serious balance of payments deficit and large accumulations of sterling in the Commonwealth and other countries. Multilateralism and convertibility posed serious difficulties. This address considers whether the American government had economic and financial hegemony after the war, or whether it was constrained; and asks how the British government was able to manoeuvre between America, Europe and the sterling area. The result was a new trade-off between international monetary policy, free trade, capital controls and domestic economic policy that was somewhat different from the ambitions of the American government and from British commitments made during and at the end of the war.

In the first age of globalisation of the late nineteenth century, a particular policy trade-off emerged in Britain: fixed exchange rates, free capital movements, free trade and an inactive domestic monetary policy. In the second address, we saw how this trade-off changed from fixed exchanges on the gold standard to competitive devaluations; from capital mobility to controls; from open markets to imperial preference; and from passive to active domestic monetary policies through the pursuit of low interest rates. The result was that Britain experienced more rapid economic recovery than many other advanced industrial economies – but there were also serious shortcomings. Unemployment remained persistently high at a minimum of 10 per cent; total volumes of world trade declined; and nationalistic economic policies throughout the world prepared the ground for warfare. The experience of the 1930s meant that attention during the war soon turned to a new trade-off within the 'inconsistent quartet' that has been discussed in this series of presidential addresses. In this address, I will focus on the outcome at the two major conferences that shaped the post-war world: the Bretton Woods conference of 1944 that created a new international monetary regime; and the Havana conference of 1948 that shaped the trade regime. Together, they set the parameters for British economic policy for the next quarter of a century, until the collapse of the monetary regime in the aftermath of Richard Nixon's decision of 15 August 1971 to suspend the convertibility of the dollar into gold, and the entry of Britain into the European Economic Community in 1973.

The task facing British politicians and officials was a formidable one: the country faced a serious economic and financial crisis, and was apparently at the mercy of a hegemonic United States which was deeply suspicious of British trade policies, urging an end to imperial preference and a swift return to non-discrimination and multilateralism. The Americans were also anxious to return to fixed exchange rates and convertibility of currencies which would be extremely difficult given the weakness of Britain's balance of payments and the scale of Britain's commitments to the sterling area. But was America quite so hegemonic in practice? Could the British government cling to imperial preference and sustain a role for sterling in the face of American pressure? The outcome involved much more than a technical issue of economic policy, for it was also intimately connected with definitions of British identity, whether as part of a dollar-denominated Atlantic world, the sterling area based on the Commonwealth or a European currency zone. The choice also had implications for domestic economic policy, for a swift return to convertibility might entail the creation of a more flexible, market-based economy and a shift away from controls and regulations. These issues were central to British politics in the decade after the war. In this address, I will focus on the outcomes of the debates at the end of the war which created the system that survived until the early 1970s, before turning next time to the dissolution of this particular trade-off and the emergence of another under which we still live – barring any immediate collapse of the world financial system.

In the Anglo-American discussions that provided the basis for the wider agreement reached between forty-four nations represented at Bretton Woods in 1944, priority was given to reestablishing currency stability as a prerequisite for the recovery of trade. In his opening address to the conference, Henry Morgenthau, US secretary of the Treasury from 1934 to 1945, explained the priority of currency disorders to the downfall of the world economy:

> All of us have seen the great economic tragedy of our time. We saw the worldwide depression of the 1930s. We saw currency disorders develop and spread from land to land, destroying the basis for international trade and international investment and even international faith. In their wake, we saw unemployment and wretchedness – idle tools, wasted wealth. We saw their victims fall prey, in places, to demagogues and dictators. We saw bewilderment and bitterness become the breeders of fascism, and, finally, of war.[1]

Why did Morgenthau and the participants at the conference give priority to currency disorders?

Morgenthau believed, and many others agreed, that the depression of the 1930s started from currency disorders and then spread to trade; it was therefore best to fix the monetary problems first in order to create financial stability for the reemergence of multilateral trade. He, and many other leading figures in the American administration, believed that the emphasis of the Department of State under Cordell Hull on reducing trade barriers in the 1930s was inadequate. Hull was a reincarnation of Richard Cobden and his belief that free trade would link together the world in prosperity and peace. The outbreak of war showed that the policy had failed. Morgenthau complained that Hull was 'obsessed by his trade agreements and. . .failed to realize that Japanese militarism and European fascism had released new and ugly forces which. . .could not be controlled politely'. Cobdenism was not enough, for in the words of Harold Ickes, secretary of the Interior, it was 'like hunting an elephant in the jungle with a fly swatter'.[2] Further, monetary policy was technical and could be left in the hands of experts, unlike trade policy which had been a highly controversial electoral issue in Britain since the days of Joseph Chamberlain's campaign for tariff reform. During the Second World War, it continued to divide economists. The economic advisers to the British government were split between believers in the virtues of free trade, such as Lionel Robbins and Roy Harrod, and adherents of protection and imperial preference such as Hubert Henderson – with Keynes steering a pragmatic course between the two.[3] It was better to start with something

[1] *United Nations Monetary and Financial Conference, Proceedings and Documents* (US Department of State, International Organizations and Conference Series, Washington, DC, 1948), I, 81.

[2] J. M. Blum, *From the Morgenthau Diaries: Years of Crisis, 1923–38* (Boston, MA, 1959), 452–3; H. L. Ickes, *The Secret Diary of Harold L. Ickes*, II: *The Inside Struggle, 1936–39* (New York, 1953), 211, and III: *The Lowering Clouds, 1939–41* (New York, 1954), 218–19.

[3] L. Robbins, *Economic Planning and the International Order* (1937), 232–7; and *idem*, *The Economic Consequences of the War* (1939), 80–5, 88–94, 99; Harrod quoted in R. Skidelsky, *John Maynard Keynes: Fighting for Britain, 1937–46* (2000), 213, 220; H. D. Henderson, 'International Economic History of the Interwar Period', in his *The Interwar Years and Other Papers: A Selection*

that could be dealt with in a reasonably dispassionate manner, and where there was a degree of consensus.[4]

The initial need was to fix monetary disorder, but the experience of fixed exchange rates in the 1920s showed a potential danger: the nationalistic backlash against globalisation arose because domestic prosperity had apparently been sacrificed on the altar of the gold standard. Many economists and politicians on both sides of the Atlantic realised that the only way to contain this threat in future was to ensure that domestic prosperity was not undermined by policies designed for international reasons. In the words of Ragnar Nurske, a leading economist at the League of Nations, 'the problem was to find a system of international currency relations compatible with the requirements of domestic stability'.[5] Hence the first article of the new International Monetary Fund (IMF) that emerged from Bretton Woods was a commitment to 'the promotion and maintenance of employment and real income, and to the development of the productive resources of all members as primary objectives of economic policy'.[6]

Our analysis of the 'trilemma' suggests that the pursuit of domestic prosperity with international currency stability was only possible by sacrificing capital mobility so that interest rates could in future be used to maintain full employment at home without provoking international capital flows and pressure on the exchanges. Keynes saw very clearly that the free movement of capital was incompatible with an active domestic monetary policy: 'The whole management of the domestic economy depends upon being free to have the appropriate rate of interest without reference to the rates prevailing elsewhere in the world. Capital control is a corollary to this.' Hence the Bretton Woods agreement followed the line of Bertil Ohlin, a leading Swedish economist and expert on trade theory: whereas the movement of goods 'is a prerequisite of prosperity and economic growth', the movement of capital was not. The Bretton Woods conference therefore sacrificed capital mobility and article VI section 3 of the articles of agreement of the IMF stated that 'members may exercise such controls as are necessary to regulate international capital movements'. As Keynes said, 'what used to be a heresy is now endorsed as orthodox'.[7]

from the Writings of Herbert Douglas Henderson (Oxford, 1955), 290, 291, 294. On Keynes's changing position, see Skidelsky, *Fighting for Britain*.

[4] G. J. Ikenberry, 'A World Economy Restored: Expert Consensus and the Anglo-American Postwar Settlement', *International Organisation*, 46 (1992), 298–321.

[5] League of Nations [R. Nurske], *International Currency Experience: Lessons from the Interwar Period* (Geneva, 1944), 230.

[6] See J. K. Horsefield, *The International Monetary Fund, 1945–1965*, III: *Documents* (Washington, DC, 1969), 187.

[7] *The Collected Writings of John Maynard Keynes*, XXVI: *Activities, 1943–46: Shaping the Post-War World: Bretton Woods and Reparations*, ed. D. Moggridge (1980), 16–17; E. Helleiner, *States and*

Of course, general agreement on the need to resolve monetary issues did not completely remove dissension between the British and the American architects of the Bretton Woods agreement. Keynes and his American counterpart, Harry Dexter White, the assistant secretary of the Treasury, had two different visions of the post-war order. The story of the negotiations leading up to Bretton Woods is well known and does not require detailed retelling here – a clash between Keynes's clearing union and White's stabilisation fund.[8] Keynes argued that the monetary system should allow adjustments by the creditor nation (the USA) to avoid the problems experienced at the end of the First World War when debtor countries bore the brunt of adjustments through deflation to force down their costs in order to be more competitive. Given the prospect of a huge American trade surplus after the Second World War, the rest of the world would lack dollars which would create a problem for liquidity to fund world trade. Keynes felt that the USA should be obliged to reduce its surplus and that liquidity should be created through an international currency or 'Bancor'.

The Americans were suspicious, fearing that the result would be inflation and manipulation of currencies for selfish ends. The White scheme was more rigid and triumphed at Bretton Woods: it did not create an international currency; adjustments were to be made by the debtors and not by the USA. Competitive devaluations which led to 'beggar my neighbour policies' in the 1930s were banned. The dollar was pegged to gold at $35 per ounce – an arbitrary figure based on nothing more than the level to which Roosevelt allowed the price of gold to rise in the 1930s.[9] Other currencies were then pegged to the dollar within a margin of 1 per cent either way. Modest devaluations were permitted, with the right to make a larger change to the rate if there were a 'fundamental disequilibrium' between exchange rates, with no right to object that domestic policies were the cause of the problem. 'Fundamental disequilibrium' was not defined, and Per Jacobssen, managing director of the IMF, later remarked that he could no more define it than he could

the Emergence of Global Finance from Bretton Woods to the 1990s (Ithaca, 1994), 34, 37; Horsefield, International Monetary Fund, III, 194.

[8] For a good account, see Skidelsky, Fighting for Britain, Part Two. Details of discussions between Britain and the USA over currency and trade are to be found in Foreign Relations of the United States, Diplomatic Papers, 1942, I: General. The British Commonwealth, the Far East (Washington, DC, 1960), 163–242; Foreign Relations of the United States, Diplomatic Papers, 1943, I: General (Washington, DC, 1963), 1054–126; Foreign Relations of the United States, Diplomatic Papers, 1943, III: The British Commonwealth, Eastern Europe, the Far East (Washington, DC, 1963), 1–110; Foreign Relations of the United States, Diplomatic Papers, 1944, I: General: Economic and Social Matters (Washington, DC, 1967), 1–135.

[9] P. Volcker and T. Gyohten, Changing Fortunes: The World's Money and the Threat to American Leadership (New York, 1992), 8.

a pretty girl – though 'you can recognize one when you meet one'.[10] In theory, all exchange controls were to be removed after a five-year transition period and full convertibility restored.

The American position largely triumphed in the negotiations leading to Bretton Woods – not surprisingly, given the economic and financial power of the United States. What happened when White's scheme collided with economic reality after the war? Could the Americans utilise their post-war economic hegemony to impose their preferred policies; or was economic hegemony constrained in ways that allowed Britain to secure more than at first sight seemed possible? The modification of White's scheme was crucial to British economic policy and to its identity after the war as an Atlantic, imperial or European nation.

The Bretton Woods agreement was not easily implemented. There were four major issues. The first was a serious shortage of dollars after the war, for the USA would have a massive trade surplus as other countries turned to it for industrial goods during reconstruction. There was a serious problem in securing dollars to pay for imports from America, and a threat to the liquidity of the world economy. How was the dollar deficit to be covered without a serious fall in living standards? Although the European Recovery Program or Marshall Aid covered some of the dollar shortfall, what would happen when it came to an end? Was the deficit transitional, or was it long term and structural? The second issue was how Britain should respond to its balance of payments deficit. The post-war export drive to earn dollars meant that domestic consumption was held down and a policy of austerity adopted. Would the swift restoration of convertibility help by imposing discipline at fixed exchange rates so that an outflow of funds would lead to deflation and cost cutting; or would this approach lead to domestic political difficulties as well as putting pressure on the exchanges? An alternative solution was to reject fixed exchanges and allow the pound to float – a strategy that would entail a rejection of the Bretton Woods scheme. This was closely connected with a third issue: the treatment of the sterling area. Other countries held large balances of sterling accumulated during the war in payment for goods, and convertibility would mean they would switch into dollars to buy American goods. So long as sterling remained inconvertible, these countries were more or less obliged to buy British goods; convertibility would threaten British exports to these 'soft' markets as well as creating a run on the pound. Further, a decision to devalue the pound would have a serious impact on these colonies and countries in the sterling area which would find that their holdings were worth less.

Initially, the American government took a firm line, pressing for a swift return to convertibility. In 1947, the American government made a loan to Britain conditional on ending the period of transition, insisting that the British government should remove exchange controls and make sterling convertible. This was a triumph of hope over experience. Holders of previously inconvertible sterling rushed to switch into dollars, the loan was rapidly used up, and convertibility was suspended within weeks.[11] The American administration now realised that the European dollar shortage needed to be solved. The problem, it seemed to them, was a lack of production in Europe and the solution was a Customs Union in western Europe to create a large single market with American assistance through the European Recovery Program. Once the European dollar deficit was overcome, it would then be possible to move to an open international economy. The attitude of the British government was different. Although aid was obviously welcome as an alternative to domestic deflation, the dollar shortage was considered to be less the fault of European production than of the USA, and there was considerable scepticism about European integration. After all, Britain had major non-European markets, imperial preference remained a central policy, and the sterling area was central to Labour's economic policy.[12]

Discussion over trade issues started from 1941 in the context of Lend Lease. Article VII of the Lend Lease agreement of 1942 laid down that the final settlement should 'be such as not to burden commerce between the two countries but to promote mutually advantageous economic relations between them and the betterment of world-wide economic relations'. Dean Acheson, who was a member of the American team, felt that the article was too idealistic: 'So far so good; here was a blow struck for the Hull liberal commercial policies open to all. Then came the apple of discord. In addition to promoting good, the final settlement should prohibit evil, or what Mr Hull thought was evil.' The article added that the settlement should 'provide against discrimination in either the United States of America or the United Kingdom against the importation of any product originating in the other country'. In other words, the article was directed against imperial preference which led Keynes to 'burst into a speech such as only he could make', complaining that 'it saddled upon the future an ironclad formula from the Nineteenth Century', and would require an imperial conference to secure the consent of the members of the Commonwealth. Acheson pointed out that the undertaking was not onerous in reality, merely promising that after the war was over, and after receiving considerable aid, Britain would not be free to take measures

---

[11] See for example A. Cairncross, *Years of Recovery: British Economic Policy, 1945–51* (1985), ch. 6.
[12] See M. J. Hogan, *The Marshall Plan: America, Britain, and the Reconstruction of Western Europe, 1947–1952* (Cambridge, 1987).

against the USA. Article VII provoked six months of discussion before it was agreed on 23 February 1942, and it continued to cause difficulties after the war. As Keynes realised from the outset, the USA would have a massive trade surplus and other countries would have difficulties in paying so that removal of preferences and quantitative restrictions would not be simple.[13]

Of course, Hull was a proponent of the 'ironclad formula' of Richard Cobden. In his memoirs, he remarked that in 1916 he embraced the views he was later to pursue as secretary of state. Until that year, he believed that lower tariffs would reduce prices for American consumers and prevent the growth of trusts and monopolies. After it, he stressed international considerations:

> unhampered trade dovetailed with peace; high tariffs, trade barriers, and unfair competition, with war...if we could get a freer flow of trade...so that one country would not be deadly jealous of another and the living standards of all countries might rise, thereby eliminating the economic dissatisfaction that breeds war, we might have a reasonable chance of lasting peace.

In 1916, he proposed a post-war international trade conference to remove 'destructive commercial controversies', and in 1917 Woodrow Wilson's Fourteen Points called for the end of international trade barriers.[14] Hull's ambitions were not fulfilled after the First World War; they had more chance of success after the Second World War. Keynes was not impressed by the 'lunatic proposals of Mr Hull', and in his initial plans for post-war institutions he still argued that Britain should retain its protectionist measures, and that anyone who abandoned them 'would be as great a traitor to his country as if he were to sign away the British navy'.[15]

One reason for the success of the conference at Bretton Woods was that Hull was absent and attention could focus on the less contentious currency schemes. However, trade policy did not disappear from consideration and was not left entirely to Hull and his Cobdenite certainties. More realistically, James Meade put forward his plan for a 'commercial union' in 1942. This scheme would complement Keynes's 'clearing union' and it was accepted by the Board of Trade and discussed with the Americans in 1943 and then again in December 1944. Meade started by pointing to Britain's commercial problems at the end of the war, with its high dependence on imports of necessities and its need to increase exports

[13] Skidelsky, *Fighting for Britain*, 126–31, 133; D. Acheson, *Present at the Creation: My Years in the State Department* (1970), 29–30. Details of the discussions over Article VII are in *Foreign Relations of the United States, Diplomatic Papers, 1941*, III: *The British Commonwealth, the Near East and Africa* (Washington, DC, 1959), 1–53; and *Foreign Relations of the United States, Diplomatic Papers, 1942*, I: *General. The British Commonwealth, the Far East* (Washington, DC, 1960), 525–37.

[14] Cordell Hull, *Memoirs of Cordell Hull*, I (1948), 81–2.

[15] Quoted in R. Skidelsky, *John Maynard Keynes: The Economist as Saviour, 1920–1937* (1992), 476–8; and *idem*, Fighting for *Britain*, 179.

of goods which other countries could more easily do without. 'If ever there was a community which had an interest in the general removal of restrictions to international commerce, it is the United Kingdom.' In the past, British trade had been multilateral: British exports went to less-developed areas (above all, India) and the proceeds were used to buy goods from the USA. Multilateral trade was therefore necessary to improve Britain's position, which meant reducing American tariffs from their high pre-war levels and the system of bilateral trade adopted by Germany in the so-called 'Schachtian' policy which was followed by many other countries. He therefore argued for a general policy of financial and economic expansion to increase purchasing power in export markets and 'a removal of those discriminations and rigidly bilateral bargains which remove the opportunities for multilateral trading'. Self-interest as well as the commitments of Article VII meant that Britain was committed to such a policy.

Hull might agree with Meade up to this point, but then they parted company. In Meade's opinion, 'Multilateral trading and the removal of trade restrictions do not. . .imply *laissez-faire*, and are in no way incompatible with a system of state trading.' Further,

> After the war we shall not be in a good position in which we can afford *unconditionally* to abandon all protective devices. We cannot readily indulge in a unilateral policy of removing our protective armour and shall thus desire to retain the right to restrict purchases from, and to discriminate against, those countries which themselves retain highly protective commercial policies or which discriminate against ours. We shall, moreover, need to retain the right to impose more general restrictions on purchases of inessential goods or on unnecessary payments abroad so long as we are faced with an acute problem of restoring equilibrium to our international balance of payments.

Meade argued that the clearing union was essential for the reduction of restrictions on commerce and that solving the currency problem came first: 'it is only in a general milieu of economic expansion that the pressure on the balance of payments of debtor countries is likely to be sufficiently relieved to make possible a really effective lowering of protective devices'. Further, the clearing union would help stimulate the general expansion of demand which was a prior condition for the removal of trade restrictions. Meade proposed an International Commercial Union to reduce trade restrictions: preferences should not be offered to one member without being offered to all; members would reduce protective duties against each other; state trading should be allowed; and an international commission should be established to adjudicate on disputes.[16]

In October 1943, meetings were held with the Americans who were drafting their own report on commercial policy. Meade and Robbins

---

[16] 'A proposal for an International Commercial Union', in *The Collected Papers of James Meade*, III: *International Economics*, ed. S. Howson (1988), 27–35.

countered American claims that preferences (as adopted in Britain) more than tariffs (used by the Americans) diverted trade from sound economic channels. Somewhat disingenuously, they argued that the USA was a federal union with 100 per cent preference between its members whereas Britain had a Commonwealth with less than 100 per cent preference. 'Why is our arrangement sinful and theirs virtuous?' The claim that the relationship between California and Massachusetts was akin to that between Britain and New Zealand was not likely to convince the Americans, and the British negotiators had to admit that unless action was taken to end their 'peculiarly wicked and dreadful' preferences, there was not likely to be progress on commercial policy.[17]

The American government hoped that solving the currency issue would soon lead to multilateral trade. Keynes differed and commented to Treasury officials in 1944 that

> currency multilateralism is quite distinct from commercial multilateralism and that the former does not imply or require the latter. Indeed, currency multilateralism has been in the past the normal state of affairs without in fact being accompanied by commercial multilateralism. The one no more implies the other in the future than it has done in the past. The fact that those who have a strong sympathy for the one are likely to have a strong sympathy for the other also seems to me to be beside the point. Moreover there is a large and important group. . .who are decidedly in favour of currency multilateralism but very dubious about commercial multilateralism.[18]

Keynes saw potentially serious political difficulties: the commercial proposals were drawn up to satisfy American public opinion which meant they were likely to provoke opposition in Britain where there was already irritation over the terms of Lend Lease. He urged White not to misinterpret any hostile response as a reaction against internationalism – rather, 'this country is immensely exhausted and has made sacrifices so far as encumbering the future goes, far beyond those of the other United Nations'.[19] Keynes hoped for a compromise but he had a very difficult task given the post-war weakness of the British economy which soon became apparent in 1945 during his negotiation of a loan from the Americans.

Hugh Dalton, the chancellor of the Exchequer, was concerned that the Americans might make elimination of imperial preference a condition for financial assistance in 1945 as they had for Lend Lease. He telegraphed

[17] *The Wartime Diaries of Lionel Robbins and James Meade*, ed. S. Howson and D. Moggridge (Basingstoke, 1990), entries for 2 Oct, 1943, 124–5, and 13 Oct. 1943, 136–7

[18] Keynes to D. H. Robertson and W. Eady, 'Monetary and Commercial Bilateralism', 31 May 1944, in *The Collected Writings of John Maynard Keynes*, XXVI: *Activities, 1941–46: Shaping the Post-War World. Bretton Woods and Reparations*, ed. D. E. Moggridge (1980), 25–6.

[19] *Collected Writings of John Maynard Keynes*, XXVI, ed. Moggridge, Keynes to White, 24 May 1944, 27; Keynes to L. Pasvolsky, 24 May 1944, 28–9.

to Keynes in Washington that

> We have repeatedly expressed our willingness to consider preferences as part of a
> satisfactory tariff settlement, but not to treat them separately. Certainly, there will be
> very violent reaction here if preference issue is formally linked, not with commercial
> talks, but with financial deal. Indeed, a financial settlement otherwise acceptable might
> be wrecked on this issue.

If the Americans did make this mistake, Dalton suggested that Keynes
should point out the difficulties of convincing the cabinet and parliament.
As Dalton remarked, 'my task would be made hopeless if anyone can
represent that a financial pistol has been held to our head on subject
of Imperial Preference'. Further, Australia and New Zealand were
committed to imperial preference, and the Americans should not attempt
to bargain away their agreements with Britain. Of course, Frederick
Vinson, the American secretary of the Treasury, denied that he was using
a financial pistol to force Britain to make concessions: rather, his concern
was to secure support in Congress. Keynes was reassured that he could
work with Vinson for a mutually satisfactory solution.

> This does not mean that the State Department does not hold strong doctrinaire views
> or that it will be easy for us to carry a satisfactory formula. But it does mean that the
> spirit and purpose of the principal negotiators on the American side are far removed
> from threats and that in the last resort they will try hard to meet us on any point which
> they believe we genuinely regard as vital.[20]

Keynes was not normally so trusting or naïve; he was soon shown to be
wrong.

In December 1945, agreement was reached for a line of credit of
$3,750 million to purchase goods and services from the USA, to meet
post-war deficits in the balance of payments, to maintain reserves of gold
and dollars and

> to assist the United Kingdom to assume the obligations of multilateral trade. This
> credit would make it possible for the United Kingdom to relax import and exchange
> controls...and generally to move forward with the United States and other countries
> towards the common objective of expanded multilateral trade.[21]

The financial pistol was indeed held to the head of the British government,
and Attlee put a brave face on the deal. On the same day that he
announced the Anglo-American financial agreement to the Commons,
the Americans published their 'Proposals for consideration by an

[20] *Documents on British Policy Overseas, Series I*, III, ed. R. Bullen and M. E. Pelly (1986),
Mr Bevin to the earl of Halifax, 8 Oct. 1945, 200, and earl of Halifax to Bevin, 12 Oct.
1945, 216–17. For the details of discussions with the USA at the end of the war, see *Foreign
Relations of the United States, Diplomatic Papers, 1945*, VI: *The British Commonwealth, the Far East*
(Washington, DC, 1969), 1–204.
[21] *Parliamentary Debates, 5th series, 1945–46, vol. 416, House of Commons*, C. Attlee, 6 Dec. 1945,
col. 2664.

international conference of trade and employment.' The proposals started with a grand statement that collective measures designed to safeguard peace must be based not only on machinery to deal with disputes but 'on economic co-operation among nations with the object of preventing and removing economic and social maladjustments, of achieving fairness and equity in economic relations between states, and of raising the level of economic well-being among all peoples'. The foundation of such a policy was 'the attainment of approximately full employment by the major industrial and trading nations' which was

> essential to the expansion of international trade on which the full prosperity of these and other nations depends; to the full realization of the objectives of all liberal international agreements in such fields as commercial policy, commodity problems, restrictive business practices, monetary stabilization, and investment; and, therefore, to the preservation of world peace and security.

But in agreeing to achieve full employment, a country could not take measures which would create unemployment elsewhere or were incompatible with a commitment to promote an expanding volume of international trade.[22]

Attlee endorsed these proposals as a basis for discussion, and agreed with the broad objectives of a code of conduct for international commerce and its expansion. However, he also made his doubts clear. His Commons statement, which was cleared with the Americans, did not make a pledge to multilateralism and he stressed the need to control imports so long as necessary to restore the balance of payments. He gave more weight to the need for domestic policies to create high and stable employment as a condition for trade expansion than did the Americans. Also, he agreed to contract imperial preference with a very significant condition, that 'there is adequate compensation in the form of improvement in trading conditions between Commonwealth and Empire countries and the rest of the world'. The Dominions were independent agents and Britain could not unilaterally surrender their preferences. Neither did the proposals lay down in advance how far the process of reducing preferences should go: much would depend on how far the Americans would reduce their tariffs. Multilateralism could not be a one-way process of Britain surrendering its preferences; the Americans needed to open their own markets.[23]

Just how much would Attlee's ministers be able to achieve as negotiations started? Article VII and the Anglo-American loan agreement had apparently committed the government to end preferences, and the British were in an extremely weak economic position. Would they be

[22] Parliamentary Papers [hereafter PP] 1945–6 XXVI, *Proposals for Consideration by an International Conference of Trade and Employment as Transmitted by the Secretary of State of the United States of America to His Majesty's Ambassador at Washington, 6 Dec. 1945.*

[23] Attlee, *Parliamentary Debates 5th series, vol. 416*, 6 Dec. 1945 cols. 2662–70.

able to limit American demands to fulfil the commitments of 1942 and 1945? The British government was in a perilous financial position in negotiating with the Americans, and also had an internal ideological difficulty in reconciling a commitment to multilateralism with a belief in planning. The issue was well expressed by Raymond Street, a leading spokesman for the Lancashire cotton industry:

> multilateralism was inconsistent with too much planning at home. In a multilateral world you could not say beforehand that the cotton industry should be of such and such a size. You had to let the efforts and ingenuities of the exporters determine what size of an export trade was obtainable and that must govern the size of your industry.[24]

The Labour party's commitment to domestic planning was complemented by a belief in international planning which led to 'a paradox long implicit in its ideology'. International forms of planning implied a loss of national sovereignty: how could this be reconciled with greater state control over the domestic economy'? Was it possible to strengthen control over the national economy and abolish economic nationalism through international planning which implied a weakening of national sovereignty? Clearly, Labour's definition of multilateralism was not the same as that of the State Department, as was already apparent in Meade's commitment to state trading. Dalton believed that multilateralism meant agreements between governments to create

> the most sensible forms of International Economic specialisation...the *ultimate* goal, must, I think, be a kind of supreme International Economic Planning Body, which would attempt to co-ordinate the various Agreements between Governments and producers, and would all the time be suggesting ways of improving agreements so as to secure a more sensible distribution of resources.

R. W. B. 'Otto' Clarke of the Treasury noted in 1946 that the combination of liberal international economic policy with planning at home led into a 'theological maze'. The tension was not only ideological but practical. A commitment to trade liberalisation was needed to secure American support, yet the British government knew the dangers to the balance of payments. The only way to proceed was to combine monetary and commercial multilateralism with a domestic policy of exchange controls, import controls and state trading for both ideological and practical reasons. As Attlee admitted in 1946, 'In certain specific points of world economic planning, we find the United States in agreement with us, but, generally speaking, they hold a capitalist philosophy which we do not accept.'[25] The tension between the two policy desiderata of

---

[24] *Lancashire and Whitehall: The Diary of Sir Raymond Street*, II: *1939–1957*, ed. M. Dupree (Manchester, 1987), 316, entry for 8 Jan. 1946.

[25] R. Toye, 'The Labour Party's External Economic Policy in the 1940s', *Historical Journal*, 43 (2000), 190, 195, 204, 215.

internationalism and domestic planning was not easily resolved and dominated the decade after the war.

The proposals on trade were initially considered in London in October 1946 and then at a conference in Geneva in April 1947. In the words of Street, the negotiations were 'a business of unbelievable intricacy and frustration. A dozen nations all engaged in cross negotiations on tariff schedules of appalling complexity: never anything final: pull baker, pull devil interminably.' The problem for the British delegation was in deciding how far to go in meeting the Americans in a compromise which would create 'a barrier against an otherwise inevitable trend to economic nationalism'. Will Clayton, the assistant secretary of state of the USA, was in the same mould as Hull. In the opinion of Harold Wilson, he was 'nice and well-intentioned but woolly in his mental processes and dominated by rigid conceptions held in a sort of self-righteous haze'; his contribution to discussions 'often seemed like discourses on points of theological dogma or morality'. When he met Stafford Cripps in 1947, Clayton complained that the terms of the loan of 1945 had not been fulfilled and that Britain had only offered a 'pitifully small' elimination of three minor preferences out of sixty-three required by the Americans. By contrast, Clayton pointed out that the Americans were willing to make a cut of 50 per cent in tariffs on British goods. For his part, Cripps was unimpressed, arguing that preferences could not be abandoned without the consent of the Dominions, and that

> The Labour Party, which a few years ago was generally opposed to preferences, has now changed its view and is substantially in favour of their retention. The great help afforded by the Dominions during the war was probably the reason for this change of view. We have, however, undertaken not to extend the preferential system and we can deal with the question of elimination by progressive reduction.

The Americans in general and Clayton in particular were treated as in need of education in the economic realities of the post-war world. Wilson was prepared to take a firm line, for he felt that the situation 'had changed a great deal since Cordell Hull saturated the State Department at Washington with his almost religious convictions on the subject of Tariff Reductions'. Wilson was therefore willing to take a robust line with Clayton and he went on the offensive at Geneva, arguing that 'the dream of multilateralism was fairly well bust', and that America had shown itself unwilling to make any real concession. This was a high risk strategy of facing down the Americans, threatening the entire success of the Geneva discussions and the future of the International Trade Organisation (ITO).[26]

---

[26] *Lancashire and Whitehall*, ed. Dupree, 408–9, 414; The National Archives [hereafter TNA], BT11/3646, record of conversation between Cripps and Clayton, 12 July 1947, FO371/62305, discussion between president of the Board of Trade and Mr Clayton, 16 July

The gamble paid off, for Clayton's demand for the total elimination of all preferences was seen as impracticable by the other American negotiators who realised that more would be lost if they did not come to a compromise with Britain.[27] The British were relatively content with their success at Geneva. The draft charter of the ITO and the General Agreement on Tariffs and Trade were then discussed at a conference held at Havana between November 1947 and March 1948. Clayton placed great hopes on the trade charter:

> Without it, nationalism would rule in the economic and political world, shattering our hopes for a prosperous and peaceful world. Between world wars I and II, nations had acted unilaterally in international economic affairs. Such action would benefit a nation only until other nations took similar action. In the end, all countries had been hurt and embittered. . .a charter for organizing the world effectively for international economic co-operation was urgently needed, as otherwise all efforts would prove futile; restored productivity would again bring unmarketable surpluses and starvation prices; any aid provided would be a mere palliative. . .The decisions taken in Havana would certainly fix the pattern of international trade for many years to come. There were only two roads open to the world, one leading to multilateral, non-discriminatory trade with a great increase in the production, distribution and consumption of goods and happier relationships between all countries; the other leading to economic nationalism, bilateralism, discriminatory practices, a lowering of the standard of living and bad feeling all around. It was up to this Conference to choose which road to take.[28]

Here was a crucial moment in the formation of the post-war world. Would Britain be able to maintain some of what it hoped to have secured in Geneva, given its own financial weakness, the economic might of the Americans and the obligations laid down in Article VII and in the Anglo-American loan agreement?

At the conclusion of the Havana conference, Wilson and Cripps commented that 'it has not on the whole gone well for us'. The terms achieved at Geneva were eroded, largely – the British complained – 'because of a tendency on the part of the United States to appease countries other than ourselves – they had appeased us fairly extensively at an earlier stage – by making concessions contrary to both American and UK interests'.[29] The final comment is interesting: it was less that the Americans imposed their will on the British than that the Americans gave way on their own position, so that their hegemony was constrained. Furthermore, despite the erosion of the American and British position

1947. For American papers on Geneva, see *Foreign Relations of the United States, 1947*, I: *General: The United Nations* (Washington, DC, 1973), 909–1025

[27] See the oral interview with Winthrop G. Brown on 25 May 1973 in the Harry S. Truman Library.

[28] TNA, BT11/5206, minutes of third plenary meeting, 26 Nov. 1947.

[29] TNA, PREM8/1416, prime minister, Havana Trade Conference, memorandum by the chancellor of the Exchequer and the president of the Board of Trade, EPC(48)16, 10 Mar. 1948.

at Havana, Britain still preserved imperial preferences in the face of everything that had conspired against them since 1942.

In the initial talks in London and in the conference at Geneva, representatives of the under-developed world demanded quantitative restrictions and preferences between neighbouring states which were inconsistent with multilateral trade. They did not make much progress at Geneva, but many more under-developed countries were represented at Havana and the balance of power changed. Development became the central issue with the under-developed countries taking it as axiomatic that the Geneva text of the Charter was heavily weighted in favour of the 'big commercial countries'. In particular, the Latin American countries played a crucial role. They were concerned that America was turning its attention to the reconstruction of Europe through the Marshall Plan and that

> the fairy godmother of the North was deserting them in favour of Europe. Their acquaintance with socialist ideas had converted them to a form of international socialism in which the richer countries were under an obligation to the poorer countries to promote the economic development of these countries and to raise their standard of living up to that of the richer countries.[30]

During the war, new industries developed in Latin America as a result of a reduction in imports from the United States and Europe; after the war, Latin Americans feared the revival of European competition. Their aim was to maintain quantitative restrictions and preferential arrangements to encourage economic development within Latin America, based on economic integration and import-substituting industrialisation. Their approach was clearly expressed by the representative of Venezuela in December 1947:

> The equality embodied in the Charter must not be of the nineteenth-century type, which actually established disequality by making it impossible, for instance, for Latin American Countries to develop new economies. During that period they had furnished raw materials and had been a dumping ground for finished products. This had now been substituted by the just idea of economic interdependence for the welfare of all. A Charter would not be possible unless the old prejudices were discarded and instead modern dynamic principles of co-operation adopted.[31]

---

[30] TNA, BT64/484, TN(48)5, Trade Negotiations Committee, Havana Trade Conference, I: Report on the Havana Conference; *Documents on Canadian External Relations*, XIV, 581, secretary of state for external affairs to heads of post abroad, 4 June 1948 and 582, chief delegate, delegation to the United Nations Conference on Trade and Employment to secretary of state for external affairs, 13 July 1948, at http://www.international.gc.ca/department/history/dcer/details-en.asp?intRefid=10321 and http://www.international.gc.ca/department/history/dv=cer/details-en.asp?intRefid=10322, last accessed 5 Apr. 2008. For American papers on Havana, see *Foreign Relations of the United States, 1948*, I: *Part 2, General: The United Nations* (Washington, DC, 1976), 802–900.

[31] TNA, BT11/5206, seventh plenary meeting, 29 Nov. 1947.

Such an approach clearly threatened multilateralism and might harm British export markets in the undeveloped economies.

The British complained that the Americans had lurched from taking too rigid a line against the under-developed countries at Geneva, where they had to be pressed into compromise, to adopting too conciliatory a line at Havana. The Americans wished to bring as many countries as possible into the ITO on the grounds that 'in the present state of the world a comprehensive International Trade Organization is more important than the securing of a Charter with only limited adherence but which safeguards our and their position more effectively'. Perhaps it was better to have the undeveloped economies inside the ITO and under control than outside. The ability of the under-developed countries to secure concessions was made possible by a shift in the voting system at Havana. In an attempt to secure a compromise, the leading industrial economies abandoned their preferred system of voting weighted by trade, and instead adopted a franchise of one country, one vote. Rather than expressing gratitude, as was naïvely assumed, the majority of undeveloped countries could instead press for greater concessions that were deeply disliked by the British.[32]

One concession was protective or development quotas designed to restrict imports in order to develop the infant industries of undeveloped countries. The Americans opposed any such concession at London and Geneva, and at this stage the British urged a compromise that would meet the needs of the under-developed countries as well as safeguarding Britain's export trade. However, the Americans offered further concessions at Havana that weakened the control of the ITO and reduced the safeguards on British exports. Despite British concerns, there seemed no alternative but to accept. The second concession was the right to introduce new preferences. At Geneva, no new preferences were allowed unless a two-thirds majority of the ITO agreed that they were needed for economic development. At Havana, new preferences could be introduced provided they were within the same economic region and were needed for development. Since Britain was committed to ending its own preferences, there was an obvious lack of symmetry if other countries were able to introduce new preferences which would hit British export markets. The issue was finally resolved by inserting a footnote to the effect that an economic region could be defined in terms of integration as well as proximity – a definition that was specifically noted to cover the

---

[32] TNA, PREM8/1416, CP(48)84, cabinet, Havana Trade Conference, memorandum by the president of the Board of Trade, H. Wilson, 12 Mar. 1948; *Documents on Canadian External Relations*, XIV, 581 and 582.

British empire. Hence Commonwealth preferences could be preserved, something at odds with the agreements of 1942 and 1945.[33]

Although the British contemplated adjourning the conference, in the end Cripps and Wilson felt that they could not stand out against the Americans and reluctantly agreed to the terms of the charter. Wilson realised that Britain could scarcely pull out at the end of a long process of negotiation after working so closely with the Americans. Such a decision would puzzle other countries which were eager to develop links outside the Russian sphere of influence, and would cause consternation in western Europe which was reluctant to threaten Marshall Aid. Wilson concluded that

> doubts that may still exist as to the lack of positive advantage to our export trade must take second place. If we were to stand out at this stage we should do so practically alone. The Americans would undoubtedly be able to cast the odium of breakdown on us and thereby gain credit with all the under-developed countries, including nearly all the Latin-Americans and probably India and Ceylon as well. We should also have increased the risk that the Americans would not be able to carry through their programme of reducing their own tariff which is very much in our own long-term economic interest...Finally we should have no support from the Commonwealth, not even on the question of new preferences.

Above all, the ITO seemed a great step forward

> as a focus for energies working in favour of a restoration of multi-lateral trade in a world which increasingly conducts its trade on a principle of bilateral barter. It is important that such a focus should exist, particularly from the point of view of this country which cannot hope to recover viability at a tolerable standard of living without a restoration of the triangular flow of trade.

Wilson argued that a rejection of the Charter would destroy the ITO which was part of Labour's commitment to international co-operation; it would also place 'a potent weapon in the hands of the forces of isolationism in the United States'.[34] In fact, Congress did not ratify the ITO which fell foul of the 'perfectionists' who felt it was insufficiently committed to free trade and the 'protectionists' who felt that it surrendered too much.[35] The Americans did not retreat into isolationism but the ambitions

---

[33] TNA, PREM8/1416, CP(48)84, cabinet, Havana Trade Conference, memorandum by the Board of Trade, H. Wilson, 12 Mar. 1948; CAB134/217/16, Cabinet Economic Policy Committee, Havana Trade Conference, memorandum by the chancellor of the Exchequer and the president of the Board of Trade, EPC(48)16, 8 Mar. 1948.

[34] TNA, PREM8/1416, EPC(48)16, prime minister, Havana Trade Conference, memorandum by the chancellor of the Exchequer and president of the Board of Trade, 10 Mar. 1948; CP(48)84, cabinet, Havana Trade Conference, memorandum by the Board of Trade, H. Wilson, 12 Mar. 1948; CP(49)114, cabinet, Havana Charter for an International Trade Organisation, memorandum by the president of the Board of Trade, 10 May 1949.

[35] S. A. Aaronson, *Trade and the American Dream: A Social History of Postwar Trade Policy* (Lexington, KY, 1996), 115; W. Diebold, 'The End of the ITO', *Essays in International Finance*, 16 (1952), 16–24.

of Hull and Clayton were frustrated, and their hegemony was more apparent than real. In the final outcome, the Havana compromise was less unfavourable to Britain than Wilson claimed and certainly than might have been expected given the terms of Lend Lease and the post-war loan. American policy had to turn away from the pursuit of multilateralism and convertibility to a more gradual and realistic programme. In one sense, this was exactly what the British had always wanted; in another, it posed a threat to British ambitions for it rested on European integration. Was such an approach compatible with the sterling area and Britain's identity as an imperial or global power? Could it cling on to this role and keep a 'two-world' system based on the dollar and sterling areas? Could it attempt to introduce convertibility by abandoning some of the central tenets of the Bretton Woods system of fixed exchange rates?

At the end of 1949 and early 1950, American and European thinking turned in a new direction – the European Payments Union (EPU) which was devised within the American's European Co-operation Administration that ran the European Recovery Program. The EPU was part of a more active American policy of European integration designed to supercede the bilateral agreements that formed the initial basis for the post-war recovery of European trade. Above all, the EPU would resolve the problems of liquidity that were holding back trade, and would be a first step towards multilateralism. The initial proposal was that each country would make a monthly return of its net balances; instead of each pair of countries settling their balances, offsetting claims would be cancelled and each country would be left with a single payment to the EPU as a whole. Payment was not needed up to a certain amount, but when the credit of the member was exhausted, payment would be required – partly in gold – and the management board could force corrective measures. These measures would impose discipline in bringing the balance of payments of deficit countries back into equilibrium.

The EPU inserted some of the elements of Keynes's clearing union into the European monetary system, helping resolve some of the problems of liquidity and assisting in the liberalisation of intra-European trade. But the EPU also posed serious problems for Britain: what would it mean for the survival of the sterling area, imperial preference and Britain's identity as a major imperial power? Should Britain join this new European venture or maintain its separate identity? The British government was wary, for it wished to reconcile the EPU with the continuation of the sterling area and its status as a reserve currency. The British government argued that the strength of sterling was vital for the liberalisation of trade and convertibility so that any action to bolster it was beneficial – a claim that was not entirely disingenuous given that about half of international payments were still in sterling. If Britain were to join the EPU, the government argued that it should be on different terms designed to retain the status of sterling as a key currency. They hoped that sterling would form a large element in European reserves and in clearings within Europe. Further, Britain wished to retain its existing bilateral agreements and above all to preserve imperial preference. The EPU also seemed to threaten British sovereignty in determining domestic economic policies. The British government was hostile to payments in gold, preferring to settle deficits through credit and wishing to have the right to discriminate against any country whose surplus went over a certain level. Such sentiments were complemented by hostility to active intervention in domestic affairs by the management board. Whether the British would join the EPU was an open question, raising as it did fundamental issues about its identity and its ability to pursue its own domestic policies.[36]

The governor of the National Bank of Belgium was rightly suspicious of the intentions of the British government: was it merely seeking to use the EPU when payments were in its interests, taking full part in its running whilst failing to carry any of the risks? He complained that

> The British proposal was unacceptable since, in essence, it meant allowing Britain to continue to enjoy the advantages of its bilateral agreements, when that is more advantageous, while giving it access to the Payments Union when a settlement through that channel is better, without its having to assume any commitments under the Union or share any of the risk involved in setting it up.[37]

The Americans were equally suspicious. If the bilateral deals continued, much trade would be outside the EPU and would evade the need to pay gold that the Americans felt necessary 'to facilitate the exercise of the classic pressures on debtors to balance their accounts'. However, the American administration wished to include Britain and the sterling area in any European system as a step towards the removal of bilateralism and discrimination. Eventually, the British government concluded that 'there was no hope of securing any material improvement on the Americans' proposals', and opted to join the EPU.[38] In the fraught negotiations

---

[36] The best account of the genesis of the EPU is J. J. Kaplan and G. Schleiminger, *The European Payments Union: Financial Diplomacy in the 1950s* (Oxford, 1989); for British perceptions and negotiations, see the files in TNA, FO371/87110-32, FO371/121925-8; CAB134/225; PREM11/1807 and T232/328-9.

[37] Letter from H. Ansiaux to P. van Zeeland, Brussels, 27 Mar. 1950, Archives historiques des Communautés européenes, Florence, Depots, DEP. Organisation de cooperation et de développement économiqes. OECD. European Payments Union/European Monetary Agreement, EPU/EMA. EPU/EMA 8 accessed 19 June 2008 at http://www.ena.lu/mce.swf?doc=10265&lang=2.

[38] Kaplan and Schleiminger, *European Payments Union*, 35–7, 49–53, 63–79; TNA, CAB134/225, Cabinet Economic Policy Committee, a new scheme for intra-European payments, memorandum by the chancellor of the Exchequer, 7 Jan. 1950; FO37/8110,

leading to British membership, who exactly won? Did the Americans impose their will or were they again constrained?

The British reported that the US Treasury felt that 'the scheme was very different from that originally proposed by the United States'.[39] Alan Milward goes so far as to see the EPU as a defeat of American ambitions to create full economic and political integration in Europe as a step towards full multilateralism. In his view, the American government shifted its attitude towards the sterling area, fearing that Britain, far from spearheading European integration as the Americans hoped, might withdraw into the sterling area and create a 'two-world' system based on 'hard' dollars and 'soft' pounds. Particularly after the devaluation of the pound in 1949, the American government realised that 'its real interests were more affected by the world-wide ramifications of British and sterling area trade than by Britain's role in Europe'. On this view, American policy was defeated and the European nation state survived.[40] Other historians believe that Milward exaggerates the extent of 'defeat', and Charles Maier is nearer the mark in seeing debates over international payments after 1944 'as a single post-war process, which comprised a passage from a sterling-based system to one of dollar ascendancy. In this transition Americans learned that they had to prop up sterling even as they partially displaced it, since it remained such an extensive international means of payment.' Meanwhile, the British realised that the pound could no longer maintain its earlier dominant role: a *modus vivendi* with the dollar had to be found. As Maier points out, 'between the British recognition that the pound could no longer dominate, and American recognition that sterling still had a role to play, there was space for compromise'.[41] The process was not so much one of defeat of American policy as pragmatic adjustments to manage the shift from one core currency (sterling) to another (the dollar) – a process that is extremely rare and potentially full of danger for the world economy.[42]

'European payments scheme', R. M. K. Slater, 5 Apr. 1950; FO37/87110, No. 79 Intel, 'European Payments Union', 22 Apr. 1950; FO37/87113, 'EPU', E. A. Berthoud, 16 May 1950; FO371/87113, 'Proposals by the UK delegation in regard to the establishment of a European Payments Union', Paris, 19 May 1950; FO371/87114, ER(P)(50)9, Organisation for European Economic Co-operation UK delegation, European Payments Union, E. L. Hall-Patch, 4 June 1950.

[39] TNA, T232/199, telegram, 23 June 1950

[40] A. Milward, *The Reconstruction of Western Europe, 1945–51* (1984), 333–4, 472–3; and *idem*, *The European Rescue of the Nation State*, 2nd edn (2000). See also S. Kelly, *The Myth of Mr Butskell: The Politics of British Economic Policy, 1950–55* (Aldershot, 2002), 116–23.

[41] C. S. Maier, 'The Making of "Pax Americana": Formative Moments of United States Ascendancy', in *The Quest for Stability*, ed. R. Ahmann, A. Birke and M. Howard (Oxford, 1994), 417–18.

[42] See B. Eichengreen, *Global Imbalances and the Lessons of Bretton Woods* (Cambridge, MA, 2007), ch. 4.

The British realised that there was more likelihood of a compromise within the European negotiations than in the discussions that were taking place between America, Britain and Canada after devaluation in 1949. Both the British and the American delegates at these ABC talks were eager to make sterling convertible and were doubtful of European integration, and there was even talk of an Anglo-American currency union. But the discussions soon stalled. The British were loathe to deflate the economy and cut expenditure on social welfare which would be necessary to make British goods more competitive, and so strengthen the balance of payments as a prerequisite for convertibility. Instead, they urged the Americans to open their markets to sterling goods and to fund some of the sterling balances or, failing this, to introduce convertibility with restrictions on American imports into Britain through trade discrimination. As the British pointed out, 'if the Americans want convertibility and non-discrimination, they will get neither. If they are prepared to take convertibility without non-discrimination there is a chance.' The Americans could not accept this position in the ABC talks, and the British realised that the European negotiations offered more room for manoeuvre. Hugh Gaitskell noted in his diary that 'in the battle we shall have to fight [with the IMF and the US Treasury over convertibility and non-discrimination], ECA might become our allies'.[43]

In the negotiations over the EPU, the British dropped their impracticable ambition to make sterling a central element in European reserves. They reached a compromise on the use of gold at the expense of Belgium which was the only economy in surplus with the whole of Europe and therefore most eager to have payments in gold. Britain also secured American acceptance of the special needs of sterling balances, and other European countries came to share British concerns over a strong management board. In the view of Kaplan and Schleiminger, a compromise was struck between the major countries involved – the USA, Britain and Belgium – in a way that 'fairly reflected a balance of the countervailing perceptions of the three major interested participants' and 'served well the interests of the community as a whole'.[44] Furthermore, the outcome should be placed in a wider context of strategic planning. Richard Toye and Till Geiger argue that British ministers decided to join the EPU as a concession to gain US support for strengthening NATO and making a greater contribution to the defence of Europe. In their opinion,

> the US administration gained the technical outcome it desired over European payments, which in turn helped the British to strengthen the US commitment to NATO. Therefore, the British decision to join EPU...was the tale of a struggle to resolve competing

[43] Kaplan and Schleiminger, *European Payments Union*, 61, 68–71; TNA, T236/2400, 'Currency Union with the US', Nov. 1949; *The Diary of Hugh Gaitskell 1945–1956*, ed. P. M. Williams (1983), 181.

[44] Kaplan and Schleiminger, *European Payments Union*, 61, ch. 4.

obligations, and, in this case, of the pragmatic subordination of economic anxieties in the interests of military security.[45]

Nevertheless, membership remained reluctant and guarded, and alternatives were soon proposed which would give a greater role to sterling, change the nature of domestic economic policy and threaten the Bretton Woods system of fixed but variable exchange rates. The EPU had made concessions to the role of sterling without removing the problems. By 1952, the issue was once more pressing. Marshall Aid was due to come to an end and the USA and Britain failed to reach an agreement on further assistance. The USA pressed for a commitment to convertibility and multilateralism which the chancellor in the new Conservative administration, R. A. Butler, was wary of giving. The US State Department was critical of British policies. In its view, the government was failing to take sufficient action against domestic inflation which was being fuelled by increases in social services' expenditure. Further, restrictive practices in industry and labour led to low productivity and hence to difficulties with the balance of payments. The Labour government's commitment to planning and to the use of agreements with unions and industrial associations to limit wages and dividends, complemented by controls over domestic and international competition, led to a 'low effort bargain'. The State Department was critical of this approach – and so were some voices at the Bank of England and Treasury. The sterling area was also seen as a source of instability. British policy was characterised as 'weak and opportunistic', and the State Department felt that 'it is difficult to provide assistance to a country without tending to accustom that country to a standard of living which depends on the continuation of US assistance and in a sense tends to postpone the necessity for becoming competitive and earning its own way'.[46] As Britain's balance of payments deficit mounted in early 1952, discussions turned to retrenchment and restrictions, but also to the more radical policies of Operation ROBOT which would restore convertibility by allowing the pound to float. This solution would have threatened the very basis of the Bretton Woods agreement and disrupted the EPU.

The initial idea of ROBOT was developed by George Bolton of the Bank of England, aided by Lucius Thompson-McCausland, and it was then modified in association with two officials from the Treasury's overseas finance division – Otto Clarke and Leslie Rowan. The acronym

[45] R. Toye and T. Geiger, 'Britain, America and the Origins of the European Payments Union: A Reassessment', available at http://eric.exeter.ac.uk/exeter/handle/10036/31032 last accessed 18 July 2008.

[46] National Archives and Record Administration, 841.00/12–2651, 'The Long-Run Economic Problem of the United Kingdom', Dec. 1951; S. N. Broadberry and N. R. F. Crafts, 'British Economic Policy and Industrial Performance in the Early Post-War Period', *Business History*, 38 (1996), 65–91.

came from their names – with the further implication that it offered an automatic, effective solution to the difficulties facing the British economy. Even Clarke admitted that the proposal was so far-reaching that 'the imagination boggles at rushing it through'.[47] The scheme underwent a number of iterations over the next few months but the essential point was that the exchange rate for the pound would be set by the foreign exchange markets within a band of 15 per cent either side of $2.80. The components of the sterling balances would then be treated in different ways. 'Overseas' or external sterling held outside the sterling area would be convertible; 80 per cent of the balances held in the sterling area would be 'blocked' and turned into government bonds; and 90 per cent of balances held in the non-sterling area outside the dollar zone would be 'blocked'. Convertibility was therefore limited. The scheme was developed unilaterally, without discussions with the Americans, the Commonwealth, Europe or the IMF – a unilateral approach which would, to put it mildly, cause some surprise.[48]

There are different interpretations of the origin of the scheme. In the opinion of Alec Cairncross, it was no more than a panic reaction of a few officials to a temporary loss of reserves which was (correctly) opposed by others, for its adoption 'would have been disastrous, politically and commercially'.[49] There is no doubt that there was a sense of crisis, for Clarke feared a collapse of confidence and a loss of effective control over the situation which would lead to 'even more unpalatable action'. Similarly, Wilfrid Eady of the Treasury took 'a "catastrophic" view of the present balance of payments crisis'.[50] However, ROBOT was more than a mere panic reaction: it involved a different perception of both international and domestic economic policy. A second interpretation makes it a battle between fractions of capital, a bid for power by finance capital which was supported by the Bank of England as a way of reasserting the role of the City of London and sterling. On this view, the central issue was the restoration of convertibility rather than a solution to the balance of payments which should instead be corrected through deflation.[51] By contrast, Jim Bulpitt and Peter Burnham argue that ROBOT owed more to Clarke and Rowan at the Treasury than it did to the Bank, and that its motivation was domestic rather than external: to

[47] TNA, T236/3240, 'Septuagesima plus', 12 Feb. 1952.

[48] For an accessible account of the scheme and its politics, see P. Hennessy, *Having It So Good: Britain in the 1950s* (2006), 199–217.

[49] Cairncross, *Years of Recovery*, ch. 9; quotation is on 270.

[50] For example, TNA, T236/3241, 'ESP: causes and consequences', R. W. B. Clarke, 26 Feb. 1952; T236/3241, W. Eady to E. Bridges, 26 Feb. 1952 . These views were expressed in the various drafts of a memorandum for the chancellor in T236/3241.

[51] S. J. Procter, 'Floating Convertibility: The Emergence of the Robot Plan, 1951–52', *Contemporary Record*, 7 (1993), 25.

create competitiveness and flexibility. By allowing the pound to float, domestic economic controls and regulations to protect the external position would no longer be needed, and a free market could be created:

> Robot is usually interpreted as an external economic strategy with awkward domestic consequences. We consider Robot to have been primarily a market-based, domestic, supply side strategy, accompanied by the necessary external economic policy supports. In other words, it is plausible to see Robot as a means fundamentally to enhance the competitiveness of the British economy.[52]

On this view, ROBOT was not a panic reaction or a bid for power by the City: it was a fork in the road between a free-market economy and a 'stultifying interventionist consensus'. It would have allowed the Conservative government to break the restrictive barriers criticised by the State Department and instil market discipline. Hence Nigel Lawson argues that the defeat of ROBOT was 'a missed opportunity of the first importance', marking the rejection of the 'liberating economic logic of Robot'. Instead, Britain continued for another twenty-seven years with 'the world's most rigorous, and thus most damaging, regime of exchange control', with 'an unhealthy obsession with the balance of payments at the expense of more important economic objectives and to the growing resort to harmful economic controls of all kinds – not least wage and price controls'.[53] On this view, what ROBOT could have done was eventually achieved by Mrs Thatcher and her chancellors – not least Lawson himself.

There is a clear danger of writing history with the benefit of hindsight. A reading of the contemporary documents indicates that the primary concern was convertibility of sterling which had implications for the restoration of free markets as a secondary consideration. Of course, this was most true of the Bank. Bolton pointed out that inconvertibility was possible during the war and post-war years when trade was largely in the hands of the government, but that the re-emergence of private trade and the growth of foreign transactions in sterling meant that the system was coming under strain. Non-residents were able to exchange their sterling by various stratagems at a 15 per cent discount so that there was already a 'leakage' from the sterling area. Controls were increasingly easy to evade as a result of the weakening of the regulation of shipping and trading, and the loss of public sympathy. Additional controls would be counter-productive for the very process of defending sterling would weaken it as an international currency, and might merely exclude British traders from international markets which would be taken over by foreigners. In

---

[52] J. Bulpitt and P. Burnham, 'Operation Robot and the British Political Economy in the Early 1950s: The Politics of Market Strategies', *Contemporary British History*, 13 (1991), 2–3.

[53] N. Lawson, 'Robot and the Fork in the Road', *Times Literary Supplement*, 21 Jan. 2005, 11–13; a similar view was taken by S. Brittan, *The Treasury under the Tories, 1951–1964* (Harmondsworth, 1964), 177.

Bolton's opinion, 'we have thus reached a point where we must recognise that inconvertibility of sterling in non-resident hands is not a policy which can long be sustained'. The choice was stark: sterling could be used as a domestic currency with the ending of its international status; or non-resident sterling should be made convertible to retain its role as an international currency. Bolton was untroubled by the consequences for the EPU which he felt (wrongly, as it transpired) was in danger of collapse because of the division between creditors and debtors. He felt that the result would be a split between those countries which were under the influence of the USA (such as Germany) and those who were identified with sterling (such as France). In other words, he hoped for a 'club' of European countries pegged to sterling. In his view, the solution was to replace the existing muddled system of theoretical inconvertibility and illicit convertibility with a clear division between inconvertible domestic sterling and convertible overseas sterling where the rate was set through the exchange markets. A secondary effect would be to 'restore the incentives of the price system'. The Bank realised that there were serious implications for 'the whole field of internal policy: – budget economy, tight monetary conditions, savings, incentive, harder work, more production, and the release of productive capacity for export – and also emergency cuts in dollar and other overseas expenditure'.[54]

Why would floating have these implications for domestic policy? On the face of it, floating could actually weaken incentives for domestic rigour, for a lack of competitiveness could be compensated by a fall in the exchange rate as happened in the 1970s. The result might be a failure to increase domestic productivity and at the same time to erode the value of sterling held outside Britain to the detriment of countries that had acquired sterling during the war. The Bank was well aware of the danger and argued that it must at all costs be avoided:

> We can only afford to consider a 'floating rate' as an additional weapon to protect the currency, against the background of determined policy in other fields and a firm budget. Without that background it would only be an admission of failure and a step towards collapse of the currency. If we are going to ask the sterling area to take sacrifices and impose sacrifices on foreign holders of sterling, we must show that we are playing our part and, rich and poor, are making sacrifices to help in restoring the value of our money.

This implied controls over government expenditure, the strengthening of incentives and the restoration of price mechanisms – a massive change in

---

[54] TNA, T236/3240, 'Inconvertible sterling', G. Bolton, 16 Feb. 1952 and 'Plan for "overseas sterling"', Bolton, 16 Feb. 1952; [?] at Bank of England to chancellor of the Exchequer, 13 Feb. 1952; T236/3241, 'The plan and Europe', 27 Feb. 1952; 'Europe – payments: note by the Bank of England', 29 Feb. 1952.

government policy. If these steps were not taken,

> a 'floating' rate is a polite name for progressive devaluation and would be even worse than devaluation to a new fixed rate...An international currency must have a high degree of stability. Unless we make this objective clear, we are wasting our time in trying to make sterling acceptable internationally by giving it a degree of convertibility.[55]

Clearly, Bolton's main concern was convertibility: changes in domestic policy were ancillary to restoring sterling to its position as an international currency. Would the changes in domestic policies be electorally acceptable given popular support for full employment, and could the commitment to discipline and competitiveness be made credible? As we shall see in the next address, Geoffrey Howe and Nigel Lawson faced this issue of imposing rules after 1979 when the medium-term financial strategy was used to impose discipline on domestic economic policies. But this strategy was only possible after the bruising experience of the 1970s when floating did indeed allow the pound to fall with a lack of control over domestic monetary policy. There is every reason to believe that the same would have happened in the 1950s when the commitment to full employment and the dread of a return to the 1930s made stringent policies electorally difficult.

At the Treasury, 'Otto' Clarke was also in favour of a swift restoration of convertibility, though he felt that the domestic benefits were more significant. The difference from the Bank of England was one of emphasis rather than a major divergence of aim. Like Bolton, he started from convertibility before articulating much more clearly a vision of the British economy that was fundamentally different from the system of planning and controls that had dominated since the war. He remarked that

> I cannot help feeling that we make very heavy weather of convertibility. The whole subject has become so overlaid with dogma from the 1944 Bretton Woods discussions onwards, and our 1947 experience was so disastrous, that we really recoil from it...The crucial issue is whether you mean convertibility at a fixed or floating rate. There is nothing sacrosanct about a fixed rate (except the decrees of the IMF Founding Fathers). It is obviously much easier to be convertible at a floating rate than at a fixed rate.

Inconvertibility was not an option: it could only work on the basis of a sterling-based system or 'two worlds' of the dollar and sterling areas which was 'fundamentally escapist' given the weakness of Britain and the impossibility of isolating the sterling area from America. The real choice, he argued, was between convertibility at a fixed rate or floating rate. A fixed rate was not likely to succeed for it would mean a loss of reserves which Britain did not have; and countries in the sterling area would need to accept painful adjustments to maintain the value of the pound. The alternative was to float.

---

[55] TNA, T236/3240, [?] at Bank of England to chancellor of the Exchequer, 24 Feb. 1952.

Clarke explained that the advantage of a floating rate was 'the fact that the rate moves sets up equilibrating pressures on the economy'. If the rate fell, import prices would rise and so reduce consumption; and exports would be more competitive. 'The whole economy feels these movements, and adjusts itself to them.' By contrast, a fixed exchange would only mean an outflow of gold 'without anybody noticing it at all – and no adjustment until the Government decrees it; and then it is the Government's fault, imposing artificial restrictions, and the *real* conditions of life go on as before'. Clarke was clear about the implications:

> These advantages of a floating rate are so terrific that formidable considerations would be needed to offset them, in present conditions. It is perfectly true that a floating rate makes for instability both in internal and external trade (it is terrible for planners). But of course when the pattern of prices, production, consumption, imports and exports is not the correct one for solvency, we can't afford to have it stable; we must have some forces at work which will set up incentives which tend to right it – and which act specifically on imports and exports (in this, unlike any fiscal or monetary measures, which are entirely universal in their application).

There was a danger of unemployment, for convertibility would allow holders of sterling to switch to dollars so that Britain would lose its 'soft' markets in the sterling area. But Clarke stressed that floating and convertibility could be combined with high employment 'if the structure and incentives are of a character which make the economy viable'. The problem, he argued, was that

> we have an economic structure which is built round a very large deficit with the dollar area, and this is the root of our balance of payments difficulties. We shall never overcome this particular difficulty if there are 'soft' markets abroad and a 'soft' home market...Once we get the structure of trade right, and the competitive power, I see no reason in principle why a floating rate should be damaging to full employment, except to the extent that our economy must always be flexible...in order to be able to adapt itself quickly. My own impression is that you need about 3% unemployment to achieve this, but if you get up to 1,000,000 or more it is self-destroying, as it was in the '20's and '30's.

Clarke was insistent that the only way to maintain the exchange rate was through 'the most vigorous action to develop our competitive power', rather than through the use of trade discrimination.[56]

Of course, the creation of 'hard' markets in the hope that it would stimulate competitiveness would entail a move away from the controls on competition that marked the post-war period. It would also involve a shift from limitation on profits and dividends designed to blunt wage demands. A positive commitment to incentives and hence to an increase in inequality went against widespread support for equality as both ethically just and economically efficient. The post-war institutional system would

[56] TNA, T236/3240, RWBC/4872, 'Convertibility', R. W. B. Clarke, 25 Jan. 1952; T236/3241, 'ESP: causes and consequences', R. W. B. Clarke, 26 Feb. 1952.

need to be modified and the low-effort bargain reconsidered. This was a major undertaking.

Not everyone at the Treasury was convinced by Clarke's arguments. The critics were led by Robert Hall who was highly sceptical at this 'leap in the dark' and troubled by 'the probable effect on our economy of the complete reversal of policy which these measures involve'. He was well aware that the decision to convert and float would upset the trade-off between international and domestic policies reached at the end of the war:

> The effect of all the measures proposed is to abandon the whole attempt to adjust ourselves to changes in world economic circumstances without resort to unemployment, to accept a serious deterioration in our terms of trade, and completely to abandon the attempt, which has in fact had only moderate success, to get some stability in internal prices. The measures are also likely to have the same effect on many other countries, ie to set up a downward spiral of the level of world trade as each country which is short of dollars tries to earn dollars by cutting its imports from other non-dollar countries. This happened during the great slump after 1929 and a great deal of thought has been devoted since then to trying to prevent it happening again. In the thirties there were serious political consequences in many countries from the unemployment and low prices which accompanied the slump, and these might again result.

ROBOT would, he feared, imply a return to the beggar-my-neighbour policies of the 1930s. As he saw it, convertibility would lead to trade restrictions and a 'downward spiral of international trade'. Countries in deficit with the dollar area would cut their imports from the sterling area for they could now convert their sterling balances into dollars with the result that Britain would have to restrict its imports. British exports would fall, and unemployment would rise from the current 400,000 to about 900,000. The depreciation of sterling would also increase the price of imports by up to 5 per cent, so reducing the standard of living.

> We would in fact be serving notice to our own people and to the rest of the world that we had been forced to abandon full employment and a high level of trade as immediate objectives, in the hope that we can get back to them later on through exchange depreciation and a considerable alteration of the terms of trade between the manufacturing countries of the non-dollar world on the one hand, and primary producers and the dollar world on the other.

Meanwhile, the 'gravest consequences' would be felt abroad, threatening the EPU and economic recovery in Europe as well as the proposals to strengthen European defence. The prospect did not appeal to Hall: 'The danger of carrying out the full plan seems to be that it might be self-defeating, ie the political effects abroad, and the industrial pressure at home, might lead to the demand for a return to the present system.'[57]

---

[57] TNA, T236/3240, R. Hall to E. Plowden, 22 Feb 1952; 'External action', R. Hall, 23 Feb. 1952; see the comment on Hall in T236/3240, E. Bridges to E. Plowden, 22 Feb. 1952; Hall to chancellor, 'Exchange rate etc.', n.d.

Treasury sceptics warned that 'There would be severe industrial unrest, and it would be political suicide for the Government – the discipline of the gold standard, the rule of Bankers etc.' Would the policy actually do any good?

> Convertibility cannot make a weak currency strong or restore confidence. Everyone would make hay while the sun shone and we should be swamped very quickly. . .If we haven't got the resolution to get ourselves out of our present difficulties, why suppose that we should have more resolution when convertible? Surely we would simply choose the slippery slope of depreciation.[58]

Indeed, the result might not be competition, incentives and a free market; it might be increased controls. 'It is all very well to say that a fall in the rate spreads through the economy and produces the necessary corrective action. But will it be allowed to do so?' Costs were sticky in Britain as a result of 'the soft markets sustained by our sterling indebtedness, and the discouragement to incentive produced by the shape and weight of personal taxation'. Failure to adjust might therefore result in 'something like war control conditions of the civil economy for a couple of years. Unless we can find a *positive* industrial policy internally, we shall be overwhelmed by the depression caused by your scheme. The exhilaration of convertibility will be slow to communicate itself to the general body of the people!'[59]

The decision was obviously intensely political, and in many ways ROBOT appealed to the Conservative government as a way of restoring free markets. The chancellor of the Exchequer, Butler, was initially supportive, remarking that 'there is something to be said, politically, for moving towards the system by which individuals are influenced by the operation of the price mechanism, to make their own adjustments to changing economic circumstances'. But he also saw 'great uncertainties and risks', with painful adjustments to domestic prices and wages, and some increase in unemployment. Initially, Butler felt the risk was worth taking and he informed his ministerial colleagues that the alternative was between 'bold action now, when we could still control the situation, and an uncontrolled devaluation later in the year which would have disastrous consequences'.[60] Churchill was attracted by the proposal, but other members of the cabinet were deeply suspicious. Lord Cherwell felt that it was 'a reckless leap in the dark', and he had a point. The adoption of the scheme would look like a panic measure, whether or not there was a longer-term ambition of changing the fundamental nature of the

[58] TNA, T236/3240 'Septuagesima plus – or Greek Kalends', 13 Feb. 1952.

[59] TNA, T236/3243, 'Robot', W. Eady [?] to L. Rowan, 17 Apr. 1952.

[60] TNA, T236/3241, third draft of memorandum by chancellor of the Exchequer: this was probably drafted by Clarke given the similarity of the phrasing to some of his own memoranda; T236/3241, notes of a meeting of ministers, 27 Feb. 1952.

economy. The immediate result would be to threaten much that had been achieved in the preceding years, for floating rates were contrary to the rules of the IMF at a time when the stability of the Bretton Woods system was seen as vital to economic recovery. Although the proponents of ROBOT argued that the Americans would be delighted to secure convertibility and non-discrimination, even they had to admit that the Americans would be annoyed by Britain's unilateral decision to renege on the agreement of 1944. Further, it would 'play old Harry with EPU' by splitting Europe into two camps, leading to the 'disintegration and economic collapse of Europe'. Anthony Eden, the foreign secretary, was alarmed by the effect on Europe, on unemployment and at the consequences for the European Defence Community – something that Lawson later dismissed as an example of Britain sacrificing its real interests to Europe. Whether Eden could so easily undermine the agreement on defence might be doubted. Further, there were potential difficulties at home. Could the Conservatives really contemplate the electoral consequences of an increase in prices and in unemployment? The dangers seemed too great and the cabinet therefore rejected the proposal in February and again in June 1952. In the words of Peter Hennessy, the post-war 'New Deal' triumphed in cabinet discussions, and 'the spectres of Beveridge's "Idleness" and "Want". . .pushed ROBOT beyond Butler's "art of the possible"'.[61] Britain, like the rest of western Europe, had struck a particular deal at the end of the war between different interest groups, and convertibility and ROBOT would have undermined the trade-off. In the words of Eichengreen and Braga de Macedo,

> Workers had to be convinced to trade lower current compensation for higher future living standards, despite uncertainty over whether management would keep its part of the bargain to reinvest the profits that accrued tomorrow as a result of labor's sacrifices today. Awareness of this problem rendered labor hesitant to agree. Governments reassured it by adopting policies and programs that acted as 'bonds' which would be lost in the event of reneging. They agreed to limit rates of profit taxation in return for capitalists plowing back earnings into investment. They provided limited forms of industrial support (selective investment subsidies, price-maintenance schemes, orderly marketing agreements) to sectors that would have otherwise experienced competitive difficulties. Workers were extended public programs of maintenance for the unemployed, the ill, and the elderly. This web of interlocking agreements – what might be called the mixed economy for short – functioned as an institutional exit barrier. It increased the cost of reneging on the sequence of concessions and positive actions that comprised the post-war settlement.[62]

[61] TNA, T236/3240, E. Bridges to E. Plowden, 22 Feb. 1952; Lawson, 'Robot'; Hennessy, *Having It So Good*, 204–8, 212–13 explains the political divergences within the cabinet. On the international impact, see P. Burnham, 'Britain's External Economic Policy in the Early 1950s: The Historical Significance of Operation Robot', *Twentieth Century British History*, 11 (2000), 379–408.

[62] B. Eichengreen and J. Braga de Macedo, 'The European Payments Union: History and Implications for the Evolution of the International Financial Architecture', *OECD*

The particular form taken by this settlement in Britain led to the low-effort bargain – but was there any realistic possibility of a different outcome?

The abandonment of ROBOT led to the emergence of the 'collective approach' – a final, impracticable, attempt to return to convertibility at a flexible rate. ROBOT was a unilateral scheme; the collective approach, as the name implied, would bring in the Commonwealth, Europe and the United States to reduce trade barriers and restore convertibility as the basis for growth in world trade. It was, claimed the British government, time for a new start with positive policies now that the immediate post-war problems had been resolved, for otherwise 'the restrictive policies which were inevitable for dealing with the initial post-war problems will become permanently embedded in the world economy'. Furthermore, a solution was vital in response to the cold war, for 'Economic instability breeds political instability. The lack of opportunities for economic progress both in advanced countries and in under-developed countries is both a check to national defence and a stimulus to Communism.'[63] Whether the other countries would agree was a moot point. The idea arose from the working party on convertibility set up by the Commonwealth Finance Ministers' Conference and was adopted at the Commonwealth conference in November 1952. The proposal rested on making European currencies and non-resident sterling convertible at the same time in order to prevent speculation. The USA was expected to provide a jointly managed support fund, and the exchange rate of sterling would fluctuate in order to reduce pressure. Import restrictions should be dismantled, though they could be retained against a persistent creditor – that is, the United States. Meanwhile, the USA should adopt good creditor policies. Imperial preferences should continue and rules against new preferences be relaxed.

The USA was suspicious given the expectation that it would provide a support fund for convertibility. Although Eisenhower initially seemed supportive, his cabinet was not and in Butler's words, they 'poured cold water on the collective approach'.[64] The USA preferred to maintain the EPU, European integration and the creation of the European Defence Community. They were now committed to a gradual return to convertibility which should, as Clarence Randall pointed out in his report for the Commission on Foreign Economic Policy, depend on 'a strong internal economy willing and able to control its money supply

Development Centre, Paris, Mar. 2001 at http://docentes.fe.unl.pt/~jbmacedo/oecd/triffin.html last accessed 20 Nov. 2007.

[63] TNA, T229/601, memorandum to the United States administration: the collective approach to freer trade and currencies, draft, 13 Jan. 1953.

[64] Quoted in B. W. Muirhead, 'Britain, Canada and the Collective Approach to Freer Trade and Payments, 1952–57', *Journal of Imperial and Commonwealth History*, 20 (1992), 114.

and its budget as safeguards against inflation, sufficiently mobile to make the best use of its resources, and willing and able to save in order to increase its productivity and improve its competitive position in world markets'. The implication was that such a state of affairs did not apply to Britain. The Europeans expressed 'widespread distrust', for convertibility would threaten the EPU. They felt that the priority was internal trade liberalisation whereas the collective approach would divide Europe between convertible and inconvertible currencies which would lead to renewed trade barriers. Not even the Commonwealth and sterling area were whole-heartedly behind the scheme. India was not willing to peg to a flexible pound which would threaten the value of its sterling balances, and other members of the sterling area were lukewarm. Not surprisingly, the collective approach came to nothing. The outcome was a slow return to convertibility which was eventually achieved in 1958. In the end, there was no alternative except EPU, despite British doubts and ambivalence.[65]

The collective approach was linked with a desire to restore capital exports which would assist those countries receiving funds, stimulate the world economy and contain the menace of Communism. Here, potentially, was a shift from Bretton Woods where capital mobility was sacrificed in the pursuit of financial stability and domestic economic policies. Attitudes to capital exports had changed from the period before the First World War, in part because of a shift in the nature of capital flows. Before 1914, most of the capital exports of the world came from Britain for investment in productive long-term projects that opened up the resources of the world. Between the wars, capital movements were widely seen as a short-term response to currency fluctuations and political uncertainties so that the result was speculative instability rather than long-term growth. Such a view appealed to one strand in American political culture. In Morgenthau's words, the aim of the Bretton Woods plan was to 'drive the usurious money lenders from the temple of international finance' – a trope in American thought that went back to Thomas Jefferson's hostility to Alexander Hamilton, continued in Andrew Jackson's 'bank war' with its opposition to the power of monopolistic financiers in an agrarian republic, and resurfaced in the People's Party of the 1880s and 1890s.[66]

This strand of thought was much less powerful in Britain where hostility to bankers was more muted. Nevertheless, Morgenthau's words chimed

---

[65] See Kaplan and Schleiminger, *European Payments Union*, 168–84; *Report of the Commission on Foreign Economic Policy* (Washington, DC, Jan. 1954), 73, cited in C. Schenk, *Britain and the Sterling Area: From Devaluation to Convertibility in the 1950s* (1994), 122.

[66] Cited in A. Eckes, *A Search for Solvency: Bretton Woods and the International Monetary System, 1941–1971* (Austin, 1975), 162.

with Keynes's dislike of 'casino capitalism' – the pursuit of speculative short-term capital gains rather than longer-term income streams. Keynes felt that Wall Street, and to a lesser extent the City of London, failed to 'direct new investment into the most profitable channels in terms of future yield' and were more concerned with liquid investment markets.[67] The problem was particularly severe because of short-term international capital movements and overseas investment. As he remarked in 1933,

> Advisable domestic policies might often be easier to compass, if the phenomenon known as 'the flight of capital' could be ruled out. The divorce between ownership and the real responsibility of management is serious within a country, when, as a result of joint-stock enterprise, ownership is broken up among innumerable individuals who buy their interest to-day and sell it to-morrow and lack altogether both knowledge and responsibility towards what they momentarily own. But when the same principle is applied internationally, it is, in times of stress, intolerable – I am irresponsible towards what I own and those who operate what I own are irresponsible towards me. There may be some financial calculation which shows it to be advantageous that my savings should be invested in whatever quarter of the habitable globe shows the greatest marginal efficiency of capital or the highest rate of interest. But experience is accumulating that remoteness between ownership and operation is an evil in the relations among men, likely or certain in the long run to set up strains and enmities which will bring to nought the financial calculation.[68]

Such an approach informed the thinking of the Labour party and its plans for a National Investment Board. The aim was to replace 'casino capitalism' and the assumed speculative and short-term nature of capital markets with what was believed to be long-sighted, rational investment in the hands of experts.[69] The policies of the post-war Labour government were designed to remove the power of capital markets in making investment decisions. The cultural meanings of speculation (short-term gambling and greed) and investment (long-term and prudential) informed debates over post-war policy, and capital movements were widely seen as disruptive of stable currencies and of trade.

However, a case could be made for the revival of capital exports, and not only for the benefit of the international bankers of the City of London. Capital exports could help resolve two serious problems which were connected though not completely identical: sterling balances and investment in development to counter Communism. A consistent policy was needed to deal with both issues. Some areas faced a threat from Communism in the absence of a sterling balance (such as Vietnam), whereas other countries had a sterling problem without a threat

[67] J. M. Keynes, *The General Theory of Employment, Interest and Money* (1936), 159–60.

[68] J. M. Keynes, 'National Self-Sufficiency', *New Statesman and Nation*, 8 and 15 July 1933, reprinted in *The Collected Writings of John Maynard Keynes*, XXI: *Activities, 1931–39. World Crisis and Politics in Britain and America*, ed. D. Moggridge (1982), 233–46, quote on 236.

[69] J. Tomlinson, 'Attlee's Inheritance and the Financial System: Whatever Happened to the National Investment Board?', *Financial History Review*, I (1994), 139–55.

from Communism (such as India). The two problems did coincide in south-east Asia and especially in Malaya where Britain was concerned by the threat of Communism. Malaya was the largest dollar earner in the empire, and raw materials from the area were vital to the British economy and to western Europe. The British government insisted that American funds were crucial for solving both the sterling balances and development, for Britain could not afford to fund the development of south and south-east Asia. Hence the Commonwealth conference would prepare a development programme to submit to the USA for assistance. The British government had sufficient self-awareness to realise that it could not approach America for direct aid for its domestic economy which would look like another scheme to help a bankrupt Britain, but it did, with only slightly more realism, hope that direct aid to Asia would appeal to the American administration as a way of resisting Communism, of relieving the world dollar shortage by strengthening the dollar-earning economies of south-east Asia, and of improving the position of sterling. By these means, the whole world economy would benefit. The collective approach was therefore complemented by the decision at the Commonwealth Economic Conference in 1952 to make 'a special effort to provide additional capital for Commonwealth development by facilitating the financing of schemes in other Commonwealth countries which will contribute to the improvement of the sterling area's balance of payments'.[70] The collective approach was linked with the Colombo Plan for Co-operative Economic Development in south and south-east Asia that was launched in 1951. It brought together Australia, Britain, Canada, India, New Zealand, Pakistan and Sri Lanka to encourage mutual help in investing in the infrastructure and in human resources. One benefit of the plan was that it allowed a reduction in the sterling balances of India that were such a cause of concern since the war.[71]

The British government's ambition of increasing capital for sound development would only be possible if it could sustain internal savings and achieve a surplus on overseas account. It was not clear that the attempt would succeed, and in 1953, Reginald Maudling, the economic secretary of the Treasury, asked his civil servants for advice on 'how much capital we shall we able to export over the next year or so, and to what

---

[70] TNA, T236/2639, 'Sterling balances and south-east Asia: memorandum submitted jointly by the working parties on the sterling area and on development in south and south-east Asia', 18 Mar. 1950. See also J. Tomlinson, 'The Commonwealth, the Balance of Payments and the Politics of International Poverty: British Aid Policy, 1958–1971', *Contemporary European History*, 12 (2003), 413–29.

[71] V. K. R. V. Rao, 'The Colombo Plan for Economic Development', *Lloyd's Bank Review*, 21 (1951), 12–32; 'The Sterling Area: I, History and Mechanism', *Planning*, 18 (1951), 65; G. Krozewski, *Money and the End of Empire: British Economic Policy and the Colonies, 1947–58* (Basingstoke, 2001), 65.

destinations this capital should go'. He was concerned by the competing claims on capital – to build up reserves, to improve the flow of funds to the Commonwealth, and the demands of foreign countries for capital which connected with the political situation in Egypt, trade negotiations with Uruguay and financial crisis in Brazil.[72] Treasury officials came to two different conclusions, following the same divides as at the time of Operation ROBOT.

On the one side was Otto Clarke, a leading 'Roboteer' who was – at first sight counter-intuitively – opposed to capital exports. A commitment to free markets might be expected to lead to support for active capital markets as occurred under Howe and Lawson after 1979. However, Clarke's approach was rather different from that of the later phase of globalisation which combined floating exchanges and capital flows. He felt that capital was better used at home. In his view, the balance of payments surplus of £300–350m desired by the government was already committed to repay debt, and that 'it is much more important from the point of view of our balance-of-payments to develop our own productivity and competitive power than to use our resources to develop other countries' productivity'. A current account surplus of £300–350m was equivalent to about 3 per cent of national income, and Clarke argued that the economy should be geared to this level in the same way that before 1914 it was geared to a current surplus of 6 per cent of the national income:

> The need for this arises *not* because we want to 'invest abroad' but because we are a debtor country on an unprecedented scale and the nature of our indebtedness involves a liability to make great repayments whenever our creditors need them. We are trying to run a world-wide international banking and financial system with wholly inadequate resources in cash and this means that the pressure has to come on our physical resources to discharge our liabilities. Fundamentally, we cannot meet the demands on our creditors in cash when they arise; we must therefore be in a position to meet them with goods...It is anomalous therefore to talk about overseas 'investment' as being a claim on our resources; it is much truer to say that overseas 'indebtedness' involves pressure on our resources. A man with a mortgage on his house is not 'paying his way' if he is failing to meet his mortgage instalments even though he may be earning enough to cover his 'current' needs...For the UK, therefore, the term 'current surplus' is a misnomer, and it is positively dangerous to think in terms of 'investing' this 'current surplus'.

In Clarke's view, 'the important thing is to be competitive and driving all round' so that British goods could secure overseas markets. In his mind, floating exchanges were combined with capital controls.[73]

On the other side was Robert Hall, a leading opponent of ROBOT, who argued that there was no incompatibility between developing British domestic competitiveness and overseas investment. He felt that there were

[72] TNA, T229/543, R. Maulding to E. Bridges, 1 Jan. 1953.
[73] TNA, T229/543, RWBC/55527, 'Overseas investment', R. W. B. Clarke, undated.

already sufficient resources to proceed on both fronts and that 'it is quite impossible to reach this surplus [that is, £300–350m on the balance of payments] unless we are *willing* to make some loans'. The main problem was selling the right goods abroad at the right price which 'involves choosing the right rate of exchange, and getting enough flexibility into the economy'. In 1949, the government devalued because costs were out of line with world costs. As Hall pointed out 'one of the strongest arguments for a floating rate is that it allows a continuous adjustment of costs. But there are strong arguments for a stable rate', as was decided at the time of the debate over ROBOT:

> The flexibility needed is secured primarily by having reasonably disinflationary conditions at home: it is a matter of judgment to get a balance between the social objective of full employment and the necessities of our foreign investment policy. In my view, we are at present somewhere near the right position now.
>
> Perhaps more important is the possession of adequate capacity. . .It takes many years to build a new factory. Thus the whole question of investment policy is involved, and in my view we do not give enough attention to our long-term needs.

It was not enough to provide the right goods at competitive prices: the rest of the world would only buy British goods if it was willing to have a deficit with Britain – and that required foreign investment. Since it was easier to earn surpluses in sterling than dollars, the lending should be in the sterling area. A mutually beneficial bargain could be struck: the Commonwealth was short of capital for development and Britain had an interest in developing their resources, particularly in producing food and materials to reduce dependence on the dollar area. Might the Commonwealth control its dollar expenditure in return for additional sterling to be spent on approved development projects? Hall denied that it was better to invest in improving British productivity. Britain had sufficient resources to do both:

> we cannot agree that sound investment in the Commonwealth does not improve our own balance of payments, just as did the 6 per cent of national income invested overseas during the first decade of this century. It will improve our invisible earnings from the Commonwealth, and should also improve the distribution of our balance of payments between the sterling and non-sterling areas, reducing our dollar deficit, which would be a valuable contribution to our balance of payments position.[74]

Hall therefore combined support for capital exports and fixed exchange rates – a different trade-off both from that struck at Bretton Woods and implemented after 1979.

[74] TNA, T229/543, 'Overseas investment: economic secretary's minute of 1st Jan. 1953', R. L. Hall, 29 Jan. 1953; 'Overseas investment', D. A. V. Allen, 3 Feb. 1953; E. N. Plowden, 'Overseas investment', 5 Feb. 1953; the debates were presented to the economic secretary in 'Overseas investment', 24 Feb. 1953; T230/226, 'Capital available for overseas investment', MFWH, 6 Jan. 1953; 'Mr Clarke's paper on "Overseas investment"', 2 Feb. 1953.

Although the sterling area was allowed to raise loans in London for general development in 1954, overseas investment was still limited and the Treasury remained cautious. Since the war, the Treasury's policy was to give exchange control approval to direct investment in the non-sterling area if there was a clear economic advantage defined as increased exports, protection of raw material supplies, and exploitation of a British technique or asset. Indirect investment in quoted foreign currency securities was only allowed if financed by the sale of other foreign currency securities in sterling area ownership.

> In general our object in applying these criteria has been to improve the balance of payments within a reasonable period of time, particularly by stimulating exports (including the invisible export of know-how), and we have therefore on the whole looked for a net short-term return above the average.

The Treasury's aim was to limit overseas investment by high domestic interest rates and tight credit in order to reduce the burden on foreign exchange resources as a result of capital export.[75] When Labour came to power in 1964, even the limited foreign investment under the Conservatives was considered to be far too high.[76]

As we will see next time, the revival of the City of London as a leading capital market was the result of a shift in American policy. As America's balance of payments weakened from the late 1950s and early 1960s, the Kennedy and Johnson administrations introduced controls on foreign investment which encouraged the holding of dollars in London. The growth of the Eurodollar market was exploited by the Bank of London and South America and its chairman, George Bolton, who had left the Bank of England. He realised that sterling could no longer survive as a major world currency and he believed that the best approach was to loosen regulations over the London financial market and exploit Eurodollars. In the 1960s, an American bank took a stake in the Bank of London and South America, and Bolton tried to build up an Anglo-American bank with a global reach. As at the time of ROBOT, Bolton was deeply suspicious of closer ties with Europe, and preferred a free trade area for the north Atlantic to membership of the EEC.[77] Here was a precursor of 'big bang' and the new global order of the close of the twentieth century – which is to look ahead to my final presidential address next year.

[75] TNA, BT213/96, 'Direct outward investment (excluding oil) in the non-sterling area', EAS (57)1, 6 May 1957.

[76] TNA, CAB47/68, 'Overseas investment', B. Reading, 17 Nov. 1964; T. Balogh, 'Foreign investment and liquidity', 15 Dec. 1964; T. Balogh, 'Foreign investment policy', 22 Dec. 1964; F. Stewart, 'Investment overseas and exports', n.d.

[77] G. Jones, 'Bolton, Sir George Lewis French, 1900–1982, banker', www.oxforddnb.com/view/article/46639 last accessed 2 Apr. 2008.

In this address, I have shown how the Americans' ambitions of the Bretton Woods conference of 1944 and the Havana conference of 1947/8 were modified in the face of economic reality. The transition to convertibility took much longer than the Americans hoped, and the return of multilateralism was delayed. The apparent American economic hegemony was constrained, and the British government was able to secure more than seemed feasible during the gloomy days of the war and post-war reconstruction. By the late 1950s, convertibility was restored and trade had recovered. Was it now possible to fulfil the ambitions of Cordell Hull and Will Clayton and return to multilateral trade – or had the emergence of the European Economic Community subverted their plans? For its part, the British government had still to decide on its economic identity: should it pursue a 'one-world' policy based on the dollar, a 'two-world' approach with the sterling area alongside the dollar, or should it throw in its lot with the Europeans? The issues that faced the Labour government in relation to the EPU were still on the agenda, though the context had changed. The dollar shortage of the post-war years was now giving way to a dollar glut as the American balance of payments weakened and the economies of Europe and Asia recovered – above all, those of Germany and Japan.

Here was the dilemma observed by Robert Triffin: liquidity for the growing world economy was provided on condition that the US economy was weak. Triffin feared that the result might be a repeat of 1931: he saw parallels with Britain's position at that time which led to the devaluation of sterling, the collapse of the gold standard and the world depression.[78] An American deficit on its balance of payments was vital in creating liquidity for the rest of the world, but could the American government allow it to continue to grow with potentially damaging results for its international standing and ability to finance its strategic ambitions? One possible response would be to deflate the domestic economy to hold down demand for imports and release goods for export, but this would have damaging electoral results for whoever embarked on the policy. Neither could the American government devalue its currency to become more competitive, for the dollar provided the foundation of the entire system of pegged currencies so that all other countries would follow it down. The USA could not devalue, and the Bretton Woods system did not oblige countries with strong currencies – above all the Deutschmark and the yen – to revalue. Was the use of undervalued currencies to secure more trade any different from the 1930s? James Schlesinger at the Bureau of the Budget remarked that 'Undervaluing the yen, for example, by a full 20 per cent is a beggar-my-neighbour policy. There is no reason that the

[78] Robert Triffin, 'Statement to the Joint Economic Committee of the 87th Congress', Washington, 28 Oct. 1959, in his *Gold and the Dollar Crisis* (New Haven, 1960).

United States should be willing graciously to tolerate such a condition.'[79] Currencies were, so it seemed, moving into disequilibrium with little ability to adjust.

By the early 1960s, the way was prepared for considerable tensions within the Bretton Woods system of monetary relations and trade policies. Shortly after his election, President Kennedy embarked on a new round of trade talks to reduce tariffs and to open up markets for American goods. How far did the 'Kennedy round' succeed in its ambitions, or did the concessions made to under-developed countries threaten American acceptance of free trade and serve to stimulate protectionism? At the same time, Kennedy and President Johnson attempted to make the American economy more efficient and productive by imposing controls over capital exports to stimulate domestic investment, as well as increasing public spending to solve some of the problems of poverty at home. In fact, the American balance of payments continued to weaken, a situation exacerbated by the mounting costs of the Vietnam war.

Triffin realised that the injection of dollars into the world economy was vital to provide liquidity, and that the only alternative was to create something like Keynes's 'Bancor'. Such an outcome depended on the ability of the international organisations created at Bretton Woods to implement reform. In the event, the IMF failed to take effective action to solve the 'Triffin dilemma'. Others adopted a more sceptical attitude to the dollar glut, seeing in it less a beneficial creation of liquidity than a form of dollar imperialism. Jacques Rueff (a leading French opponent of Keynes and member of the Mont Pelerin Society devoted to economic liberalism) and Charles De Gaulle complained that America was able to pay its deficits by printing dollars so that, in Rueff's words, it had found the 'marvellous secret of a deficit without tears'. It did not need to restrict domestic demand to deal with the balance of payments, and was instead exporting inflation, printing greenbacks to fund its military adventures and to buy European businesses. Rueff feared that there would soon be speculation against the dollar, leading to panic, deflation, tariffs and an inability to counter Communism. The Bretton Woods system, he remarked in 1962, 'places the whole economy in the situation of a man falling from the tenth floor: everything goes well at the start, but he can be sure that he is going to crash to the ground'. The system was, in De Gaulle's phrase, 'abusive and dangerous'. The answer was to

---

[79] Memorandum from the assistant director of the Office of Management and Budget (Schlesinger) to the president's assistant for international economic affairs (Peterson), 20 July 1971, *Foreign Relations, 1969–1976*, III: *Foreign Economic Policy, 1969–1972: International Monetary Policy, 1969–1972*, document 161, http://www.state.gov/r/pa/ho/frus/nixon/iii/5348.htm last accessed 26 July 2004.

return to gold to contain the inflationary potential of democracy.[80] More realistically than a return to gold, the European Economic Community developed a plan for monetary integration: in 1970, the Werner Report set out a three-stage plan to create Economic and Monetary Union (EMU) within a decade, starting with a reduction in the fluctuations of margins between member currencies, proceeding to integrate financial and banking markets, and eventually fixing rates between the member countries with a convergence of economic policies.[81] The Europeans had little confidence in the dollar as the basis of the world economy, for in the words of the French President Georges Pompidou 'one could not eternally ask people to set their watches by a defective clock'.

Just how would the British government respond to these strains of the 1960s as its own balance of payments weakened, and the pound was devalued in 1967? Was it any longer feasible to maintain sterling's international position, and, if not, should it look to the United States or join the European initiatives? Should Britain turn away from the 'soft' markets of the sterling area towards Europe? These issues became particularly pressing when the fixed but variable exchange rate regime of Bretton Woods experienced a mortal blow in 1971: Richard Nixon suspended the convertibility of the dollar into gold. Attempts to restore the Bretton Woods currency regime through the Smithsonian agreement later in the year failed, and by 1973 the pound was floating. Both in America and in Britain, the fears expressed by the anti-Roboteers came to pass: the ability of the pound and dollar to float downwards removed the need for monetary and fiscal restraints which led to inflation and to mounting budgetary deficits. By the late 1970s, it was clear that new 'rules of the game' were needed to impose discipline: the European monetary system, the Federal Reserve's tight money policy and Howe's medium-term financial strategy which set strict limits to the growth of money supply. Lawson argued that the new policy was 'a belated unlearning of what were mistakenly believed to be the lessons of the war' – a rejection of the Bretton Woods consensus that fixed rates were the cure to the problems of competitive devaluations and beggar-my-neighbour policies of the 1930s. His view, following the work of Milton Friedman on the monetary history of the USA, was that the real lesson of the depression was that the Federal Reserve made a serious mistake in reducing the monetary supply in 1929–33, so turning a financial problem into a serious disruption

[80] Some of Rueff's writings were translated: see *The Age of Inflation* (Chicago, 1964), and *Balance of Payments: Proposals for the Solution of the Most Pressing World Economic Problem of Our Time* (New York, 1967); C. S. Civvis, 'Charles de Gaulle, Jacques Rueff and French International Monetary Policy under Bretton Woods', *Journal of Contemporary History*, 41 (2006), 701–20.

[81] Council-Commission of the European Communities, *Report to the Council and the Commission on the Realisation by Stages of Economic and Monetary Union in the Community, 8 Oct. 1970* [Werner Report], Supplement to Bulletin 11 – 1970 of the European Communities.

of the economy. The correct lesson, he argued, should have been to ensure stable monetary growth rather than to reject orthodoxy. After the war, excess monetary growth was held in check by fixed exchange rates but was then threatened in the 1970s by the loss of constraints imposed by fixed exchanges.[82] The re-imposition of these constraints from the late 1970s through tight money led to domestic pain. Not only had White's and Keynes's adherence to fixed exchange rates been abandoned. Now, their commitment to capital controls to allow an independent domestic monetary was dropped. The policy choice in 1979/80 was a crucial turning point in the story, with a different pattern of beneficiaries and losers. It forms the subject of my final address.

[82] N. Lawson, *The New Conservatism: Lecture to the Bow Group* (1980).

Transactions of the RHS 18 (2008), pp. 43–68 © 2008 Royal Historical Society
doi:10.1017/S0080440108000650   Printed in the United Kingdom

HIGH AND LOW: TIES OF DEPENDENCE IN THE FRANKISH KINGDOMS*

By Alice Rio

The Alexander Prize Essay

ABSTRACT. Our understanding of ties of loyalty and dependence formed at the level of the Carolingian political elite has been much improved by a great deal of excellent recent research. As mutually beneficial relationships freely entered into, they tend to be sharply distinguished from ties of dependence involving members from the lower echelons of society: the latter ties, on the contrary, are usually seen as the result of coercion, and they were long seen as emblematic of the increasingly oppressive control of local lords. Commendation for these less powerful members of society is thus often seen as tantamount to forfeiting free status. Because oppression, for legitimate reasons, has been so strongly emphasised in historical treatments of this type of relationship, paradoxically little attention has been given to what influence the lower-status party may have had on the proceedings, the extent of their negotiating ability or the range of duties and benefits involved in such agreements. But not all lower-status people made the same deals: the Frankish formularies, an important source of evidence regarding such arrangements, show a complicated situation, indicating that ties formed at this lower level need to be treated with as much nuance as higher-status relationships.

Studies of ties of service and dependence in the early middle ages have traditionally been split into two main directions of enquiry: slavery and unfree labour on the one hand, and free military or political service on the other. Both, in different ways, have been the object of fierce debate. In the case of slavery, the historiography has by and large told a story of endings rather than beginnings, with most arguments relating to identifying the date by which the classical model may be said to have died out. The question of free military service has proved equally controversial, but has generally been approached more from the perspective of later developments of the central medieval period. Arguments initially focused on the birth of vassalage as an institution and on the early signs auguring the advent of 'feudalism' (in the Ganshofian sense of formalised military

* I would like to thank Jinty Nelson, Chris Wickham and Paul Fouracre for being kind enough to read drafts of this paper, and for the helpfulness and generosity of their comments. I also thank all those present at the Medieval History seminar at All Souls, Oxford, on 5 November 2007, when I gave a preliminary version of this paper.

service), emphasising its novelty and uniqueness, and its heralding of a crisp new way of defining and formulating power relationships, wholly distinct from the earlier, institutionally messier late antique system of patronage and clientelism. This teleological approach was firmly refuted by Susan Reynolds, in her ground-breaking *Fiefs and Vassals*.[1] Concurrently, the reevaluation and discrediting, during the 1990s, of arguments positing a major turning-point around the year 1000 has also emphasised continuity between Carolingian lordship and that of later periods.[2] This has resulted in an interpretation of the Carolingian era as a period of unprecedented aristocratic growth, coupled with an acknowledgement, at least in the British historiography, that Carolingian military dependence cannot be said to constitute an origin-point for an inexorable progression towards feudalism (though, as we shall see, Carolingian 'vassalage' as an institution remains alive and well in much continental historiography).

Most examples of ties of dependence found in the sources have thus tended to be interpreted as falling into one of the following two categories: dependence is either characterised as fully consensual and as a mark of enhanced status, in the case of free military dependants, or as coerced and degrading, in which case it is assimilated to unfree status. Beyond the legally unfree, this latter category has been seen as extending progressively to all low-status people, technically free but in practice subjected, with dependence in all these cases linked with the constitution of a new, more diffuse and inclusive servile category ('serfdom' as defined by Marc Bloch). The divide is also historiographical: slavery and unfreedom have mostly been studied by social historians, while military service has tended to fall more within the remit of political and constitutional history. Partly as a result of the dearth of source material, however, social 'history from below' and analyses of 'top-down' political structures tend not to stray very far from their initial starting-point, and only rarely meet in the middle. As a result, the terms of these debates have rarely been combined effectively, except in the Marxist model, which, at its best, has perhaps been most successful at articulating the two, though it too posits a deep structural divide between them as radically different spheres of dependence, the one high-status and honourable, the other low-status

---

[1] S. Reynolds, *Fiefs and Vassals: The Medieval Evidence Reinterpreted* (Oxford, 1994).

[2] On this issue, see in particular the famous debate in *Past and Present*: T. N. Bisson, 'The "Feudal Revolution"', *Past and Present*, 142 (1994), 6–42, and the resulting debate involving Dominique Barthélemy (*Past and Present*, 152 (1996), 197–205), Stephen D. White (*Past and Present*, 152 (1996), 205–23), Timothy Reuter (*Past and Present*, 155 (1997), 177–95) and Chris Wickham (*Past and Present*, 155 (1997), 196–208), with Bisson's reply (*Past and Present*, 155 (1997), 208–25). See also D. Barthélemy, *La société dans le comté de Vendôme de l'an mil au XIVe siècle* (Paris, 1993); D. Barthélemy, *La mutation de l'an mil a-t-elle eu lieu? Servage et chevalerie dans la France des Xe et XIe siècles* (Paris, 1997).

and humiliating. Put in the starkest terms, these two categories could be said to represent the putative winners and losers of the 'crucial period of aristocratic affirmation' associated with the Carolingian period, which, Chris Wickham has recently argued, allowed all-out oppression by this aristocracy of the lower echelons of society, and of the peasantry in particular, thereby bringing to an end a period of relative autonomy enjoyed by the peasantry after the breakdown of the Roman taxation system.[3] There may, however, be some value in considering them not as natural opposites, but as two ends of a spectrum, by looking for broader underlying principles and examining in more concrete terms how and why people across the social scale entered into such ties of dependence, and what this meant to them – in short, what lords and dependants expected to get out of them, and from each other.

I

One text in particular may serve as a useful starting-point, since over the years it has successively been taken as evidence for both high-status military service and low-status dependence. It is a legal formula, no. 43 of a formulary (that is, a collection of models for legal documents) compiled in Tours at some point during the eighth century:

> For someone who is putting himself under the power of another man. To the magnificent lord A, I, B. Since it is known to all that I do not have the means from which to feed and clothe myself, I therefore asked your piety, and this was my decision (*et mihi decrevit voluntas*), that I should put and transfer myself under your protection (*me in vestrum mundoburdum tradere vel commendare*), which I did in this manner, in such a way that you should provide me with help and comfort with both food and clothing, according to how much I may deserve in serving you; and for as long as I live in dependence (*in caput advixero*), I should pay you service and obedience (*servitium et obsequium*) as a free man (*ingenuili ordine*), and I may not have the power to withdraw myself from under your power and protection in my lifetime, but I should remain all the days of my life under your power and protection (*defensio*). And it was decided that if one of us wants to change this agreement for himself, he should pay *n. solidi* to the other, and let this agreement remain firm; and it was decided that they should make and sign for each other two documents regarding this copied with an identical content, which they did.[4]

Long associated with the origins, from the eighth century onwards, of the 'triumphal march of vassalage' (in the words of Gerd Althoff), this text has been said to constitute the earliest surviving evidence for an embryonic 'vassalic' relationship between a secular lord and his dependant, and taken as a prototype for later developments.[5] It is often referred to in

---

[3] C. Wickham, *Framing the Early Middle Ages: Europe and the Mediterranean, 400–800* (Oxford, 2005), 570–5.

[4] *Formulae Turonenses* no. 43 (K. Zeumer, *Formulae Merowingici et Karolini Aevi*, Monumenta Germaniae Historica [hereafter MGH] Legum V (Hanover, 1886), 158).

[5] G. Althoff, *Family, Friends and Followers: Political and Social Bonds in Early Medieval Europe*, trans. C. Carroll (Cambridge, 2004), 104; M. Bloch, *Feudal Society*, trans. L. A. Manyon, 2nd

textbooks on feudal relationships as if it presented few or no problems of interpretation: the clear outline of such elements as the service of the dependant, the duties of the lord and the lifelong and irrevocable nature of the agreement seemed enough to interpret it as showing an example of vassalage, which may be why it has proved so enduringly attractive to historians. A closer reading, however, shows clear weaknesses in this interpretation.

The lack of any mention of ritual, such as the oath and symbolic touching of hands generally thought to have been typical of 'vassalic' entry into service,[6] is not in itself enough to deal a death-blow to the hypothesis that this formula involved a bond of vassalage. Rituals of this sort tend to be little emphasised in sources beyond relationships directly involving the king in a formal court setting.[7] This could of course be due only to the limits of the available evidence, but it could also imply that the symbolism of power at lower levels remained more fluid.

More worryingly for those who want Tours no. 43 to be the foundation-text of feudal relations, however, this text also makes no mention of the most important structural feature normally associated with vassalage: the performance of military service in return for land. Our Tours formula does not mention military service as the specific occupation of the new dependant; nor does it contain any reference to his being granted any land by his new lord.

The representativeness of this text may also be called into question, in view of its very limited impact on the manuscript tradition of the Tours collection. This text is a legal formula, that is, a model prepared by a scribe on the basis of an existing legal document to help him with his future work or in teaching his pupils.[8] Although some of these

edn (London and New York, 1962), I, 149; F.-L. Ganshof, *Qu'est-ce que la féodalité?*, 5th edn (Paris, 1982), 23–8; R. Boutruche, *Seigneurie et féodalité* (Paris, 1968), II, 166–70; W. Kienast, *Die fränkische Vassalität. Von den Hausmeiern bis zu Ludwig dem Kind und Karl dem Einfältigen*, ed. P. Herde (Frankfurt, 1990), 9–10; P. Depreux, , *Les sociétés occidentales du milieu du VIe à la fin du IXe siècle* (Rennes, 2002), 161; J.-P. Devroey, *Puissants et misérables: système social et monde paysan dans l'Europe des Francs (VIe–IXe siècles)*, Classe des Lettres series 3, vol. 40 (Académie royale de Belgique, Brussels, 2006), 164.

[6] Kienast, *Die fränkische Vassalität*, 1; Depreux, *Les sociétés occidentales*, 161; Devroey, *Puissants et misérables*, 172; on this point, see Reynolds, *Fiefs and Vassals*, 19 and 28–9.

[7] Compare, for instance, the formula relating to the king's *antrustio*, in which ritual is much more emphasised than in this formula: *Formulae Marculfi* I, 18 (Zeumer, *Formulae*, 55; A. Uddholm, *Formularum Marculfi libri duo* (Uppsala, 1962), 86–7). On this formula, see Depreux, *Les sociétés occidentales*, 158; Devroey, *Puissants et misérables*, 162. On the possible reasons for the transition from 'antrustions' to 'vassals', see P. Fouracre, *The Age of Charles Martel* (2000), 152.

[8] The standard edition is Zeumer, *Formulae*; see also K. Zeumer, 'Über die älteren fränkischen Formelsammlungen', *Neues Archiv*, 6 (1881), 9–115, and 'Über die alamannischen Formelsammlungen', *Neues Archiv*, 8 (1883), 473–553. The classic synthesis on formulae is H. Brunner, *Deutsche Rechtsgeschichte*, 2nd edn (Leipzig, 1906), I, 575–88. More recent work includes W. Bergmann, 'Die Formulae Andecavenses, eine Formelsammlung auf der

models were first compiled in the Merovingian period, they survive only in Carolingian manuscripts, which often give vastly different versions of the same collections. Charting the development of these texts over time can give us an impression of what models the scribes who copied our surviving manuscripts felt they would need in the course of their professional careers. The surest way to establish the general usefulness and relevance of any given formula during this period is therefore to see how many later scribes, working on the basis of the collection of which it was part, chose to copy or reuse it themselves in their own manuscripts.[9] By this standard, Tours no. 43 does not score very highly, since this text can only be found in a single manuscript, the fullest and most comprehensive out of the seven or so containing material relating to this collection: it was therefore clearly far from being a favourite of later scribes in the process of compiling their own selections. This once again points to the fragility of this text's status as the founding-stone of feudalism; perhaps a founding-pebble would be more accurate.[10]

All this can only cause the gravest doubts regarding Tours no. 43 as evidence for anything that might be thought of as straightforward vassalage.[11] Indeed, the particular arrangement made in the Tours formula and the wording used to describe it may have owed less to the observance of a preexisting, standard way of entering into someone else's service 'as a free man' (or as a vassal), and more to negotiations

Grenze zwischen Antike und Mittelalter', *Archiv für Diplomatik*, 24 (1978), 1–53; W. Bergmann, 'Verlorene Urkunden nach den *Formulae Andecavenses*', *Francia*, 9 (1981), 3–56; I. N. Wood, 'Disputes in Late Fifth- and Sixth-Century Gaul: Some Problems', in *The Settlement of Disputes in Early Medieval Europe*, ed. W. Davies and P. Fouracre (Cambridge, 1986), 7–22; C. Lauranson-Rosaz and A. Jeannin, 'La résolution des litiges en justice durant le haut Moyen-Âge: l'exemple de l'*apennis* à travers les formules, notamment celles d'Auvergne et d'Angers', in *Le règlement des conflits au Moyen-Âge, XXXIe Congrès de la SHMES (Angers, juin 2000)* (Paris, 2001), 21–33; W. Brown, 'When Documents Are Destroyed or Lost: Lay People and Archives in the Early Middle Ages', *Early Medieval Europe*, 11 (2002), 337–66; W. Brown, 'Conflicts, Letters, and Personal Relationships in the Carolingian Formula Collections', *Law and History Review*, 25 (2007), 323–44; P. Depreux, 'La tradition manuscrite des "Formules de Tours" et la diffusion des modèles d'actes aux VIIIe et IXe siècles', in *Alcuin de York à Tours: Écriture, pouvoir et réseaux dans l'Europe du Haut Moyen Âge*, ed. P. Depreux and B. Judic (Rennes and Tours, 2004), 55–71; A. Rio, 'Freedom and Unfreedom in Early Medieval Francia: The Evidence of the Legal Formularies', *Past and Present*, 193 (2006), 7–40; A. Rio, 'Les formulaires mérovingiens et carolingiens: tradition manuscrite et réception', *Francia* (forthcoming). For a translation of two of the most important collections, see also A. Rio, *The Formularies of Marculf and Angers: Two Merovingian Legal Handbooks* (Liverpool, 2008).

[9] Brown, 'When Documents Are Destroyed or Lost'; Rio, 'Freedom and Unfreedom', 13–16; Rio, 'Les formulaires mérovingiens et carolingiens'.

[10] The manuscript is Warsaw BU 1; see Depreux, 'La tradition manuscrite des "Formules de Tours"' (with a table of the formulae contained in each manuscript at 68–9).

[11] See P. Geary, 'Extra-Judicial Means of Conflict Resolution', in *La giustizia nell' alto medioevo (secoli V–VIII)*, Settimane di studio del centro italiano di studi sull' alto medioevo 42 (Spoleto, 1995), I, 569–601, at 586–8.

and bargaining in the particular case which had formed the basis for this formula, in a similar way to those which could lead to unfree service (as in self-sales), or even, as in another formula, to a man handing over 'half' his free status to another in exchange for a loan:[12]

> Here begins a loan security concerning a man. To the magnificent lord brother A, I, B. Let it be established by this deed of security that I received from you, as I did indeed receive, a loan of *n*. ounces of silver. I give to you as a pledge (*in loco pignoris*) half my free status (*statum meum medietatem*), so that I will have to do whatever appropriate work (*qualecumque operem legitema*) you order me to do for *n*. days out of every seven. After *n*. years have elapsed, I will have to return your property, and I will recover my deed of security. And if I am slow or negligent regarding this work or in returning this property at the appointed *placitum*, or if I do not act according to your wish in this matter, I am to pay you back twice the amount of the loan you gave me, either to you or to whomever you will have given this deed of security to enforce.[13]

As with the 'half-freedom' emphasised in this case, the insistence on 'free' service in the Tours formula may simply have been intended to ensure better terms for the dependant; it may have meant, for instance, that the lord could not inflict corporal punishment on him, as he could have on an unfree dependant.[14]

The absence of most of the classic features of vassalage from the Tours formula could not but be noticed in the end, and this text has recently experienced a fall from grace in historians' eyes, if not in general textbooks, at least in new research. In his recent book on Frankish social history, *Puissants et misérables*, Jean-Pierre Devroey thus correctly pointed to similarities between Tours no. 43 and documents relating to unfree service. These similarities, however, led him to suggest that this example could not be considered as dealing with truly free service in any real sense.[15] This is a little strange given the text's insistence on the dependant's service 'as a free man' (*ingenuili ordine*, literally 'as a man in the free order'); Devroey takes this as having only been a 'pathetic' attempt to save face by hiding the humiliation inherent in such dependence. In spite of the apparent general thrust of this text, Devroey thus associated it with what he saw as virtually unfree 'clientelism', by which previously free people would have been pushed, by poverty and the harshness of the times, into offering their service to a lord in exchange for protection and legal responsibility; he contrasted this with vassalage as a freely chosen and mutually beneficial association.[16] His interpretation of Tours no. 43

---

[12] See Rio, 'Freedom and Unfreedom', 30–1.

[13] *Formulae Andecavenses* no. 38 (Zeumer, *Formulae*, 17). For a discussion and translation of this collection, see Rio, *Marculf and Angers*.

[14] See Rio, 'Freedom and Unfreedom', 29.

[15] Devroey, *Puissants et misérables*, 164–5.

[16] *Ibid.*, 269: 'la pression exercée par la misère et l'incertitude du temps a précipité... un nombre croissant d'individus libres dans le rang des clientèles personnelles... dans un

echoes Detlef Liebs's recent evaluation of the reasons for self-sales, which he considered a last resort in cases of extreme poverty.[17] Devroey therefore paradoxically takes this text as evidence for a very strong differentiation between truly free (or 'vassalic') service, in which the duty of obedience would have been only 'symbolic', and unfree or not-so-free service, as in the Tours formula, in which the duty of obedience would have been more 'real'. Any resemblance between the two he views as merely superficial, which allows him to preserve the rift between free and unfree service which has remained a persistent trend in the historiography.[18]

Tours no. 43 has thus so far been interpreted in two mutually exclusive ways: either as evidence for the origins of the highest-status type of dependence (vassalage), or as evidence for the lowest-status type (unfree or nearly unfree service). Either way, it has been seen as paradigmatic: for vassalage, in defining the relationship as mutually beneficial and the result of a free decision for both parties; for low-status dependence, in stressing such features as the poverty of the dependant, his willingness to give service not in exchange for land, but with food and clothing as his only reward, and his desire to secure legal protection, all of which have been seen as typical of exclusively low-status concerns. As we have seen, the first interpretation is virtually impossible to sustain, since this text manifestly differs from vassalage in several highly significant ways; whether the second one proves to be any more convincing remains to be seen. The fact that our Tours formula could be interpreted in such radically different ways indicates the need to investigate what it was, if anything, that made these two types of dependence so fundamentally distinct.

The best way to make such comparisons is to set Tours no. 43 against the background of other legal formulae produced during this period. As I argued earlier, the continued copying of some of these texts indicates that they remained broadly relevant across the alleged chronological divide between structures of lordship before and after the affirmation of aristocratic domination under the Carolingian kings: they therefore provide useful evidence for continuity as well as renewal. Since they could relate to almost any situation for which a scribe might be expected to have to write a document, their wide range of subjects means that they can effectively be seen as handbooks setting out the ways in which legal, social and economic relationships could be formulated in the Frankish

---

rapport de réciprocité brutalement hiérarchique'. See also Kienast, *Die fränkische Vassalität*, 9 ('Bittere Not bedrängt den Freien'), for a similar view of the reasons for entry into service in this formula, if not of their institutional significance.

[17] D. Liebs, 'Sklaverei aus Not im germanisch-römischen Recht', *Zeitschrift der Savigny-Stiftung für Rechtsgeschichte. Romanistische Abteilung*, 118 (2001), 286–311. Cf. Rio, 'Freedom and Unfreedom', 27–8.

[18] Althoff, *Family, Friends and Followers*, 103; Depreux, *Les sociétés occidentales*, 161.

kingdoms. They are also especially valuable in that they deal not only with the king and his great men, but with a much bigger slice of the social spectrum, since most scribes were only marginally involved in drawing up royal documents, and were more often called on to prepare documents for their own religious institution or for the lay community in its neighbourhood. Legal formulae also document the construction of particular relationships through explicit agreements, rather than merely referring to them as self-explanatory, as do most other sources. This allows us to focus on the relationship being expressed, rather than on the identity of the protagonists or the use of words expressing particular titles or functions (*leudes, fideles, vassi* and others), the precise meaning of which is always difficult to ascertain; the use of the word *commendatio* in sources is similarly both vague and non-systematic, so that fixing on that word does not tell us as much as we might wish either.[19] Since status itself did not follow a precisely and coherently defined system in this period, this terminology was not used by early medieval authors in as systematic or technical a manner as may have been suggested in modern analyses.[20] As Susan Reynolds has convincingly argued, deriving conclusions from the use of such terms is therefore problematic, since their own meaning is far from clear.[21] Formularies, by contrast, give room for a different, more structural, approach, and may thus offer us a better chance of understanding relationships of domination and dependence across the whole of Frankish society.

II

Let us begin with poverty as a motivation for entry into service, and the lack of free choice that this supposedly implied. Do parallels with self-sales mean that Tours no. 43 is not 'really' dealing with a free man? Poverty is certainly mentioned in the text, as it often is in self-sales, but is it all that it seems?

The process of comparison is complicated by the difficulty of finding such a thing as a standard, generally applicable model for entry into unfree service in our sources: the specific rights and duties which unfree service could involve seem to have themselves been eminently negotiable

---

[19] Devroey, *Puissants et misérables*, 164. The same can be said of the word *beneficium*, which similarly did not always take on the technical meaning associated with precarial grants (Devroey, *Puissants et misérables*, 187–8).

[20] The most thorough study of this kind is Kienast, *Die fränkische Vassalität*. For critiques of this approach, see Reynolds, *Fiefs and Vassals*, 82–3; Wickham, *Framing the Early Middle Ages*, 184 and 198; Devroey, *Puissants et misérables*, 138–9; on *beneficium*, see especially P. Fouracre, 'The Use of the Term *beneficium* in Frankish Sources: A Society Based on Favours?', in *The Language of Gift in the Early Middle Ages*, ed. W. Davies and P. Fouracre (forthcoming). I am grateful to Professor Fouracre for allowing me to read this article ahead of publication.

[21] Reynolds, *Fiefs and Vassals*, 83.

throughout the early medieval period.[22] Nor were self-sales necessarily the result of coercion; this was demonstrably the case only when people who had been found guilty of a crime effectively had to sell themselves to whomever agreed to pay their fine, if they could not afford to pay it themselves. Poverty is certainly often mentioned as a motivation for entry into service, in self-sales as in our Tours formula; but it is difficult to know how seriously to take such claims in either case. Take, for instance, the following formula, from a collection compiled in Angers during the Merovingian period, but preserved in a late eighth-century manuscript copy, in which a couple sold their freedom along with their land:

> To the magnificent lord brother A and his wife B, we, C and his wife D. Let it be established that we sold to you (as indeed we did) our free status along with all the possessions that we may own or rent, *mansus* and land and vineyards, however much we are known to possess at this present day on the land of the villa of E, on the territory of the church of Angers, together with everything that we are known to have anywhere. For this we received from you the price that pleased us, worth *n. solidi* in gold, so that from this day the said buyers may have the free power to do whatever they want with us and our heirs.[23]

The property described here is not large, but then the model documents found in this formulary hardly ever deal with large estates or with a villa in its entirety. Although this couple may not have been particularly well off, they were therefore clearly not completely destitute either, at least in comparison with the other lay people whose transactions were included in this collection. The future conditions under which they were to live as a result of this sale are not stated, but they may well subsequently have received their property back as a precarial grant, or farmed it as tenants. Whatever the reason for this couple's decision to give up their free status, they must have been expecting it to bring about an improvement on their situation as free smallholders, for instance by providing ready cash or securing enhanced protection.

Earlier evidence for this type of arrangement can be found in a famous passage of Salvian of Marseilles's vociferous tract on the state of the late Roman empire, the *De gubernatione Dei*, in which he shows 'poor' people handing themselves and their property over to more powerful persons, against the backdrop of the fifth-century invasions. Salvian considered this practice as yet another sign of the decadence of the empire and of the injustice of the late Roman taxation system, but his only explanation for this behaviour was that these people had been driven to these measures by their desire to retain their property and stay with their families; otherwise, according to Salvian, they would happily have fled to the barbarians. This certainly suggests they could keep their

---

[22] Rio, 'Freedom and Unfreedom'.
[23] *Formulae Andecavenses* no. 25 (Zeumer, *Formulae*, 12).

land under these new arrangements, and contradicts Salvian's claim that precisely these arrangements were causing such people to be despoiled. The discrepancies in his account may have arisen because the only type of right over land which he seems to have acknowledged as worth having (and, indeed, the one most heavily privileged in Roman law, though, perhaps precisely because its status was uncontroversial, it was subject to fewer regulations) was that of full ownership, rather than any right to exploit the land or retain its revenues. Entry into service in these cases could therefore similarly be interpreted as involving people who were not necessarily in financial extremities, but in search of protection and patronage.[24] Salvian in fact went on to say that many of his *pauperes* were 'of not obscure birth, and educated like gentlemen'.[25]

These texts reflect the tendency to use the discourse of poverty to represent weaker social and political status rather than to indicate an actual financial situation. As Karl Bosl showed over forty years ago, the word *pauper* did not mean 'poor' so much as 'weak', and could also refer to those without the protection of a lord.[26] Formulae describing entry into service were therefore bound to cite 'poverty' as a motive; this does not in itself constitute supporting evidence for nightmare scenarios postulating slavery and famine as the only two possible alternatives for the majority of early medieval people. The literary sources seldom specify the actual socio-economic situation of protagonists, but instead tend to offer shades of moral characterisation linked with status; historians are therefore left to guess at the underlying circumstances of their actions, and in so doing often reproduce the assumptions of medieval authors in equating legal subjection with complete powerlessness and financial destitution, and vice versa. This, however, reveals much more about what the rather grand persons who wrote these sources considered to be a truly free and dignified life than about social reality for the majority of the population. The self-sale formulae should therefore be seen not as

---

[24] Salvian, *De gubernatione Dei* v, 9. R. Van Dam, *Leadership and Community in Late Antique Gaul* (Berkeley and Los Angeles, 1985), 42–4. The same observation could perhaps be made regarding the episode described by Caesarius of Arles, Sermon 154, ed. G. Morin, *Sermones*, Corpus Christianorum Series Latina 103–4 (Turnhout, 1953), II, 629; translated in W. E. Klingshirn, *Caesarius of Arles: The Making of a Christian Community in Late Antique Gaul* (Cambridge, 1994), 205–6; J. Smith, *Europe after Rome: A New Cultural History, 500–1000* (Oxford, 2005), 161.

[25] 'Multi eorum, et non obscuri natalibus editi et liberaliter instituti' (*De gubernatione Dei* v, 21).

[26] K. Bosl, '*Potens* und *pauper*: begriffsgeschichtliche Studien zur gesellschaftlichen Differenzierung im frühen Mittelalter und zum "Pauperismus" des Hochmittelalters', in K. Bosl, *Frühformen der Gesellschaft im Mittelalterlichen Europa* (Munich and Vienna, 1964), 106–34; Depreux, *Les sociétés occidentales*, 142; Devroey, *Puissants et misérables*, 317–20. For the Byzantine side, see R. Morris, 'The Powerful and the Poor in Tenth-Century Byzantium: Law and Reality', *Past and Present*, 73 (1976), 3–27.

a last-resort option, of which only the most desperate would ever have considered availing themselves, but as a deliberate choice (which does not, of course, imply that it was necessarily a pleasant one); the same may be said of our Tours formula.[27] Entering someone's service of one's own free will cannot, therefore, be seen as a feature exclusive to free military service; nor, conversely, can coercion be seen as necessarily typical of unfree service. In this sense at least, the opposition between these two types of dependence is not a useful one.

Let us now consider the smallness of the reward envisaged in Tours no. 43, and whether it can really be considered as typical of near-unfree service, and only of near-unfree service. The new dependant's concern, according to this text, was only to obtain material support 'according to how much I may deserve' in the form of food and clothing (*me tam de victu quam et de vestimento, iuxta quod vobis servire et promereri potuero, adiuvare vel consolare debeas*). This, however, does not fit unfree service more than it does any other type of service, since greater rewards at the discretion of the lord could also be expected by unfree dependants, who, as other formulae show us, could even hope for grants of land, whether under precarial tenure or in outright ownership. One formula from the Marculf collection thus shows us a *mansus* being given to an unfree military retainer (*gasindus*; Marculf added *servus* as its Latin equivalent), though this unfree status did not constitute a salient feature of the text, and the same formula could easily have been used regardless of the legal status of the recipient.[28] Another formula from the Angers collection, in which a man gave a small estate to his *nutritus*, displays a similar ambiguity between free and unfree.[29]

It is striking that the two texts which come closest in the surviving corpus of formulae to using the classic vocabulary of a land grant in exchange for service (without, however, using the word *beneficium*) should concern people who seem to have counted as technically unfree: these are two ninth-century formulae dealing with grants of land by a bishop to a *serviens* of his church.[30] The word *serviens* is again vague, but it does seem, at least in formulae, to have mostly been used to refer to the unfree:

---

[27] For a similar point on self-sales in the eleventh century, see D. Barthélemy, 'Qu'est-ce que le servage, en France, au XIe siècle?', *Revue historique*, 287 (2) (1992), 233–84.

[28] Marculf II, 36 (Zeumer, *Formulae*, 96–7; Uddholm, *Formularum Marculfi libri duo*, 284–7); see Rio, 'Freedom and Unfreedom', 25–7.

[29] *Formulae Andecavenses* no. 56 (Zeumer, *Formulae*, 24). On this formula, see Devroey, *Puissants et misérables*, 133; R. Le Jan, *Famille et pouvoir dans le monde franc (VIIe–IXe siècle): essai d'anthropologie sociale* (Paris, 1995), 343.

[30] *Addenda ad Formulae Senonenses recentiores*, nos. 18 and 19 (*Formulae*, ed. Zeumer, 723–4). These two texts were copied in Tironian notes at the end of Paris BnF lat. 4627. Some of these are illegible, resulting in some gaps in the text.

servientes are thus sometimes opposed to *ingenui* in lists of property, and are often found in manumissions.[31]

> *Prestaria.* A, archbishop of the church of Sens. We decided, with the agreement of all my canons, that we should grant a *mansus* to a certain serving-man (*serviens*) of Saint B named C, which he had...to pay for his...riding (*ad cavalicandum*) and his...[in the *pagus*] of D, in the villa which is called E, for this service; which we did, in such a way that both he and his heirs [should hold] the said *mansus*, as he [held it] in this manner..., and they are to hold this *mansus* from this day by right of inheritance (*iure hereditatis*). And if they appear to be slow or negligent in this service, [let them] pay [a fine?] according to the law, and let them not lose this *mansus* as a result of this. And we ask and beg our successors that all...and that this [document] made for them should remain firm, so that they should take care to keep our [document] in their favour. I signed this document below in my own hand, and decided to have it confirmed by our canons. *Explicit.*

> Here begins a *prestaria.* Thus I in God's name A, archbishop of your holy church. We decided, with the agreement and the decision of our brothers and B, the abbot (*rector*) of the monastery (*cella*) of Saint C in our gift (*ex nostro dono*), that we should grant in exchange for an annual rent (*ad censum concedere*) to a certain man, our servant (*serviens*) named D, an urban property within the city of E, out of the property of Saint C, and [situated] in this place; which we did, in such a way that every year, on the feast of Saint C, he should take care to pay *x* amount to this abbot, and he may hold and use the said urban property through the days of his life in exchange for the said annuity (*census*). And if he is slow or negligent in [paying] this annuity (*census*), let him promise [to pay it] (*fidem exinde faciat*), and having made his promise, let him pay [a fine?] according to the law, and let him not lose this urban property as a result of this. But after his death, let the abbot of this monastery recover it under his power and authority with all its increased and added value. And we ask our successors that [this document] in his favour may remain valid. B, abbot of this monastery, consented [to this].

The second text seems to depict a more or less straightforward precarial arrangement: the use of the property is granted in exchange for an annual payment (which had become a standard feature of precarial tenure in the Carolingian period)[32] and the property was to revert to the monastery after the death of the servant. The servant is not said to fulfil a military function. The formula preceding it is more unusual: the reference to providing for his riding service may suggest it dealt specifically with a military retainer, though this could also have referred to bearing messages. The land was here granted in full ownership, rather than as a benefice in exchange for continued service: in spite of the title describing this text as a 'prestaria', the servant was to hold it *iure hereditatis*, so that, as in the two formulae from the collections of Angers and Marculf mentioned earlier, he would have had the right to leave it to his heirs (though the land had

---

[31] For the opposition of *servientes* with *ingenui* in lists of property, see *Formulae Marculfi* I, 2–4; for manumissions of *servientes*, see *Formulae Marculfi* I, 39, II, 3, II, 34 and II, 52; *Formulae Salicae Merkelianae* no. 13a; *Formulae Bituricenses* no. 8; *Formulae Extravagantes* I, 19 (all of these texts may be found in Zeumer, *Formulae*).

[32] On the payment of a *census* in precarial formulae, see H. J. Hummer, *Politics and Power in Early Medieval Europe: Alsace and the Frankish Realm, 600–1000* (Cambridge, 2005), 92–4.

apparently been held by the same servant as a benefice beforehand; on what terms is unclear because the text here is partly illegible). Both texts stipulate that the land could not be recovered by its original owners if these servants proved negligent in performing their duties; this mention suggests that the land *could* have been taken away under a different arrangement, but that this was decided against in these two cases. The coupling of these two texts in the manuscript points to an association in the mind of the scribe between these different ways of granting land as a reward for service (whether as a benefice or in full ownership), without laying much emphasis on the distinction between either military and non-military service or free and unfree dependence.

The fairly small reward for service, limited to food and clothing, envisaged in Tours no. 43 therefore does not in itself bring this text closer to unfree service, since even unfree servants could sometimes hope for more than this. Conversely, the concern to ensure provision for daily sustenance was not limited to the unfree, but seems to have been widely shared. Tours no. 43 shares features not only with self-sales and unfree service, but also, in some ways, with arrangements made within a family context, in particular those dealing with adoptions and provision for family members:

> I, in God's name A, living in the villa of B, have determined in my mind to give two [thirds] of all the property which I am seen to own in this life to my son [C] by this document, so that he may have it in his possession from this day. . .in recognition of his assiduous services and kindness (*pro adsidua servicia sua vel benevolentia*). . .with this condition, that while I live, he should take care of me, and feed and clothe me (*mihi in omnibus tam de victo quam et de vestito soniare mihi debiat*).[33]

The focus on reward for service and the provision of food and clothes echoes the concerns of the Tours formula. A degree of assimilation seems to have existed between the service offered by junior family members and that offered by servants in the mind of at least one scribe, who curiously merged in his collection two formulae taken from Marculf, one dealing with a man giving property to his grandchildren in exchange for their support in his old age and 'poverty', the other concerning entry into unfree service.[34]

Gifts of land could also be made by parents to reward a son's performance of military service above and beyond what would be included in his inheritance, as in the following case provided by a formula

---

[33] *Formulae Andecavenses* no. 58 (Zeumer, *Formulae*, 24–5).
[34] *Formulae Salicae Merkelianae* nos. 25–6 (= Marculf II, 11 and II, 28); Zeumer divided this into two distinct formulae, though it was copied as a single text in the manuscript (Vatican reg. lat. 612) (Zeumer, *Formulae*, 251).

from the Angers collection:

> I, in God's name A, and my sweetest wife B, to our son C, loved by us with full affection. Since you are seen to serve us faithfully in all things and in every way, and have endured on our account many hardships and injuries in various places, and went in my place to fight the Bretons and Gascons in the service of our lords, we therefore decided to give you something from our property; which we did. Therefore we give to you in writing our small estate (*mansellus*) of D. . .And when anything else from our property which is not entered in this charter is left to our children, you should share it with them equally.[35]

The link between ties of service and obligation and family support is nowhere more clear than in cases of adoptions, in which non-family members took on the responsibilities of sons. These, at least in formularies, always included a gift of land in exchange for material support:

> If someone adopts a stranger (*extranio homine*) as his son. To my lord brother[36] A, B. Since, for my sins, I have long been bereft of sons, and poverty and infirmity are seen to afflict me, I was seen to adopt you in the place of my sons, according to what was decided and agreed between us with good will, so that, while I live, you will spare and provide in sufficient quantity food, clothing, both for my back and for my bed, and shoes (*victum et vestimentum tam in dorso quam in lecto seu calciamentum mihi in omnibus sufficienter inpercias et procures*); and you are to receive in your power all my property, whatever I am known to have, including *mansus*, vineyards, meadows, cattle and every other content of my house, on the condition [that you observe] this right while I live. I therefore decided to have this document made for you, so that neither myself nor any of my heirs nor anybody may be able to change this agreement made between us, but, as mentioned above, you must provide for my necessity while I live, and all my property will remain in your power, both at present and after my death, and you will have the free power to do whatever you please with it.[37]

The claim of poverty is here again undermined by the property listed immediately afterwards. This contradiction is a more or less constant feature of such documents: another formula of adoption, which made similar claims of poverty, thus transferred a fairly substantial amount of property, including a number of *mansi*, in exchange for the provision of food, drink, clothes and shoes.[38]

This type of arrangement, offering land rather than service in exchange for material support, did not necessarily take the form of adoption as part of a family, but could also characterise relationships with a lord or a religious community: the choice between these two different forms of bond, adoption or dependence, no doubt depended on the relative social positions of the parties involved, with adoption only a possibility when comparable social status made it acceptable to both parties. In purely material terms, however, their consequences may not have been that

---

[35] *Formulae Andecavenses* no. 37 (Zeumer, *Formulae*, 16–17).

[36] As elsewhere in this formulary, 'brother' is meant in the Christian sense rather than to indicate an actual family tie.

[37] *Formulae Marculfi* II, 13 (Zeumer, *Formulae*, 83–4).

[38] *Formulae Lindenbrogianae* no. 18 (Zeumer, *Formulae*, 279–80).

different. One formula from the late ninth century shows us the model to follow when a man handed over all of his property to a religious house (*qualibet locum*) or, alternatively, 'to any powerful man' (*vel cuiquolibet potenti viro*), in exchange for material support, again ascribing his need to poverty and old age, 'which often go together'. What this lord was supposed to provide in exchange is here described in far more detail than in most such cases: this included

> two sets of clothes each year, one of wool, one of linen, and sufficient provisions, including bread, beer, vegetables and milk, and meat on feast days; and, every three years, a blanket, gloves, shoes, leg-bands, and soap and a bath-tub, which are very necessary for the sick, and the tools with which to work, as they promised me.

The arrangement was to last only if they received and treated him well (*si, ut reor, benignius me voluerint habere*); if they failed to do this, the man was to recover his property.[39] No reference is made to the status under which he was to live, so we can assume he would certainly have counted as free, since he was not subject to any future obligations.

Such arrangements to provide material support in exchange for land also seem to have been perceived as equivalent, or at least comparable, to land grants and *precariae*, generally seen as the hallmark of military or political dependence. One collection, perhaps originating from Reichenau, contains a series of formulae describing the different possible options that could be followed to establish the terms of the counter-favour expected from a monastery in exchange for a couple's gift of their entire property, with variations depending on the preferred arrangements.[40] The counter-favour could take the form of a precarial grant, but could equally well involve instead the promise to provide food and clothing for the lifetime of the party who made the gift.[41]

Obtaining the basic necessities of life on the best possible terms from the persons or institutions best able to provide them, whether directly, in the form of food and clothing, or indirectly, through the granting of land allowing such sustenance, thus seems to have been a very general concern during the early medieval period, and to have remained central to a great many people's decisions and choices. The arrangements into which people could enter to achieve this were not limited to relationships

---

[39] *Collectio Sangallensis* no. 15 (Zeumer, *Formulae*, 405–6). This arrangement is similar to one recorded in a document from St Gall (Wartmann, *Urkundenbuch der Abtei Sankt Gallen* (Zurich, 1863), no. 221, *a*. 816), in which a man named Cozbert gave a detailed list of all the things he expected the monastery to provide for him every year, including shoes and clothing. I thank Jinty Nelson for drawing my attention to this text.

[40] *Formulae Augienses coll. B* nos. 2 to 12 (Zeumer, *Formulae*, 348–53).

[41] *Formulae Augienses coll. B* no. 11 (Zeumer, *Formulae*, 353). The next formula in the collection gives another possibility, in which the giver reserved the right to join the monastery should he wish to at a later date (which would also have involved the provision of food and clothing, though on an admittedly different basis).

of service in any strict sense, whether specifically military or not, but were framed according to whatever possibility would secure the most favourable outcome: sometimes in exchange for service, sometimes in exchange for a gift of land; sometimes within the family unit, sometimes with persons outside it, whether a lay or ecclesiastical lordship or a person of more or less equal status whom one could adopt (thereby effectively assimilating the tie to a family link). In any case, the concern to secure a regular supply of food and clothing seems to have been widespread, and not to have been restricted to the unfree or quasi-unfree, nor even to the very poor: Hincmar's *De ordine palatii* thus refers to food and clothing among the appropriate rewards to be given to the king's military followers.[42] A variety of people seem to have been interested in forming such relationships with more powerful persons, as long as the cost of ensuring that person's support remained proportionate to the advantage they would get out of it. Such arrangements included a great number of variables; for instance, offering one's land in exchange for material support, judging from this evidence, seems to have been a solution chosen mostly by elderly people, presumably because they were no longer able to exploit their land directly, and could not otherwise easily obtain such sustenance through service: this limited the range of what they had to offer, and may sometimes have led them to pay a more hefty price to secure their entry into a relationship of support and dependence. The size of the reward for service (or in exchange for gifts of land) thus seems to have depended much more on complex appraisals of what each party had to offer than on a strict distinction between high- and low-status types of dependence.

III

Next to obtaining basic sustenance, the need to obtain protection constituted a comparably important and generally shared concern. I will now turn to the last defining characteristic of dependence included in our Tours formula: the question of legal protection, and whether the need for it would have been limited to the powerless and the unfree. Tours no. 43 includes this aspect of relationships of dependence in its reference to *mundeburdium* and its Latin equivalent *defensio*, emphasising the legal protection afforded to the dependant by his new lord. Devroey takes such legal protection to have been an essentially low-status concern, leading vulnerable free people to abandon their liberties and hand themselves over to lords.[43] It is true that most references to *mundeburdium* in formulae

[42] Hincmar of Rheims, *De ordines palatii*, ed. T. Gross and R. Schieffer, MGH *Fontes iuris Germanici antiqui in usum scholarum separatim editi* III (Hanover, 1980), *cap.* 22 and 27, at 72 and 80.
[43] Devroey, *Puissants et misérables*, 164–5.

are found in deeds of manumission and relate to freedmen. This may not mean, though, that such protection applied only to unfree or semi-free people, but rather that those were the circumstances in which it was most likely to need mentioning: since unfree persons would automatically have been under the protection and legal responsibility of their master,[44] exactly who would fulfil these functions after their manumission needed to be clarified. Sometimes freedmen were allowed to choose their own protector;[45] sometimes their choice was restricted by the terms of the manumission. An ex-master could for instance require his freedmen to choose their protector from among his heirs,[46] or, more frequently, assign them to the protection of a particular church.[47] The latter solution seems to have become widespread during the Carolingian period, at least in the Eastern Frankish kingdom, where manumission apparently grew increasingly assimilated to the transfer of unfree dependants to a church; so close was this conceptual association that a manumission which allowed a freedman to choose his own protector came to be referred to specifically as being made 'extra ecclesiam'.[48] The transfer of dependants to a church presumably gave added value to the spiritual benefits of making a manumission. Manumission in such cases may only have implied slightly better terms for the dependant under his new ecclesiastical lord. Either way, manumissions in which a particular protector was assigned to the freedman certainly suggest that responsibility for legal protection was understood to give protectors certain rights over the beneficiary.

These rights could include the payment of dues in money or in kind: while the duty to provide wax candles or a supply of hosts for a church or for the tomb of one's ex-master, if the freedman had been assigned one

---

[44] See, for instance, *Formulae Senonenses recentiores* nos. 3 and 6 (Zeumer, *Formulae*, 212–14), in which an abbot represents a *colonus* of his monastery in court.

[45] As in *Formulae Arvernenses* nos. 3 and 4 (Zeumer, *Formulae*, 30); *Formulae Marculfi* II, 32 (Zeumer, *Formulae*, 95); *Formulae Turonenses* no. 12 (Zeumer, *Formulae*, 141–2); *Formulae Bituricenses* no. 8 (Zeumer, *Formulae*, 171–2); *Cartae Senonicae* nos. 1 and 6 (Zeumer, *Formulae*, 185–6 and 187–8); *Formulae Salicae Lindenbrogianae* nos. 10 and 20 (Zeumer, *Formulae*, 273–4 and 281). *Formulae Morbacenses* no. 19 (p. 334) shows the same solution in the case of a *carta conculcatoria*, guaranteeing the continuing free status of a woman and her future children after her marriage to an unfree man; the language of such documents often mirrored that found in manumissions (Rio, 'Freedom and Unfreedom', 17–20).

[46] As in *Formulae Marculfi* II, 34 (Zeumer, *Formulae*, 96).

[47] As in *Formulae Andecavenses* nos. 20 and 23 (Zeumer, *Formulae*, 11–12); *Formulae Salicae Bignonianae* no. 2 (Zeumer, *Formulae*, 228–9); *Formulae Salicae Lindenbrogianae* nos. 9 and 11 (Zeumer, *Formulae*, 273–4); *Formulae Salicae Merkelianae* no. 14 (Zeumer, *Formulae*, 246); *Formulae Argentinenses* no. 2 (Zeumer, *Formulae*, 337); *Formulae Augienses coll. B* nos. 21 and 34 (Zeumer, *Formulae*, 356 and 360); *Formulae Extravagantes* I, 19–20 (Zeumer, *Formulae*, 545–6). For a later example in Marmoutier's *Book of Serfs* assimilating manumission with the transfer of an unfree person to the church, see Barthélemy, 'Qu'est-ce que le servage', at 255–7.

[48] As in *Formulae Augienses coll. B* no. 42 (Zeumer, *Formulae*, 363).

of his heirs as protector, seems to have been fairly common,[49] protection was sometimes also afforded in exchange for a yearly payment or *census*.[50] One formula gives an example of a testament in which a couple's gifts to some freedmen whom they had entrusted to the protection of a church were automatically to go to that church after the death of these freedmen,[51] which suggests that protectors acquired a measure of control over the property held by the people assigned to them in manumissions. One way or another, such protection can therefore still be said to have constituted a tie of dependence, albeit perhaps a less demanding one than unfree service. Indeed, people seem to have been conscious, in making manumissions, of the possible abuses or over-interpretation of such ties by the freedmen's new protectors: ex-masters thus sometimes felt the need to protect the free status of their freedmen in the future by specifying that this duty of protection was to be 'non ad adfligendum sed ad defensandum' or 'ad defensandum non ad inclinandum'.[52] Such distinctions suggest the existence of grey areas in what could be demanded of someone under one's protection, and of a level of anxiety on the part of masters about the risk that the spiritual impact of their gesture would effectively be annulled as a consequence.

There is therefore little doubt that legal protection could constitute a powerful tool of domination. On the other hand, acknowledging such limitations on a freedman or dependant's autonomy did not mean that these arrangements were wholly one-sided: taking someone under one's protection also involved a degree of responsibility for the welfare of the dependant, and a certain amount of give and take. In Tours no. 43, an explicit link is made between giving protection (*mundeburdium*) and bearing responsibility for the provision of support and sustenance for the dependant. Another formula may suggest a similar link, this time by describing what happened when such arrangements went wrong: in this case, a monastery which had previously enjoyed royal protection

---

[49] As in *Formulae Marculfi* II, 34 (Zeumer, *Formulae*, 96); *Formulae Salicae Merkelianae* no. 14 (Zeumer, *Formulae*, 246); *Formulae Augienses coll. B* nos. 21 and 34 (Zeumer, *Formulae*, 356 and 360); *Formulae Extravagantes* I, 20 (Zeumer, *Formulae*, 545–6). As Paul Fouracre has shown, such dispositions were not necessarily of a symbolic nature, but could be an important part of material support for churches (P. Fouracre, 'Eternal Lights and Earthly Needs: Practical Aspects of the Development of Frankish Immunities', in *Property and Power in the Early Middle Ages*, ed. W. Davies and P. Fouracre (Cambridge, 1995), 53–81).

[50] *Formulae Argentinenses* no. 2 (Zeumer, *Formulae*, 337); *Formulae Extravagantes* I, 19 (Zeumer, *Formulae*, 545). *Formulae Extravagantes* I, 26 (Zeumer, *Formulae*, 548–9), a manumission-like document described as a *carta traditoria* in its title, oddly makes the freedman owe a *census* to the church of St-Maximin, Trier, while apparently allowing him the freedom to choose his own protector outside it.

[51] *Collectio Flaviniacensis* no. 8 (Zeumer, *Formulae*, 476).

[52] *Formulae Salicae Bignonianae* no. 2 (Zeumer, *Formulae*, 228–9); *Formulae Salicae Lindenbrogianae* no. 11 (Zeumer, *Formulae*, 274).

(*mundeburdium*) had later been given by the king to someone else as a
favour (*nos ille beneficiasti*); since then, as the monks bitterly complained to
the king, begging him to take them back under his own direct protection,
'we have not received clothes, shoes, ointment, soap or food, as we used to
(*sicut antea fuit consuetudo*)'.[53] Rights to protection, and the level of control
accorded to those who provided it over those who received it, thus seem to
have been intimately linked with the concerns of dependants to secure an
adequate living, as discussed earlier. Although these were, by and large,
highly unequal relationships, and we may assume that lords had more to
gain from them than dependants (since they would have had no reason
to enter into them otherwise), we should therefore not underestimate
dependants' ability to define and claim the rights which the establishment
of these relationships also afforded them. The particular terms of such
arrangements would no doubt have been down to bargaining, depending
on the relative position of strength of each party, how much they had to
give and how much each thought they could reasonably expect from the
other in exchange.

The variables involved in such negotiations are central to understanding how fundamentally similar ways of formulating relationships
of dependence could be applied in such a wide range of circumstances.
As already seen in the case of the monastery cheated of its food and soap,
protection was far from being exclusively the mark of the socially weak,
or of unfree or quasi-unfree service: on the contrary, it too seems to have
been a very widely shared concern.

Lords' duty of protection and legal responsibility for their dependants
seems to have been a commonly accepted idea in formulae documenting
already established relationships as well as in those documenting the
creation of new relationships through entry into service. One small
cluster of formulae in the Marculf collection provides good evidence
for the crucial importance of a lord's personal legal action on behalf of
his dependants. One, for instance, shows the king issuing a document
ensuring that no legal cases could be brought against a lord's dependants
while he was away on state business:

> We therefore decide and order by the present charter that, until he returns from these
> parts, all his legal affairs and those of his friends (*amici*), both those who are going with him
> and those who are remaining in their homes, or of anyone for whom he is legitimately
> answerable (*undecumque ipse legitimo redebit mitio*), should remain on hold, and afterwards
> he is to make right every legal accusation on their behalf, and in a similar manner obtain
> justice from others.[54]

---

[53] *Formulae Salicae Merkelianae* no. 61 (Zeumer, *Formulae*, 261–2).
[54] *Formulae Marculfi* I, 23 (Zeumer, *Formulae*, 57; Uddholm, *Formularum Marculfi libri duo*,
96–7). See Wickham, *Framing the Early Middle Ages*, 439.

Who had legal responsibility for whom could become a fairly intricate matter, as in the following royal mandate, in which one lord was authorised to assume legal responsibility for another, who himself was responsible for his dependants:

> Our *fidelis* A, with God's favour, having come into our presence, put it to us that due to his ignorance he could not pursue his legal cases or enter a plea before a court (*mallus*). He asked the clemency of our rule that the illustrious man B should take up all his legal cases on his behalf, in local as well as our royal courts, and pursue them and enter pleas regarding them before a court. He was seen to delegate them to him presently by the rod (*per fistuca* [*sic*]). Therefore we order that, since this was the will of both parties, the said man B must pursue and enter pleas regarding all of A's legal cases everywhere, and must do right concerning legal accusations (*unicuique. . .de reputatis condicionibus et directum faciat*) on his behalf and on that of his men (*pro ipsum vel ominibus suis*), and in a similar manner obtain justice from others, for as long as this is the will of both parties.[55]

The vocabulary used in royal documents to refer to people under a lord's protection tends to refer to *amici, pares, gasindi*,[56] or *homines*, all of which could imply a military context, but not necessarily so: A's *homines* could have included both military retainers and his other dependants, including rural tenants and freedmen. The absence of lower-ranking dependants in this cluster of texts is probably due to the higher social and political sphere in which these documents were being produced, and ought not to be taken to imply that such dependants were not also meant to be included in these arrangements.

This same text also shows that legal protection could be sought by socially more prominent persons, as in the case of 'A' himself. He is described as a *fidelis*, and clearly had access to the king; B seems to have been of higher status, since, unlike A, he is described as *inluster*. A's plea of ignorance may or may not have been real; either way, he clearly thought that B would be better able than himself to uphold his interests. Although this arrangement gave B a level of control over A's affairs, in this case the relatively high status of both parties meant that the relationship was framed as one of patronage, in which the counter-favour was left vague or to be called in at a later date, rather than as a wider-reaching tie of dependence, in which the precise terms of the relationship tended to be defined more strictly. The practice of enlisting the support of a more powerful person through mandates, however, was not merely a feature of the royal court, and there are clear equivalents at a more local level.[57]

Should legal protection at this higher level be construed as similar to *mundeburdium*, or did *mundeburdium* imply a fundamentally different, more constraining type of relationship? The majority of known cases in which

---

[55] *Formulae Marculfi* I, 21 (Zeumer, *Formulae*, 56–7; Uddholm, *Formularum Marculfi libri duo*, 92–3).

[56] On this word, see Rio, 'Freedom and Unfreedom', 25–6.

[57] See, for instance, *Formulae Andecavenses* no. 52 (Zeumer, *Formulae*, 22–3).

kings made specific grants of their own *mundeburdium* do seem to relate to members of less dominant groups, such as women, freedmen or Jews.[58] It is likely, however, that royal grants of this kind arose out of a particular interest in being seen to defend such groups for reasons that were primarily ideological. In one formula reproducing the text of a letter addressed to Charlemagne at some point after his imperial coronation, a woman who did not have a man to represent her in court, and who did not yet have a charter of royal *mundeburdium*, wrote to the king asking for the rights such a charter would have extended to her, emphasising the protection of helpless women (in this case perhaps a widow) as a Christian virtue. Although her situation was contrasted in the title of the formula with the kind of automatic access to the king afforded to *fideles* in his service (the title suggests she was not technically allowed to speak directly to the king, though she could submit a written petition: 'if you do not have the permission to speak with the king, these are the words you should send to him regarding your case'), she clearly felt she too had a legitimate claim to his protection, and made her case by explicitly tapping into the protective streak of the Christian discourse of Charlemagne's regime.[59] The fact that most surviving charters of *mundeburdium* should relate to people belonging to less powerful categories does not mean that protection in their case was in any way more onerous or less effective than that offered to the king's *fideles*: although it was given for different reasons, that is, out of Christan duty rather than as a reward for service, there is no reason to assume that royal protection in the case of such groups would have had fundamentally different effects in practice. This could explain why grants of this kind could also be made to religious houses.[60] Royal grants of *mundeburdium* do not, therefore, constitute evidence for a lower-level form of protection, though they may well have been used more often in the case of certain special categories (churches, widows and orphans in particular), the protection of which was, in this world of 'little patriarchs', as Jinty Nelson has evocatively put it, seen as a fundamental cornerstone of Christian kingship.[61] In the case of charters of this kind given to Jews, the recipients are described as 'serving the king' ('partibus palatii nostri fideliter deservire'), which could suggest that *mundeburdium* was simply

---

[58] See *Formulae Imperiales* nos. 30, 31, 48, 52 and 55 (Zeumer, *Formulae*, 309–11, 323 and 325–7).

[59] *Formulae Bituricenses* no. 14 (Zeumer, *Formulae*, 174): 'Vestra pietas hoc emendare compellat, qualiter elimosina atque mercis seu mundeburdum vester semper adcrescat.'

[60] See *Formulae Marculfi* I, 24 (Zeumer, *Formulae*, 58; Uddholm, *Formularum Marculfi libri duo*, 98–101); Marculf *Add.* 2 adapts it to a monastery only, with very slight changes (Zeumer, *Formulae*, 111; Uddholm, *Formularum Marculfi libri duo*, 354–7).

[61] J. L. Nelson, 'Gender, Memory and Social Power', in *Gendering the Middle Ages*, ed. P. Stafford and A. Mulder-Bakker (Oxford, 2001), 192–204, at 192.

meant to extend to them in a more secure and explicit manner the same sort of protection available to other men in the king's service.[62]

Legal protection, far from being an essentially low-status concern, was an almost universal factor in the workings of both society and the state. Warren Brown has confirmed in a recent article the fundamental importance of personal relationships and connections in the settlement of disputes as evidenced in Carolingian formularies, with particular reference to letters of intercession.[63] As we have seen, evidence for this is not only to be found in letters, and relationships of legal protection were also formally recognised in legal documents throughout the Merovingian and Carolingian periods: public and private power and jurisdictions complemented rather than limited each other.[64] This is at odds with Devroey's hypothesis of a fundamental opposition between service to the king and service to a patron, and of vassalage as opposed to other kinds of service:

> The relationship of reciprocity initiated by royal protection did not directly threaten the dignity and freedom of his subjects. By contrast, the relationship of protection / dependence between a humble man and his patron entailed the irremediable degradation of the 'poor' and a rupture of the link between them and the ruler (whereas the Carolingian vassal remained among the king's faithful because he was his subject).[65]

But there is actually very little in the sources to support such a distinction: 'poor' people would certainly not have had much direct involvement with the king, but this would have been true whether they were in the dependence of a lord or not. Whether the concept of 'subject' can be said to have been relevant at all in relation to early medieval kingship is debatable,[66] and there is no evidence to support the notion that low-status people who put themselves under the protection of a more powerful party were somehow removed altogether from the authority of the king as a matter of principle. Simon MacLean has shown that succession crises played a greater role in the end of the Carolingian empire than any

---

[62] *Formulae Imperiales* nos. 31 and 52 (Zeumer, *Formulae*, 310–11 and 325).

[63] Brown, 'Conflicts, Letters, and Personal Relationships in the Carolingian Formula Collections'.

[64] See J. L. Nelson, 'Review: Head and Landes (eds.), *Peace of God*', *Speculum*, 69 (1994), 168; cited in C. Wickham, 'Debate: The Feudal Revolution', *Past and Present*, 155 (1997), 196–208, at 197–8.

[65] 'le rapport de protection/dépendance d'un faible vis-à-vis d'un patron entraînait la dégradation irrémédiable des "pauvres" et la rupture du lien entre eux et le souverain (alors que le vassal carolingien demeurait le fidèle du roi parce qu'il était son sujet' (Devroey, *Puissants et misérables*, 330).

[66] See J. L. Nelson, 'Kingship and Empire', in *The Cambridge History of Medieval Political Thought c.350–c.1450*, ed. J. H. Burns (Cambridge, 1988), 211–51, at 223.

increasingly rampant pauperisation leading free people to put themselves under 'private' ties of dependence, as Devroey suggests.[67]

IV

In many respects, the opposition between free military service on the one hand as honourable and all other forms of dependence on the other as dishonourable thus seems somewhat artificial. Devroey's interpretation of Tours no. 43 as not 'really' dealing with free service rests on the assumption that there was such a thing as classic vassalage for lords and their men in this period, but that Tours no. 43 does not correspond to it. Yet dismissing this formula leaves us with very little evidence for the existence of vassalage as such a neatly separate institution, at least outside the sphere of the very highest political elite. Devroey correctly points to the inappropriateness of identifying this formula as relating to vassalage, but then tries to reduce the relationship involved here to a concealed form of humiliation: he imagines the position of free people putting themselves in the dependence of someone else as 'irrémédiablement dégradée', no better than that of children or slaves, and altogether precluding any claim to personal independence.[68] Such an interpretation is linked to a wide assumption in the modern historiography that dependence in the case of the less powerful sections of society would necessarily have been shameful or demeaning, and could therefore only have been the result either of coercion or of abject poverty. However, there is in fact little to suggest that people were faced with such a stark choice between complete freedom and complete lack of freedom: as formulae show us, in particular with Tours no. 43, there were many kinds of middle ground. What comparison between our Tours formula and self-sales shows is that early medieval people perceived free and unfree service as *similar*, not as opposites.

The flexibility and negotiability of arrangements over service could explain why even lower-status people could think that they might have something to gain from entering a relationship of dependence with a lord. Rather than forcing them into a status lower than that of independent free peasants, association with a lord may in fact have given dependants a distinct edge in competing with other members of their local communities, particularly in relation to the legal protection such a relationship involved, since it would have increased their ability to win court-cases against their neighbours. Lower-status types of service and dependence were therefore

---

[67] Devroey, *Puissants et misérables*, 330–1; S. MacLean, *Kingship and Politics in the Late Ninth Century: Charles the Fat and the End of the Carolingian Empire* (Cambridge, 2003).

[68] Devroey, *Puissants et misérables*, 331.

not necessarily the result of coercion, but of individual decisions based on calculations of short-term benefits.

The distorting elite viewpoint of most of our sources is what led them, and consequently has led modern historians, to turn vassalage and military service into an exception, by considering them as more honourable in principle, and allowing them a unique status as the only positive form of service. But medieval views on dependence may not have been so rigid as that, except at the very highest echelons of society which brought forth the authors of all our literary sources. It is certainly important to distinguish military service from other kinds of service in political and cultural terms, but it was still part of wider social structures: historians should perhaps be wary of following their lead entirely in this respect, and of isolating free military service from this surrounding background as a distinct and wholly self-contained type of relationship.

Einhard's letters show us that a similar interplay in the language of pressure and protection, of exploitation and the recognition of rights, as that observed earlier for low-status dependants could also be at work for higher-status dependants. In one letter, for instance, he effectively ordered one of his *fideles*, who was clearly not low-status, to allow his daughter to marry a *vassalus* of Einhard's: although the father's decision was free in principle, Einhard took it for granted that he would follow his instructions, and applied pressure by referring to the support he had given him:

> I do not doubt that you recall how you commended yourself and yours to me. Since you decided to do this of your own will, it is also my wish in turn and by all means to supply you and yours, whenever the opportunity arises, with fitting support to the extent that I know how and possess the ability. Thus, let it be known to your kindness that my *vassalus* and your daughter desire with the Lord's approval and your permission to take each other in marriage...To conclude this business [all] that remains is either for you not to defer coming yourself at the present time in order to bring this matter to a close or to allow me to finish it.[69]

Other letters back up Einhard's claim regarding the support he gave to his dependants, showing him helping to secure their benefices and actively interceding on their behalf in legal cases.[70] High-status dependence did not necessarily imply a less hands-on approach or a lesser degree of intereference on the part of the lord: here as in the other cases discussed in this paper, patronage implied control.

Judging from the evidence of formularies, no single feature seems to have been exclusively characteristic of either high- or low-status service, whether in terms of freedom of choice in entering service, of the types of reward on offer or of legal protection and the level of control it afforded

---

[69] Einhard, *Epistolae*, ed. K. Hampe, MGH *Epistolae* V (Hanover, 1898–9), no. 62, 140; translation (with some minor alterations) from P. E. Dutton, *Charlemagne's Courtier: The Complete Einhard* (Broadview, 1998), letter no. 58, p. 159.

[70] See, for instance, Einhard, *Epistolae*, ed. Hampe, nos. 1, 7, 24, 39 and 51.

to lords. Ties of dependence at all levels seem to have been contracted on a largely *ad hoc* basis, depending on the outcome of negotiations. There was no sudden break on the social scale on either side of which power relationships could be said to have worked themselves out in fundamentally distinct ways: what we see instead is a continuum. Considering military service as the only form of truly free dependence and everything else as either explicitly or virtually unfree thus obscures similarities in the basic concerns shared across the social spectrum, and in the level of control that the establishment of relationships of patronage could involve: the very ambiguity and conflicting interpretations associated with Tours no. 43 show just how similar the terms of either relationship could be. In this context, it might be more fruitful not to worry so much about whether such free service as is described in the Tours formula 'really' corresponded to vassalage or to unfree service, but to examine this evidence against the broader background of the various ways in which ties of obligation and dependence could be formulated and understood during this period.

A useful comparison with the Tours formula may be made in the case of a group of tenth-century charters from northern Spain, recently studied by Wendy Davies, recording gifts of land made in exchange for future support, with the expectation that the recipient would 'do good' (*bonum facere*) for the donor.[71] These charters, like our Tours formula, were for a long time interpreted as straightforward acts of formal commendation.[72] As Wendy Davies has convincingly shown, however, such agreements were far from forming part of 'a general European post-Roman process, in which small-scale free proprietors submitted their persons and gave up their property to great landlords in order to secure assistance and protection in an increasingly unstable world': they did not always involve all of the donor's property; they were not always meant to create a lifelong relationship; and donors in these cases could be aristocrats as well as peasants.[73] Instead, Davies places these texts in the realm of 'light-touch' patronage, 'lining up and getting supporters, in an altogether looser, less autocratic, framework than the "commendation" model', epitomised by the use of the ambiguous term *gubernare*, which could mean 'to rule', but also 'provide' and 'support'.[74]

---

[71] W. Davies, *Acts of Giving: Individual, Community, and Church in Tenth-Century Spain* (Oxford, 2007), 149–54.

[72] See C. Sánchez-Albornoz, 'Las Behetrías: la encomendación en Asturias, León y Castilla', in *Viejos y nuevos estudios sobre las instituciones medievales españolas*, ed. C. Sánchez-Albornoz (Madrid, 1976), I, 15–84. For a critique of this view, see C. Estepa Díez, *Las Behetrías Castellanas* (Valladolid, 2003), I, 41–5; further references in Davies, *Acts of Giving*, 150 n. 43.

[73] Davies, *Acts of Giving*, 153.

[74] *Ibid.*, 154.

The reevaluation of this Spanish evidence could in turn help us to revisit our Frankish material. If these charters are not about formal commendation, perhaps we should revise our interpretation of the Tours formula and of similar texts from the Frankish kingdoms along these lines. Susan Reynolds has already dealt a death-blow to the modern conception of vassalage as a fixed, self-evident construct; perhaps it is now time to free ourselves from another tyrannous construct, and to abandon the idea of lower-status 'commendation' as a rigid, formal process. If we are to understand them properly, the need to allow for a similar level of complexity and ambiguity in the formulation of power relationships in the case of ties of dependence at lower social levels is just as crucial as in the case of vassalage. The negotiations over the rights and duties owed to and by peasants and lower-status dependants, documented in formulae as well as in other sources, implies a level of recognition of their rights by lords.[75] As with most human relationships, some degree of oppression and some degree of reciprocity were both nearly always part of the deal; the real question lies in the balance between the two, and this seems to have been governed not by hard and fast rules so much as by improvisation and opportunity. These different ways in which ties of dependence and protection allowed people to obtain what they needed from each other, which overwhelmingly involved the provision of support and security, certainly point in the direction of a strong consciousness of power relationships, but not ones that were fixed in a conceptually very systematic way: a *range* of dependent relationships are best viewed within a single, broad, social and legal context of need and support. Strategies of patronage, support and control could take many different forms and include people from virtually all sections of society, and it is consequently very hard to find a single form of dependence which could be called typical for this period. That is why historians should be wary of attributing to lower-status dependence as an undifferentiated whole such strong connotations of humiliation and powerlessness: early medieval people were, after all, familiar with ideas of honourable dependence and empowering service.

---

[75] J. L. Nelson, 'England and the Continent in the Ninth Century: III, Rights and Rituals', *Transactions of the Royal Historical Society*, sixth series, 14 (2004), 1–24.

Transactions of the RHS 18 (2008), pp. 69–99 © 2008 Royal Historical Society
doi:10.1017/S0080440108000662   Printed in the United Kingdom

TEXT, VISUALISATION AND POLITICS:
LONDON, 1150–1250*
By Derek Keene

READ 2 FEBRUARY 2007

ABSTRACT. Focusing on London, the paper discusses the interaction between theoretical, descriptive and quasi-historical writing about cities, a growing capacity to visualise city landscape and activities, and forms of graphic representation that drew on those ideas. Reading this interplay as a political space, the paper explores the structure, content and purposes of the 'London Collection' of national laws, pseudo-laws and city customs put together in London at about the time of Magna Carta. Though no more than a preliminary investigation, the exercise reveals the extent to which London interests, especially with regard to the politics of international trade, the 'law of London', earlier episodes of communal activism and a sense of London's historic destiny within that of the nation pervade the collection as a whole. This casts some doubt on the supposed antiquity of some of the London laws in the collection, which may well have been adjusted for the occasion.

The starting point of this paper is the proposition that in the twelfth and early thirteenth centuries the writings of philosophers and others on the city, its visual representation and its politics occupied a common space that historians can profitably explore. This approach to an understanding of urban culture is familiar enough in later medieval studies, most notably concerning Italy,[1] but it has not been adopted for London, especially in this much earlier period. Some of the texts concerning London are marked by a distinct visual sensibility, while the stories they told had an impact on the way in which the city was portrayed graphically. Some of those stories gave Londoners a strong sense of their past and

---

* I am grateful to John Gillingham, Lindy Grant, Judith Green, Bruce O'Brien, Richard Sharpe and Susan Reynolds for conversations which have helped shaped my thinking for this paper.

[1] For a wide-ranging discussion of related themes, see C. Frugoni, *A Distant City: Images of Urban Experience in the Medieval World*, trans. W. McCuaig (Princeton, 1991), an updated version of C. Frugoni, *Una lontana città: sentimenti e immagini nel Medioevo* (Turin, 1983); and also Q. Skinner, 'Ambrogio Lorenzetti: The Artist as Political Philosopher', *Proceedings of the British Academy*, 72 (1986), 1–56, and *idem*, 'Ambrogio Lorenzetti's Buon Governo Frescoes: Two Old Questions, Two New Answers', *Journal of the Warburg and Courtauld Institutes*, 62 (1999), 1–28.

were influenced by responses to the physical environment of the city, which thereby became an object for structured thought. That sense of history informed ideas of what was appropriate political action in the present, while at the same time political objectives informed rhetorical manipulations of texts concerning history, custom and law with a view to justifying what was currently desired.

London's politics in this period were complex and, as today, shaped by internal conflicts and by relations with powers outside the city itself. While some of the personal and family interests of Londoners and a few dramatic incidents emerge clearly from the records, much of the city's political life remains obscure and cannot be explored here.[2] A key relationship was that between London and the Crown, which drew heavily on the city for financial and other material support and exercised an undisputed lordship over it, while the same time acknowledging the collective rights of a large but ill-defined group of 'citizens' and allowing a degree of self-determination to certain specialised groups. This relationship was close, tense, ambiguous and sometimes confrontational, especially in periods of wider conflict, as during the baronial opposition to King John. Internally, the city's politics were structured in part by interests associated with commerce, manufactures and hierarchies of wealth and power, and in part by loyalties which could cut across class or family concerns. This paper's approach to the politics is through some of the London concerns apparent in that great collection of national laws, pseudo-laws and London customs which was put together around the time of Magna Carta and for more than a century afterwards remained intact within the city's archive. For convenience, it is described here as the 'London Collection'.[3] The compilation illuminates the political struggle which led up to the charter, but also strongly indicates the way in which London's elite pursued its interests and defined and visualised them within a broad historical and geographical landscape.

Most parts of Europe in the eleventh and twelfth centuries witnessed a remarkable growth of towns and cities.[4] In England, the material evidence for rapid growth seems more apparent for the eleventh century

---

[2] For London in this period, see C. N. L. Brooke and G. Keir, *London 800–1216: The Shaping of a City* (1975), and D. Keene, 'London from the Post-Roman Period to 1300', in *The Cambridge Urban History of Britain*, I: *600–1540*, ed. D. M. Palliser (Cambridge, 2000), 187–216. For recent accounts of family and political interests, see D. Keene, 'fitz Ailwin, Henry', 'fitz Osbert', in *Oxford Dictionary of National Biography* (Oxford, 2004); *idem*, 'English Urban Guilds, c. 900–1300: The Purposes and Politics of Association', in *Guilds and Association in Europe, 900–1900*, ed. I. A. Gadd and P. Wallis (2006), 3–26.

[3] See below, n. 36.

[4] For a recent survey, see D. Keene, 'Towns and the Growth of Trade', in *The New Cambridge Medieval History*, IV: *c. 1024–c. 1198, Part I*, ed. D. Luscombe and J. Riley-Smith (Cambridge, 2004), 47–85, 758–76.

than for the twelfth, but development picked up again rapidly from about 1180 onwards. Overall, however, the twelfth century was marked by the proliferation of literary and philosophical writing on the city. One strand focused on neo-Platonist ideas of the city or the state, and developed an organological notion of the hierarchical structure of these institutions, a model that became most widely known through John of Salisbury's *Policraticus* written in the 1150s. There were significant spatial and material elements in these discussions. Thus the *arx* or citadel was associated with the wise men or elders – the Senate – who governed the city under the prince, while the suburb outside the city was the preserve of those who tilled the fields and served as the feet of the body politic. Several treatises included, in the same low position, those craftsmen whose mechanical arts, sometimes listed in detail, sustained the city.[5] This indicates a striking scholarly engagement with everyday aspects of urban life. Another important strand was the revival of the literary genre of the description and praise of cities, of which an influential example was the *Mirabilia Urbis Romae* compiled at about the time of the establishment of the Roman commune and the restoration of the Senate in 1143.[6] Many such texts, though incorporating accurate observation of the urban scene, were rhetorical, idealising constructions that drew on ancient models and a standard repertoire of themes. These included the status of the city by comparison with notable places such as Rome; origins and heroic founders; the character and institutions of the inhabitants; and the appealing nature of the site and its landscape setting, which were often characterised with acute visual awareness.[7]

It is hardly surprising that the most compelling of the twelfth-century visualisations of urban landscape is that of a poet, Chrétien de Troyes, who about 1180 adopted a viewpoint that reminds modern readers of

[5] T. Struve, 'The Importance of the Organism in the Political Theory of John of Salisbury', in *The World of John of Salisbury*, ed. M. Wilks (Oxford, 1984), 303–17; T. Gregory, 'The Platonic Inheritance', in *A History of Twelfth-Century Western Philosophy*, ed. P. Dronke (Cambridge, 1988), 54–80, esp. 62; John of Salisbury, *Policraticus: Of the Frivolities of Courtiers and the Footprints of Philosophers*, ed. C. J. Nederman (Cambridge, 1990), 81, 125.

[6] *Mirabilia Urbis Romae*, ed. F. M. Nichols (1889), xi–xii, 86–7; M. Accame Lanzillotta, *Contributi sui Mirabilia Urbis Romae* (Genoa, 1996), preface.

[7] J. K. Hyde, 'Medieval Descriptions of Cities', *Bulletin of the John Rylands Library*, 48 (1965–6), 308–40; J. Scattergood, 'Misrepresenting the City: Genre, Intertextuality and William fitz Stephen's *Description of London* (c. 1173)', in *London and Europe in the Later Middle Ages*, ed. J. Boffey and P. King (1996), 1–34; J. M. Ganim, 'The Experience of Modernity in Late Medieval Literature: Urbanism, Experience and Rhetoric in Some Early Descriptions of London', in *The Performance of Middle English Culture: Essays on Chaucer and the Drama in Honour of Martin Stevens*, ed. J. J. Paxson, L. M. Clopper and S. Tomasch (Cambridge, 1998), 77–96; K. Arnold, 'Stadtelob und Stadtbeschreibung im späteren Mittelalter und der Früen Neuzeit', in *Städtische Geschichtsschreibung im Spätmittelalter und in der frühen Neuzeit*, ed. P. Johanek (Städteforschung: Veröfentlichungen des Instituts für vergleichende Städtegeschichte in Münster, Reihe A, Bd. 47; Cologne, Weimar, and Vienna, 2000), 247–68.

the passage in de Certeau's *La pratique de la quotidienne*, concerning visual engagement with the city as seen from above and as a walker in the street.[8] De Certeau was inspired by the skyscraper view of New York, while Chrétien, in a work containing many allusions to the commerce and politics of towns, describes how Gawain observed a town as if from above, his gaze traversing the streets and squares, and encountering the variety of tradesmen with their specialised commodities and skills:

> [Gawain] gazes on site of the castle, which sat on an arm of the sea, and saw that the walls and the tower were so strong that they feared no assault. He gazes on at the entire town, thronging with many fair people and the tables of the moneychangers all covered with gold and silver and coins. He sees the squares and streets all full of good workmen engaged in different crafts according to their various skills. One makes helmets and another coats of mail; one saddles and another shields; one bridles and another spurs; here they furbish swords. Here they full cloths and here they weave them; here they teasel them and here they shear them. Here they forge and cast silver, and they make fine and expensive things: chalices, cups and bowls and vessels worked in niello, rings, belts, and buckles. One might well believe and declare that the town held a fair every day, filled as it was with so many riches: wax, pepper, grain [an expensive dye], ermine and grey furs, and all kinds of merchandise. They gaze on all these things, looking here and there.[9]

This evocation echoes contemporary philosophical concerns with the mechanical arts and prefigures thirteenth-century and later attempts to find a language for the exciting world of specialised luxury goods. Chrétien's repetition of verbs denoting seeing (*esgarder, voire, regarder*) emphasises the visual engagement both with city space and with the selection and consumption of commodities, a feature of later texts dealing with such topics.[10] Moreover, mundane legal and administrative records of English and French towns in the period confirm the essential veracity of Chrétien's account, which could easily concern English cities such as London or Winchester, both of which he probably knew.[11]

Several twelfth-century texts engaged directly with London's landscape. The most popular and influential of them was Geoffrey of Monmouth's fictional 'History of the Kings of Britain', completed about 1136, a major theme in which is the destiny of the city and

---

[8] M. de Certeau, *L'invention du quotidien*, I: *Arts de faire*, ed. L. Giard (Paris, 1990), 139–42.

[9] *Chrétien de Troyes: Le Conte du Graal ou le Roman du Perceval*, ed. C. Méla (Paris, 1990), lines 5680–710, pp. 406–8; translation by the author.

[10] Especially in the Parisian *Dictionarius* of Jean de Garlande and Jean de Jandun's later description of *Les Halles*, discussed in D. Keene, 'Cultures de production, de distribution et de consommation en milieu urbain en Angleterre, 1100–1350', *Histoire Urbaine*, 16 (août 2006), 17–38.

[11] E. Chapin, *Les villes de foires de Champagne des origines au début du XIVe siècle* (Paris, 1937); *Winchester in the Early Middle Ages: An Edition and Discussion of the Winton Domesday*, ed. M. Biddle (Oxford, 1976); U. T. Holmes and M. A. Klenke, *Chrétien, Troyes, and the Grail* (Chapel Hill 1959), 23–4.

its association with a single realm of Britain.[12] In a careful exercise of literary construction, Geoffrey placed the 'Prophecies of Merlin' in his work just before his account of Arthur, thereby sacralising the prophesied events which subsequently unfolded in his story, including the fortunes of London.[13] Like later urban historians, Geoffrey includes among his starting points the real monuments and place-names of the city. By associating these landmarks with events in an invented history from his alleged Trojan foundation of London onwards and by connecting his fable in this way to the known world, Geoffrey lent an air of verisimilitude to his fable and at the same time invited his audience to reflect on the events and experiences of his own time.[14] Thus, Ludgate gives us King Lud, buried next to the gate, while Billingsgate gives us Belinus, the prince who had built a marvellous (but fictional) tower there with a gate opening on to the port where ships tied up, as indeed they actually did in Geoffrey's time at Billingsgate's distinctive harbour.[15] In a prophetic passage attributed to Merlin he seems to allude to plans to strengthen the defences by introducing the river into an enlarged city ditch, a project that was to be attempted at the Tower of London in 1190.[16] John Clark has noted that archaeological discoveries in London of Roman bronze statues, not in themselves unlikely, could explain Geoffrey's story of the embalmed body of Cadwallo being encased in a bronze equestrian statute placed on Ludgate.[17] On the other hand, awareness of the comparable statue of Constantine (as was then believed, but which we now know to be one of Marcus Aurelius) outside the Lateran palace in Rome, described in the *Mirabilia*,[18] may be a sufficient explanation and one which would allow an assertion of London's status by association with Rome. Geoffrey's account

---

[12] Unless otherwise stated, references to Geoffrey's 'History' are given to the chapter and section numbers assigned in the 'Vulgate' version edited from the Bern MS in vol. I of *The Historia Regum Britannie of Geoffrey of Monmouth*, ed. N. Wright and J. C. Crick (5 vols., Cambridge, 1985–91), and to page numbers in *The History of the Kings of Britain*, trans. L. Thorpe (Harmondsworth, 1966).

[13] C. Daniel, *Les prophéties de Merlin et la culture politique (xiie–xiiie siècle)* (Turnhout, 2006), 16–17; for the impact of Geoffrey's work on ideas of English and British history, see J. C. Crick, 'Geoffrey of Monmouth: Prophecy and History', *Journal of Medieval History*, 18 (1992), 357–71, and *eadem*, 'British Past and Welsh Future', *Celtica*, 23 (1999), 60–75.

[14] M. Otter, *Inventiones: Fiction and Referentiality in Twelfth-Century English Historical Writing* (Chapel Hill and London, 1996), 69–80; J. Clark, 'Trinovantum – The Evolution of a Legend', *Journal of Medieval History*, 7 (1981), 135–51.

[15] *Historia Regum*, ed. Wright and Crick, 44, 53; *History*, trans. Thorpe, 100, 106.

[16] *Historia Regum*, ed. Wright and Crick, 116(37); *History*, trans. Thorpe, 178; *The History of the King's Works*, II, ed. H. M. Colvin (1963), 708–9.

[17] J. Clark, 'Cadwallo, King of the Britons, the Bronze Horseman of London', in *Collectanea Londiniensia: Studies in London Archaeology and History Presented to Ralph Merrifield*, ed. J. Bird, H. Chapman and J. Clark (London and Middlesex Archaeological Society, Special Paper 2, 1978), 194–9; *Historia Regum*, ed. Wright and Crick, 201; *History*, trans. Thorpe, 280.

[18] *Mirabilia*, ed. Nichols, 42.

suggests a special interest in St Paul's cathedral and its environs, not least in the matter of the cathedral's claim to metropolitan status, but also in his mention of London as the burial place of kings and his references to Ludgate and the adjacent church of St Martin.[19] His audience of courtiers and clergy would have included its learned canons. A later dean, Ralph de Diceto, drew on Geoffrey's writings in his own historical work and John of Salisbury mocked the metropolitan pretensions of the see in a quasi-Galfredian remark about the bishop's intention to convert the cathedral into a Temple of Jupiter.[20] Such links may explain the fact that by the early thirteenth century a property between St Paul's and the river was known as 'the house of Diana', possibly an allusion to the goddess who in Geoffrey's story had prophesied that the Trojan Brutus would found a new city in a distant island. Brutus called his city 'New Troy', a notion that quickly became embedded in London's historical identity.[21]

Today, the most famous twelfth-century account of London is that which William fitz Stephen wrote about 1173 and placed at the beginning of his life of Thomas the recently martyred archbishop of Canterbury, the city's most famous son and soon to be adopted by the citizens as their special patron.[22] This relentlessly rhetorical work in its idealisation of London deploys a horde of Latin tags and covers virtually the entire repertoire of city praise. Nevertheless, it contains much that is demonstrably true and is notable for its sense of the landscape of the city, the specialised trades there and the surrounding territory.[23] In these

---

[19] *Historia Regum*, ed. Wright and Crick, 112(4), 115(19)(24), 201; *History*, trans. Thorpe, 172, 175–6, 280.

[20] *Radulfi de Diceto Decani Lundoniensis Opera Historica*, ed. W. Stubbs (2 vols., Rolls Series, 1876), I, 10–15, 36, II, 222–32; *Gilbert Foliot and his Letters*, ed. A. Morey and C. N. L. Brooke (Cambridge, 1965), 151–62; *The Letters of John of Salisbury*, II: *The Later Letters (1163–1180)*, ed. W. J. Millor and C. N. L. Brooke (Oxford, 1979), 666–7.

[21] *Historia Regum*, ed. Wright and Crick, 21; *History*, trans. Thorpe, 64–5; *Early Charters of the Cathedral Church of St Paul, London*, ed. M. Gibbs (Camden Society, 3rd series 58, 1939), nos. 79–80. By the fifteenth century the house, then in the possession of the cathedral, was known as 'Diana's Chamber': H. C. Maxwell Lyte, 'Report on the Manuscripts of the Dean and Chapter of St Paul's' (Appendix to the Historical Manuscripts Commission, *Ninth Report*, 1883), 1–72 at 4–5.

[22] For Becket's life, see F. Barlow, *Thomas Becket* (London 1986). For texts of the description of London: *Materials for the History of Thomas Becket*, ed. J. C. Robertson and J. B. Sheppard (7 vols., Rolls Series, 1875–85), III, 2–13; the text was incorporated in J. Stow, *A Survey of London* (1598); in his edition of the 1603 edition of Stow's *Survey*, Kingsford included a new edition of the description which notes significant textual variations: J. Stow, *A Survey of London*, ed. C. L. Kingsford (Oxford, 1908; reprinted 1971), 219–29, 387–8. Translations and commentaries include: F. M. Stenton, *Norman London, an Essay* (1934), including a translation by H. E. Butler; Butler's translation is reproduced in *Norman London by William fitz Stephen*, ed. D. Logan (New York, 1990).

[23] Scattergood, 'Misrepresenting the City', provides a valuable critique from these points of view; see also Ganim, 'The Experience of Modernity', and C. A. M. Clarke, *Literary Landscapes and the Idea of England, 700–1400* (Cambridge, 2006), 90–8.

respects, William's text can be associated with a style of historical and quasi-historical writing in twelfth-century England that displays a special concern with the geography and landscape of the kingdom, associating them with a new interpretation of the structure of British and English history marked by successive phases of order and disorder and by new senses of the western and northern frontiers of the realm and of the lesser, barbarous peoples beyond.[24] William's reading of snippets from Virgil and other classical authors may have stimulated his visual imagination, but he also drew on twelfth-century writing in a way that indicates familiarity with discourses concerning London and cities in general. From Geoffrey of Monmouth he adopted the city's Trojan origin and the prophecy concerning its status as a metropolitan see, while Geoffrey's stories of the city walls and towers perhaps influenced his own detailed description. Notions of hierarchy and authority, which inform William's emphasis on good lordship, may also lie behind his use of the phrase *arx palatina* to denote the Tower of London, which is clearly intended to pair it with the *palatium regium* at Westminster. The other great fortresses at the west end of the city, no longer in royal hands, were simply *castella*.[25] Though proudly noting that London was older than Rome, he points out that both cities used ancient laws and had institutions in common, such as a Senate, lesser magistrates, separate courts and regular assemblies. The London senators were its aldermen, whom the archbishop of Rouen, perhaps thinking of contemporary events in Rome, had addressed by that title when he wrote to the London commune at a date between 1141 and 1144.[26] Claims specific to London lie behind William's mention of the citizens' hunting rights in the surrounding territory, detailed in the charter of Henry I to the Londoners, which has been claimed as a genuine royal charter issued in 1133 but is more likely to be a later compilation

---

[24] A.Gransden, 'Realistic Observation in Twelfth-Century England', *Speculum*, 47 (1972), 29–51; *Henry, Archdeacon of Huntingdon, Historia Anglorum, the History of the English People*, ed. D. Greenway (Oxford, 1996), esp. lvii–lviii; J. Gillingham, *The English in the Twelfth Century: Imperialism, National Identity and Political Values* (Woodbridge, 2000); cf. J. Green, 'King Henry I and Northern England', *Transactions of the Royal Historical Society*, 6th series, 17 (2007), 35–55.

[25] For the scale of the western fortresses, or fortress, see *St Paul's: The Cathedral Church of London, 604–2004*, ed. D. Keene, A. Burns and A. Saint (New Haven and London, 2004), 18 and Fig. 9.

[26] He addressed the *senatoribus inclitis, civibus honoratis et omnibus communie Londoniensis*: *Reading Abbey Cartularies*, ed. B. R. Kemp (2 vols., Camden 4th series, 31 and 33, 1986–7), I, no. 463. Brihtmær of Gracechurch, a mid-eleventh-century donor of London property to Canterbury Cathedral, was described in a rental of *c.* 1100 as *senator*. *Anglo-Saxon Charters*, ed. A. J. Robertson (Cambridge, 1939), 217, 468–9; B. W. Kissan, 'An Early List of London Properties', *Transactions of the London and Middlesex Archaeological Society*, new series 8 (1938–40), 57–69.

based on a charter of Stephen and possibly, as suggested below, further elaborated after William wrote his account of London.[27]

To judge from the number of surviving manuscripts, William fitz Stephen's praise of London was not widely circulated, although it seems to have influenced some later writing, perhaps including a mid-thirteenth-century verse abridgement of Geoffrey's History, which elaborated the account of the setting of the city founded by Brutus by detailing the surrounding fields, meadows and woodland.[28] William's text was certainly known to thirteenth-century Londoners and was used to preface a later collection of the city's customs.[29] Moreover, the last quarter of the twelfth century was remarkable for a proliferation of brief descriptions of London's landscape, wealth and trade, most of which drew on Geoffrey of Monmouth's History and to a lesser extent on fitz Stephen's description, but in some cases added distinctive characterisations of their own. They include one perhaps by Hugh of Montacute and so dating to about 1170;[30] metrical descriptions by Alexander Neckam of about 1200, which emphasise London as the burial place of kings and especially note the fish of the river Thames;[31] and Gervase of Tilbury's remarkable account, which noted the stability of London's food supply, described the way in which the Thames at high tide flowed around the Tower and characterised the Thames as being more like a sea than a river, thereby suggesting a link with Chrétien's description of his fictional town. Gervase's description is embedded in a text that he addressed to the Emperor Otto IV about 1215, a critical period for the emperor's interest in the city.[32]

---

[27] C. N. L. Brooke, G. Keir and S. Reynolds, 'Henry I's Charter for the City of London', *Journal of the Society of Archivists*, 4 (1973), 558–78; C. W. Hollister, 'London's First Charter of Liberties: Is It Genuine?', *Journal of Medieval History*, 6 (1980), 289–306; J. Green, 'Financing Stephen's War', in *Anglo-Norman Studies*, 14, ed. M. Chibnall (Woodbridge, 1992), 91–114, at 106–7. The earliest surviving text of the 'charter' is as a copy in the early thirteenth-century London Collection, where it is inserted immediately after Henry I's coronation charter near the beginning of the text of the *Leges Henrici Primi*: Rylands Latin MS 155, fos. 78–9 (formerly numbered 77–8). The 'charter' itself is not mentioned in the otherwise comprehensive list of the city's royal grants of privileges surviving in the citizens' custody in 1212–14, also part of the London Collection: British Library [hereafter BL], Add MS 14252, fo. 106. See also *Leges Henrici Primi*, ed. L. J. Downer (Oxford, 1972), 81; J. H. Round, *The Commune of London and Other Studies* (1899), 256.

[28] The *Gesta Regum Britanniae*, being *Historia Regum*, ed. Wright and Crick, V, at 32–3.

[29] *Liber Custumarum*: pt 1 of *Munimenta Gildhallae Londoniensis: Liber Albus, Liber Custumarum et Liber Horn*, ed. H. T. Riley (3 vols., Rolls Series, 1859–62), II, pt 1, 1–15.

[30] A. B. Scott, 'Some Poems Attributed to Richard of Cluny', in *Medieval Learning and Literature: Essays Presented to Richard William Hunt*, ed. J. J. G. Alexander and M. T. Gibson (Oxford, 1976), 181–99, text at 197. A. Rigg, *The History of Anglo-Latin Literature, 1066–1422* (Cambridge, 1992), 135–6 n. 231.

[31] *Alexandri Neckam De naturis rerum libro duo: With the Poem of the Same Author, De laudibus divinae sapientia*, ed. T. Wright (Rolls Series, 1863), 410, 414–15, 458–9.

[32] *Otia imperialia: Recreation for an Emperor, Gervase of Tilbury*, ed. S. E. Banks and J. W. Binns (Oxford, 2002), 398–403.

Figure 1 Seal of the barons of London, c. 1220, drawings from surviving impressions.

Texts such as these almost certainly informed the earliest surviving graphic representations of medieval London, in what one could describe as reverse ekphrasis. The earliest of them are on the city's common seal, the 'seal of the barons of London', recently characterised as 'one of the outstanding civic seals of medieval Europe' (Figure 1). On one side it displays St Paul and on the other St Thomas, each in relation to the city landscape. Its style suggests that the seal was commissioned about 1220, the year of the translation of Thomas's remains at Canterbury on the Jubilee of his martyrdom, when the citizens were initiating an effort to commemorate him at his birthplace in the city.[33] It includes a striking and in many ways realistic panorama of London. St Paul's occupies a central position with its tall spire, probably the 'tower' completed in 1221. To either side are substantial fortifications, representing the Tower of London to the east and Baynard's Castle to the west. The view seems to show the river Thames lapping against the city wall. Roman London had been walled against the river, but visible traces of that part of the walled circuit had probably disappeared long before 1100, so the image may rather have been inspired by fitz Stephen's account of a wall with towers which had once enclosed the city on the south but had been washed away, a notion itself perhaps derived less from observation or from knowledge of actual events than from Geoffrey of Monmouth's story of how King

[33] For a good photograph of an impression of the obverse and a note by T. A. Heslop on the style of the seal, see *Age of Chivalry: Art in Plantagenet England, 1200–1400*, ed. J. Alexander and P. Binski (1987), 273, no. 193. For a photograph of an impression of the reverse, see *St Paul's*, ed. Keene *et al.*, Fig. 11. For the citizens' commemoration of St Thomas: D. Keene and V. Harding, *Historical Gazetteer of London before the Great Fire*, I: *Cheapside* (Cambridge, 1987), no. 105/18.

Figure 2 London as depicted by Matthew Paris in his itinerary from London to Apulia, c. 1252. (© British Library Board. All Rights Reserved. BL, Royal MS 14 C.VII, fo. 2).

Lud had entirely surrounded the city with walls and towers. Certainly, the accounts and depictions of this period convey the idea, common in representations of cities, that London's wall made a complete and perfect circuit. The great tower with the gate opening towards the river shown on the seal may be intended to represent Belinus's tower at Billingsgate. In this way Geoffrey's History both shaped perception of the city and became entwined with expressions of its political identity. The other side of the seal portrays the Londoners before St Thomas, in what seems to be a group of men on one side and a group of women, apparently portrayed as Roman matrons, on the other. This portrayal may refer to fitz Stephen's text, where there is a comparable juxtaposition between an account of the dignity of the citizens and a statement in praise of London's matrons as *ipsae Sabinae*.

Matthew Paris's famous sketch of London (Figure 2) conveys similar messages.[34] Again, St Paul's is the focal point within a circuit of walls.

[34] S. Lewis, *The Art of Matthew Paris in the Chronica Majora* (Aldershot, 1987), 332–5 and Fig. 204.

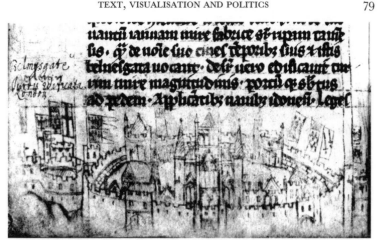

Figure 3 Drawing of London c. *1300, added to a text of Geoffrey of Monmouth's 'History of the Kings of Britain', below the story of Billingsgate. (© British Library Board. All Rights Reserved. BL, Royal MS 13* A.*iii, fo. 28v).*

The text above describes the city as *chef dengleterre* and founded by Brutus who called it New Troy. Below, six city gates are named and are indicated by distinctive signs. This underlines the fact that the drawing serves as an ideograph rather than an exact representation, for one important city gate, Aldersgate, is omitted and Billingsgate, which was not a gate at all, is included. The mythical 'tower of Billingsgate' may be intended by the words *la tur* just west of London Bridge (*punt*), while the Tower of London itself is shown on the other side of the river. This total of seven gates, one of them mythical, may justify William fitz Stephen's allusion to Thebes in his account of London's defences, which he said included seven double gates in the city wall. Indeed, Matthew Paris's signs indicate double gates. An equally meaningful graphic representation is an early fourteenth-century sketch added below the Billingsgate section of an earlier text of Geoffrey of Monmouth's History (Figure 3). Again, the view is south, with St Paul's at the centre and the Tower of London to the left. The city walls are shown as a complete circuit. Against the river, to the west of the Tower of London, the large gate-tower is presumably intended as that erected by Belinus.

The consistency in these representations suggests that this image of London and its expressions in historical or quasi-historical texts was widely appreciated. They also relate to an understanding of London as the capital and organising principle of the kingdom. This idea had been current for some time and in particular was articulated during the 1140s in accounts of the events in King Stephen's troubled reign: London was the 'queen metropolis of the kingdom' and the 'head of the whole kingdom', while the Londoners were 'in effect magnates because of the greatness of their city in England'.[35] For fitz Stephen, some decades later, the city was the 'seat of the kingdom of the English' and the bishops and lay magnates were 'almost to be counted as citizens because of their frequent attendance there for councils and on their own business'.

This conjunction of text and image brings us to the London Collection and politics. The collection now survives in two parts, one in Manchester and the other in the British Library, each containing about 130 folios.[36] The text is largely intact, but not without some damage and possible disordering in the final section of the work. It was written by two scribes. The first, using a script of an older style than that of the second, was at work after 1204 and wrote the whole of the Manchester part and the first four-fifths of the British Library part, carrying the collection of materials into the reign of John. The ruling and layout of the text demonstrates that the second scribe's work (beginning on fo. 104v, immediately below the final lines written by the first scribe) was intended as part of the same overall project. He copied several items originating before 1204 and others datable to 1205–6 and later, the latest of which is a list of the city's sheriffs holding office between the years 1188–9 and 1216–17.[37]

---

[35] *Gesta Stephani*, ed. K. R. Potter and R. H. C. Davis (Oxford, 1976), 4, 112; *William Of Malmesbury ca 1090–1143, Historia Novella: The Contemporary History*, ed. E. King, trans. K. R. Potter (Oxford, 1998), 94–5; cf. *The Chronicle of Jocelin of Brakelond*, ed. H. E. Butler (1949), 75–7.

[36] The first part is now Manchester, the John Rylands University Library, Rylands Latin MS 155, and the second, BL, Add. MS 14252. See F. Liebermann, *Über die Leges Anglorum saeculo xiii ineunte Londiniis collectae* (Halle, 1894), and *idem*, 'A Contemporary Manuscript of the Leges Anglorum Londiniis collectae', *English Historical Review*, 28 (1913), 732–45. A selection of the London material in Add. MS 14252 is printed and discussed in M. Bateson, 'A London Municipal Collection of the Reign of John', *English Historical Review*, 17 (1902), 480–511, 707–30, which also identifies the remaining materials previously printed elsewhere from this or later MSS. The London laws, customs and memoranda from the collection are more comprehensively printed and described in M. Weinbaum, *London unter Eduard I. und II.* (2 vols., Stuttgart, 1933), II, 5–91, which remains the most convenient and accurate version of that material so far published. The way in which the collection, for some of its contents, appears to have drawn on earlier and perhaps more accurate, but no longer surviving, transcripts is discussed in Brooke *et al.*, 'Henry I's charter'. Recent discussions of aspects of the collection are: P. Wormald, '"*Quadripartitus*"', in *Law and Government in Medieval England and Normandy: Essays in Honour of Sir John Holt*, ed. G. Garnet and J. Hudson (Cambridge, 1994), 111–47; J. Gillingham, 'Stupor mundi: 1204 et un obituaire de Richard Coeur de Lion depuis longtemps tombé dans l'oubli', in *Plantagenêts et Capétiens: confrontations et héritages*, ed. M. Aurell and N.-Y. Tonnerre (Turnhout, 2006), 397–411. The quires of the MSS are briefly described in N. N. R. Ker, 'Liber Custumarum and Other Manuscripts Formerly at the Guildhall', *The Guildhall Miscellany* 1.3 (1954), 37–45, at 37.

[37] The list of sheriffs is printed in Weinbaum, *London*, II, 48–9; see also Brooke *et al.*, 'Henry I's charter', n. 7, where its last part is described as 'corrupt'. Allowing for normal variations

The second scribe probably worked over a short period, perhaps at some time between 1214 and 1216, and at least a part of his text was completed after Prince Louis's invasion or even after the death of King John. His role was to order and copy texts relating specifically to the citizens of London and their objectives at that time. The first scribe's work, perhaps undertaken immediately before that of the second scribe, had consisted mostly of copying earlier laws, but it included linking material specially composed for the occasion. The many 'London interpolations' in the texts of the laws, especially those in the 'Laws of Edward the Confessor', may have been made at that time. Adjustments, and even additions, to an existing text of the supposed charter of Henry I to the citizens may have been part of this programme. The laws of Henry II are represented by a distinctive and somewhat confused version of Glanville.[38] The resonances between the two parts of the collection seem to be a deliberate literary and polemical device, indicating that the compilation as a whole and the interpolations in the earlier texts were planned and executed as a single programmatic scheme, most likely in London and during the years immediately before and after the granting of Magna Carta in June 1215.

Although the text is well ordered and decorated overall, it is clear that both scribes were hasty and sometimes inaccurate, necessitating marginal corrections and additions. Haste is also indicated by the leaving of gaps for text to be inserted later. Insertions sometimes turned out to be too large for the space available and some gaps were not filled (Figure 4). The high incidence of ruled but unwritten gaps in the folios of the second scribe's section suggests that the project of gathering London's laws and customs was both hasty and not so much completed in 1216–17 as abandoned on the death of King John. The appearance of the manuscript thus conveys the drama of time in which it written, with much of the linking material or introductory material placed between sections apparently not having been fully composed by the time that the copying of those sections had been completed. Parts of a run of several blank folios left by the first scribe were used by a third for transcripts of two additional texts.[39] These were documents of London interest, but the folios were ruled and written in a format and style very different from that of the other two scribes and so the texts presumably were inserted after, but perhaps not long after, 1216–17. These two documents have been discussed as if they were an integral part

in name forms and the haste with which the whole of the last part of the collection was compiled, the list overall is an accurate one and it is not necessary to postulate that it was compiled or copied after 1217.

[38] *The Treatise on the Laws and Customs of the Realm of England Commonly Called Glanville*, ed. G. D. G. Hall, with further notes by M. T. Clanchy (Oxford, 1993), lv–lvii.

[39] BL, Add. MS 14252, fos. 88v–89, 90v–91.

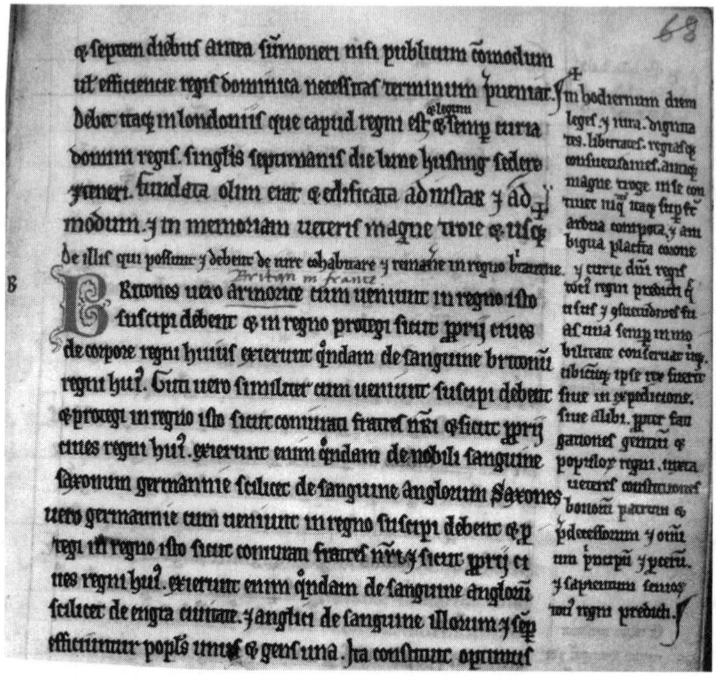

Figure 4 The hasty composition of the 'London Collection', showing how the account of London's foundation in memory of Troy was added after the description of the city's court of Husting and then continued in the margin. The description of Husting relates to a clause in Henry I's supposed charter to the citizens of London copied earlier in the collection. All the material on this folio is part of the longest of the 'London interpolations' in the text of the 'Laws of Edward the Confessor'; for this section of the text, see Gesetze, ed. Liebermann, I, *657. (Manchester, the John Rylands University Library, Rylands Latin MS 155, fo. 69).*

of the collection and had a bearing on its purpose, but that was clearly not the case.[40] They are the only suggestion of any later use of the manuscript as a place for collecting additional material relevant to the city, although marginal annotations show that it was carefully scrutinised during the

[40] Bateson, 'Municipal Collection', 483–6; Weinbaum, *London*, II, 10–17. The full significance of these additions is not clear. One, referring back to a dispute in the 1130s, concerns the rights of the lord of Baynard's Castle over the water of the Thames; the other, interpreted by Bateson and Weinbaum as a record of civic property, is in fact an extract from an early thirteenth-century rental of property belonging to Canterbury Cathedral Priory on the London waterfront to the west of Queenhithe (see D. Keene and V. Harding, *A Survey of Documentary Sources for Property Holding in London before the Great Fire* (London Record Society, 22, 1985), 72). A concern with the river is perhaps the connection between them.

late thirteenth and early fourteenth centuries by those interested in the city's laws.

The overall context and purpose of this collection has long been appreciated, not least as a result of the careful analysis and pithy comments of Felix Liebermann. It served the purpose of the barons, of the mayor and leaders of London and of the canons of St Paul's in their confrontation with King John, as a statement of established laws and customs of the case against kings who acted unjustly and without due forms of consent, and of an ideal of responsible government by counsel. These principles underlay Magna Carta. Apart from the close involvement of London in the opposition to John, there are direct links between parts of the collection and the Articles of the Barons and clauses in Magna Carta. Secondly, the collection presents a providential sweep of British history emphasising the extent of what English rule should be and tracing elements of that dominion to the time of King Arthur. This vision drew on Geoffrey of Monmouth, but with an additional emphasis, which reflects mercantile interests (presumably those of the leading Londoners) and a concern for the links between the inhabitants of Britain and other peoples.[41] Ralph Hanna has recently drawn attention to the fact that this document is far more than a simple collection of laws and customs, which is how historians have tended to exploit it so far, and that its literary and rhetorical structure reveal much about its purpose and meaning. When Hanna's book appeared,[42] I was thinking on similar lines about the choices which determined the content of the collection, the light they threw on London interests outside the immediate context of the baronial opposition and what implications this might have for our understanding of the London customs as recorded in the document. My subsequent thinking has benefited greatly from Hanna's ideas.

The arrangement of the material in the collection is striking (Figure 5). Laws are gathered in a chronological succession of groups according to the kings associated with them, from Ine, the king of Wessex who died in 726, through Alfred, Athelstan, Cnut, Edward the Confessor (said to have been confirmed by William I, decrees attributed to whom are entered before Edward's laws), to Henry II, who died in 1189. Several of these groups conclude with a few lines of praise on the monarch in question, perhaps inspired by the characterisations of kings from Arthur onwards that Henry of Huntingdon had included in his history.[43] Though not totally formulaic these encomia have much in common, stressing the

[41] Gillingham, 'Stupor mundi', 399–400, summarises views on this purpose. See also J. C. Holt, *Magna Carta* (Cambridge, 1992), 20, 55–7, 93–5, and Wormald, '"*Quadripartitus*"'.
[42] R. Hanna, *London Literature* (Cambridge, 2005), 56–8, 70–2, 84–9; Hanna mistranslates a few passages.
[43] *Historia Anglorum*, ed. Greenway, 98–9, 226–7, 298–9, 318–19, 366–7.

Tribal Hidage and Burghal Hidage
(Rylands, fo. 3v-4)

approx 66 folios: laws, Ine to Edward the Confessor

Description of the realm of Britain (Geoffrey of Monmouth)
(Rylands, fo. 70)

approx 73 folios (to end of Rylands MS): laws, Edward the Confessor (cont.)
to Henry II

approx 87 folios (from beginning of Add MS 14252): laws etc, Henry II
('Glanville') to Richard I

Prester John's Letter
(Add. MS, fos 92-97v)

4 folios: London laws mostly concerning foreigners

Description of Britain (largely Henry of Huntingdon)
(Add. MS, fos 101-104)

approx 21 folios: London customs, laws and memoranda (possibly divided at
14th folio by lists of counties in the judicial circuits,1208-9), articles for a royal
charter, descent of the honour of Boulogne

Hidage of Middlesex
(Add. MS, fos 126-7)

4 folios: Cornhill family, fitz Ailwin's building assize (London heroes?)

*Figure 5 The geographical framing of the London Collection. The texts in bold are the
framing element.*

military vigour of the king and the extent of his rule, sometimes using the
adjective *inclitus* which, significantly, is deployed in connection with King
Arthur in the most significant of the London additions to the version of
the 'Laws of Edward the Confessor' contained in the collection.[44] The
encomium on Athelstan, for example, declares that he ruled up to the
limits of the kingdom established by Arthur, while the longer statement on
Henry II emphasises his conquest of Ireland and the numerous territories

---

[44] These London additions are identified in Liebermann's edition of the laws: *Die Gesetze
der Angelsachsen*, ed. F. Leibermann (3 vols., Halle, 1903–16), I, 627–70, with these references
to Arthur at 655, 659. The text in *Gesetze* should be read in conjunction with Liebermann,
'Contemporary Manuscript'.

that he ruled between Norway and Spain. There follows a brief but strikingly warm encomium on Richard I, informed by knowledge of the later loss of Normandy, and a rubric and a blank space indicate that at this point it was intended to include at least an extract from Geoffrey of Vinsauf's extravagant praise of that king.[45] After this the final section of the collection focuses on the reign of John, although without identifying him as king. These sections are framed by a sequence of texts of a different type, the purpose of which is to provide a geographical description or idealisation, indeed a visualisation, of the territory over which the monarchs ruled. Although the text is not illustrated, there is a strong visual element in this structure, recalling that of a narrative sequence of images, each defined by a frame (as in a mural or manuscript history of the world), or of a gallery of sculptures portraying kings or prophets holding the texts or tables of their laws, such as can be seen on Romanesque or early Gothic cathedrals.[46] Visual or architectural framing was an important mnemonic and cognitive device in rhetoric and oratory, adding expressive force to narratives which, as in the case of the London Collection, were often composed of multiple stories, interrupted but interlaced.[47] Sculptural programmes of this type sometimes portray the forerunners of Christ. The rather different message of this collection, compiled after the loss of Normandy in 1204, is that King John had much to live up to.

The choice of geographical texts is illuminating (Figure 5). At the beginning, before King Ine's laws, are placed texts of the Tribal and of the Burghal Hidages, early lists of territories and towns which serve to introduce the realm. Towards the end of the longest of the London interpolations in the 'Laws of Edward the Confessor' is a description of the kingdom of Britain, derived from Geoffrey of Monmouth. Significantly, this description marks a transition from an encomium on King Ine to an account of the 'right and appendages of the crown of Britain' containing praise of Arthur, the 'most glorious of the kings of the Britons', and a

---

[45] Gillingham, 'Stupor mundi', 400–8. Gillingham is mistaken in the statement (at 410–11) that the collection's favour towards King Richard is further indicated by its inclusion of the text of Richard's charter concerning Portsmouth issued in 1194: the text is not included, although, for different reasons, a copy forms part of later London collections.

[46] G. Zarnecki, *Later English Romanesque Sculpture, 1140–1210* (1953), 48–9; idem, *Romanesque Lincoln: The Sculpture of the Cathedral* (Lincoln, 1988); *The Romanesque Frieze and its Spectator: The Lincoln Symposium Papers*, ed. D. Kahn (1992), *passim*, and esp. W. Sauerläder, Romanesque sculpture in its architectural context', 17–43, and W. Cahn, 'Romanesque Sculpture and the Spectator', 45–60.

[47] H. R. Broderick, 'Some Attitudes towards the Frame in Anglo-Saxon Manuscripts of the Tenth and Eleventh Centuries', *Artibus et Historiae*, 5 (1982), 31–42; M. Carruthers, *The Craft of Thought: Meditation, Rhetoric and the Making of Images, 400–1200* (Cambridge, 1998), 122, 151–3, 201–4, 237–41; A. Fowler, *Renaissance Realism: Narrative Images in Literature and Art* (Oxford, 2003), 27–8, 45–6, 77.

long list of the territories he had ruled.[48] At a later important transition point in the collection, the brief section on King Richard is followed by a copy of one of the earliest versions of Prester John's letter to the Emperor Manuel Comnenus, a fictitious text composed a generation so earlier. This introduces the controversial reign of King John and the part of the collection which explicitly focuses on London. As a piece of exotica, the letter may have been chosen for its appeal to an audience of barons and wealthy merchants who would have had some knowledge of the east and its commodities, including the pepper carefully described in the letter and mentioned in the documents which immediately follow it as one of the commodities brought to London. The letter is also a powerful statement of a 'moral utopia', a well-ordered, wealthy and extensive territory, where seventy-two kings and their provinces were subject to a priestly ruler.[49] In key respects this resembled the realm of King Arthur as presented in the interpolations and it certainly offered a model for John's kingdom of England, while its image of Christian rule, like Arthur's, would underline criticism of John's failure to protect the church. After the letter, there is entered the first of the texts which detail the laws and customs of London. This is in Anglo-Norman, in contrast to all previous and the majority of subsequent texts, which are in Latin. My current hypothesis is that the texts in Anglo-Norman, the vernacular of the leading citizens and the barons, deal with matters which might be specifically contested by the king and were in some sense drafts for internal discussion, rather than statements for public consumption or straightforward copies of earlier texts from the city's archive. This Anglo-Norman text, which occupies a crucial position in the collection, is in three distinct, but not strongly separated, sections. The first deals with legal procedures and rules concerning landholding and debt in the city's Husting court, with the roles of the sheriffs and aldermen and with the relationship between foreigners and the 'law of London'; the second details regulations concerning merchants from Lorraine and elsewhere overseas; and the third deals with the city Folkmoot and its relation to the Husting. The concern with foreigners is emphasised by the text's proximity to the letter of Prester John. This text is followed immediately by another geographical description of Britain, in Anglo-Norman but largely drawn from Henry of Huntingdon, a description of the territory clearly paired with that of Prester John's exotic realm. The first scribe then

---

[48] For the interpolation, see *Gesetze*, ed. Liebermann, I, 655–9.

[49] B. Hamilton, 'Prester John and the Three Kings of Cologne', in *Studies in Medieval History Presented to R. H. C. Davis*, ed. H. Mayr-Harting and R. I. Moore (1985). For the date of the particular version used in the collection, see M. Gosman, *La lettre du Prêtre Jean* (Groningen, 1982), 32–4, and B. Wagner, *Die 'Epistola Presbiteris Johannis': Lateinisch und Deutsch; Überlieferung, Textgeschichte, Rezeption und Übertragungen im Mittelalter* (Tübingen, 2000), 55. I. Bejczy, *La lettre du prêtre Jean* (Paris, 2001), *passim*. See also Hanna, *London Literature*, 82–6.

completed his work by introducing the final section of the collection as 'a part of the laws of the city of London and of its franchises'. At that point the second scribe took over. At the beginning of his, or his instructor's, selection of London material he placed the Latin text now known as the *Libertas Londoniensis*, which deals with some of the same matters, including Folkmoot, Husting and rules for foreign merchants, including one limiting their stay in the city to forty days. This text seems to be based on a mid-twelfth-century exemplar. At the end of his London material the scribe copied the Hidage of Middlesex, listing the components of the territory immediately subject to London. After that he added two more items, which, as we shall see, may have been intended as a heroic conclusion.

The clearest statements of political principle in the collection are to be found in the interpolations in two earlier sets of laws, those of King Henry I, originally compiled about 1117, and those attributed to Edward the Confessor, which in their first version appear to have been compiled in the 1130s or a little earlier.[50] The more extensive interpolations were in the latter, which seem very likely to have been made specifically for the purpose of this collection, and presumably resulted in the 'laws of St Edward' that the barons were said to have sought from King John in 1215.[51] Recurrent themes in the London interpolations to Edward's laws[52] emphasise the rights of the Crown, the unity and extent of the kingdom, and the king's responsibility to protect the church and the realm, to promote good laws and abolish bad ones and to do justice according to counsel. They also outline an ideal, but historically based structure of local government and political assembly, informed by common counsel, communes and an oath of brotherhood which united nobility, townsmen and all people for the utility of the realm. This system was older than Arthur, who used it to consolidate the kingdom of Britain and drive out enemies. These ideas seem to have been informed by a memory of the great council convoked by John in London in 1205, following which the adult population was to be organised into a commune for the defence of the realm.[53] The interpolations emphasise the leading role of London as *caput regni . . . et legum et semper curia domini regis* and the way in which it had been founded and built in the 'manner, form and memory of old, great Troy', whose laws and liberties it still contained (Figure 4). These would have been the laws that Arthur found. In addition there were more or less direct allusions to London in the identification of aldermen as senators,

[50] *Leges*, ed. Downer, 34–7; B. R. O'Brien, *God's Peace and the King's Peace: The Laws of Edward the Confessor* (Philadelphia, 1999), 44–8.

[51] Holt, *Magna Carta*, 115.

[52] *Gesetze*, ed. Liebermann, I, 635–7, 639–40, 655–60, 664.

[53] *The Historical Works of Gervase of Canterbury*, ed. W. Stubbs (2 vols., Rolls Series, 1870–80), I, 96–7.

in the mention of folkmoots being summoned by a bell and in references to hunting rights and to local armies being led by aristocratic constables or *heretocii*.

The term 'common counsel' (*commune consilium*) used several times in the interpolations may have a had a particular resonance for Londoners, for the copy of a city inventory, datable to between 1212 and 1214 and forming part of the collection, lists a 'seal of the common council' kept with some of the charters 'in the treasury' (*in thesauro*). This 'common council' (to be distinguished from the later medieval common council of the city) may have been identical with the body of twenty-four which in 1205–6 swore that it would legally see to counselling (*ad consulendum*) according to its custom by the right of the king and that no member of the body would take a bribe when giving judgement.[54] The oath taken by this body, which presumably comprised the twenty-four aldermen of the city, was perhaps influenced by the statute arising from the great council which John had summoned in London in 1205, according to the terms of which it would have represented the commune of the city. An alternative interpretation is that the 'common council' of this period also included a number of *probi homines*, who are recorded from time to time in this period as supporting the mayor and aldermen and who appear to be distinct from the larger body which constituted the commune.[55] The building code of 1212, for example, was made *per consilium proborum virorum* and refers to the way in which scotales could be licensed *per commune consilium civitatis apud Gildehallam*, although the code itself was enacted at Guildhall by 'the mayor and other barons of the city'.[56] The 'seal of the barons of London', discussed above, appears stylistically to be later in date and so the 'seal of the common council' was presumably its predecessor, although it may not have been owned by a body precisely comparable to the 'barons'. A letter from the mayor and *universitas* of London in 1219 was said to be sealed with the *communi sigillo civitatis Londonie*, a phrase which could denote either of the seals, if indeed there were two.[57] The treasury where this seal and the charters were kept is usually assumed to have been at the city guildhall, but given the close association between St Paul's and the London folkmoot and between the canons and the leading citizens at this time, plus the role of cathedrals as custodians of archives relating to

---

[54] Bateson, 'Municipal Collection', 507–8; Round, *Commune*, 237; Weinbaum, *London*, II, 49–50. The inventory's phrase *cum sigillo de communi cons* cannot refer to a seal attached to the charter which precedes it in the list since that charter was a royal one.

[55] Bateson, 'Municipal Collection', 509–11.

[56] Weinbaum, *London*, II, 89–91.

[57] *Patent Rolls 1216–1225* (1901), 211.

county administration,[58] it is at least equally likely that the 'treasury' was the cathedral treasury at St Paul's.

The interpolations indicate the particular interest that Edward's laws had for the Londoners and the way in which that interest extended back beyond their commune of 1191 to Stephen's reign and the city's earlier commune of 1141 which had united citizens and barons in a common cause. In that year, when the Londoners were negotiating terms with the Empress Matilda, they had asked that they might be allowed to live under the excellent laws of King Edward rather than the severe ones of her father, King Henry. Matilda harshly refused and London turned against her.[59] Perhaps the idea of a distinctive London law of some antiquity was consolidated at that time, for the story that Brutus had given the Londoners their law was added to the original version of Geoffrey's History before 1155.[60] With regard to the kingdom as a whole, the laws of King Edward had by 1100 or soon after achieved a status as the best of all laws, but in 1141 it seems that the Londoners were seeking laws which would apply specifically to them. Moreover, there were reasons why rulers of London might have a particular regard for King Edward as the source of their law. Thus, the first mayor, Henry fitz Ailwin, members of the Cornhill family and possibly other leading families at the time of the 1191 commune could count among their ancestors members of the London guild of *cnihtas*, which had received from King Edward a writ confirming its jurisdiction and good laws. In 1125 that writ was placed on the altar of the London priory of Holy Trinity Aldgate as confirmation of the guild's gift of land and rights, and the writ would still have been at the priory when fitz Ailwin was buried there in 1212.[61] It may be that the two documents added at the very end of the collection (Figure 5) were intended to signal this Edwardian link, for the first of them was a genealogy, in Anglo-Norman, of the Cornhill and supposedly related London families and the second named fitz Ailwin in relation to his most well-known act as mayor, the city building code drawn up after the Great Fire of London in July 1212 and written in Latin. This code, as we shall see, may also have been included in the collection as a concluding expression of the effectiveness of the city's government based at Guildhall. This pairing may deliberately underline one of the collection's pervading themes, the

[58] Cf. R. L. Poole, 'The Publication of Great Charters by the English Kings', *English Historical Review*, 28 (1913), 444–53.

[59] *The Chronicle of John of Worcester*, ed. P. McGurk, II and III (Oxford, 1995–8), III, 296–7.

[60] *Historia Regum*, ed. Wright and Crick, II (the 'first variant version'), cap. 22.

[61] *Anglo-Saxon Writs*, ed. F. E. Harmer (Manchester, 1952), 231–5; *The Cartulary of Holy Trinity Aldgate*, ed. G. A. J. Hodgett (London Record Society 7, 1971), 168. The members of the guild in 1125 included Robert and his brother Ailwin, sons of Leofstan (of whom the latter was probably Henry fitz Ailwin's father) and Edward Hupcornhille, ancestor of the Cornhills.

unity of different peoples within the kingdom, for Henry fitz Ailwin was of English descent and, according to the genealogy, the Cornhills had a Norman ancestor.

Given primacy among the foreign groups named in the London interpolations to Edward's laws who by right should live in the kingdom of Britain as *proprii cives* were Bretons from Armorica. Here the interpolator drew on Geoffrey of Monmouth's account of the close connections between Britain and Brittany and of the prophecy that the *cives* (that is the Bretons) of the island shall return to it, a prophecy that William fitz Stephen related to London. From its context, later readers could relate this prophecy to the eventual loss of Normandy.[62] Thus the interpolator's highlighting of the Bretons might form part of the case against John, not least on account of his role in the murder of his nephew, Arthur of Brittany, in 1203.

The collection conveys a sense that the rules by which Londoners governed their public lives were regarded as law rather than custom, that is with a general and binding purpose rather than of merely local application. Such a distinction was made by the Pisans in the late 1150s when they envisaged a double code for their city, one of *leges* and one of *usus*.[63] Even in Pisa, however, the distinction between law and custom was fuzzy and some London rules were described as customs, while in a few other towns of the period the rules were described as 'laws and customs'. Among English towns, only London, so far as I am aware, was marked by references to its 'law' in the singular alone.[64] Moreover, London customs were widely employed as models for those granted to other towns and this may have contributed to their standing as 'law'. This actual or perceived special status of London's customs seems to explain certain choices concerning the documents that were included in the collection. For example, it was clearly not the aim to assemble a set of the citizens' royal grants of privileges, of which twelve (or seven, excluding duplicates) were listed in the inventory of 1212–14 already mentioned. The collection includes texts of only two such grants, that of Henry I, which, if it had ever existed, survived only as a copy in 1212–14, and that of Henry II, both copies of which were then in the custody of private citizens. In the London Collection, the texts of Henry I's and of Henry II's charters to the citizens are placed immediately after the monarch's 'coronation charter', as if to emphasise the high standing and wider significance of the privileges enjoyed by London. The former mentioned the law of London and the latter confirmed to the Londoners the law

[62] Daniel, *Les prophéties*, 43–4; Brooke and G. Keir, *London 800–1216*, 120–1.

[63] C. Wickham, *Courts and Conflict in Twelfth-Century Tuscany* (Oxford, 2003), 108, 112, 114–16.

[64] Up to 1216, 'laws' or 'laws and customs' are mentioned only in royal charters to Lincoln, Newcastle, Northampton, Oxford and Hartlepool (following Newcastle).

of his grandfather's day, seemingly authoritative statements which may have been the charters' principal value for the compiler. They would have resonated with the several references to the 'law of London' in the important first text detailing London customs which was entered in the collection immediately after Prester John's letter. Later royal charters to London which mention its law simply repeat the phrase from Henry II's charter, while in the thirteenth century, as the difference between what was fixed and general and what was local became more clearly established, references to London law faded away. It may be relevant here to note the royal letter of 1235 which directed the mayor and sheriffs to suppress the teaching of 'laws' in the city. Paul Brand suggested that this may relate to some developing synthesis of Roman and English laws,[65] but it seems possible that instead, or perhaps as well, it concerned the complex laws of London itself, perhaps as yet only imperfectly recorded in writing, the teaching of which could be viewed as subversive.

Important elements in the collection's argument concern trade. Especially significant is what is clearly an early thirteenth-century statement copied by the first scribe into a gap he had left in an early section.[66] This statement drew on earlier sources, but also included new ideas and some notions contrary to those favoured by the king. It affirmed the unity of weights, measures, currency, tolls and mercantile customs (possibly an allusion to London law) throughout the ports and the entire kingdom of Britain. In addition, it affirmed the freedom of merchants (presumably foreign merchants) to enter and return through the ports, with the qualification that they could neither go with their goods beyond the legal limits of the ports out into the kingdom nor stay in the ports more than forty days, restrictions which clearly allude to the customs of London recorded near the end of the collection. Magna Carta also stated merchants' freedom of entry and departure but, reflecting what had been royal policy since the time of Richard I, added that they were free to move about England and said nothing about restricting them to the ports, thereby ignoring what appears to have been older custom, at least in London. The statement notes the restriction on exporting materials of war, customary by 1200, but makes a significant addition by declaring that wool cannot be taken overseas out of the kingdom of Britain without having been woven into cloth. There was no royal policy of restricting the export of wool, except during periods of warfare, and so this prohibition must reflect the interest of native merchants who were active in the production and export of cloth and their fears concerning the loss of trade in the face of competition from Flemish towns. Here too, the

---

[65] P. Brand, 'Westminster Hall and Europe: European Aspects of the Common Law', in *London and Europe*, ed. Boffey and King, 55–83.

[66] Rylands Latin MS 115, fo. 10v; Liebermann, *Leges Anglorum*, 12–14.

London interest was strong, for the latter part of the collection includes, in Anglo-Norman, the 'law of the weavers and fullers' of Winchester and other towns which asserted weavers' subjection to merchants and was said also to be the custom of London, where in 1202 the citizens briefly managed to suppress the weavers' independence.[67] London was, or had been within living memory, a major centre of cloth manufacture and finishing and Henry fitz Ailwin and his family appear to have been active in that business since at least the early twelfth century.[68] The compiler of the collection endowed this powerful statement of London mercantile interests with special authority as long-standing custom in Britain by placing it among the laws of Ine. Thus, Liebermann named it 'Pseudo-Ine'.

Commercial interests, especially London ones, were in several respects at variance with royal policy overseas during this period. Dynastic ties and periodic alliances between Plantagenet and German Welf kings, together with the position of Cologne as a focus of Welf interest and a major trading partner of London, shaped a diplomatic environment in which English and German monarchs manoeuvred to protect their interests against French kings by building up regional alliances which where possible included Cologne. Cologne merchants had long enjoyed special privileges in London, which in 1194 Richard I had extended by freeing them of a rent due from their guildhall in the city and allowing them freedom to travel throughout England and to visit fairs. This grant deprived Londoners of profitable distributive trade. John, in a letter to the mayor and commune of London in the first year of his reign, declared the freedom of all foreign merchants to travel in England, while immediately after the loss of Normandy in 1204, he acknowledged the freedom of the Cologne merchants to travel in his realm. After 1207, in association with Otto IV, John attempted to build up a Rhineland alliance against France, and in 1213, when both he and Otto were in weak positions, he confirmed Richard I's quitclaim to the citizens of Cologne in the rent they had been accustomed to pay from their London guildhall and in all customs, but with the caveat that it was to be 'saving the liberty of London'.[69] That

---

[67] Bateson, 'Municipal Collection', 509; F. Consitt, *The London Weavers' Company* (Oxford, 1933), pp. 1–6, 180–1.

[68] His uncle had been responsible for the London weavers' guild and his own city establishment was in the cloth-making district of Candlewick Street, surrounded by cloth tenters and dubbers (probably dyers): Keene, 'fitz Ailwin, Henry', in *Oxford Dictionary of National Biography*, s.n.; *Cartulary of Holy Trinity*, ed. Hodgett, no. 426; Corporation of London Records Office, Bridge House Deed, F35.

[69] J. P. Huffman, *Family, Commerce and Religion in London and Cologne* (Cambridge, 1998), 9–22; idem, *The Social Politics of Medieval Diplomacy: Anglo-German Relations (1066–1307)* (Ann Arbor, 1999), 168–222; H. Stehkamper, 'England und die Stadt Köln als Wahlmacher König Ottos IV', in *Köln das Reich und Europa: Abhandlungen über weiträumige Verflechtungen der Stadt Köln*

phrase and the assertion in Pseudo-Ine that foreign merchants were to remain in the ports indicates that despite the benefits of Rhineland trade, the Londoners' political programme at this time included opposition to the rights that Cologne merchants enjoyed in London and elsewhere. The importance of these issues is also indicated by the appearance in the final part of the collection of a genealogy of the counts of Boulogne, for Renaud of Damartin, count of Boulogne, was John's chief agent in building up an alliance against France in the Low Countries, and in 1212, in London, he and John publicly agreed not to make a separate peace with France.[70] It was presumably a few years later – following the defeat of Otto and the capture of Renaud at Bouvines and when London interests came to the fore in England – that the Cologne merchants lost possession of their guildhall, for in 1219–20 they had to pay 30 marks to recover it.[71]

Although the London Collection for its Anglo-Saxon laws draws on the twelfth-century Latin collection known today as 'Quadripartitus', which probably originated during the reign of Henry I,[72] it includes no laws of Æthelred II, whose legislation is included in 'Quadripartitus'. The reason for this may have been the London compiler's desire to present his collection of laws as the works of a succession of heroic kings and so to pass directly from Athelstan to Cnut omitting Æthelred. On the other hand, the London Collection contains one text which relates to legislation which at present is commonly attributed to Æthelred. That text is the highly commercial second part of the Anglo-Norman account of London customs placed in the collection after the letter of Prester John. The relevant material attributed to Æthelred is the set of regulations concerning the city and port of London, and in particular the well-known 'Billingsgate tolls', which form the opening part of the code known since 1840 as 'IV Æthelred' and so dated to c. 1000.[73] It is clear that 'IV Æthelred' is a composite document, its London element being of a very different character to the rest. Moreover, 'IV Æthelred' is not present in the earliest manuscripts of 'Quadripartitus' and appears only in those of the mid-twelfth century and later.[74] This raises the possibilities that the materials comprising 'IV Æthelred' were not put together before the

in *Politik, Rech und Wirtschaft im Mittelalter* (Mitteilungen aus dem Stadtarchiv von Köln, 1971), 213–44; *Rotuli Cartarum*, ed. T. D. Hardy, I.i (1837), 60, 194; *Hansisches Urkundenbuch*, ed. Verein für Hansische Geschichte (11 vols., Halle and Leipzig, 1876–1916), I, nos. 40, 84.

[70] Bateson, 'Municipal Collection', 728; A. L. Poole, *From Domesday Book to Magna Carta, 1087–1216* (Oxford, 1955), 449–53; Huffman, *Social Politics*, 209, 211, 214.

[71] *The Great Roll of the Pipe for the Fourth Year of the Reign of King Henry III, Michaelmas 1220*, ed. B. E. Harris (Pipe Roll Society, new series 47, 1981–3), 136.

[72] P. Wormald, *The Making of English Law: King Alfred to the Twelfth Century*, I: *Legislation and its Limits* (Oxford, 1999), 236–44.

[73] *Gesetze*, ed. Liebermann, I, 232–5; *The Laws of the Kings of England from Edmund to Henry I*, ed. A. J. Robertson (Cambridge, 1925), 70–3, 322–4.

[74] Wormald, *Making of English Law*, 240–1, 320–2, 371.

twelfth century, that there was no earlier Old English version and that the London element may not have been composed until the twelfth century, possibly even in the reign of Stephen when the original version of the document we now know as Henry I's charter to London may also have been compiled. Furthermore, there now seems to be some uncertainty as to whether the towns in the Meuse valley (Huy, Liège and Nivelles) mentioned in 'IV Æthelred' were sufficiently developed as commercial centres by the year 1000 for their merchants to be regular visitors to England, as implied by the record of Billingsgate tolls.[75]

One of the features of the account of Billingsgate tolls is the favoured position said to have been enjoyed in London by 'the men of the Emperor', merchants from Lorraine and the lower Rhineland and so essentially those trading through Cologne, especially by comparison with those from Rouen, Flanders, Ponthieu, Normandy, France and the Meuse valley towns. This part of the document was written in the imperfect tense. The men of the emperor who came to London in their ships were 'held worthy of good laws, like us' (*bonarum legum digni tenebantur sicut et nos*). This presumably means either that they were subject to the same laws as the Londoners or that, like the Londoners, they enjoyed good laws of their own. The reference here may be to the privileges in the city enjoyed by the men of Cologne, which were confirmed and extended by two royal charters granted in the 1170s, one of which enjoined the Londoners to give perpetual protection to the men of Cologne.[76] That privilege would have been acceptable in twelfth-century London and suggests a possible context for the Billingsgate toll record (although the men of Cologne could have enjoyed similar rights in London long before the royal charters), but it would have been a privilege too far for London merchants of the early thirteenth century.

The Anglo-Norman statement in the London Collection that includes a copy of regulations concerning Lorraine merchants in the city is usually assumed to belong to the mid-twelfth century or even much earlier,[77] but it now seems possible that those rules were drafted for the specific purposes of the Londoners during the early thirteenth century or that they were a heavily manipulated version of some earlier, probably twelfth-century, text or texts. The first part of the statement need be no earlier than the reign of John.[78] Dealing with procedures of the city's court of Husting concerning affray, rents and debts according to 'the law of London', it

---

[75] M. Suttor, *Vie et dynamique d'une fleuve: la Meuse de Sedan à Maastrich (des origines à 1600)* (Brussels, 2006), 15, 182–3, 242, 302–6, 346–51.

[76] Huffman, *Family, Commerce and Religion*, 14–17.

[77] Bateson, 'Municipal Collection', 495–502; Weinbaum, *London*, II, 29–38; cf. Brooke and Keir, *London*, 266–8; P. Nightingale, *A Medieval Mercantile Community: The Grocers' Company and the Politics and Trade of London, 1000–1485* (New Haven and London, 1995), 7–10, 44–5.

[78] Bateson, 'Municipal Collection', 485–95; Weinbaum, *London*, II, 13–17.

makes no mention of privileges enjoyed by foreigners, but it does define a specific procedure for a foreigner (*forein*) taking an oath concerning debt and then states that by the law of London no foreign merchant (*marchant forein*) has soke there 'neither at the guildhall nor elsewhere' (*ne gildhalle ne aillurs*).[79] This is usually is taken to be a reference to the guildhall of the citizens of London, but is more likely to concern the guildhall of the Cologne merchants on the Thames waterfront, described in one of Henry II's charters as their 'house' and subsequently as their guildhall. In this text the Londoners appear to be challenging the rights of the Cologners to an independent jurisdiction, contrary to the provisions of the Billingsgate toll record. As we have seen, the Cologners subsequently lost their guildhall for a while. The second part of this statement, which reads as a continuation of the first, opens with a statement concerning the 'law of the Lorrainers', clearly intending to differentiate it from the 'law of London' and thus perhaps alluding to the Billingsgate toll record, on which it draws in other ways but with some significant changes. Thus the toll record's statement that the men of the emperor could purchase *unloaded* (*discarcata*) wool (perhaps meaning wool that had been shipped down river to London and was available in the open market) and melted fat and three live pigs for their ships becomes more restrictive in the Anglo-Norman version of the same passage which asserts that no Lorrainer can purchase *unworked* (*desfaite*) wool, a variety of other goods (including 'broken wines', *vinz descusuz*, evidently derived from the *dissutum unctum* of the earlier text) or any more than three live pigs as provisions. In its aim to protect London's clothing industry and in its rule that the Lorraine merchants could stay in the city no longer than forty days, this statement is immediately comparable to Pseudo-Ine. Moreover, the first part of the statement, with references to Husting and to procedures concerning lands and debts seems to make a similar reference to another supposedly historic authority in the collection, Henry I's supposed charter to the citizens, which affirmed the procedure of Husting and the city's law concerning lands and debts. The conclusion of this Anglo-Norman section of the collection, with its account of the Folkmoot and its summoning by the authoritative bell at St Paul's, just possibly reflects the dramatic events at St Paul's between 1212 and 1216.[80] It certainly resonates with the account of folkmoots in the London interpolations to the Laws of Edward the Confessor,[81] which like this statement mention a bell and the need there to make provision against fire, a point reinforced by the inclusion later in the collection of the building code implemented after the fire of 1212.

---

[79] Weinbaum's reading and translation are here preferable to Bateson's.
[80] *St Paul's*, ed. Keene *et al.*, 31.
[81] *Gesetze*, ed. Liebermann, I, 657.

Texts on later folios,[82] the majority of them in Latin and so perhaps long-standing records of city custom, are more in the nature of evidential memoranda concerning city procedures. Their selection and ordering are careful and relate to points made in the preceding section of the collection: the analysis of these connections is for another occasion. After the *Libertas Londoniensis*, they include further texts concerning merchants, oaths relevant to the commune, material associated with the citizens' right to choose their sheriffs (but, significantly, not John's charter granting them that right), statements concerning the ways in which the commune could levy money for collective purposes, a matter which been a cause of bitter conflict within the city, and articles which informed Magna Carta.

Finally, it is worth noting the collection's distinctive attention to Norway and its significance for London interest in that period. This reflects Norway's close trading,[83] religious and cultural relations (not least through the foundation of Cistercian monasteries)[84] with England during the twelfth century and Geoffrey of Monmouth's stories of Arthur's conquest of Norway and his overlordship of Gotland. It also builds on the emphasis in the original version of the 'Laws of Edward the Confessor' on Danish and Norwegian laws and customs being among those observed in England.[85] But the London Collection went much further, adding references to Norway to several texts, stressing the way in which Arthur had caused the one God to be venerated throughout Norway,[86] and providing a detailed listing, derived from German sources, of places in eastern Baltic regions which Arthur was supposed to have ruled.[87] Moreover, Edward the Confessor was credited with having established the Norwegians, once immigrants, as 'sworn brothers' and 'almost citizens' of the realm. Indeed, the collection's 'law of the Lorrainers' ends with an implication that Norwegians should enjoy the same freedom to trade in London as the Danes, that is a greater freedom than the Lorrainers. By the late twelfth century, London had seven churches dedicated to St Olaf (d. 1030) and one to St Magnus (d. 1116), while its four churches dedicated to St Botolph suggest indirect Norwegian connections via Boston. Trade

---

[82] Add. MS 14252, fos. 106–28; Bateson, 'Municipal Collection', 505–730; Weinbaum, *London*, II, 39–91.

[83] See E. Miller and J. Hatcher, *Medieval England. Towns, Commerce, and Crafts, 1086–1348* (1995), 188 (includes errors); *The Cambridge History of Scandinavia*, ed. K. Helle (Cambridge, 2003), 385.

[84] J. France, *The Cistercians in Scandinavia* (Kalamazoo, 1992), 77–98, 119–22, 281–4, 322–4, 328, 493, 522–5, 535.

[85] O'Brien, *God's Peace*, 186–7, 190–3.

[86] E.g. *Gesetze*, ed. Liebermann, I, 635, 659–60.

[87] L. Muir, 'King Arthur's Northern Conquests in the *Leges Anglorum Londiniis Collectae*', *Medium Aevum*, 37 (1968), 253–62.

in eastern Baltic goods to England, in which the Norwegians and Gotlanders were significant intermediaries, was increasing and Cologne merchants were attempting to gain a foothold there. In 1186 King Sverri of Norway came to Bergen where there was a great number of merchant ships and the 'Southmen' (evidently Germans from the Rhineland) had imported so much wine that it was cheaper than ale. This led to fighting between the Northmen and the Germans. Sverri then spoke at a public assembly against the evils of drink and the Germans' attempt to corner trade, contrasting them with the English, whom he thanked for bringing wheat, honey, flour and cloth. For Sverri St Botolph's day was a special feast and two Norwegians named in the saga were named Botolph.[88] The Norwegian references in the London Collection thus seem to reflect the Londoners' antagonism towards Cologne and a preference for dealing with a friendly people who had more direct access to Baltic trade. This explains a reference to *Engra civitas*, named in one of the interpolations to Edward's laws as the origin of the 'Saxons of Germany' who were one of the groups claimed as potential 'sworn brothers' and 'proper citizens' of the English. *Engra* was presumably Schleswig, at the neck of the Angeln peninsula and under the authority of the king of Denmark, who also periodically controlled Lübeck, its successor as a hub for Baltic trade.[89] It is especially striking, therefore, that a year after the death of John a commercial treaty was concluded with the king of Norway. That was made possible by the recent reconciliation of warring parties in Norway, but the terms, stating that the two lands shall be common so that their men and merchants shall have freedom to come and go, express the ideal of quasi co-citizenship stated in the London Collection and in Magna Carta.[90] Lübeck's imperial charter of less than a decade later indicates that Cologne had attempted to control that trade at the mouth of the Rhine, blocking the Lübeckers' access to markets in England, from which the charter released them.[91] Geoffrey of Monmouth had structured his history as the fulfilment of prophecy. Prophecy had informed William fitz Stephen's view of the city. The compiler of the London collection followed a similar prophetic line. Many of those London aspirations expressed in the collection came to fruition between 1215 and 1217, while there are

---

[88] *Sverissaga: The Saga of King Sverri of Norway*, trans. J. Sephton (1899), 49, 166, 128–30, 198; for the reliability of this source, see *History of Scandinavia*, ed. Helle, 502.

[89] *Gesetze*, ed., Liebermann, I, 658; D. Kattinger, *Die Gotländische Genossenschaft: der frühansisch-gotländisch Handel in Nord- und Westeuropa* (Cologne, Weimar and Vienna, 1999), 13–23, 155–87; *Codex Diplomaticus Lubecensis: Urkundenbuch der Stadt Lübeck*, ed. Verein für Lübeckische Geschichte (11 vols., Lübeck, 1843–1905), I, nos. 11–15, 20, 23, 27–8.

[90] *Foedera*, ed. T. Rymer *et al.* (3 vols. in 6 parts, 1816–30), I.i, 149; *History of Scandinavia*, ed. Helle, 375–6.

[91] *Codex Diplomaticus Lubecensis*, no. 35; Huffman, *Family Commerce and Religion*, 23–4.

signs that around 1220 a new settlement was made in the city's internal affairs and in its relations with Cologne and Lübeck.

This paper has argued that the resemblances and echoes between a variety of writings concerning cities in general, and London in particular, indicate that in the late twelfth and early thirteenth centuries there developed a widely shared community of ideas about London and its physical, cultural, social, historical, mythological and political identity. A developing capacity to visualise the city and to respond to its depiction was part of this process. Literary and visual modes of expression, two forms of story telling not so distinctly separated as they are today, informed both an appreciation of city landscape and strategies for achieving political ends. It is not necessary to assume that all involved in the process read the texts or even listened to readings from them: ideas, stories and vocabulary could circulate in many informal ways, including the visual. So far as Londoners were concerned, St Paul's and its environs was in this period probably the most important site for such exchanges. The cathedral linked them to the circles in which key texts were composed and debated. Some of its canons were members of leading London families and the cathedral and its precinct constituted the citizens' principal site of assembly, for religious, political and military purposes. Moreover, some of the writers involved wrote for a wide audience, 'for the many ... the less educated', as Henry of Huntingdon had put it.[92] The 'less educated' middling groups in London, outside the ruling elite, certainly included people of some learning who engaged in controversial political debate, not least at St Paul's.[93] Those politics were informed by a strong sense of the city's standing and its role in relation to the nation (or Britain) and to ideas of law. The great collection of laws and other texts put together in London during the reign of John, itself a complex literary construction informed by spatial and visual principles, unites these aspects of the city's identity, not least by means of its historical and geographical breadth. Moreover, it indicates how the citizens, or their leaders, in rehearsing the legitimacy of their claims not only focused on contemporary concerns but also drew on their awareness of ideas developed in earlier episodes of communal crisis, on the documented rights of deeply entrenched groups and on an imaginative visualisation of the past. In the compilation of this collection, texts were selected, manipulated and fabricated to further the interests of those groups. This paper has done no more than scratch the surface of this particular topic, dealing with only a few elements in a single collection and leaving many problems unresolved. The findings raise serious questions as to how we should address this and other such collections of laws and

---

[92] *Historia Anglorum*, ed. Greenway, lviii, 584–5.
[93] Keene, 'fitz Osbert, William'.

customs in the future. It seems that those historians of London, including the present author, who have used some of these texts as evidence for much older city law and custom, should be more cautious from now on. For all its great achievements, the positivistic, decontextualising approach of the past, seeking to establish the 'uncorrupted' text, has missed more than a trick or two. At the same time we should rejoice at the new insights that these and other sources of the time continue to offer us into London's complex cultural and political identity.

Transactions of the RHS 18 (2008), pp. 101–28 © 2008 Royal Historical Society
doi:10.1017/S0080440108000674   Printed in the United Kingdom

CENTRE AND PERIPHERY IN THE EUROPEAN BOOK WORLD

By Andrew Pettegree

READ 19 OCTOBER 2007 AT THE UNIVERSITY OF ESSEX

ABSTRACT. The rapid spread of print in the fifteenth century masks considerable difficulties that faced the industry in adapting to the new disciplines of mass production. Many early print shops were short-lived. Within two generations production of printed books was concentrated in a comparatively small number of major centres of production. This paper explores the implications of these developments for our understanding of the 'print revolution'. It considers in particular the contrasting fortunes of three major markets: France, one of the largest centres of production; the Netherlands, a major hub of international trade; and England, which lay towards the periphery of the European book world.

I

The printed book plays a fundamental role in any presentation of the culture of European society in the centuries of the Renaissance and the Reformation. In all general treatments of the transition from the medieval to the modern, print emerges as one of the crucial determinants. It is thereby firmly embedded as one of the foundation stones of a progress-orientated view of western society, not least through Elizabeth Eisenstein's seminal presentation of print culture as a catalyst in the development of an enlightened humane society: *The Printing Press as an Agent of Change.*[1] It is curious that as other teleological progress-orientated historical interpretations have fallen out of favour, this view of print and progress has proved so remarkably tenacious. This is not all down to Eisenstein: it also owes something to the fact that the first producers of printed books themselves maintained a constant litany in praise of print. Martin Luther's hymn to print, which he famously describes as 'God's highest act of Grace', is well known – but in fact Luther's view fitted comfortably

---

[1] Elizabeth Eisenstein, *The Printing Press as an Agent of Change. Communication and Cultural Transformations in Early Modern Europe* (Cambridge, 1979); *idem*, *The Printing Revolution in Early Modern Europe* (Cambridge, 1983). The argument is summarised in preliminary form in *idem*, 'Some Conjectures about the Impact of Printing on Western Society and Thought: A Preliminary Report', *Journal of Modern History*, 40 (1968), 7–29.

within a framework of analysis that stretched right back to the first ecstatic responses to the new invention, when print was effortlessly aligned with the discoveries of the Renaissance, turning darkness into light. Such a view, refined by scholarship, has essentially defined educated opinion in the centuries since.

In the fifteenth century curiosity and enthusiasm for the new invention appeared to be universal. Until 1455 printing by moveable type had been experimental technology, not necessarily destined to succeed. Within twenty years printing was an established part of the book world in almost every part of Europe. From Mainz it spread very rapidly to the other towns of the German Empire, and throughout Europe. Itinerant German artisans introduced printing to Italy by 1465, and Paris by 1470. It spread swiftly to the Low Countries, and thence across the Channel to England. Eastwards it reached Poland (Cracow) by 1473, and the Iberian peninsula (Barcelona and Valencia) in the same year. These first bridgeheads were usually in major centres of commerce, government or established centres of medieval manuscript book production. But a defining feature of this new book world would be the rapidity with which this productive capacity was diffused. In the Netherlands printing presses were established in over twenty towns throughout the northern and southern provinces before 1501; in the Francophone world the figure was closer to forty. From Mainz print spread throughout the German Empire, and to points further east. The first book in Czech was published before 1475, in Pilsen; the first book in Croat, a Breviary of the Roman Rite, in 1483.[2] This latter project was indicative of the extraordinary ambition of some of these earliest ventures, since the Breviary was printed in two colours, red and black (necessitating a skilled process of double impression) and in glagolitic characters. This type was specially designed and cut for the Breviary, probably in Venice.[3]

In all, a printing press had been established at some point in over 250 different locations throughout Europe by the end of the fifteenth century.[4] Nevertheless this confident narrative of expansion is only one part of the story. In fact, it masks a severe crisis that afflicted the new industry in the last decades of the fifteenth century, a crisis that necessitated a swift and brutal restructuring of the industry even before the first generation of experimental works had been concluded.

It is well known that the printed book owed part of its spectacular early success to the manner in which print emulated familiar physical features of the manuscript. As far as the visual appearance of the new

---

[2] Eliska Ryznar, *Books in Czechoslovakia, Past and Present* (Wiesbaden, 1989), 5.

[3] Alexander Stipcevic, 'Aspects de la production du livre croate au XVe siècle', in *Les croates et la civilisation du livre*, ed. Hernik Heger and Janine Matillon (Paris, 1986), 35–46.

[4] Philippe Nieto, 'Géographie des impressions européennes du XVe siècle', *Revue française d'histoire du livre*, 118–21 (2004), 125–73.

printed book was concerned this was greatly to be welcomed: purchasers welcomed a product that was both eye-catchingly new and reassuringly familiar. But what was not immediately clear was that the familiar business of manuscript production offered a model of distribution and sales that was wholly inappropriate for print. The manuscript functioned, in effect, through a system of on-demand reprint.[5] There were, in late medieval Europe, some major centres of production, where manuscripts were turned out almost in industrial quantities. University towns such as Paris and Bologna dealt in school books; major commercial centres, such as Bruges, Florence and Paris, catered for the luxury market.[6] But manuscript production was also very widely dispersed: any place where there was both a competent scribe, and an available text, could contribute to the supply of manuscripts.

This experience of local production set up an utterly unrealistic expectation for the organisation of the print industry. At first, every city, every court and every episcopal see aspired to its place in the new art. Print spread with astonishing rapidity, often to places of relatively modest size. Whereas such places could deal with the disposal of relatively modest numbers of manuscripts, the disposal of whole print runs of printed books was a very different matter.

The difficulties that print would face in this regard were not immediately apparent, since the early expansion was supported by the enthusiasm of the ruling elites. But when the novelty wore off, printing presses were functioning in many places where they were not economically viable.[7] The result was a rapid contraction in the market. Many towns that had boasted a printing press from early in the incunabula age disappeared from the printing map of Europe for several generations. To take some examples from Italy, Treviso was one town where printing was introduced in 1471 and where eleven separate presses operated in the next twenty years. Yet when the last of these closed in 1493 printing in the town ceased until 1589. In Udine the press established in 1484 lasted just two years; the next press did not appear there until 1592.[8] In France around thirty places boasted a printing press at some point in the incunabula age; after the late century crisis, perhaps only three cities,

---

[5] Curt F. Bühler, *The Fifteenth-Century Book. The Scribes, the Printers, the Decorators* (Philadelphia, 1960).

[6] Peter Spufford, *Power and Profit: The Merchant in Medieval Europe* (2002), 281–3.

[7] Martha Tedeschi, 'Publish and Perish', in *Printing the Written Word. The Social History of Books circa 1450–1520*, ed. Sandra L. Hindman (Ithaca, 1991), 41–67; Susan Noakes, 'The Development of the Book Market in Late Quattrocento Italy. Printers' Failure and the Role of the Middleman', *Journal of Mediaeval and Renaissance Studies*, 11 (1981), 23–55.

[8] Neil Harris, 'Italy', in *The Oxford Companion to the Book*, ed. Michael J. Suarez and Henry Woudhuysen (Oxford, 2009).

Paris, Lyon and Rouen, could sustain a press continuously through the first half of the sixteenth century.

This amounted to a complete restructuring of the publishing industry. This took place between about 1485 and 1520. From the 1490s printing was concentrated in a far smaller number of well-capitalised ventures established for the most part in Europe's major trading cities. These larger firms were able to take on the larger, more ambitious works that required either a strong local market or, in the case of Latin books, a trans-European distribution network.[9] The larger firms were able to support the very considerable investment often required to bring an edition to the press; they could finance the storage of unsold copies, often for considerable periods before an edition would be exhausted; and they were able to develop the sophisticated networks of transportation and exchange necessary to bring their products to a readership spread throughout Europe.

Thus by the first two decades of the sixteenth century, the production of printed books was characterised not by the extraordinary diversity suggested by the enumeration of the multiple locations that had experienced print, but by a high degree of concentration. In France, Paris emerged not only as a major centre of European production, but as the dominant force within the French industry. In Italy, Venice would be responsible for half the total output of books published throughout the whole Italian peninsula in the sixteenth century. An extraordinary proportion of the entire output of European printing in the next hundred years would be concentrated in fewer than a dozen large centres of production: a steel spine that ran along Europe's major trade routes from Antwerp and Paris to the north, through Cologne, Basle, Strasbourg and Lyon to Venice in the south. Within these printing behemoths was concentrated much of the investment capacity of the industry, and the most sophisticated mechanisms of financing, warehousing and distribution. These cities were the natural focus of projects that required substantial investment. They utterly dominated the market in scholarly books. This applied particularly to the production of books in the scholarly languages, for notwithstanding the eye-catching experimentation with vernacular publication throughout Europe, books in Latin remained the core business of the sixteenth-century book trade.

The true importance of this Latin trade has been somewhat obscured by the undoubted success of early ventures in vernacular print, books that were often significant cultural milestones, and often played a significant role in the development of a local vernacular culture. Caxton's experiments in English printing are a striking example. But in many

---

[9] Oscar von Hase, *Die Koberger: Eine Darstellung des Buchhändlerischen Geschäftsbetriebes in der Zeit des Überganges vom Mittelalter zur Neuzeit* (Leipzig, 1885).

parts of Europe the vernacular reading community was not at this time large enough to sustain on its own a substantial publishing business. Book production was sustained over the first century of print by established and rather traditional markets, with Latin continuing as the overwhelmingly most important medium of publication.

In this Latin market, the locus of production mattered far less than the establishment of an efficient distribution network. It mattered not to a purchaser whether a book was published in Paris or Basel, so long as they could obtain the desired title, at a price they could afford, and in a timely fashion. At an early stage in this history of print there developed a market of great efficiency and sophistication to ensure that books could be transported around Europe in this way. At least with regard to Latin books the sixteenth-century book world was to a large extent one integrated market. The salvation of print lay in the development of an efficient market of exchange and distribution that enabled books to be transported to a readership community widely dispersed around Europe.

This was achieved, building around two critical features of the late medieval economy: the system of international trade fairs, and the development of efficient credit mechanisms. The wholesale market in books was built very largely around exchange, focused on the strategically situated twice yearly book fairs at Frankfurt.[10] The success of Frankfurt and subsidiary markets in places like Lyon, Basel and Leipzig (an important gateway mart for eastern Europe) further reinforced the supremacy of the industry giants, who could rely on Frankfurt to dispose of a major part of their print runs to a small number of clients within months of publication.

Through these developments of marketing, finance and production strategy, Europe's printers had achieved the structural changes necessary to ensure the long-term viability of print. They had also reshaped the European book world in a manner almost unrecognisable from the exuberant dispersed production of the early years. The mature print world of sixteenth-century Europe can helpfully be understood as a series of concentric circles. By far the most important, both intellectually and in terms of book production, was an inner core comprising France, the German Empire and the towns of northern Italy. These were joined by, and articulated around, two centres of exchange and production in the Netherlands and the Swiss Confederation. These five centres of production between them accounted for more than 80 per cent of all

---

[10] Alexander Dietz, *Frankfurter Handelsgeschichte* (Frankfurt, 1921), III, 1–178; *idem*, *Zur Geschichte der Frankfurter Büchermesse, 1462–1792* (Frankfurt, 1921); Bruno Recke, *Die Frankfurter Büchermesse* (Frankfurt, 1951).

books published throughout Europe before 1601, and an even higher proportion of scholarly books and books in Latin.[11]

Outside this central core lay a number of more peripheral markets, in Spain and Portugal, England and southern Italy. These secondary markets were characterised by a relatively robust production serving a vernacular reading community of sufficient size to sustain a printing industry of some significance. But most books published in these places were for local consumption. Because they did not publish extensively for export these places did not command a significant proportion of the production of Latin books. Rather they relied for most scholarly and more expensive editions on imports, supplied through the long-established trade connections with the major centres of production elsewhere in Europe. These import markets worked very effectively, as the large numbers of imported books in early English collections will testify; but the dependence on larger continental centres of production placed a distinct limit on the ambitions of the local printing industry.[12]

Beyond these secondary markets lay a still more remote outer periphery. Most of the lands of northern and eastern Europe belonged to this third outer circle in the first century of print. These were places where printing was often established rather late, and where it struggled to put down firm foundations. The lands of this outmost circle were often relatively sparsely populated, with few towns of any great size, at least compared to the great cities of the more urbanised parts of Europe. Their vernacular reading communities were often too small to justify heavy investment in print technology. To an even greater extent than in Spain and England, the establishment of a printing industry relied on foreign investment and expertise: sometimes books intended for these markets were even printed in the larger printing centres in Germany, Italy or the Netherlands. Faced with these relatively daunting circumstances, sustaining a viable local print industry relied to an unusual extent on the interest of local political elites, who would often support the establishment of a printing press, or sustained it when not strictly viable in economic terms, more from motives of cultural national pride.

The cultural consequences of this very starkly differentiated print network would be very significant. In the larger centres of production

---

[11] See Appendix.

[12] Lotte Hellinga, 'Importation of Books Printed on the Continent into England and Scotland before c. 1520', in *Printing the Written Word. The Social History of Books, circa 1450–1520*, ed. Sandra Hindman (Ithaca, 1991), 205–24; Elizabeth Armstrong, 'English Purchases of Printed Books from the Continent, 1465–1526', *English Historical Review*, 94 (1979), 268–90; Margaret Lane Ford, 'Importation of Printed Books into England and Scotland', in *The Cambridge History of the Book in Britain*, III: *1400–1557*, ed. Lotte Hellinga and J. B. Trapp (Cambridge, 1999).

publishers could undertake more ambitious works in a whole variety of fields: not only in the Latin works they placed in the international market, but also in their vernacular production. In the smaller, less highly capitalised print domains, the absence of large-scale print enterprises encouraged a more cautious and conservative approach. Yet, even within this broad pattern there was room for significant local diversity. The development of a local print industry was shaped not only by its part in the international Latin trade, though this was critical, but also by the size of the local vernacular reading community. The attitude of the local governing power was also critical in shaping how print would respond to the different opportunities and dangers posed by political events over the course of the century.

II

The remainder of this paper will explore these questions in greater detail with a comparison of the three most substantial print cultures of north-western Europe: France, England and the Low Countries. The three were closely linked by established trade connections, especially in the book world, where the mutual trade in books was extensive in the manuscript age. But in the sixteenth century each of these three places' experience of print would take a sharply divergent course. France was one of the three major print centres of Europe, home both to northern Europe's largest print metropolis, Paris, but also, as the century wore on, an increasingly vibrant tradition of provincial print. In England, in contrast, a much small print world was concentrated almost entirely in one location, London. The Low Countries present in many respects the most singular case. Here a number of centres generated a large volume of printed books catering explicitly for an international market, and this allowed the publishing houses of the Netherlands to subvert the limitations of a small vernacular reading community. They also succeeded, in the second half of the century, in riding out political storms that might have obliterated a less robust printing culture. These investigations will allow us to elucidate our themes of centre and periphery in two different but interlocking ways: with respect to the European print world as a whole, and with regard to centre and periphery in each individual print domain: here, especially with regard to their largely separate vernacular reading communities.

This work rests on an analysis of data for print production that for many parts of Europe has only recently become possible. It might seem at first sight extraordinary that so much interpretative weight has been placed on 'the coming of the book' in the absence of reliable production data.[13] But this is indeed the case. It is only now, at the beginning of the twenty-first century, that we are in a position to say with any degree of confidence how many books were published in Europe, where and when.

This salient if surprising truth has been somewhat obscured for historians of the Anglo-American tradition by the early precocious success of bibliography in charting the history of early print in England. It is now eighty years since Pollard and Redgrave first published their *Short Title Catalogue of Books of Books Printed in England and in English Abroad before 1640*. The early publication of this bibliographical milestone has allowed British bibliography to achieve a state of development unrivalled for other parts of Europe, through successive refinements of the STC, the extension of coverage to the seventeenth and eighteenth centuries and on-line and full text editions.[14]

The study of other sixteenth-century print cultures has lagged seriously behind. We now have a serviceable survey of two of the most significant European print domains of the sixteenth century, the German and Italian.[15] But bibliographical coverage of France and the Netherlands has been fragmented and patchy, and there has been no attempt at all to create a survey of books published on the Iberian peninsula. These substantial lacunae are now finally being made good in a series of projects initiated by the publication in 2007 of a full survey of all books published in French: a substantial body of some 52,000 works.[16] The remarks in this paper, and the overall figures for European production presented in the appendix, are underpinned by the ongoing bibliographical analysis for these projects, timed to conclude in 2012 with an integrated on-line catalogue of all books published throughout Europe before 1601: the *Universal Short Title Catalogue*.

With that, at last, our knowledge of the European world of print will rest on reasonably secure foundations. The U-STC will also make possible a whole new generation of research on texts, authors and genres with trans-national appeal and influence: a class of work whose impact has inevitably been obscured by the fragmentary tendency of the national bibliographical tradition.

[13] Lucien Febvre and Henri-Jean Martin, *The Coming of the Book: The Impact of Printing 1450–1800* (1976).

[14] The English Short-Title Catalogue: http://www.bl.uk/collections/early/estc1.html; Early English Books Online: http://eebo.chadwyck.com/home.

[15] *Edit 16. Le edizioni italiane del XVI secolo: censimento nazionale* (5 vols., Rome: Istituto centrale per il catalogo unico delle biblioteche italiane e per le informazioni bibliografi che, 1989–), continued as an on-line resource at http://edit16.iccu.sbn.it/web_iccu/ihome.htm. *VD 16. Verzeichnis der im deutschen Sprachbereich erschienenen Drucke des XVI. Jahrhunderts* (25 vols., Stuttgart, 1983–2000). An enhanced version now available on-line at http://bvbd2.bib-bvb.de/cgi-bin/bvb_suche?sid=VD16.

[16] Andrew Pettegree, Malcolm Walsby and Alexander Wilkinson, *FB. French Vernacular Books. Books Published in the French Language before 1601* (Leiden, 2007).

III

It was always likely that France would play a distinguished part in the early history of the printed book. Paris had been one of the major centres of the medieval book world for two centuries before print. The core of this market, which approached industrial mass production, was the market in school books for university students, but the tastes of the Court also ensured a healthy demand for luxury items.[17] Rumours of the new art perfected in Germany thus posed something of a challenge to the French Court, and in 1458 the French king dispatched Nicolas Jensen, one of the leading booksellers of Paris, to Mainz to discover its secrets.[18] The wily Germans proved understandably reluctant to admit Jensen to their confidence; rebuffed, he is next found in Venice where he went on to found a major printing house. It was therefore not until 1470 that print made its way to Paris, and then courtesy of three émigré Germans.

Once print was established, however, France swiftly reclaimed a leading role in the provision of books, both for a local and international market. Within a decade Paris had established a place as one of the major European centres of print: a position it would not relinquish through the next three centuries. Equally remarkable is the speed with which print spread around France. Before the end of the fifteenth century printing presses had been planted in over thirty locations in the Francophone world: not only in the kingdom of France itself, but in Flanders, the Franche Comté (both under Habsburg rule) and the kingdom of Brittany (independent until 1532). In Brittany alone some six places briefly sustained a printing press: here the new art played an important part in celebrating a rich and at this point independent intellectual culture.[19]

Despite this France was not immune from the late century crisis of print. The production of printed books disappeared entirely from over half the places that had experienced print in the fifteenth century, and effectively the production of books was concentrated in a still smaller number of places. Lyon, Rouen and Poitiers, important regional centres, could to some extent sustain a viable press, concentrating for the most part on staples of school books, ecclesiastical texts and local legal handbooks. In the south Toulouse performed a similar function.[20] But in terms of

---

[17] Richard H. Rouse and Mary A. Rouse, *Manuscripts and their Makers: Commercial Book Producers in Medieval Paris, 1200–1500* (London, 2000).

[18] A thorough review of the evidence concerning this much reported episode is provided by Lotte Hellinga, 'Printing Types and the Printed Word. Considerations around New Insights into the Beginning of Printing', *Archiv für Geschichte des Buchwesens*, 57 (2003), cols. 249–65.

[19] Malcolm Walsby, *Books and Book Culture in the First Age of Print: Brittany, 1484–1600* (Leiden, 2009).

[20] *Bibliographie des livres imprimés à Lyon au seizième siècle*, ed. S. von Gültlingen (10 vols., Baden-Baden, 1992–2006). *Répertoire bibliographique des livres imprimés en France au seizième siècle*

overall production, in the period Paris emerged as the overwhelmingly dominant centre.

This consolidation of print, characteristic of much of Europe, in no way diminished the impact of French typography in the European book market. Indeed, the concentration of capital and expertise in Paris, and to a lesser extent Lyon, facilitated the production of books of ever greater quality and sophistication. Paris in this period emerged as a recognised centre of high-quality typography: this era saw not only the rise of outstanding printing dynasties, but also significant advances in printing of the learned languages. Parisian printers were also in the vanguard in refining techniques for the publication of musical notation, a development enthusiastically supported by the French king, Francis I.[21]

Paris also played a notable role in the emergence of a market in news publication. It is sometimes suggested that the development of printed news publications was essentially a seventeenth-century phenomenon, but this is an observation based largely on the English experience.[22] Elsewhere in Europe the thirst for information generated a lively market for printed news publications almost from the first years of print.

These were not necessarily ephemeral prints, still less the preserve of marginal figures in the publishing industry.[23] In Paris, until at least the 1530s, most news publications emanated from close to the Court.[24] They played an important role in efforts to engage the political nation in active support of crown policies. Leading Court poets and authors were expected to play their part in hymning the king's triumphs in war and peace.[25] This propaganda offensive reached its apogee in the period 1537–44, when the long-running conflict between Francis I and the

(32 vols., Baden-Baden, 1968–80), V (Poitiers), XX (Toulouse). The bibliography of Caen and Rouen was resigned to a separate section of this project, but remains very incomplete. Pierre Aquilon, *Bibliographie Normande. Bibliographie des ouvrages imprimés à Caen et à Rouen au seizième siècle* (Répertoire bibliographique des livres imprimés en France au seizième siècle. Fascicule hors série, 1992). These projects are now substantially superseded by *French Vernacular Books*.

[21] Daniel Heartz, *Pierre Attaingnant, Royal Printer of Music: A Historical Study and Bibliographical Catalogue* (Berkeley, CA, 1969).

[22] Joad Raymond, *Pamphlets and Pamphleteering in Early Modern Britain* (Cambridge, 2003), 25.

[23] As is demonstrated also for Germany by the important book of Hans-Jörg Kunast, '*Getruckt zu Augspurg'. Buchdruck und Buchhandel in Augsburg zwischen 1468 und 1555* (Tübingen, 1997).

[24] Jean-Pierre Seguin, 'L'information à la fin du XVe siècle en France. Pièces d'actualité imprimées sous le règne de Charles VIII', *Arts et traditions populaires*, 4 (1956), 309–30, 1–2 (1957), 46–74; idem, *L'information en France de Louis XII à Henri II* (Geneva, 1961); Michael Sherman, 'Political Propaganda and Renaissance Culture: French Reactions to the League of Cambrai, 1509–1510', *Sixteenth Century Journal*, 8 (1977), 97–128, an article based on material drawn from his unpublished dissertation: 'The Selling of Louis XII: Propaganda and Popular Culture in Renaissance France' (Ph.D. dissertation, University of Chicago 1974).

[25] Jennifer Britnell, *Jean Bouchet* (Edinburgh, 1986).

emperor, Charles V, reached its most intense phase. In this period the numerous pamphlets charting the ebb and flow of the conflict even found their echo in the provincial press, anticipating the greater upsurge of pamphlet publications in the second half of the century.[26]

In these decades Lyon also established itself as a second major printing centre within France.[27] As a print town Lyon had many advantages. Strategically placed along several of Europe's major trade routes, it was a gateway to commerce towards both Italy and Spain.[28] The establishment of a major printing industry indeed owed much to a number of émigré Italian merchant families, who brought with them the capital resources necessary for the production of high-quality printed works. Lyon also quickly established a significant reputation in several important markets, such as the production of texts of Roman law, and modern humanist works of scholarship.

The production of books in Paris and Lyon in the twenty years after 1540 – elegant in appearance, varied in scope and immensely profitable – gives a fair indication of how the French book world might have remained but for the mid-century crisis that stimulated the French Wars of Religion. It is of course in marked contrast to the situation in Germany – and our familiar paradigm of print and Reformation – that the impact of Protestantism on the French printing industry should have been so long delayed. There had been interest in the German controversies, especially in Paris, in the years immediately following Luther's protest. But conservative opinion rallied quickly to inhibit the expression of evangelical views. Paris's publishing community was warned off the printing or sale of Luther's works, and from 1525 the publication of the Scripture in the vernacular was also forbidden. Few were prepared to risk their livelihoods by challenging the ban; the publication of Protestant books (and editions of the Bible in French) necessarily moved abroad.[29] In fact only very modest amounts of evangelical literature in French were published before the 1540s, when Calvin's definitive establishment in Geneva permitted the establishment of a new centre for the production of Protestant texts.

---

[26] Andrew Pettegree, 'A Provincial News Community in Sixteenth-Century France', in his *The French Book and the European Book World* (Leiden, 2007), 19–42. For the equally energetic propaganda on the Imperial side see now Steven Gunn, David Grummitt and Hans Cools, *War, State, and Society in England and the Netherlands 1477–1559* (Oxford, 2007), ch. 18.

[27] Gültlingen, *Bibliographie des livres imprimés à Lyon*, replacing H.-L. and J. Baudrier, *Bibliographie lyonnaise. Recherches sur les imprimeurs, libraires, relieurs et fondeurs de lettres de Lyon au XVIe siècle* (12 vols., Lyon, 1895–1921).

[28] James B. Wadsworth, *Lyon 1473–1503. The Beginnings of Cosmopolitanism* (Cambridge, MA, 1962); Richard Gascon, *Grand commerce et vie urbaine au XVIe siècle: Lyon et ses marchands (environs de 1520 – environs de 1580)* (Paris, 1971).

[29] *Le livre évangélique en français avant Calvin*, ed. Jean-François Gilmont and William Kemp (Turnhout, 2004); B. T. Chambers, *Bibliography of French Bibles. Fifteenth- and Sixteenth-Century French-Language Editions of the Scriptures* (Geneva, 1983).

For the next two decades Geneva completely dominated the output of Protestant literature in French, to the fury of the royal authorities, who took stern measures to inhibit all contact with the town.[30]

All this changed very rapidly with the crisis of the French monarchy that followed the death of Henry II in 1559. Events gave French Protestantism its opportunity; the evangelical churches grew very rapidly. Protestant printing also increased exponentially, and, crucially, moved back within the borders of France. Major Protestant presses were established in Lyon, Orléans, at Caen in Normandy and, more discreetly, within Paris itself.[31] But most of the capital's printers remained loyal to Catholicism. Crucially, and again in marked contrast to Germany, the evangelicals did not dominate the printing press. Rather, the crisis of 1559–64 produced a torrent of passionate polemic on both sides of the religious divide. Catholic authors matched their Protestant opponents tract for tract, sermon for sermon.[32] The fierce and murderous passions unleashed during the French wars had their origins in these polemical exchanges.[33]

The end of the first war in 1563 fatally interrupted the momentum of Protestant growth. Catholic France had rallied effectively; although the French wars would drag on another forty years, the outcome was never seriously in doubt. For the crown the issue was how to heal the wound opened by the conflict, and promote harmony between an enflamed Catholic majority and an entrenched Protestant minority. To this purpose they made much use of the press.

Through 1564 and 1565 the regent, Catherine of Medici, toured the nation, introducing the young king to his people, and promoting reconciliation. This involved numerous edicts and proclamations, and these were published not only in Paris and Lyon, but in numerous other locations throughout the kingdom. This process, pursued through

---

[30] Jean-François Gilmont, *Le livre réformé au XVIe siècle* (Paris, 2005). The output of Genevan editions is now fully documented in Gilmont's on-line bibliography of Genevan imprints GLN 15–16, www.ville-ge.ch/bge/bibelec/e/gln15–16.htm.

[31] Louis Desgraves, *Elie Gibier imprimeur à Orléans (1536–1588)* (Geneva, 1966); the different editions of Gibier's political tracts are more precisely identified in Jean-François Gilmont, 'La première diffusion des Mémoires de Condé par Éloi Gibier en 1562–1563', in his *Le livre & ses secrets* (Louvain-la-Neuve and Geneva, 2003), 191–216. For Lyon and Caen see now Pettegree, *The French Book and the European Book World*, chs. 3 and 4. For Paris, Eugénie Droz, 'Le curé Landry et les frères Langelier', in E. Droz, *Chemins de l'heresie: textes et documents* (4 vols., Geneva, 1970–6), I, 283–394.

[32] Luc Racaut, *Hatred in Print: Catholic Propaganda and Protestant Identity during the French Wars of Religion* (Aldershot, 2002); Émile Pasquier, *Un curé de Paris pendant les guerres de religion: René Benoist, le pape des Halles* (Paris, 1913).

[33] Natalie Davis, 'The Rites of Violence', in her *Society and Culture in Early Modern France* (1975), 152–87; Barbara B. Diefendorf, *Beneath the Cross: Catholics and Huguenots in Sixteenth-Century Paris* (New York, 1991).

several subsequent eruptions of hostilities and repeated efforts to fashion a lasting peace, stimulated a new beginning for provincial printing in France. The crown's wishes were relayed through a network of newly established printing houses in places like Tours, Orléans, Bordeaux, Dijon and Bourges. It is easy to overlook the importance of this apparently mundane trade in small official ordinances: usually, in France, octavo pamphlets rather than broadsheet placards. But for printers such work was often the mainstay of their trade.[34] Once reestablished they quickly developed a secondary market in pamphlets retailing the convolutions of the tangled conflict, the sieges, battles and the fate of prominent casualties.

This renewed pamphlet publication reached its apogee with the tumultuous triangular conflict between Henry of Navarre, the Catholic League and the embattled king, Henry III. When the king made a last desperate effort to reassert his authority by assassinating the leader of the League, the duke of Guise, the shock waves of this treacherous act reverberated through the French press.[35] Months later the same presses celebrated the king's own assassination. This unlikely series of events brought the Protestant Henry of Navarre to the throne but he faced a kingdom reluctant to accept his authority. Among his many problems in making good his rights was the fact that his leaguer enemies controlled every major printing centre throughout the kingdom, including Paris, Lyon, Rouen and Toulouse. Henry's response was to establish his own presses in smaller loyalist towns.[36] Over the next five years the military struggle for supremacy was accompanied by a parallel polemical warfare in the public prints.

The accumulated impact of the French conflicts was thus to effect a profound and lasting transformation in the nature and locus of French printing. The domination of Paris, never entirely complete, was in the second half of the century eroded by a revitalised provincial press. By the last decades of the century these presses were responsible for a substantial proportion of the total printed output. Events also effected a transformation of the industry so that it would now serve both the established market for high-quality and scholarly books, and an animated local industry dealing in news, official mandates and current events. This dense network of printing towns was in marked contrast to the situation that would prevail across the Channel in England.

---

[34] See *Répertoire bibliographique*, XXVIII, 87–93, for the Le Mans printer Jêrome Olivier whose output was utterly dominated in the 1560s by the production of local reprints of royal edicts.

[35] Denis Pallier, *Recherches sur l'imprimerie à Paris pendant le Ligue (1585–1594)* (Geneva, 1975).

[36] As for instance at Tours: *Répertoire bibliographique*, XXIII.

IV

In its first beginnings the introduction of print in England conformed reasonably closely to the normative experience of Europe. Print was introduced to England by William Caxton, an imaginative merchant and diplomat who had experience of the book trade in Bruges, a major centre of commerce and, not coincidentally, of the medieval manuscript trade.[37] In his zeal to bring printing to England Caxton, as was often the case, made liberal use of the expertise of those with experience of printing in the newly established continental houses: this established a pattern that would continue for much of first century of English print, with workmen from Germany, France and the Low Countries playing an influential role in the establishment and development of printing houses in England's capital.[38] Caxton introduced his first printing press at Westminster in 1476. A press was established in Oxford in 1478 and in St Albans the following year. But neither of these ventures could be sustained. Within a decade both the Oxford and St Albans press had failed, and henceforth the craft of printing would be concentrated almost entirely in the capital.

The failure of undercapitalised provincial presses was not, as we have seen, unusual in the last two decades of the fifteenth century, the years following the first exuberant age of expansion. But it was only in England that provincial printing died out altogether. In the four decades between 1500 and 1540, the period during which the early printed book achieved its final, definitive form, the domination of London over the English book trade was complete. Attempts to revive printing in York and St Albans lasted scarcely a year. Even the university towns of Oxford and Cambridge, with their healthy markets for educational texts, could not sustain a printing press.[39] For the very first time the English printing industry embarked on a course that was utterly at variance with the mainstream experience of European print.

There are several plausible reasons why this should have been so, but the most fundamental was the failure to establish a substantial part in the production of books for the international Latin trade. Where printing survived, and sometimes flourished, away from the emerging centres of production along the Rhine, then this local trade was sustained, very

---

[37] George D. Painter, *William Caxton: A Quincentenary Biography of England's First Printer* (1976); Janet Backhouse, Mirjam Foot and John Barr, *William Caxton: An Exhibition to Commemorate the Quincentenary of the Introduction of Printing into England* (1976). The most recent list of Caxton editions is in Paul Needham, *The Printer & the Pardoner: An Unrecorded Indulgence Printed by William Caxton for the Hospital of St. Mary Rounceval, Charing Cross* (Washington, 1986).

[38] E. Gordon Duff, *A Century of the English Book Trade: Short Notices of All Printers, Stationers, Book-Binders and Others Connected with it from the Issue of the First Dated Book in 1475 to the Incorporation of the Company of Stationers in 1557* (1905).

[39] William K. Sessions, *A Printer's Dozen: The First British Printing Centres to 1557, after Westminster and London* (York, 1983).

largely, by local production of books in Latin. This was so of France, and would be so of the Netherlands, as we shall see.[40] If England's publishers were forced to rely largely on the vernacular trade, then the volume would be small, given that the community of those who required books in English was relatively restricted. It meant that English publishers would take only a modest role in an exceptionally valuable part of the book trade: the steady recurrent trade in school books, and the production of liturgies and Books of Hours. These were a staple part of the trade in books in the manuscript era, and would be also in the new age of print.[41] A common feature of the book trade across Europe was that the profits created by easy best sellers helped create venture capital for other projects. Yet so swiftly did England's printers lose ground to continental competitors that it soon became convenient to print abroad liturgical works with a largely, if not exclusively, English market, such as books according to the Sarum rite. Books of Hours for England were printed extensively in Paris and Rouen, in the Low Countries and as far away as Venice, though often with the name of a London bookseller on the title-page (which is why many are listed in the English STC).[42]

If English printers were limited to the relatively slim pickings of the vernacular market, then other constraints soon emerged. A large part of this residual market was made up by what one might broadly describe as official publications: proclamations, statute books and later church orders and service books. Publications of this nature made up the undramatic bedrock of the trade in many parts of Europe, and the right to publish such works was keenly sought after. By and large they offered steady returns, particularly the most ephemeral edicts and proclamations, where the entire print run was often supplied to a single client.[43] But this close relationship with officialdom imposed its own limitations, since printers and publishers who enjoyed such patronage were unlikely to take on any project that would jeopardise the continuing flow of work. If one considers that the London print fraternity was in any case small, where everyone tended to know everyone else's business, then there was little incentive for a printer to involve themselves with disapproved, or, after

---

[40] P. M. H. Cuijpers, *Teksen als koopwaar: vroege drukkers verkennen de markt* (Amsterdam, 1998).

[41] Mary C. Erler, 'Devotional Literature', in *The Cambridge History of the Book in Britain*, III, ed. Hellinga and Trapp, 495–525; Eamon Duffy, *Marking the Hours: English People and their Prayers, 1240–1570* (New Haven, 2006).

[42] Erler, 'Devotional Literature', 501ff. A search of the electronic version of the E-STC (02.2008) produced 150 hits for Rouen and 86 for Paris. Most are Sarum Missals, or Books of Hours, in English or Latin. In the Henrician period many were produced for the London based Cologne printer/ bookseller Arnold Birckman.

[43] For England, numerous examples in Paul L. Hughes and James F. Larkin, *Tudor Royal Proclamations* (3 vols., New Haven, 1964–9), e.g. I, nos. 73, 181 (warrants for payment to R. Pynson), 128, 151 (Thomas Berthelet).

the Reformation, heretical, publications. This was even more the case when one considers that all printing paper was imported, and therefore passed through the well-regulated Tudor ports.[44] Even if members of the printing fraternity had had some sympathy with Protestantism, few would have been prepared to risk their existing business. And for any newcomer tempted to set up specifically to print evangelical literature, accumulating type, ink and paper, let alone printing heretical texts unobserved, was logistically almost inconceivable.

Thus it was that at the point that the eruptions caused by Martin Luther were transforming the print industry in central Europe, London's printers were unable to take advantage of the economic opportunities that presented themselves. In two decades during which Wittenberg was transformed from a sleepy backwater to one of Europe's major print capitals, demand for evangelical books in English was met largely by printers abroad – mostly in Antwerp.[45]

That London's printers did include many with sympathy for the new doctrines was amply demonstrated during the reign of Edward VI, when the new regime not only removed restrictions on printing, but actively encouraged the publication of works of Protestant theology.[46] The reign of Edward VI also saw the only significant attempt to encourage provincial printing in England. During the course of 1547–8 presses were established in four strategic locations outside the capital, at Canterbury, Ipswich, Worcester and Dublin.[47] But this experiment was short-lived. When Mary Tudor ascended the throne in 1553, all of these presses were forced to close; English provincial towns would play no further significant role in the production of printed books until the end of the eighteenth century.

The new Marian government made a determined effort to control the English printing industry. The new regime had dealt the industry a shrewd blow by requiring all non-naturalised foreigners to leave the country, since many of the more prominent London printers relied heavily on foreign expertise in their workshops; some, indeed, chose to join the expelled foreigners in withdrawing to the continent. A further decisive moment came in 1557, when the king and queen issued a charter that completed

[44] Rhys Jenkins, *Paper-making in England, 1495–1788* (1958).

[45] For English printing in Antwerp see *Antwerp. Dissident Typographical Centre. The Role of Antwerp Printers in the Religious Conflicts in England (16th Century)* (Antwerp, 1994); Willem Heijting, 'Early Reformation Literature from the Printing Shop of Mattheus Crom and Steven Mierdman', *Nederlands Archief voor Kerkgeschiedenis*, 74 (1994), 143–61.

[46] Diarmaid MacCulloch, *Tudor Church Militant: Edward VI and the Protestant Reformation* (1999); John N. King, 'John Day: Master Printer of the English Reformation', in *The Beginnings of English Protestantism*, ed. Peter Marshall and Alec Ryrie (Cambridge, 2002), 180–208.

[47] Sessions, *A Printer's Dozen*; idem, *The First Printers at Ipswich in 1547 and Worcester, 1549–1553* (York, 1984); Janet Freeman, 'John Oswen', *Oxford Dictionary of National Biography* (Oxford, 2004).

the formal organisation of the craft of printing under the control of the Stationers' Company of London.[48]

In itself the instinct for control did not mark out the English situation from that of other European nations. All over Europe printers and publishers, assessing the investment required to bring a new book to the market, wanted the assurance that this market would not be spoiled by a second, competing edition. This prompted the development, in each printing market of Europe, of a system of privilege, granting printers exclusive rights to a text, or class of texts, in which they had invested.[49] What was unique to the English case was the delegation of these responsibilities to a single commercial body. In addition the Stationers were given national powers of regulation and search. These two peculiarities of the English system put astonishing power in the hands of a single trade guild. How they would exercise this power would shape the English book market for centuries ahead.

But first the Stationers had to negotiate one final convolution of English politics, with the death, a mere year after the Charter had been granted, of their patroness, Queen Mary. But the new queen stopped short of reinstating the experiment in press freedom that had characterised the Edwardian years. Rather, in 1559 the new administration issued Articles that not only confirmed the Stationers' charter, but further reinforced their control over the industry. The Articles of 1559 extended the Stationers' control over booksellers, and ordered that all books to be published in London should first be registered with the Company. Further proclamations of 1566 and 1580 reaffirmed the ban on unauthorised printing. A new order of 1586 made explicit the ban of printing outside the capital, with the exception of one press each in Oxford and Cambridge. In 1605 the Company added the monopoly in the production of Common Law books, and in due course also the right to print Bibles; the University presses were paid a cash fee not to enter into competition with the Stationers in this respect. These negotiations were the climax of an immensely successful period, during which the Stationers' Company entrenched its position at the heart of the English book trade.[50] It is interesting to consider what impact this very particular history – both with respect to the Stationers and other developments – had on the intellectual life of England during this period.

First, it must be noted that by European standards the English book world remained very small. The regulations of 1586 put a limit on the

---

[48] Cyprian Blagden, *The Stationers' Company: A History, 1403–1959* (1960).

[49] Elizabeth Armstrong, *Before Copyright: The French Book-Privilege System 1498–1526* (Cambridge, 1990).

[50] Blagden, *Stationers' Company*, 92–5; James Raven, *The Business of Books: Booksellers and the English Book Trade, 1450–1850* (New Haven, 2007), 73–4.

number of printing houses to be permitted in London: only twenty. This limit was reiterated by the regulations of 1615, which further elucidated that of twenty printing houses, fourteen might run two presses and the other six just one. This created an upper limit of thirty-four presses operating, to meet the needs of the whole kingdom. This was only marginally more than had been authorised in the single city of Geneva in the middle decades of the sixteenth century, or, indeed, than the twenty-four presses operated by the single firm of Plantin in Antwerp in the 1580s.[51] Even so, according to James Raven, these regulations may not have been unduly restrictive, since his survey of output for this period suggests that even this limited number of presses would not have been running at full capacity.[52] All told English presses account for 1.5 per cent of the editions published throughout Europe before 1501; and around 4 per cent of those produced in the sixteenth century.[53]

Secondly the English industry was characterised by a unique degree of concentration on one centre of production: London. This was the single respect in which England deviated most entirely from the European norm. Provincial printing was almost negligible: in fact there were more books printed for the English market abroad than there were books printed in England outside the capital.[54] Production was also concentrated very heavily on vernacular books. Vernacular titles outnumbered Latin by over 5:1, against a European norm nearer 1:1. The consequence of this was that for England the trade in learned texts was essentially an import trade. And this trade was very largely one way: there was no substantial export trade to balance the books. To make an international impact English authors had generally to be published abroad, and in Latin. This was certainly possible, as John Fisher would demonstrate in the early Reformation controversies.[55] And one could certainly make a case that the size and organisation of the industry did not impact greatly on the range of books available to English readers. English libraries and collectors availed themselves freely of the easy and long-established connections with the continent to obtain the best books that continental suppliers had to offer. The accounts of the Plantin press in Antwerp reveal regular transactions with a large range of London booksellers, supplying

[51] Colin Clair, *Christopher Plantin* (1960).

[52] Raven, *The Business of Books*, 46–9.

[53] See Appendix.

[54] By a margin of more than two to one; search of the electronic version of the STC (2.2008) yielded 469 books printed before 1601 in England outside London or Westminster, and 1,122 books printed abroad.

[55] M. A. Shaaber, *Check-List of Works of British Authors Printed Abroad, in Languages other than English, to 1641* (New York, 1975), nos. 41–103. Fisher's works were also translated into German and Dutch.

especially maps and topographical works not published in England.[56] Leedham-Green's Cambridge inventories and the English Renaissance Libraries series reveal that students in Oxford and Cambridge had little difficulty in obtaining such books as they required.[57]

It was more in the range of books available in the vernacular trade that the particular circumstances of the English market had most impact. The management of the trade by the Stationers' Company encouraged a definite conservatism. The trade was very heavily concentrated on religious books. But London's output was conspicuously low in several areas which formed an important part of the European vernacular trade. One area of the market that seems somewhat underdeveloped in England was what one might call polite recreational literature. Domestic readers could avail themselves of any number of sermons, but more secular pleasures were not catered for with such assiduous care. Major milestones of European literature made their way into English only very haltingly. Ariosto's *Orlando Furioso* was not translated into English until 1591, Machiavelli's *The Prince* was not rendered into English until 1640.[58] The market in news print also seems to have been substantially less developed in England than in continental places; a consequence, in part, of the absence of provincial presses. England also lagged substantially behind in what one might describe as the scholarly vernacular: books of science, mathematics, topography, botany and medicine aimed at a vernacular audience. This was a direct result of the relative size of the London industry, which simply did not generate the capital resources necessary for such projects.

V

The case could be made that the differences identified between France and England were to some extent inevitable. France was a nation of many more million inhabitants and many substantial towns. The vernacular reading community extended over the borders to the Low Countries and parts of the Empire. This accounts for some, but not all, of the differences. It was not inevitable that France would appropriate so significant a share in Latin production, but it had very significant consequences for the overall sophistication of the French print world. In any case, any easy determinism is subverted by the undoubted success of print in the sixteenth-century Low Countries. The Seventeen Provinces boasted a population of less than two million, and the larger of its two

[56] Colin Clair, 'Christopher Plantin's Trade Connections with England and Scotland', *The Library*, 5th ser., 14 (1959), 28–45.

[57] E. S. Leedham-Green, *Books in Cambridge Inventories: Book Lists from Vice-Chancellor's Court Probate Inventories in the Tudor and Stuart Periods* (2 vols., Cambridge, 1986).

[58] STC 746 (Ariosto), 17168 (Machiavelli).

vernacular reading communities (Dutch) was much smaller than this. Nevertheless the publishers of Flanders and Holland appropriated a significant proportion of Europe's printing trade, a role they sustained in often adverse and difficult political circumstances.

Print was established in the Low Countries at an early date. Given all that we know about the vibrancy of schools' culture and commerce in the Low Countries this is hardly a surprise, and the Netherlands would soon emerge as an important centre of print. The first dated editions published in the Low Countries appeared at Alost, a small town in Flanders, and Utrecht, both in 1473. Yet interestingly, print seems from a very early stage to have pursued two divergent courses, reflecting different strands of interest in the new art. In the commercial towns of the south, printers specialised in the types of books popular with the nobility and wealthy merchants, chivalric romances, moralities and chronicles.[59] This was notably so in the case of Bruges, a major centre of the medieval manuscript trade, where Colard Mansion established his shop. Other presses were established in Brussels, at Louvain, where the university sustained demand, and at Antwerp. In the north, Utrecht soon ceded primacy to Deventer, where the copying trade of the Brethren of the Common Life promised an established market in school books. This became a foundation stone of the trade in the north: the bibliography of Low Countries' incunabula lists an astonishing 280 surviving examples of the two staples of the school curriculum, the *Doctrinale* of Alexander de Villa Dei and the *Ars Minor* of Donatus.[60] Presses were also established in other towns with notable schools, such as Zwolle, Nijmegen and 's Hertogenbosch.

These strongly developed specialised markets allowed regional print in the Netherlands to resist the full impact of two potentially destructive tendencies: the late fifteenth-century crisis of European print, and the magnetic pull of the emerging print metropolis, Antwerp. Printing in the dispersed towns of the north was not entirely immune from these tendencies. Print shops in Delft, Haarlem and Bruges ceased operation; Gerard Leeu moved his press from Gouda to Antwerp; even Pafraet in Deventer was forced temporarily to close his doors. Nevertheless it was not until the 1520s that Antwerp's proportion of the print production of the Netherlands reached 50 per cent, and Antwerp never attained the total domination of the market that Paris had temporarily achieved in the early sixteenth century, and London on a permanent basis.[61] Regional print centres of some importance survived, largely through the pursuit

[59] Wytze Gs Hellinga, *Copy and Print in the Netherlands* (Amsterdam, 1962), 11–13.

[60] Gerard van Thielen and John Goldfinch, *Incunabula Printing in the Low Countries* (Nieuwkoop, 1999), nos. 85–214, 739–886.

[61] Cuijpers, *Teksten als koopwaar*, 71–4.

of significant specialism: Latin theological works in the case of Louvain, school books in the case of Deventer. At Louvain, in particular, Thierry Martens conducted a business of some significance, turning out numerous editions of the classics and modern authors.[62] He was the first to introduce italic type in the Netherlands, and also experimented with Greek and Hebrew characters; he also enjoyed the patronage of Erasmus for editions of his works published in the Netherlands. Martens's spiritual heir was Rutgerus Rescius, the learned scholar/printer who from 1518 occupied the Chair of Greek at the Trilingual College in Louvain.[63] Although Deventer's influence would fade in the second half of the century, other northern print towns would emerge to take its place.[64]

Antwerp's influence in the print culture of the Netherlands was nevertheless significant and growing. The print metropolis on the Scheldt also developed significant specialisms of its own. Reflecting the cosmopolitan nature of its mercantile population, the city became a precocious centre of news publications, relaying first intelligence of events in central Europe and the Orient to a local audience, and also, at one remove, to France and England.[65] The connections with the English book market were particularly close and long established. It is therefore no surprise that when the English authorities moved to impede publication of evangelical texts, Antwerp became a major centre of production for Protestant works in English, destined for clandestine distribution across the Channel. This is all the more remarkable given the stringent measures enacted against the publication of heretical literature for domestic consumption. It was, for Charles V, emperor and hereditary ruler of the Low Countries, a matter of personal honour to ensure that the Lutheran heresies did not secure a foothold. This was no small task. Luther's teaching found a distinct resonance in the towns of the Netherlands and his works were discussed, and initially published, quite freely.[66] To inhibit the spread of heresy Charles V insisted on the enactment of a range of controls over the printing and dissemination of heretical books as stringent as any in Europe.[67] From 1530 the possession of unauthorised texts was a capital crime. Printers found to have printed

---

[62] *Dirk Martens, 1473–1973* (Aalst, 1973); Anne Rouzet, *Dictionaire des imprimeurs, libraires et éditeurs des XVe et XVe siècles dans les limites géographiques de la Belgique actuelle* (Nieuwkoop, 1975), 140–3.

[63] Rouzet, *Dictionaire*, 186–7.

[64] Paul Valkema Blouw, *Typographia Batava 1541–1600: repertorium van boeken gedrukt in Nederland tussen 1541 en 1600* (2 vols., Nieuwkoop, 1998).

[65] Carl Göllner, *Turcica: Die europäischen Türkendrucke des XVI. Jahrhunderts. I. Band MDI–MDL* (Berlin, 1961).

[66] C. Ch. G. Visser, *Luther's geschriften in de nederlanden tot 1546* (Assen, 1969).

[67] Alastair Duke, 'Building Heaven in Hell's Despite: The Early History of the Reformation in the Towns of the Low Countries', in his *Reformation and Revolt in the Low Countries* (1990), 71–100.

such items could expect severe treatment. From 1546 the emperor, in cooperation with the University of Louvain, issued detailed lists of texts and authors that could not be read or published.[68]

Despite these measures, the control of the output of presses in the Netherlands was extremely patchy. In truth the continuing diversity of printing in the Netherlands, spread through more than a score of different centres, made control of heretical printing far more difficult than in places where print culture was more centralised. It is also relevant that the publication of the Bible in vernacular languages was not specifically forbidden, as was the case in France. In consequence Antwerp was able to capture a significant part of this market, publishing Bibles and New Testaments in French, English and Danish, as well as in Dutch and Latin.[69] The first Dutch translation based on an evangelical model was published in 1526, and this was the first of a sequence of distinguished translations intended for a public eager to embrace the reading of Scripture.

The erosion of royal authority after Philip II's departure for Spain in 1559, together with the rise of Calvinism, precipitated a political crisis that resulted, in 1566, in the outbreak of the Dutch Revolt. Not surprisingly these events brought an immediate reaction from the press. Printers, both within and outside the Netherlands, turned out multiple editions of the rebel manifestos, and of catechisms, Psalters and church orders for the rapidly growing evangelical congregations.[70] The first revolt was quickly extinguished, but the polemical fury of 1566 established a pattern that would continue for much of the century. Over three decades when the rebellion first established a foothold back in Holland, then painfully established a free northern state, the printing presses of Antwerp, Brussels and latterly Leiden and Amsterdam chronicled each twist and turn of events. Alongside the manifestos and denunciations of the opposing parties, a large part of this literature was made up of official publications: orders of the king, his successive viceroys and later the States General, acting as a *de facto* independent sovereign power.[71] The magistrates in Antwerp also made extensive use of print in their administration of the city.[72] Although much of this regulatory literature

---

[68] J. M. de Bujanda *et al.*, *Index de l'Université de Louvain, 1546, 1550, 1558* (Geneva, 1986).

[69] A. A. Den Hollander, *De Nederlandse Bijbelvertalingen, 1522–1545* (Nieuwkoop, 1997); Chambers, *Bibliography of French Bibles*.

[70] W. Heijting, *De catechismi en confessies in de Nederlandse Reformatie tot 1585* (2 vols. Nieuwkoop: De Graaf, 1989).

[71] W. P. C. Knuttel, *Catalogus van de pamfletten-verzameling berustende in de Koninklijke Bibliotheek* (9 vols., The Hague, 1882–1920); Valkema Blouw, *Typographia Batava 1541–1600*; Elly Cockx-Indestege, Geneviève Glorieux and Bart op de Beeck, *Belgica typographica 1541–1600: catalogus librorum impressorum ab anno MDXLI ad annum MDC in regionibus quae nunc Regni Belgarum partes sunt* (Nieuwkoop, 1968–94).

[72] Léon Voet, *The Plantin Press (1555–1589): A Bibliography of the Works Printed and Published by Christopher Plantin at Antwerp and Leiden* (6 vols., Amsterdam, 1980–3), I, 89–157 (nos. 68–569).

was a direct consequence of the turbulence of war, a lot was of a more mundane character, reflecting the growing power and administrative reach of officialdom. This was a common feature of administration throughout Europe, and print became a powerful auxiliary tool. In the Netherlands much of this official literature was also devoted to the regulation of commerce: a reflection of its special position as a fulcrum of European trade.

It says much both for the resilience of the local economy and the special place of the Low Countries in Europe's scholarly networks that local printers continued, through all the disruptions of war, to command a major portion of the market in serious scholarly literature.[73] By the second half of the century the Low Countries had become the leaders in the production of high-quality woodcuts and copper-plate engravings.[74] And Antwerp had by this point become a major gathering place for scholars and those engaged in experimental investigations, many attracted by the religious eclecticism of its mercantile culture.

In the second half of the century this market in high-quality publications is inevitably associated with the printing house of Christophe Plantin. Plantin, originally an immigrant from France, first established a press in Antwerp in 1555.[75] He quickly established a profitable specialism in several genres in which Antwerp already excelled, such as small format versions of the classics and popular modern literature. An unwise flirtation with forbidden evangelical texts almost brought shipwreck, but despite a potentially ruinous financial penalty Plantin found investors willing to help rebuild his business. Through the 1570s and 1580s Plantin built a publishing house that matched any in Europe. At its peak the workshop at the House of the Golden Compasses sustained twenty-four presses. Plantin matched this prodigious output with a keen business sense, and a restless ambition to publish books of outstanding aesthetic quality. So while the firm and its agents in Paris, London and Frankfurt moved phenomenal quantities of books on to the international market, Plantin himself was increasingly preoccupied with projects that would secure his reputation.[76] Much of his profits were invested in a long-term contract to supply liturgical books to Spain, a contract for which

---

[73] A. Geerebaert, 'De Antwerpse uitgevers en de Nederlandsche vertalingen van klassieke schrijvers in de XVIe eeuw', *De Gulden Passer*, 3 (1925), 131–48.

[74] Karen L. Bowen and Dirk Imhof, *Christopher Plantin and Engraved Book Illustrations in Sixteenth-Century Europe* (Cambridge, 2008); Jan Van der Stock, *Printing Images in Antwerp. The Introduction of Printmaking in a City: Fifteenth Century to 1585* (Rotterdam, 1998).

[75] Clair, *Plantin*; Léon Voet, *The Golden Compasses: A History and Evaluation of the Printing and Publishing Activities of the Officina Plantiniana at Antwerp* (2 vols., Amsterdam, 1969–72).

[76] R. Lauwaert, 'De handelsbedrijvigheid van de Officina Plantiniana op de Buchermessen te Frankfurt am Main in de XVIe eeuw', *De Gulden Passer*, 50 (1972), 124–80, 51 (1973), 70–105.

Plantin never received more than a fraction of the promised payment. His masterwork, the magnificent Polyglot Bible, was an enterprise equally fraught.[77] The book was eighteen months in the press, and cannot have recouped more than a fraction of the money Plantin invested in the project. Yet Plantin had no regrets. The Polyglot Bible was a literary and scholarly achievement that sealed the reputation of its printer, and confirmed Antwerp's status as the capital of the northern Renaissance.

For all the lustre of such prestigious ventures, the steady bedrock of profit came from more mundane projects. Antwerp's place in the world of commerce not only greatly assisted the circulation of books around Europe's market places, it also created a market for certain specific categories of books. From early in the century the Netherlands took a leading role in the publication of books of exchange: documenting coins in circulation and their relative values, often with illustrative woodcuts. Later printers developed a lucrative new line in dictionaries and phrase books, often with a choice of phrases specifically directed towards the needs of merchants.[78] For those wishing to improve their command of these languages printers in the Netherlands also developed a range of literary texts, with texts in two, three or even four languages arranged in parallel across two facing pages.[79]

Antwerp's place at the crossroads of many voyages also allowed its printers to gain a foothold in many distant markets. Antwerp's printers published books in more than fifteen different languages, including several vernaculars not native to the Low Countries. Books were published in German, Italian, Swedish and Danish, as well as the large trade in Spanish and English books.[80] As a result of the religious controversies of the Reformation, Netherlandish printers commanded a not insignificant portion of the English market, publishing Protestant books in the first half of the century, and Catholic recusant works during the reign of Elizabeth.[81] Spain represented a major export market for printers in the

[77] Clair, *Plantin*, 57–86.

[78] J. Hoock and P. Jeannin, *Ars Mercatoria. Handbücher und Traktate für den Gebrauch des Kaufmanns*, I (Zurich, 1991).

[79] Pettegree, 'Translation and the Migration of Texts', in *French Book and the European Book World*, 216–17.

[80] Voet, *Plantin Press*, VI, 2521–56; Wouter Nijhoff and Maria Elizabeth Kronenberg, *Nederlandsche bibliographie van 1500 tot 1540* (3 vols., 's-Gravenhage, 1965–71; reprint of The Hague, 1919–42), for the editions in the first part of the century. The editions published in Danish, mostly in Antwerp between 1529 and 1531, are listed in L. Nielsen, *Dansk bibliografi 1482–1550* (Copenhagen, 1919), nos. 271–2 (editions of the New Testament), 146, 147, 155, 158, 159 (Luther translations), 22, 215.

[81] A. F. Allison and D. M. Rogers, *A Catalogue of Catholic Books in English Printed Abroad or Secretly in England, 1558–1640* (1968); *idem*, *The Contemporary Printed Literature of the English Counter-Reformation between 1558 and 1640: An Annotated Catalogue* (2 vols., Aldershot, 1989–94).

Netherlands.[82] The two most important figures in this trade were Martin Nutius and Christophe Plantin. Nutius, later succeeded by his widow and then his son Philip, may be credited with developing this important trade.[83] Later Plantin would supply the Spanish market with enormous quantities of liturgical books under exclusive contract. The volume of this production, to which Plantin devoted twelve presses between 1571 and 1576, was stupendous. In these six years, according to his very precise reckoning, he shipped some 47,445 Breviaries, Missals, Books of Hours and Hymnals to the peninsula.[84]

In 1585, after a long siege, the city of Antwerp capitulated to the armies of the duke of Parma, and returned to Spanish obedience. Printers and members of the ancillary book trades were among the many thousands who left the south and settled in Holland; the close blockade maintained by the rebel provinces was a further inducement to abandon the former Scheldt metropolis.[85] The impending catastrophe had already induced the ever shrewd Plantin to establish a branch of his business in Leiden, where printing had been reestablished along with the foundation of a new university in 1575. Although Plantin himself moved back to spend his last years in Antwerp, the Leiden branch continued under the management of his son-in-law, Raphelenghien. The presence of the university, and a notably distinguished cadre of professors, allowed Leiden to become a major centre of scholarly publishing. Other notable publishing ventures flourished in Holland in these years in Amsterdam, Dordrecht, Delft and Haarlem, and elsewhere in the United Provinces at Franeker, Leeuwarden, Kampen, Deventer and Utrecht. In Franeker the distinguished Academy provided a steady line of work in the publication of academic dissertations.[86] At the other geographical extremity, in Middelberg in Zeeland, Richard Schilders continued the established tradition of publishing for critics of the English church, in this case Puritan adversaries of the Anglican establishment. In all, more than twenty towns in the north found a place on the printing map of the Low Countries in the last two decades of the century.

---

[82] Jean Peeters-Fontainas, *Bibliographie des impressions espagnoles des Pays-Bas méridionaux* (2 vols., Nieuwkoop, 1965), lists 600 editions printed in Spanish in the sixteenth-century Low Countries.

[83] Jean Peeters-Fontainas, *L'officine espagnole de Martin Nutius à Anvers* (Antwerp, 1957); B. A. Vermaseren, 'De Spaanse uitgaven op godsdienstig gebied van M. Nutius en J. Steelsius', *De Gulden Passer*, 50 (1972), 26–99.

[84] Clair, *Plantin*, 87–104.

[85] J. G. C. A. Briels, *Zuidnederlandse boekdrukkers en boekverkopers in de Republiek der Verenigde Nederlanden omstreeks 1570–1630: een bijdrage tot de kennis van de geschiedenis van het boek* (Nieuwkoop, 1974).

[86] Ferenc Postma, *Auditorium Academiae Franekerensis. Bibliographie der Reden. Disputationen und Gelegenheitsdruckwerke der Universität und des Athenäums in Franeker 1585–1843* (Leeuwarden, 1995).

The success of printers in the Netherlands was based on a number of complementary factors. They boldly appropriated markets in which they had no natural place. They shrewdly developed special niche markets, although the largest printers were also notable generalists. They exploited their position at the hub of Europe's commerce both for distribution and transportation of books, and to develop new types of publication specifically for merchant readers. Finally they applied their experience of complex financial transactions to underwrite some of Europe's finest and most ambitious printing projects. In these ways the printers of the Low Countries not only subverted the constraints of a relatively small population, but also made light of the restrictions imposed by successive rulers, and the disruption of the Dutch Revolt.

VI

This sustained success is a warning against excessive determinism in interpreting the development of print culture in different parts of Europe. There was always room for the enterprising entrepreneur, such as the Lübeck merchant who supplied Breviaries and Missals to Livonia.[87] A notably successful printing tradition was sustained for much of the century in Königsberg (now Kaliningrad) in East Prussia.[88] The planting of print in the Spanish American colonies was another successful example of a carefully planned venture that overcame daunting logistical difficulties.[89] But if we consider the central core of the European book world, the long-term success of print culture in sixteenth-century Europe depended ultimately on a paradoxical relationship between concentration of production and diversity of output. The wide dispersal of production that followed the first enthusiastic engagement with print in the fifteenth century represented a critical misunderstanding of the new dynamics of the book industry. This was a model of production appropriate for the manuscript age that could not work for print. Once this was recognised, after a painful period of adjustment, the restructured industry could achieve a wonderful diversity of production, in terms of both type and price. By the end of the sixteenth century Europe's printing industry could meet the needs of a large and ever expanding reading community,

---

[87] Hellmuth Helwig, 'Das Buchbinderhandwerk in Riga vom 16. bis 18. Jahrhunderts', *Archiv für Geschichte des Buchwesens*, 8 (1967), cols. 485–904.

[88] *VD 16* lists 537 works printed in Königsberg during the sixteenth century.

[89] Joaquín García Icazbalceta, *Bibliografía mexicana del signo XVI* (Mexico City, 1954), lists 179 items fully described; a further 85 not known from surviving copies; 48 from fragments. Carlos E. Castañeda, 'The Beginning of Printing in America', *Hispanic American Historical Review*, 20 (1940), 671–85; Lawrence S. Thompson, 'Some Reconsiderations of the Origin of Printing in Sixteenth-Century Mexico', in his *Essays in Hispanic Bibliography* (1970).

for books on an ever increasing range of subjects, and in a huge variety of prices and formats.

Appendix

Estimate of total numbers of known books published in different parts of Europe before 1601, divided by country or region (March 2008)

'Core' zone

	Vernacular	Latin	Total
France	45,344	34,000	79,344
Italy	50,800	47,000	97,800
Germany	62,600	70,016	132,616
Swiss Confederation	4,757	9,270	14,027
Low Countries	14,161	13,452	27,613
Total	177,662	173,738	351,400
Proportion of European total	86.1%	93.3%	89.5%

'Peripheral' regions

	Vernacular	Latin	Total
England	11,616	1,816	13,432
Spain	10,200	4,800	15,000
Scandinavia	873	793	1,666
Eastern Europe	6,000	5,000	11,000
Total	28,689	12,409	41,098
Proportion of European total	13.9%	6.7%	10.5%
Total for whole of Europe	206,351	186,147	392,498

For **France**, vernacular editions are fully documented in *FB*. The figure for Latin editions is an estimate based on ongoing work for the third and fourth volumes of *FB: Books Published in France in Latin and Languages other than French*.

For **Italy**, the totals given here are based on a survey of the on-line edition of *Edit 16*. This is an ongoing survey; the 63,000 records analysed have been scaled up to account for holdings in libraries not yet surveyed (not least the British Library, the largest single collection of early Italian books). The I-STC database contributes a further 9,803 editions published in Italy.

For **Germany**, the *VD 16* reports 100,432 entries [August 2007], against an anticipated final total of around 128,000, and the I-STC a further 9,861 editions for Germany and German-speaking Europe. Entries for Basel, Zurich and Bern have been transferred to the Swiss Confederation, below. The *VD 16* also does not include single-sheet items or printed music, and a further adjustment has been made to include data from these separate surveys.

For the **Swiss Confederation** sixteenth-century imprints from French centres of production (Geneva, Lausanne and Neuchâtel) are fully documented in *FB* and by Jean-François Gilmont in his GLN database. These generate records for 2,047 editions in the vernacular and 2,624 in the learned languages. The sixteenth-century editions from German-speaking parts of the Confederation are included in the *VD 16*; a search for Basel, Zurich, Bern and other marginal centres of production generates 8,400 records. The I-STC records 956 editions, divided between Geneva and Basel.

For the **Low Countries**, the figures are derived from the ongoing project to replace the existing Netherlandish and Belgian bibliographies: *NB. Books Published in the Sixteenth-Century Low Countries and in Dutch Abroad* (forthcoming, Brill, 2009).

For **England**, a search has been made of the electronic E-STC, searching for place and language. An additional filter (country = England) ensures that false imprints are excluded.

For **Spain**, the figures are derived from the ongoing project, *IB. Books Published in Spain and Portugal before 1601 and in Spanish and Portuguese Abroad*, ed. Alexander Wilkinson (forthcoming, Brill, 2009).

For **Scandinavia** the figures are derived from existing national bibliographies.

For **Eastern Europe** use has been made of existing national bibliographies, refined for the ongoing project *ENB. Books Published before 1601 in Northern and Eastern Europe* (forthcoming, Brill, 2009).

Transactions of the RHS 18 (2008), pp. 129–63 © 2008 Royal Historical Society
doi:10.1017/S0080440108000686   Printed in the United Kingdom

A TALE OF TWO EPISCOPAL SURVEYS: THE STRANGE FATES OF EDMUND GRINDAL AND CUTHBERT MAYNE REVISITED

The Prothero Lecture

By Peter Lake

READ 4 JULY 2007

ABSTRACT. This article seeks to relate the course of Edmund Grindal's disgrace to the formulation and enforcement of policy against catholics. It argues that the two were integrally related and that the nature of that interrelationship can be seen as a function of certain manoeuvres and debates about a range of issues involving the queen and her councillors and bishops and indeed members of the wider regime. The resulting exchanges were conducted in terms of the nature and relative significance of the popish and puritan threats. The aim here is to reveal the dynamics of the resulting mode of ideological politics and to show how very serious differences of approach, priority and world view could be both canvassed and contained within the consensual mechanisms and assumptions of the Elizabethan regime. Through a close analysis of one political moment the paper also hopes to demonstrate the extent to which a series of conventionally separately told stories – about ecclesiastical affairs, about foreign policy, about puritans and about catholics, about both court and local politics – need to be seen as parts of a unitary political narrative or process, the nature of which this paper is an attempt to reveal.

I

It has become fashionable, of late, to decry the effects of academic specialisation. Since most of these complaints are in some way self-interested – designed either to recall a lost golden age of generalists, or else to sell hoary old narratives to television companies – I have never taken the resulting jeremiads too seriously. But there can be no doubt that the creation of myriad sub-fields and specialisms can result in a sometimes unfortunate fragmentation of the object of study. Certainly, the literature on Elizabethan England has come to be marked by a series of parallel narratives; religious and political; diplomatic and domestic; local and national; and, perhaps most notably and destructively of all, protestant and catholic. This last dichotomy is not, of course, only, or even mainly, a function of academic specialisation, but also of long-standing confessional divisions and cultural assumptions. Here the central conceit is of an 'England' that is, almost by definition, protestant and of catholics and catholicism as consequently always already peripheral to the 'mainstream' story. Certainly, for the Elizabethan and Stuart periods, that assumption is wrong, and has been shown to be so by a great deal of both revisionist and post-revisionist writing, but the divisions and exclusions in the literature that result from it are, to a surprising and entirely unhelpful extent, still with us and need to be broken down. What follows is an attempt to do that through a close analysis of what I hope will emerge below as integrally connected events, central to both the religious and political history of the reign of Elizabeth I.[1]

The events in question took place between the summers of 1576 and 1578. Of the two strange fates and episcopal surveys of my title, one of each concerned things protestant and the other, things catholic. My first, protestant, fate involved Edmund Grindal. Grindal, of course, was the first, and, at least so far, the only, post-Reformation archbishop of Canterbury to have been first suspended from office by the monarch, and then to have expired years later, still under house arrest. My second, catholic, fate involves Cuthbert Mayne, the first seminary priest to be executed for treason by the Elizabethan regime. Mayne went to his doom at Launceston in Cornwall in November 1577. He is therefore something of an outlier from the main body of clerical martyrs slaughtered by the regime subsequent to the Campion/Parsons debacle of 1580/1. It has never been clear just what – if anything – Mayne had done to bring this fate upon himself or why he met his end just when and how he did. In so far as it has been explained, it has been seen (by A. L. Rowse) as a purely local affair, a function of Cornish rivalries between Sir Richard Grenville and his protestant allies and local catholics, between (protestant) coastal and inland (catholic) interests.[2]

As for my two surveys, again, one concerned protestants, the other catholics. The first was instituted in the summer of 1576, by Grindal and concerned the prophesyings, often monthly meetings of ministers in market towns and other population centres, designed to generate a number of expositions of the same text, before both clerical and lay, elite

---

[1] I should say at the outset that what follows is a product of what has now been a rather long ongoing conversation with Michael Questier on how best to reintegrate things catholic into the master narratives of post-Reformation English history. It is Michael's work that has done most to re-centre the doings and sayings of English catholics in the political and religious histories of late Tudor and early Stuart England. Typically, it was Michael who first suggested that I read the 1577 recusant survey against the survey of the prophesyings of the previous year. This paper also draws on the work of three other scholars – Patrick Collinson, Simon Adams and Diarmaid MacCulloch – the extent of whose contribution to its argument cannot properly be indicated through occasional references in the footnotes. It is a pleasure to be able to acknowledge here the extent to which my own work has been informed by theirs over the past thirty years.

[2] A. L. Rowse, *Tudor Cornwall* (New York, 1969), 346–51.

and popular audiences. The prohesyings can be said to have had three main functions; first to use the expertise of the best preachers to train their less talented, learned and experienced colleagues in the ministry; secondly, to maximise the number and quality of sermons and sermon hours produced by the limited number of trained preachers available to the Elizabethan church; and thirdly, to foster, perform and exhibit the social, cultural and spiritual power of the gospel and of the protestant godly.[3]

The second survey of autumn 1577 concerned catholics. It was organised by Walsingham and the Privy Council, in collaboration with Grindal's *de facto* successor John Aylmer. A round robin letter was sent to the bishops asking them how many recusants were to be found in their dioceses and what those recusants were really worth financially. It represented a new departure – indeed a more or less unprecedented initiative – and as such bulks large in studies of recusancy which see it, accurately enough, as the first real attempt to map the extent of the catholic threat and actually put a number on the recusant population.

These events – the fates of Grindal and Mayne and the two surveys – are seemingly unconnected; and, for all that they took place in the same weeks, months, indeed in one instance even on the same day, have certainly remained unconnected in the existing literature. They have been discussed separately, as admittedly central events, in what have been, to date, two more or less hermetically sealed, protestant and catholic narratives. The seminal account of the fall of Grindal by Patrick Collinson (upon which, for the most part, this paper relies implicitly) does not mention Mayne or the recusant survey.[4] As for the survey of recusants it has remained embedded in accounts of catholicism and of recusant policy largely untouched by the storm over the prophesyings, which, on the 'catholic' view, was clearly an intra-protestant spat of no particular relevance to the study of English catholicism.[5]

In this paper, I want to argue that these events were in fact connected in ways that have much to tell us about the nature of Elizabeth politics; about the relation between the queen and her councillors, about the relation between 'politics' and 'religion', between national and local politics and between politics and ideology and, in particular, about the complex,

[3] On the prophesyings see P. Collinson, *The Elizabethan Puritan Movement* (1967), 168–79, 182–3, 191–6; *idem*, 'Lectures by Combination: Structures and Characteristics of Church Life in 17th-Century England', in Collinson's *Godly People* (1983); *Conferences and Combination Lectures in the Elizabethan Church, 1582–1590*, ed. P. Collinson, John Craig and Brett Usher, Church of England Record Society, 10 (Woodbridge, 2003), xxvi–xxxii, xxxvii–xxxviii.

[4] P. Collinson, *Archbishop Grindal, 1519–1583: The Struggle for a Reformed Church* (1979), chs. 3, 14, 15; *idem*, 'The Downfall of Archbishop Grindal and its Place in Elizabethan Political and Religious History', ch. 14 of his *Godly People*.

[5] W. R. Trimble, *The Catholic Laity in Elizabethan England* (Cambridge, MA, 1964), 72–90.

dialogic and dialectical relations between anti-popery and that emergent ideological mode – anti-puritanism.

II

Let us start with the issue of the prophesyings and our first survey of summer 1576. This was organised by Grindal to provide him with material to protect the prophesyings from royal assault. Elizabeth's intermittent attempts to have the prophesyings suppressed started in 1574 and, to use Collinson's resonant phrase, had 'been kicked into the long grass' by the collusive efforts of both bishops and lay councillors. In the summer of 1576 Grindal learned from Leicester and others that the issue was back on the royal agenda.

It is not clear just who it was that first raised the prophesyings with the queen but we can reconstruct the outline of the case against from the questions put by Grindal to his episcopal colleagues and indeed from the contents of some of the replies. First, it was claimed that the prophesyings were 'puritan' institutions; set up and run by puritans, they were occasions for non-conformist behaviour and for the public venting of complaints about the ceremonies and structures of the church and of appeals for further reformation. Secondly it was alleged that they were not under proper episcopal control; the local clergy (often the local puritan clergy) ran them themselves, with no proper discipline or oversight from the bishops. They thus represented exercises in self-government by self-selected clerical (puritan) elites, protected by local lay (puritan) interests. Thirdly, it was claimed that the prophesyings were both popular and divisive in their form and effects. Their dialogic form put different expositions of the same scriptural text before promiscuously mixed, clerical and lay, elite but also popular, audiences. Even more than the most contentious sermon the prophesyings could thus be taken to be constructing an intellectually active and critical audience, an audience called upon, in effect, to judge between different positions. Not an attempt to stop discussion and division by informing opinion, instructing the laity, telling people what they ought to believe, they were rather attempts to start discussion, provoke opinion, raise questions and thus to create division. These propensities were intensified, of course, if the topics under discussion included contentious issues like the controverted ceremonies or the need for 'further reformation'. Moreover, it was further claimed that the prophesyings were overtly popular in form; that they actually and actively involved 'the people'. Not just the laity, but the humble laity, artisans even, were involved, not only as spectators, but as active participants in discussion.

On this account, the prophesyings were an emanation of a popular puritan threat to the parochial and hierarchical structures of the church and, as such, agents of religious division, stirrers up not only of dissension but also of disobedience. We know from what the queen said, when she acted personally to suppress the prophesyings, that this was how she saw the matter.[6] Moreover, it is clear from some of the episcopal replies to Grindal's questionnaire that this was what a dissident minority amongst the bishops also thought.[7] We can also tell from the nature of the other replies, that is to say, from the anxiety of many of Grindal's respondents to explain just when it was that they had stopped beating their wives, what the nature of the accusations against the prophesyings were.

On non-conformity, some replies were insistent that prayers from the prayer book were used both before and after proceedings; that contentious issues were never discussed; that there was no non-conformity, no complaints about the ceremonies or pleas for further reformation either performed or canvassed at their prophesyings.[8] Or, alternately, it was conceded that while there used to be some – quite a lot, in fact – of that sort of thing going on, everything was now under control. Others still (and here Bishop Cooper is the best example) admitted that there still was more than a hint of puritanism about some of the prophesyings on his patch and that he would like to, indeed that he would, quash it – if only certain nameless but powerful lay interests would let him.[9]

On lay involvement, it was claimed, by Bishop Curtis for example, that there was no lay in-put, and certainly no artisans active in prophesyings in his diocese.[10] Or it was admitted that there were some laymen involved – but only learned ones – like George Gifford, then a school master and soon to be a leading puritan minister;[11] or again that if there were no laity involved, there seemed to be no good reason why there should not be, provided they were learned. Again, it was readily affirmed that the prophesyings were under episcopal control; in some cases admittedly the prophesying in question had not been set up by the bishop himself, but

[6] Lambeth Palace Library [hereafter LPL] MSS 2003, fo. 40r–v, Elizabeth to John Whitgift, bishop of Worcester, 7 May 1577. For another copy see British Library [hereafter BL], Lansdowne MSS 25, fo. 94r.

[7] Here Bishop Scory of Hereford's response to Grindal was perhaps the most outspoken. LPL MSS 2003, fo. 10r–v, Scory to Grindal, 18 July 1576.

[8] *Ibid.*, fo. 13r, Archdeacon Walker of Essex to Bishop Sandys; *ibid.*, fo. 16v, Archdeacon Kemp of St Albans to Sandys.

[9] *Ibid.*, fo. 5r–v, Bishop Bentham to Grindal, 16 July 1576; *ibid.*, fos. 29r–30r, Bishop Cooper to Grindal, 27 July 1576.

[10] *Ibid.*, fo. 5r, Bentham to Grindal, 16 July 1576; *ibid.*, fo. 29v, Cooper to Grindal, 27 July 1576; *ibid.*, fo. 4r, Curtis to Grindal, 15 July 1576.

[11] *Ibid.*, fo. 12r, Walker to Sandys; *ibid.*, fos. 31r–v, Bishop Davies of St David's to Grindal, 24 July 1576. 'I think it were not amiss to give the moderators and interpretors authority to all and admit a learned lay man to interpret or oppose if they see cause.'

he had approved the arrangements. (Thus Cooper.)[12] Or, as Bradbridge claimed, while the prophesyings in his diocese had been set up by his predecessor, he was closely involved, sometimes attended himself and even moderated from time to time. But unfortunately, just at the moment, he could not tell you which ministers were actually involved in the exercises – he would have to get back to Grindal on that one.[13] Or finally, as we have seen, Cooper was reduced to claiming that he was in control, except where he was not, but that was decidedly not his fault.[14]

We can see here not only the thrust of the anti-puritan, anti-popular critique of the prophesyings but also, if not its literal truth, then certainly the origin of its purchase. These straws in the wind certainly do not confirm the prophesyings as the puritan, populist, if not crypto-presbyterian, then inherently anti-episcopal, institutions that their critics claimed them to be – but they do show that there was some truth in the allegations of puritanism and popularity lodged against prophesyings. But even if those claims themselves were – in some sense, at least in some places, some of the time – 'true', they were then couched and circulated in such heightened and hyperbolic terms as to render them obviously untrue, as well. That, of course, was what this sort of religio-political caricature and stereotyping did (and does); it exaggerates, pumps up for polemical purposes, elements of the 'real', until the resulting picture is not 'true' at all, at which point those on other side of the argument, those being denounced and stereotyped, seek to denounce the stereotype itself as simply false and its disseminators as downright, self-interested and possibly subversive liars.

Grindal's survey was designed to expose the untruth of the critics' claims. It was to provide him with ammunition to defend not quite the prophesyings as they actually were but rather as he desired them to be and, indeed, as they might well have become, after a good dose of Grindalian reform and episcopal oversight. His other aim was almost certainly to line up episcopal opinion behind his stand on the prophesyings. As we have seen he was not completely successful here; Scory was positively vituperative on the subject and even Cox had reservations about the prophesyings, both name and thing.[15]

Scory apart, the most overtly anti-puritan response came from John Aylmer. In many ways he was the exception that proved rule, for he was not a bishop but a mere archdeacon and he responded to Grindal's enquiry about the prophesyings in really quite scathing anti-puritan terms. Aylmer

---

[12] *Ibid.*, fos. 106r–109v, order for the prophesying in Hertfordshire, see especially Cooper's postscript, fo. 109v.

[13] *Ibid.*, fo. 8r, Bradbridge to Grindal, 9 July 1576.

[14] *Ibid.*, fos. 29v, 30r, Cooper to Grindal, 27 July 1576.

[15] For Cox's opinion see BL, Additional MSS 29546, fo. 47r–v.

had been a candidate for episcopal preferment since the beginning of reign, but had been frozen out and may have become something of a malcontent.[16] He was certainly denounced as such by his diocescan, Cooper, who, in what was almost certainly a reference to Aylmer, dropped dark hints about the activities of those who hoped to rise by criticising the well doing of others.[17]

If not every school boy, then every moderately informed undergraduate student of Elizabethan England, knows what happened next – Elizabeth told Grindal to suppress the prophesyings and in December 1576, in an elaborately scholarly letter of some 6,000 words, he told her where to go and she told him to get out – first out of the room – 'it was not your majesty's pleasure then, the time not serving thereto, to hear me at any length concerning the said two matters propounded'[18] – and then out of office, from which he was sequestered.

As Grindal left others came in – John Whitgift – who had made his name as an opponent of puritan non-conformity and Cartwrightian presbyterianism in the early 1570s got Worcester; Aylmer, no less, became bishop of London, in which role he succeeded the suspended Grindal as the *de facto* episcopal leader of the national church. Also rising in and through these events – making his final breakthrough from favourite/courtier to councillor – was Sir Christopher Hatton. Aylmer, for one, thought he owed his job to Hatton.[19] We are seeing here the emergence, at least in outline or prospect, of a new ecclesiastical establishment, pushing a new model ecclesiastical policy. From later letters from Aylmer to Hatton we learn that Aylmer had learnt from Elizabeth herself that 'it was her majesty's pleasure that I should understand her mind by you in such things'. What the queen wanted apparently was a policy designed 'to cut off (even as her majesty termed it) and to correct offenders on both sides', disciplining 'both the papist and the puritan in anything, wherein disobeying her majesty's laws, they may be indifferently touched'.[20] Such a policy of even-handed severity to both papists and puritans had provided the rationale for the crack down on the prophesyings, and was now to be put into wider practice by the Hatton/Aylmer nexus. At least in Elizabeth's mind, it represented a radical break from Grindalian dispensation, a dispensation that was personified by the archbishop himself, and given its most obvious

---

[16] LPL MSS 3470, fo. 22r–v, Aylmer to Grindal, 28 Sept. 1576. On Aylmer's career see Brett Usher's article on Aylmer in ODNB.

[17] LPL MSS 2003, fo. 29v, Cooper to Grindal, 27 July 1576, 'I suspect there be some that seek to creep in favour not only by their own well doings but by the discrediting of other's well doings, and so to suspect I have greater cause than I may conveniently put in writing.'

[18] *The Remains of Edmund Grindal* (Parker Society, Cambridge, 1843), 376.

[19] BL Additional MSS 15891, fos. 41v–42r, Aylmer to Hatton, 8 June 1578.

[20] *Ibid.*

institutional form by the prophesyings, but that was also a product of a clique of lay councillors, an inner circle often thought to constitute the so-called 'monarchical republican' core of the Elizabethan regime.[21]

Elizabeth was applying to the prophesyings an emergent anti-populist anti-puritanism that had been developed to its highest pitch of coherence and aggression by John Whitgift in his assault on Cartwrightian presbyterianism in the first half of decade. But the logic of Whitgift's anti-puritan case was not limited to the Elizabethan puritan movement, as its application here to the prophesyings showed.[22] For, for all their links with puritanism and popularity, identified by their critics, as Patrick Collinson has argued, the prophesyings were anything but exclusively or distinctively 'puritan' institutions. Rather, as Collinson has shown, they were a place where the devolved power of the episcopate and the zeal of the godly clergy, and of some local lay elites, met in the furtherance of true religion as those groups understood it.[23] Now the prophesyings were being denounced as popular and puritan. Anti-puritanism was being used here as an aggressive ideological solvent, to disrupt the smooth running of the Elizabethan regime, and the institutions, connections and assumptions of an emergent hot protestant political nation, by none other than the queen herself. In so doing Elizabeth might be thought to have been trying to loosen the cloying control over policy of her leading councillors, both clerical and lay, and to impose her own notions of political and religious order on her church and realm. She was doing it, moreover, via men who, at the start of these events, had not been a part of the real inner circle – via Hatton, not yet a councillor, Aylmer, not yet a bishop – on the basis of an ideology developed by man, John Whitgift, who, at the time he had developed it had not been a bishop but rather merely master of Trinity College, Cambridge.

III

Grindal had been suspended from office in May. By June 1577 diverse elements within the regime were turning their attention to the catholic issue with the aim, it appears, of turning up the heat on the catholics and of turning the attention of the regime, and particularly of the queen, on to the extent and nature of the catholic threat. The initiative came

---

[21] P. Collinson, 'The Monarchical Republic of Queen Elizabeth I', ch. 2 of his *Elizabethan Essays* (1994); now also see *The Monarchical Republic of Early Modern England: Essays in Response to Patrick Collinson*, ed. J. F. McDiarmid (Ashgate, 2007).

[22] On Whitgift's anti-puritanism see P. Lake, *Anglicans and Puritans: Presbyterianism and English Conformist Thought from Whitgift to Hooker* (1988), ch. 1; *idem*, 'The Monarchical Republic of Queen Elizabeth I (and the Fall of Archbishop Grindal) Revisited', in *Monarchical Republic*, ed. McDiarmid.

[23] See material cited in n. 3.

from both the lay and clerical establishments; first we have a letter from Aylmer to Walsingham. He had consulted with Grindal and the other bishops; there was agreement that the catholic threat was on the rise; the existing means of dealing with it were not working. Aylmer proposed a scheme whereby increased fines could be levied on recusant catholics, without the need for a new law. This was the continuation of an approach pushed in the previous parliament, where it had been backed by Grindal, amongst others, but blocked by the queen.[24] On the one hand, this was conciliar and Grindalian business as usual. But, on the other, we can see Aylmer advising Walsingham just how to pitch it under the new ideological circumstances; her majesty must be 'given to understand that it is meant hereby as well to touch the one side as the other indifferently, or else you can guess what will follow'.[25]

Second, we have another letter from Walsingham to Aylmer, summoning him and other bishops to a meeting with the Council over the catholic issue, and a more extended memorandum on 'how such as are backward and corrupt in religion may be reduced to conformity and others stayed from corruption'. This features as a central proposal that 'letters be sent to the bishops and others well affected in each diocese to make inquiry by such means as by them shall be thought meet after such as refuse to come to church, especially such as are of countenance and quality and do offend in example'. The offenders were to be conferred with for some months by 'men sufficiently learned, after a charitable sort'. Those that remained recalcitrant were to be treated 'according to the laws of the realm'. As 'the number of the recusants is so great as the places of restraint are not able to hold them', only the 'most corrupt' of the recusants of each diocese should be 'first dealt withal' and 'the principal persons such as by law are to be reached unto'.[26]

The outcome of all these discussions seems to have been the second survey of October. Another round robin was sent to all the bishops, this one asking not about prophesyings and puritans but about how many

---

[24] Collinson, *Archbishop Grindal*, 213–14.

[25] The National Archives [hereafter TNA] (Public Record Office [hereafter PRO]), State Papers [hereafter SP], 12/114/22, Aylmer to Walsingham, 21 June 1577.

[26] There is an undated copy of this letter in Walsingham's letter book (*ibid.*, 12/45/21). For a discussion of the likely provenance and date of the letter see Conyers Read, *Mr Secretary Walsingham and the Policy of Queen Elizabeth* (3 vols., Oxford, 1925), II, 280–1. For the memorandum see TNA (PRO), SP12/45/10. This likewise is undated but, as Read pointed out, what links both documents together and to the summer of 1577 is a common concern with what to do with 'Watson, Feckenham and the rest upon whose advice and consciences the said recusants depend'. For this see *Acts of the Privy Council* [hereafter *APC*], *1577–8*, X, 4, Council to the bishop of Lincoln, 28 July 1577. (By a slip of the pen Read appears to have identified the recipient of the letter in Walsingham's letter-book – which is clearly addressed to the 'bishop of London' – as the bishop of Lincoln, the recipient of the Council's letter about the custody of Feckenham *et al.*)

recusants there were out there and about how much they were really worth.[27] The results would enable the Council to identify and then to target the most substantial recusants and thus gain both a proper sense of the scale of the popish threat and of the extent of the revenue that they might be able to raise by realistic fines levied upon the wealthiest recusants. Both of which were, of course, likely to be subjects of interest to the queen.[28]

Here we have councillors and bishops turning the queen's rhetoric of a 'middle way' of equal opportunity repression to be directed at both catholics and puritans against her anti-puritan, and in favour of their own distinctly anti-papal, agenda. If the queen wanted, or at least said that she wanted, an even handed policy towards catholics and puritans, the least they could get out of the demise of the prophesyings was more stringent measures against the papists. But if popery could be established as *the* problem, then these men could present themselves and, of course, Grindal, as rather a large part of the solution. Thus the two issues – the gravity of the popish threat and the rehabilitation of the archbishop became very closely associated; so closely that the second half of Grindal's reply, as archbishop of Canterbury, to the Council's letter about recusancy was another plea for them to intercede on his behalf with the queen.[29]

The political and ideological logics at work here were impeccable; when Grindal had been in control the line had been that popery, too, was under control; in 1574 Grindal had told Burghley, about the diocese of York of all places, that 'only five persons have been committed for their obstinacy in papistical religion. For the number of that sect (thanks be to God!) daily diminisheth, in this diocese especially.'[30] Again, one argument in favour of the prophesyings had been that the papists disliked them; as a crucial means to suppress popery and spread true religion you could show how well they were working by how much papists hated them and you could show that because the only people who complained about them were papists and fellow travellers, who were, of course, not to be listened or pandered to.[31] If you suppressed the prophesyings, the

[27] BL Additional MSS 48018, fo.184r, a copy of the Council's letter to the bishops, dated 15 Oct.

[28] The fiscal aspects of the scheme were still being pursued in December 1577, when on the 3rd of that month it was reported that the judges had met to discuss the matter and concluded that 'the law ecclesiastical is plain that a pecuniary pain may be put upon such recusants' by the bishops without recourse to further legislation. BL Lansdowne MSS 27, fos. 46r–47v.

[29] TNA (PRO), SP12/117/9, Grindal to the Council, 24 Oct. 1577. 'I trust God will ... move her Majesty's heart to consider of my afflicted estate in which I now live and that the rather by your Lordships' good mediation.'

[30] *Remains of Edmund Grindal*, 350–1, Grindal to Burghley, 13 Nov. 1574.

[31] For such arguments see LPL MSS 2003, fo. 5v, Bentham to Grindal, 16 July 1576, where Bentham remarked that 'the fretting and fuming which the papists have at this exercise

argument went, you would only be giving aid and succour to papists and popery and that was the very opposite of what you should be doing.

Now, however, with the prophesyings suppressed and Grindal disgraced, those who had made that case could come back with reports of renewed catholic activity and threat. Under the circumstances this represented something like a discrete 'I-told-you- so', with the unspoken message clear; if you insist on doing things like this, then the recent upsurge of recusant recalcitrance is precisely what you are going to get. And, just as with the anti-puritan allegations about the prophesyings, there was a good deal of truth to such claims. Diarmaid MacCulloch has shown that one of the main effects of the anti-puritan activities in the diocese of Norwich of that anti-Grindalian, the wonderfully named Bishop Freake, had been the alienation of the local puritan magisterial elite and the consequent reliance, by Freake, on catholic and crypto-catholic figures amongst the local gentry. This had, in turn, prompted complaints about the increase of catholicism from Freake's puritan enemies and victims; and concern amongst the conciliar allies and contacts, indeed in some cases the relatives, of the local puritan magistrates.[32]

This is where Cuthbert Mayne enters the story. During the summer of 1577, Sir Richard Grenville, in his capacity as sheriff of Cornwall, 'accompanied with nine or ten justices of the peace and with them well near a hundred persons' had raided the house of a prominent local papist, Francis Tregian. After a full scale search of the premises they had seized the persons of Tregian himself, 'sundry other his servants', and 'one Mr Cuthbert Mayne, a priest'. They then took their charges off to Truro where, conveniently enough, Bishop Bradbridge, one of the most enthusiastic of the defenders of the prophesyings during the previous summer, was on visitation. Bradbridge interviewed Tregian and found him to be a catholic. Both Tregian and Mayne were imprisoned in Launceston castle. Tregian was later bound over to the sum of £2,000 to appear before the Council and lodged thereafter in the Marshalsea. Mayne, however, remained in the county, charged with treason under the 1571 statute, 'for a bull which was found in his custody, and by him, as they said, procured from the bishop of Rome concerning matter of absolution'. However, the bull found in Mayne's possession had not been procured at Rome but rather printed at Douai where Mayne had bought

causeth me the rather to like and allow of it'; also see *ibid.*, fo. 30r, Cooper to Grindal 27 July 1576, where Cooper opined that 'the general dissolution of them [the prophesyings] will raise a great triumph and expectation among the adversaries and an offense to all them that favour religion'.

[32] D. MacCulloch, 'Catholic and Puritan in Elizabethan Suffolk: A County Community Polarises', *Archiv für reformationsgeschichte*, 72 (1981).

it from a bookseller as a sort of souvenir.[33] Moreover, the papal jubilee which it announced had long since expired. It was however a papal bull which Mayne had indeed brought into England and therefore he was technically guilty under the statute. On the other hand, of course, it was perfectly possible to argue that Mayne's was hardly the sort of offence which the statute had been designed to punish and that it was thus unjust to condemn a man on a mere technicality. When Mayne made this case to his judges, Manwood brushed him aside but his colleague, Sir John Jeffreys, demurred. Mayne was sentenced to death at Manwood's insistence, only later for the case to be referred to the Council.[34] There were clearly very public doubts about the equity of the treatment being dished out to Mayne and Tregian. Tregian meanwhile had already been up to London to be interviewed by the Council where, having had his appeals to the integrity of his conscience brusquely dismissed by Walsingham, he had been taken to dinner by the earl of Sussex.[35] Sussex proceeded to offer Tregian and his servants their liberty, and Mayne his life, if Tregian 'would have yielded only for a fashion sake, as they said, to have shown himself at the church'. Tregian, however, resolutely refused, 'always preferring Christianity before his own immunity or his servant's liberty. And concerning the life of Cuthbert Mayne, always alleging that he would not hazard his own soul unto hell to withhold his man's from heaven.'[36]

Crucial to the argument being pursued here is timing. The discussions between Walsingham and Aylmer, the Council and the bishops took place in June/July 1577. Tregian and Mayne were seized in June and the case dealt with by the Council in August.[37] The survey of recusant numbers was instigated on 15 October. The letters sent to the bishops wanted a reply in a week.[38] This was a decidedly odd way to run even an early modern state. The replies varied, as had those to the survey of 1576.[39] Some were ideologically framed. Bishop Cheney talked as much about puritans

---

[33] J. Morris, *The Troubles of our Catholic Forefathers*, first series (1872), 65–7, for the initial arrest; 77–8, 90–1 for the bull found in Mayne's possession.

[34] *Ibid.*, 79, 91, for the differences amongst the judges. The account of the proceedings against Mayne and his co-defendants given in Morris garbles some of the technicalities of the case. For an exemplary reconstruction based on the indictments themselves see Leslie Ward, 'The Law of Treason in the Reign of Elizabeth I, 1558–1603' (Ph.D. thesis, Cambridge University, 1985), 222–31.

[35] Morris, *Troubles*, 69–70, 97–8.

[36] *Ibid.*, 97.

[37] *APC, 1575–7*, IX, 390, Council order, dated 4 Aug. 1577, requiring Mayne and others to be examined at the next assizes not only about their own offences 'but also to understand what others there are of that condition lurking in this realm, and in what place'.

[38] The letter from the Council, dated 15 Oct., required an answer 'within seven days also after your receipt hereof'. BL Additional MSS 48018, fo. 184r.

[39] The replies are reprinted in *Catholic Record Society, Miscellanea*, 12 (1921), 1–113.

as about papists, remarking 'that the third sort [of recusants] commonly called puritans' wilfully refuse to come to church 'as not liking the surplice, ceremonies and other service now used in the church, whereupon they have been arraigned and indicted in diverse and several sessions upon the statute and now remain in prison upon the same'.[40] But other anti-puritan figures – Whitgift, for instance – while pleading his lack of knowledge of his new diocese – ended with a typically Whitgiftian reminder of 'how much harm lenity did the last time that the like certificates were made', and by 'most earnestly beseeching your honours, even for God's sake, to provide some discipline for them, [the recusants whose names he had returned] lest others, by their example, fall into the like contempt'.[41] Many did their best, but the replies remained patchy and many excuses were made; most about the rapid turn around time. At least some of these seem not to have been mere excuses. When we find life-long anti-popish zealots like Francis Hastings or the earl of Huntingdon claiming that they had done their 'best as the short time would suffer', claiming that the task placed upon them 'will hardly be performed in so short a time' and asking for more time so that they could turn 'suspicions', which 'against sundry are very great', into 'certain knowledge' we can, I think, believe them.[42]

And so the obvious question to ask is, why so fast? If we are dealing here with a bureaucratic initiative, the culmination of months, if not years, of planning and thought about what to do about popery, why take three months to think about it, and then give the bishops only one week to reply? The answer, I want to argue, is that Grindal's case was coming to what looked like its climacteric point and his allies on the Council needed information about the nature and extent of the popish threat to make their pitch to the queen about what a genuinely even-handed policy towards papists and puritans would look like and about the necessity, in the current situation, of a unified episcopate; unified by the values and in the person of a suitably repentant and rehabilitated Archbishop Grindal.

The replies to the Council's letter started to come in late October and early November. Grindal's reply to the survey and petition for the intercession and support of the Council was dated 24 October.[43] On 2 December 1577, Grindal told Matthew Hutton that 'about six weeks ago' – i.e. in the middle of October, when the push against the papists was being unleashed – 'I was put in assured hope of liberty, etc.' That state

[40] TNA (PRO), SP 12/117/12, Cheney to the Council, 24 Oct. 1577.

[41] Ibid., 12/118/11, Whitgift to the Council, 5 Nov. 1577.

[42] Ibid., 12/117/19, Francis Hastings and Adrian Stokes to the Council, ibid., 12/117/19, 27 Oct. 1577; ibid., 12/117/20, earl of Huntingdon and others to Archbishop Sandys, 27 Oct. 1577.

[43] Ibid., 12/117/9.

of happy expectation had lasted, Grindal explained, until 'the 26th of November', about which 'time arose a sudden contrary tempest, which had brought me to have appeared in the Star Chamber 29 November last, if God had not laid me up two days before of my old disease, the stone'.[44] As for Mayne, his fate was sealed on 12 November, when the Council not only confirmed his sentence but sent detailed instructions into the county about how he was to be dispatched and what was to be done with his remains. He was to be executed in Launceston

> upon a market day, where after he shall be dead and quartered, his head to be set upon a pole and placed in some eminent place within the said town of Launceston and his four quarters to be likewise set upon four poles and placed the one at Bodmin, the second at Torquay, the third at Barnstaple and the fourth at Wadesbridge, and this letter to be his warrant in that behalf.

As it happened, the meeting of the Privy Council that issued this command also witnessed the swearing in as 'Vice-Chamberlain and one of the Privy Council' of Sir Christopher Hatton and the meeting of Star Chamber in which Grindal's fate was to have been decided coincided – and clearly these were just coincidences – with the execution in far-away Cornwall of poor Cuthbert Mayne.[45]

IV

The hastily arranged hearing of Grindal's case was to have taken place in Star Chamber on 30/31 November. Grindal was prevented from attending by an attack of the stone. But the issue did not go away. The queen was still seriously upset and by January/February 1578, the prospect of the archbishop's removal from office was back on the table. On 23 January Sir Walter Wilson can be found writing to Burghley to tell him that 'the queen is much offended with the archbishop and disliketh our darings for dealing with him so at large, whom her highness would have deprived for contempt committed'. By 22 February 1578 the scare seemed over, with Killigrew reporting that 'there is hope that the bishop of Canterbury shall do better and better daily'.[46] Between those two observations two more catholics had followed Mayne to a traitor/martyr's death. At Tyburn on 3 February and then on 7 February 1578 first the priest John Nelson and then the layman Thomas Sherwood had both suffered a traitor's death. Nelson, who had been taken in London on 1 December 1577, was brought to trial on 1 February and killed on the 3rd. Sherwood had been in custody for some six months prior to his death.

---

[44] *Remains of Edmund Grindal*, 394–5, Grindal to Hutton, 2 Dec. 1577.

[45] *APC, 1577–8*, X, 85.

[46] TNA (PRO), SP, 12/122/15, Wilson to Burghley, 23 Jan. 1578; *ibid.*, SP 15/25/74, Killigrew to Davison, 22 Feb. 1578.

Both are described in various catholic accounts as having been trapped by their captors into treasonous words. According to Cardinal Allen, Nelson had readily agreed that the English church was both 'heretical and schismatical'. At this point his interrogators had moved in for the kill, asking him 'what thinkest thou of the Queen, is she a schismatic or no?' Nelson

answered that he never so called her, for reverence of her high dignity; nor could tell (for he knew not Her Majesty's meaning) whether this religion were established by her special commandment and authority or no; and, therefore, humbly prayed them not to urge him wittingly to commit any crime, wherein hitherto he had never offended.

But his captors persisted, badgering him on this one point by insisting that 'this English religion was established by her and by her maintained'. Still Nelson would not bite, having recourse now to the evil counsellor manoeuvre. But his tormentors would not let go; '"but what", say they, "if she were the author of this religion, then whether were she a schismatic or heretic, or no?"' This was the point at which Nelson broke, or rather at which his conscience betrayed him; finally he said: '"If she be the setter-forth and defender of this religion, then she is a schismatic and heretic indeed."' And those, of course, were the fatal words for which he swung at Tyburn on 3 February.[47]

A similar story is told of Sherwood, who was actually put to torture on the orders of the Privy Council in December when he threatened to take back his treasonable words about the queen being a usurper and a heretic.[48] Later Cardinal Allen would recall that 'young Sherwood' 'was the first in our memory that was put to the rack for matters of conscience, then when no man dreamed of any these feigned new conspiracies'.[49] It is surely to these events that Mendoza the Spanish ambassador was referring later in 1578 when he claimed that a few months earlier Walsingham himself had had the devil's own job to entrap a catholic prisoner into treasonous words; so much so that he had been forced actually to falsify the man's replies, which replies he had then immediately taken off to the queen to persuade her that that was how all English catholics really regarded her. Fortunately, we do not have simply to believe the claims of the Spanish ambassador as literally true to get the picture or to reconstruct the penumbra of rumour surrounding the treatment of these prisoners

[47] *The Execution of Justice in England by William Cecil and A True, Sincere and Modest Defense of English Catholics by William Allen*, ed. Robert M. Kingdon (Ithaca, NY, 1965), 131–2.

[48] *Calendar of State Papers Spanish, Elizabeth, 1568–1579* (1894) [hereafter *CSPSp, 1568–1579*] 2, 595, item 512, Mendoza to Zayas. *APC, 1577–8*, X, 92, 94, 111. On 4 Dec. 1577, the Council instructed 'Mr Lieutenant, Mr Attorney, Mr Solicitor and Mr Recorder, or any three of them', that since 'Sherwood' was now proving refractory 'they are therefore to assay him at the rack upon such articles as they shall think meet to minister unto him for the discovering either of the persons or of further matter'.

[49] Allen, *A True, Sincere and Modest Defense*, ed. Kingdon, 73.

and the wider political purposes to which their fate was being put. On 12 December Killigrew told Davison about the execution of Mayne and the apprehension in London of Nelson and Sherwood.

> I think they be of the number of the twenty four priests sent lately out of those parts. . . into this country to reconcile men . . . with the pope. If you have not advertised of them to Mr Secretary I pray you learn thereof what you can and write the same both to him and to my Lord of Leicester because it may be occasion of much good.[50]

In a later comment on these same events Killigrew spelt out to William Davison what seems to have been at least part of the intended message; 'the papists are so stout and arrogant that one Sherwood' 'being brought before the bishop of London' behaved himself so 'stubbornly' that Killigrew thought that the bishop would henceforth show the more favour 'to such as, of malice', were called 'by the name of puritans'.[51]

Catholic accounts of the confessions extracted from Nelson or Sherwood are confirmed by the official record of what Mayne had been induced to say in a statement taken the day before his execution. Determined not to incriminate his friends, patrons or co-religionsts, Mayne, to the last, had named no names, but he did make a crucial admission, to the effect that

> the people of England may be won unto the catholic religion of the see of Rome by such secret instructors as either are or may be within the realm, but what those secret instructors are he will not utter and hopeth that when time serveth they shall do therein as pleaseth God.

Suspicious words were found in a book of his, signifying that 'though the catholics did now serve, forebear and obey, yet, if occasion were offered, they should be ready to help the execution etc.'. Badgered about what that might mean, Mayne had finally explained that they

> were annexed to a text taken out of a general council of Lateran for the authority of the pope in his excommunications and ratified at the last council at Trent where there was a consent of the catholic princes for a reformation of such realms and persons as had gone from the authority of the bishop of Rome, where it was concluded that, if any catholic prince took in hand to invade any realm, to reform the same to the authority of the see of Rome, that then the catholics in that realm so invaded by foreigners should be ready to assist and help them to the uttermost of their powers and this was the meaning of the execution as he saith, which he never revealed to any man before.[52]

In the words of an infamous headline, Gotcha!

The survey of recusants of October 1577 – intended to establish the extent of the popish threat in England – and the interrogations and executions of Mayne, Nelson and Sherwood – intended to establish the

---

[50] TNA (PRO), SP 15/25/49.

[51] *Ibid.*, 15/25/74, Killigrew to Davison, 25 Feb. 1578.

[52] *Ibid.*, 12/118/46, 'the examination of Cuthbert Mayne, taken at Launceston the 29th day of November'.

treasonous nature of English popish opinion and clerical activity – can thus be put together, as two sides of the same campaign to garner evidence of the nature and extent of the popish threat to lay before the queen. To them can be added the arrest of the long-time Spanish agent, Antonio de Guerras. This too took place in October 1577. At midnight on 19/20, to be exact, when de Guerras's house was raided, he, his secretary and others were arrested and his papers seized.[53] The ostensible reason was de Guerras's contacts with Mary Stuart and the very rude comments and intelligences about both the queen and her Council that he had been sending to don John of Austria in Flanders. If the questions being put to his secretary the following summer are anything to go by, just like Nelson and Sherwood, de Guerras was asked whether he had defamed the queen and her councillors as heretics and schismatics; about why so many English catholics resorted to him; and about his contacts with Mary Stuart, with Westmoreland and, of course, with Don John himself.[54]

The letters which occasioned de Guerras's arrest had been intercepted early in March 1577, the code in which they were written had been broken by the end of that month[55] and the regime's anxiety about alienating don John as a negotiating partner dissipated by the middle of the summer;[56] why, then, had it taken until October for the regime to act? Again the answer seems to be that material was now needed in a hurry to establish the true nature and extent of the popish threat, and it was hoped that de Guerras would provide the clinching evidence that linked the burgeoning numbers of English catholics and the traitorous opinions and activities of the missionary priests, like Mayne, with the political machinations and conspiracies of English catholic exiles, Mary Stuart and the Spanish

[53] *CSPSp., 1568–1579*, 550–2, item 471, de Guerras to Zayas, 29 Dec. 1577, reporting his arrest at midnight 19/20 Oct. Unable to make a case against him, de Guerras explained, they were trying to fabricate plots involving the queen of Scots and the exiled earl of Westmoreland.

[54] *Ibid.*, 571–3, item 486, Mendoza to the king of Spain, explaining that when he raised the matter of de Guerras's arrest with the queen 'she was very much irritated, and said that it was only because he was a subject of your majesty that she had not hanged him, as he had been in correspondence with her rebel subjects and the queen of Scotland and she had letters of his greatly prejudicial to the peace of her country'. Quote at p. 573. Also see *ibid.*, 602–4, item 517, de Guerras's account of his examination by Sir Walter Mildmay and Dr Wilson who asked him, amongst other things, whether he had had 'any understanding with the earl of Westmoreland' or any correspondence with Mary Stuart about Westmoreland. Also see *ibid.*, 607, item 522, document headed 'Juan de Aguirre was examined on the 25th of June by the governor of the Tower, and master Herll, on the following points'.

[55] *Calendar of State Papers, Foreign Series, Elizabeth, 1577–1578* (1901), 542–3, item 1325, Sir Thomas Wilson to Burghley, dated 10 Mar. 1577, informing him about de Guerras. *Ibid.*, 546–7, item 1335, Wilson to Burghley, 17 Mar. 1577, remarking on the difficulty of breaking de Guerras's code. *Ibid.*, 551–2, item 1360, Wilson to Leicester, 22 Mar. 1577, announcing that St Aldegonde 'has deciphered Guerras' letters first into Spanish and then into French'.

[56] A point I owe to the kindness of Simon Adams.

crown. Here was convincing evidence not merely for a popish threat but for a veritable popish conspiracy, against which the queen was now being urged to act on a variety of fronts.

All of these bursts of activity occurred, first in October/November 1577 and then again in January/February 1578, clustered around the crucial moments when Grindal's fate appeared to be in the balance. At each point, the fate of Grindal was associated by contemporary commentators with the decision whether to intervene in the Low Countries or not. In September Edward Cheke had conjoined the happy news that 'I am promised my master's liberty' with rumours of Leicester's 'full determination' to lead the men to be sent to the Low Countries himself, but this is 'yet unknown to her highness, neither shall she be acquainted with it until she be fully resolved to send'.[57] In late January the same letter in which Killgrew informed Davison that 'the bishop of Canterbury is like to be deprived' also contained the news that 'it is hardly believed that an army will be sent there'.[58] Conversely the letter of 22 February which contained welcome news of Grindal's improved prospects also contained the claim that Lord Buckhurst had come from 'court and said that it was resolved in council to send my Lord of Leicester over with 10,000 men'.[59] Might we conclude, then, that whenever pressure to act on the Low Countries became too intense the queen turned up the heat on Grindal and whenever Grindal's job seemed to be really in danger (and the question of whether to intervene in the Low Countries seemed about to be decided) the archbishop's allies on the Council simply topped another priest?

I am not arguing for a coherent conspiracy, a concerted and centrally coordinated campaign. On the contrary, what we have here is a mixture of coincidence, cock-up and hastily extemporised expedient, entirely typical of the workings of Elizabethan government. The roots of the raid on Tregian's house and the taking of Mayne were no doubt as much local as national; the interception of de Guerras's letters prompted by fears about international intrigue, Spanish plotting and policy towards the Low Countries. Conversely, the taking of Sherwood, arrested when the son of his catholic patron, 'whose faith and manners were widely distant

---

[57] TNA (PRO), SP 15/25/35, Cheke to William Davison, from the court, 19 Sept. 1577.

[58] Ibid., 15/25/71, Killigrew to Davison, 29 Jan. 1578. I cite here from the *Calendar of State Papers, Elizabeth, 1566–1579, Addenda* (1871), 530, since the original is so badly damaged as to be illegible on the microfilm.

[59] Ibid., 15/25/74, Killigrew to Davison, 22 Feb. 1578. The ideological timbre of the circles producing this commentary is rendered clear by the fact that the same correspondence between Killigrew and Davison contains detailed machinations to secure Walter Travers employment in the Low Countries (see, for instance, ibid., 15/25/68, Killigrew to Davison, 8 Jan. 1578, or ibid., 15/25/79, Killigrew to Davison, Mar. 1578) and casual references to the doings of one John Field. (Ibid., 15/25/74, Killigrew to Davison, 22 Feb. 1578.)

from those of his mother', followed him through the streets of London shouting '"stop the traitor, stop the traitor"', seems to have been pretty much an accident.[60] The recusant survey was clearly the culmination of discussions that dated from at least the previous summer, and of failed anti-popish initiatives that went back years, even if the decision to conclude it in a week does not betoken the culmination of some long-planned bureaucratic reform.

If anything in their origins united these events it was no more than a sense that popery was on the march; a sense heightened, no doubt, by the suppression of the propheysings and the sequestration of Grindal, and emanating from the centre of the regime, from the godly in the provinces, and indeed from reports from and about the continent. The result was a climate in which it appeared that a variety of both personal and political ends and agendas could be furthered through talking up the popish threat. The resulting discrete incidents then became associated together in a hastily assembled series of manoeuvres designed to push the queen to do things, that (left to her own devices) she did not want to do. Put another way, Sherwood's capture might have been an accident, the product more of certain tensions between his patron and her heretic son, than of any concerted government crack down, but what happened to him next was not.

What we have got here is neither a conspiracy nor a concatenation of mere coincidences, but rather a series of dialectically patterned contingencies. Discrete events, set off by or within a particular ideological moment, were associated together, glossed and deployed, to further a set of increasingly pointed and coherent ideological and political purposes, central to which were the rehabilitation of Grindal and the support of the Dutch rebels. In a memo of December 1577 we can watch Burghley assembling such material to formulate arguments in favour of intervention in the Low Countries to take to the queen. A long list of arguments for the ill-will of the Spanish is topped off by 'the practises of Guerras with the Scottish queen'.[61] Burghley also asserted that 'in all men's judgements that desire change of religion in England' – a company, of course, now rendered far more numerous and threatening by the recusancy survey and the examinations of Nelson, Sherwood and Mayne – a marriage between don John of Austria and Mary Stuart 'is the best and only means to restore the realm of England to the church of Rome'. By marriage to Mary Stuart, Burghley alleged, don John will

make his title to her right to the crown of England, whereunto both the pope, the French king, the king of Spain and all potentates catholic will give aid; the pope for religion,

[60] Bishop Challoner, *Memoirs of Missionary Priests* (1880), 19.

[61] Kervijn de Lettenhove, *Relations politique des Pays Bas et de l'Angleterre sous le reign de Philippe II* (11 vols, Brussels, 1882–1900), X, 128.

the French king by solicitation of the house of Guise, and thereby to avoid all sequel of comforting his subjects of the religion in France; the king of Spain for advancement of his brother don John.[62]

Thus were the dastardly plots of the papists made manifest, the subject changed from the puritan to the popish threat, the need for action emphasised and – perhaps as a side effect, perhaps not – the bacon of Edmund Grindal saved.

V

Extemporised and hastily put together, the resulting mode of queen-centred, anti-papal manoeuvre can be observed operating through another set of contingencies, those set off by the queen's summer progress of 1578.[63] Starting out from Greenwich in July, the queen wound a circuitous course through Essex and Suffolk to Norwich. As Professor MacCulloch has shown, whether by accident or design, the gentlemen at whose houses the queen stayed represented a wide ideological range; some were puritans, others were overtly catholic, indeed recusant, and still others bare conformists.[64] The crucial *coup de théâtre* was played out at Euston Hall, the house of Edward Rookwood. The occasion was described by Richard Topcliffe in a famous letter to the earl of Shrewsbury.[65] According to Topcliffe, Rookwood was 'a papist of kind newly crept out of his late wardship'. The royal visit to his house culminated in the queen giving 'to Rookwood ordinary thanks for his bad house and her fair hand to kiss; after which it was braved at'. But what looked like an extraordinary gesture of royal favour conferred on a known catholic was then transformed by the lord chamberlain, Sussex, who called Rookwood before him; denounced him as an excommunicate papist, 'demanded of him how he durst presume to attempt her real presence, he, unfit to accompany any Christian person; forthwith said he

---

[62] *Ibid.*, 153. Lettenhove prints the memorandum as three distinct documents (*ibid.*, 125, 127, 152). They are read by Read as one and dated to December 1577, see Conyers Read, *Lord Burghley and Queen Elizabeth* (New York, 1960), 185–7.

[63] For a narrative account of the progress see Zillah Dovey, *An Elizabethan Progress: The Queen's Journey into East Anglia, 1578* (Stroud, 1996). Now see the definitive account of the religio-political background by Patrick Collinson, 'Pulling the Strings: Religion and Politics in the Progress of 1578', in *The Progresses, Pageants and Entertainments of Queen Elizabeth I*, ed. Jayne Elizabeth Archer, Elizabeth Goldring and Sarah Knight (Oxford, 2007). It is entirely typical that I should have discovered this article in the week before I delivered this lecture.

[64] MacCulloch, 'Puritan and Recusant'.

[65] E. Lodge, *Illustrations of British History* (1838), II, 119–25. Mendoza reports rumours of these events in a letter to Zayas of 8 Sept. 1578; 'during her progress in the north the queen has met with more catholics than she expected, and in one of the houses they found a great many images which were ordered to be dragged round and burnt.' *CSPSp., 1568–1579*, 609–11, item 524, quote at 610–11.

was fitter for a pair of stocks; commanded him out of the court, and yet to attend her council's pleasure'. Later, on the pretext that there was a piece of plate missing from the court, Rookwood's premises were searched and

> in the hay rick such an image of our lady was there found, as for greatness, for gayness and workmanship, I did never see a match; and after a sort of country dances ended, in her majesty's sight the idol was set behind the people who avoided . . . her majesty commanded it to the fire, which, in her sight, by the country folks, was quickly done, to her content, and unspeakable joy of every one but some one or two who had sucked of the idol's poisoned milk.

Here, then, was a physical display of the prevalence of the catholic threat and of the queen's personal repugnance in the face of popish idolatry.

The progress culminated at Norwich where the Council called before them a large number of suspected catholic gentry, including Rookwood, and consigned most of them to prison or house arrest where they were to be forced to confer with protestant ministers.[66] This was to realise, *in parvo*, and on the back of the practical lessons learned in the course of the summer progress, the sort of comprehensive anti-catholic policy, concentrated on the confinement, forced consultation with learned divines and eventual exemplary punishment of selected recusant gentry, that we have seen being discussed in the summer and autumn of 1577.

On the other side of the equation, other of the gentlemen with whom the queen had stayed were knighted; some of these were notorious puritans, others conformist crypto-catholics. As Professor MacCulloch observes, there could scarcely have been a clearer enactment either of the rewards of obedience and conformity or of the costs of defiance. Thus, what in prospect must have looked not just like a signal mark of royal favour, conferred on a known catholic, but even a tacit royal acceptance of the possibility of a genuinely and overtly catholic loyalism – the take-home message being that even an acknowledged recusant and excommunicant like Rookwood could enjoy royal favour, if he demonstrated his personal devotion and loyalty to the queen – had suddenly been converted into its polar opposite. What could or should have been an occasion for catholic celebration – as Topcliffe observed Rookwood's kissing the queen's hand

---

[66] *APC, 1577–8*, X, 310–13, an account of the Council's treatment at Norwich of a large number of recusants. Rookwood was made a particular example of, being committed 'close prisoner to the gaol of the county of Norfolk', 'without conference, saving of such as should be thought meet by the Bishop, either for his better instructions or for direction of the necessary business of his living and family'.

was much 'braved at'[67] – had been converted into an occasion for the public performance of the queen's loathing for all things popish.

As ever, a shift in policy towards papists involved a change in attitude towards puritans. 'Shortly after', Topcliffe remarked,

> a great sort of good preachers who had long commanded to silence for a little niceness, were licensed and again commanded to preach, a greater and more universal joy to the countries, and the most of the court, than the disgrace of the papists; and the gentlemen of those parts, being great and hot protestants (almost before by policy discredited and disgraced) were greatly countenanced.[68]

These sentiments were echoed by Sir Thomas Heneage who told Walsingham that 'my lord, with the rest of her Majesty's Council, have most considerately straightened divers obstinate and arch papists that would not come to the church. And by good means her Majesty is brought to' think well of 'divers most zealous and loyal gentlemen of Suffolk and Norfolk whom the foolish bishop had maliciously complained of to her majesty as hinderers of her proceedings and favourers of preciseness and puritans, as he calls them'.[69]

The uses to which the lessons taught by the summer progress were subsequently put can be gleaned from a quite remarkably wide range of sources. On the one hand, we have a letter from the Council which informed the bishop of London of the queen's knowledge of and displeasure at the prevalence of recusancy. This knowledge had been gained on 'this late progress', when, 'having had occasion to repair into sundry shires', the queen had learned

> (to her majesty's no small grief), that sundry persons, being in commission of the peace within diverse counties, have, of late years, foreborn to come to the church to any

---

[67] The extent to which the queen's visit to the houses of overt catholics may actually have raised catholic hopes can be gleaned from a typically garbled account of these events by Mendoza, who in a letter of 14 Aug. reported that 'in the north where the queen is traveling' 'there are many catholics' and that on 'her entering the house of a gentleman where she was to lodge, her people found an altar with all the ornaments thereupon ready for the celebration of mass, whilst the gentleman, his wife and children received the queen with crucifixes round their necks. There is not as much severity against them as usual' (*CSPSp. 1568–1579*, 606–7, item 521). On this account, taking the visit of the queen to their house as a mark of royal favour and acceptance, known and recalcitrant catholics had not only taken no real precautions to hide the physical evidence of their religious identity – the altar prepared for the mass – they had actually paraded certain outwards signs of that identity – the rosaries – before the queen. Rather than any elaborate advance planning, it may have been some such display of catholic over confidence or indiscretion that both prompted and enabled the extemporised display of anti-papal zeal played out by and before the queen at Euston Hall. These, of course, are typically garbled versions of already garbled rumours. But if we cannot use Mendoza's account to establish what really happened at Euston Hall, his version of events certainly reveals the extent to which the queen's itinerary served to raise catholic hopes and expectations; just as Topcliffe's shows how the subsequent course of the progress was used to dash them again.

[68] Lodge, *Illustrations*, 121–2.

[69] TNA (PRO), SP 15/ 25/113, Heneage to Walsingham, 2 Sept. 1578.

> common prayer and divine service, whereby not only God is dishonoured, the laws infringed but very evil example given to the common sort of people, as in time (if it be not looked unto) may be feared will tend to a division and disturbance of the common quietness of the whole realm.

Moreover, despite repeated conciliar promptings to the bishops, 'neither have the said persons been, by good conference of the ordinaries, brought to any conformity, nor we advertised of their contempts, as appertaineth to their [the bishops'] callings and special trust reposed in them for such matters to have been done'. Having 'espied this fault in some shires ourselves' the councillors were sure that the 'like may be committed in other places'. Thus, if blame were to be apportioned for the current (shocking) state of affairs, it lay with the bishop/s and not with the Council. But the Council was now on the case, and they instructed Aylmer

> upon secret conference with such persons as be well affected to religion within your diocese and you shall think can inform you of such persons as, being justices of peace, refuse to come to the church in any shire under your jurisdiction, to send unto us a particular certificate of their names, qualities and dwelling places and further what time they have been noted to have foreborn to frequent the said divine service.

In other words, Aylmer was being told to cabal with and to rely on the local godly, people who to their enemies, indeed very probably to Aylmer himself, not to mention to poor, embattled Bishop Freake, were 'puritans', in order the better to defend the state against 'popery'.[70]

Here was the Council doing to Aylmer on the catholic issue what others had done to Grindal over the prophesyings. Having convinced the queen of the existence of a threat to the 'common quietness of the whole realm', a threat emanating this time from popish recusancy rather than from puritan prophesyings, they were using the royal ire to induce the bishops to pursue anti-popish policies very similar to those discussed and formulated during the summer and autumn of 1577. Here was anti-popery trumping anti-puritanism and royal and episcopal policy being pushed in a direction far more conducive to the interests of the 'protestant cause', as at least some members of the Council understood it, than had seemed likely when the disorderly nature of the prophesying and the presumption and disobedience of Grindal had been the business of the hour.

But we can also see the lessons of the summer progress being driven home in an altogether different sort of text and context; in a court entertainment performed before the queen at the earl of Leicester's house at Wanstead, where the progress ended in September. Known as *The Lady of May*, the piece consisted of a petition to the queen from various country folk to decide between two rival suitors for the hand of the Lady

---

[70] *Ibid.*, 12/45/16, an undated letter 'from the council to the bishop of London'.

of May.[71] The discussion of the relative merits of the two suitors became the occasion for a rehearsal of that common topos, the comparison of the active and of the contemplative lives, with the former personified by the hunter, Therion, and the latter by the shepherd, Epilus. The consequent debate was moderated by a pedantic old schoolmaster, Rombus. There are two versions of the piece, one of which concludes with a speech by Rombus who, in presenting the queen with a jewel, in a clear reference to the earl of Leicester, delivered a disquisition on

> a certain neighbour, they call him master Robert of Wanstead. He is counted an honest man, and one that loves us doctified men *pro vita* . . . But so stays the case that he is foully commaculated with the papistical enormity, *O heu Aedipus Aecastor*. The *bonus vir* is a huge *catholicam*, wherewith my conscience being replenished, could no longer refrain it from you, *proba dominus doctor, probo inveni*. I have found *unum par*, a pair, *papisticorum bedorus*, of Papistian beads, *cum quis*, with the which, *omnium dierum*, every day, next after his *pater noster* he *semper* suits 'and Elizabeth', as many lines as there are beads on this string.[72]

This, of course, was to recall in jest, in Leicester's house an earlier occasion, at Euston Hall, when the queen had indeed found herself staying in a house in which all the impedimenta of popish superstition had come to light. But Leicester, of course, was known not for his catholic, but rather for his puritan, sympathies.

What seems to have happened here is that after the scene at Euston Hall, Sidney had added the concluding speech to the entertainment – and here it is worth remembering that the speech occurs only in one of the two extant versions – to reflect back on the events of the summer, when the entertainment was performed before the queen when she returned to Wanstead, in September, that is to say, at the end, rather than at the beginning of the progress (when some commentators take the entertainment to have been performed). In September, the speech would have operated as a very pointed reminder of the significance of what had just happened to the queen and of the stark difference between Leicester's real, and entirely protestant, devotion to the royal person, and the entirely false professions of loyalty of her catholic subjects.

Not that the pointed topicality of the piece was limited to this reminder of the lessons of the summer about the catholic threat. For, as Louis Montrose has argued, the choice presented to the queen, by the central organising conceit of Sidney's entertainment was one between a virtuous, valorous mixture of the active and the contemplative lives, personified by the hunter, and the passive, languorous, voluptuous and, ultimately, both constraining and corrupting, life of contemplation and withdrawal,

---

[71] *The Miscellaneous Prose of Sir Philip Sidney*, ed. K. Duncan-Jones and J. van Dorsten (Oxford, 1973), 13–32.
[72] *Ibid.*, 31.

personified by the shepherd.[73] That choice was, of course, being offered to a queen confronted, at that very moment, with another choice: whether actively to intervene in the Low Countries, or rather to watch passively from the sidelines, tending her own flock at home, while the fate of the gospel was being decided by others, elsewhere.[74] Offered what was surely a lightly coded version of this choice in Leicester's garden at Wanstead, we are told the queen opted (predictably enough) for the shepherd as the appropriate husband for the Lady of May.

VI

I want now to draw the argument thus far together and reach some preliminary conclusions. First, I want to argue that the preceding analysis shows the extent to which we cannot hope to understand the catholic narrative in isolation from the protestant one, and vice versa. The stories recounted above have traditionally been told in hermetically sealed compartments, but they cannot be properly understood until placed in relation the one with the other. Secondly, by putting these stories together we can watch the conversion of Elizabethan politics into a ruthless struggle for advantage. If we include the experience of at least some catholics – of Mayne, certainly, but also of his patron, Tregian – who was to rot in prison for another twenty years – the nastiness of Elizabethan politics did not have to wait until 1590s to emerge. The result was a no holds barred struggle in which – and I cannot resist this sound bite – Cuthbert Mayne was publicly eviscerated to save Edmund Grindal's job.

When I first thought about this paper I was tempted to lace such a conclusion with glancing references to the propensity of governments, if not to invent, then certainly to exaggerate, manipulate and exacerbate threats and plots to suit their own wider purposes and hold on power.[75] I remain tempted enough by that conclusion not to want to give it up altogether, but while, if you live in America, and perhaps even if you live in England, it is easy, and even salutary, these days, to subject official claims about external threats and plots to a certain bracing scepticism, scepticism on its own is not enough.

And so I do not want to end by saying 'look what those dreadful men did to those nice, innocent catholics' or, at least, if I do end up saying

[73] Lois Adrian Montrose, 'Celebration and Insinuation: Sir Robert Sidney and the Motives of Elizabethan Courtship', *Renaissance Drama*, n.s., 8 (1970); also see his *The Subject of Elizabeth* (Chicago, 2006), 107–9.

[74] As ever, the queen preferred peace and delay to active and overt intervention and war. On all this see Collinson, 'Pulling the Strings'.

[75] In this case, however, the main focus of the political pressure was not some version of 'the public', so much as the queen herself. For it was Elizabeth who needed to be persuaded, by other central elements in her own regime, of the necessity of certain actions for the security of the state, herself and the protestant cause. On this point see n. 85.

something like that, I want to do so with a full acknowledgement of what the people doing these dreadful things thought the stakes were; that is to say, with a realisation that the people at the centre of these events believed in the master narratives and organising tropes, the claims, assumptions and prejudices, that they were also instrumentally, perhaps even rather cynically, manipulating, to force others to do what they wanted. For if there really was a threat, then doing whatever you needed to do to convince people of that fact was not manipulation, intimidation and hyperbole, or, still less, dissimulation and tyranny. It was, rather, a necessary service to the common good and the defence of the realm. As ever, what looked, to insiders, like the operations of good counsel in an increasingly dangerous world – the monarchical republic doing what it was supposed to do – appeared, to those observing events from the outside – particularly to those on the receiving end of many of these manoeuvres, that is to say to catholics – very much like a self-serving conspiracy of evil counsel.[76] Either way, it was the combination of conviction and manipulation, of realpolitick with ideologically enflamed fantasy, that rendered the resulting political mode simultaneously so sinister and so formidable, so transparently manipulative and so effective.

And, of course, there was more involved here than just Grindal's job, but rather the whole notion of 'the protestant cause', a view of the world identified by Simon Adams over thirty years ago as capable of integrating events and issues at home – the fates of puritans and papists, of Grindal, and of the cause of further reformation – with the fate of the gospel abroad and indeed with the independence and integrity of the realm.[77] As ever Collinson has been here before, in two seminal articles relating the Grindal affair, and domestic religious politics more generously conceived, to policy towards the Low Countries.[78] We might even go further than that and argue that at issue in the Grindal affair at least seemed to be the continuing hold over the queen of those committed to a unitary vision of the catholic threat and of the need for action, in England and the Low Countries, to meet that threat. (This, we might speculate, was why the Grindal affair occasioned so much muttering within the elite about the queen listening to private men rather than to accredited counsellors and about the effects of nameless evil counsellors, called by Sir Francis Knollys, at one point, 'Richard II's men'.)[79]

[76] On this point more generally see P. Lake, '"The Monarchical Republic of Elizabeth I" Revisited (by its Victims) as a Conspiracy', in *Conspiracies and Conspiracy Theory in Early Modern Europe*, ed. B. Coward and J. Swann (Aldershot, 2004).

[77] S. L. Adams, 'The Protestant Cause: Religious Alliance with the Western European Calvinist Communities as a Political Issue in England, 1585–1630' (D.Phil. thesis, University of Oxford, 1973).

[78] Collinson, 'Downfall of Archbishop Grindal', and *idem*, 'Pulling the Strings'.

[79] BL Harleian MSS 6992, no. 44, fo. 89, Knollys to Wilson, 9 Jan. 1578.

So the stakes were very high and the events described here amount to a no holds barred multi media campaign to get the queen to do the right thing/s both at home and abroad; a campaign to which the fates of Mayne and Nelson, on the one hand, and of Grindal, on the other, were integral; with the former providing irrefutable evidence of the nature and extent of the popish threat, and the latter acting as a symbol for the more general fate of 'the protestant cause' in the counsels of the queen. As Walsingham observed to Burghley in May 1577 'howsoever he hath offended', a stay in the queen's 'proceedings against the Archbishop' was, 'at this time', 'in true policy most requisite'.[80]

Thus was the fall of Grindal connected to the capture and execution of Cuthbert Mayne and to the botched survey of October 1577. Thus were the mid-night raids, the torture and intimidation, the public executions and coerced confessions, visited on the likes of Mayne, Sherwood and de Guerras, connected to the bizarre outbreak of royally sponsored iconoclasm at Euston Hall, and the public shaming of various catholic gentry at Norwich, in August 1578. Thus were the disgusting acts committed in the defence of the realm in the torture chamber and at Tyburn connected, in their turn, to the pastoral whimsy of the 'Lady of May'.

But to stop even here would still perhaps not be entirely adequate to the extraordinary nature of this story; for while its initial victims were real, live, and then rapidly enough dead, catholics, the resulting exercise in anti-papal vituperation and positioning was not being directed first and foremost at catholics at all; rather it was being directed at other protestants, and, in particular, at the queen herself. Anti-popery was being used by elements in the Council to respond to the newly virulent strain of anti-puritan and anti-popular invective being employed by the queen and her agents – Hatton and Aylmer, and whoever else had stoked the fires of her ire against the prophesyings.

This was a form of intense, court- and queen-centred politics, but it is not anything that we could or should call a factional politics, but rather an intensely ideological politics, conducted in and through the ideological codes of anti-popery and anti-puritanism. Since Simon Adams definitively banished the notion of faction and of factional rivalry from our account of high Elizabethan politics, there has been a tendency to assume that, along with faction, has gone any really serious conflict within the central workings of the regime.[81] The assumption seems to have been that, with no faction to speak of, there can be no sustained conflict, and, of course, after revisionism, we all know that the opposite of conflict is

---

[80] BL Additional MSS 5935, fo. 68, Walsingham to Burghley, 31 May 1577, quoted in Collinson, *Archbishop Grindal*, 250.

[81] S. L. Adams, *Leicester and the Court* (Manchester, 2002), chs. 1–4.

consensus. This does not seem to me to be a necessary consequence of Adams's argument but it is what a number of people have taken that argument to mean. All we are left with are certain tensions between the queen and an inner core of her councillors about a number of issues – marriage, the succession, Mary Stuart, further reformation, what to do about English catholics, whether and how aggressively to intervene in the struggle against popery abroad – all of them integrally bound up with the furtherance of the protestant cause.

But another way of stating this is to remark, not on the absence of 'faction', but, rather, on the presence of ideological division and to register that perhaps the most significant and pressing ideological fault line in Elizabethan England did not run between a unified establishment and a puritan opposition, nor between competing factions, or rivals for the queen's favour, at court, but between the queen and an inner core of her own councillors. At stake here were fundamental differences of view about both politics and religion and about the relations between them, differences which the issue of the prophesyings and the subsequent Grindal affair threatened to bring both to the surface and to a head.

The Grindal affair also showed what was likely to happen if these differences of priority and principle were addressed directly; if, in a series of claims and counter claims, they were raised to greater and greater levels of coherence, of explicit articulation and of overt disagreement. Arguably, in his letter to the queen, Grindal had laid before the queen many of the foundational assumptions of the so-called 'monarchical republic of Elizabeth I'. At stake were not merely religious differences about the nature of true religion and the role of the national church in fostering it, but questions of royal authority and of counsel. Moreover, the results of Grindal's exercise in plain speaking had been (at least potentially) disastrous, not merely for the archbishop himself but also for his allies on the Council and for the wider protestant cause. If indeed monarchical republicanism ever rose to the status of an explicit ideology, it was clearly an ideology that dared not speak its name at the business end of affairs at court and in counsel.[82]

In the exchanges described in this paper we can see these issues being canvassed, a debate being conducted, as it were, in code, via recourse to anti-popery and anti-puritanism. I am decidedly not claiming here that the *real* issues were 'political' – concerned with royal authority and counsel, the balance of power within the mixed polity of the monarchical republic – and that the religious ideologies of anti-popery and anti-puritanism merely provided outward polemical forms, obfuscatory languages, in and through which the real (political) issues

---

[82] For this case see Lake, '"Monarchical Republic of Queen Elizabeth I"'.

could be discussed. But I am arguing that anti-popery and anti-puritanism nearly always operated as repositories of political (as well as of religious) values and priorities – and that their use almost always involved the assertion and legitimation of some sort of political programme or policy agenda. Which mode predominated at any given moment could shift the ideological spectrum, reordering, as it did so, priorities and policy options. For what was happening when these ideologies were put in play was not merely the defence, from external threat, of a stable regime about the nature of which all could agree, but rather a debate about what sort of regime this was and about what it needed to do now and next to protect and perpetuate itself.[83]

But while anti-popery and anti-puritanism very often brought with them different priorities, values and programmes, they were not anything like mutually exclusive. On the contrary, they overlapped, claiming to defend similar, if not identical, visions of protestant and monarchical order from similar sorts of extreme religious threat. And, in so doing, they used similar means and media in order to mobilise very similar, overlapping, if not identical, publics or constituencies.[84] In a political and polemical scene in which no one could be overtly pro-papist or pro-puritan, the successful invocation of either anti-popery or anti-puritanism could induce, even coerce, consensus. It could make people who in many ways, or on other issues, did not agree at all, collaborate and cooperate behind a common front or policy. Debate about what the terms puritan and papist might mean and thus about who precisely might be included within those categories was entirely possible and permissible. That was what was going on when the likes of Killigrew or Heneage or Huntingdon referred to 'puritans as they call them' or as 'out of malice, they are called', or when Sussex tried to get Francis Tregian to at least pretend to conform. But, at the end of the day, everyone had to agree that real puritans and real papists (whoever they were) were very bad things indeed.[85]

What we have here, then, are sharp disagreements about what the real threats were and about what it was best to do about them – debates about principles and policy – being conducted via ideological forms

[83] P. Lake, 'Anti-Popery: The Structure of a Prejudice', in *Conflict in Early Stuart England*, ed. R. Cust and A. Hughes (1987), and *idem*, 'Anti-Puritanism: The Structure of a Prejudice', in *Religious Politics in Post-Reformation England*, ed. K. Fincham and P. Lake (Woodbridge, 2006).

[84] For an explication of how such ideological codes could both prompt and enable certain groups to 'go public' in their attempts to push royal policy in the desired direction see P. Lake, 'The Politics of Popularity and the Public Sphere: The "Monarchical Republic of Elizabeth I" Defends Itself', in *The Politics of the Public Sphere in Early Modern England*, ed. S. Pincus and P. Lake (Manchester, 2007).

[85] It is perhaps worth remembering here that, if we include separatists in the category puritan, then, when push came to shove, even presbyterians could become quite virulently anti-puritan.

which induced, indeed enforced, consensus rather than division. In the course of the events I have been describing an opening, anti-puritan, anti-popular, bid had been made by the queen, in the course of which even Grindal's natural allies and patrons on the Council had been forced not merely to embrace but to make, in open court, the official case against the archbishop. That opening move had been countered by a renewed playing of the anti-papal card. Putting popery front and centre was a way to bring anti-puritans – Hatton, Aylmer and Whitgift – on board, recruiting them for a reassembled pro-Grindal, pro-protestant cause and anti-papal establishment. The resulting re-jigged common front could then confront the queen about what she needed to do next in order to preserve what Leicester called in a letter to Walsingham 'her self and her estate'.[86] Thus it is surely not without significance that, while the likes of Mildmay and Bacon were chosen to make the official case against Grindal,[87] it was Sussex, who had been so anxious to play down the popish threat and save both Tregian and Mayne from the consequences of their own rigourism in the autumn of 1577, who, in the summer of 1578, had been forced, as lord chamberlain, to unmask the popish Rookwood and expel him from the royal presence, thus underlining the ubiquity and seriousness of the popish threat. What was involved in such manoeuvres and exchanges was partly ideological coercion or cooption – the exploitation of the fact that now, especially, men like Hatton, Aylmer or Whitgift, or indeed Sussex, could not afford to look soft on popery – but it was also, perhaps rather more, a matter of activating or appealing to another, parallel, set of (anti-popish) convictions to which, in their own way, such men were as subject as even the most enthusiastic of Grindal's backers.

VII

As ever, the inner workings of such manoeuvres showed most clearly not when they worked but when they met resistance and I want to conclude with an instance when the Council's insistence on the anti-papal mode broke down before the defiant deployment of anti-puritanism. In a situation in which 'the friends of Grindal' had decreed that everyone play up the threat of popery and play down that of puritanism, anyone caught sedulously mentioning the puritan threat was liable to be identified immediately, not as a loyal servant of the queen and defender of the church, but rather as a covert enemy of the archbishop. Thus we find the earl of Huntington complaining bitterly to Matthew Hutton that just at the point when the good offices of (the successfully coopted?)

[86] De Lettenhove, *Relations politique*, x, 772, 29 Aug. 1578.

[87] For Mildmay's case against Grindal see Northamptonshire Record Office FM PB. For Bacon's 'speech used to Edmund Grindal the Archbishop of Canterbury being in her Majesty's displeasure' see BL Harleian MSS 5176, fo. 95.

Hatton (of all people) had been about to spring Grindal, 'the bishops of Durham and York have written to her majesty', not to complain, in the approved manner, about the prevalence of popery, but rather to report the presence 'of such sects and puritans', which reports 'hath made a stay of his deliverance'. Incensed, Huntington had put Sandys to the test.

> I told him a piece of this matter, but said no word of Canterbury, and I did ask him what infection he found in all his diocese, especially for puritanism, as they term it. He answered that he found none to offend that way, neither saith he, have I written any thing thereof.

A couple of now contained instances of puritan defiance aside, 'of other matters he did not write, but of the increasing of the papists, etc.'.[88] Sandys, then, knew what the rules were, and, at least to Huntington, claimed to be playing by them.

Not so Bishop Barnes of Durham, who, in a remarkable letter to Burghley, responding to similar allegations that he too had stabbed Grindal in the back, steadfastly refused to say the right, anti-papal, things. On the extent of the popish threat, he gave Burghley the ostensibly happy (but surely also at this point entirely unwelcome) news that in the 'short space' 'since my last letters' Barnes's poor efforts had met with such 'very good and prosperous success and effect' that 'truly I doubt not but that within this half year your good lordship shall see a wonderful reformation there'. The wild talk 'in private assemblies' of some 'that were of late rebels and some dissolute gentlemen' aside,

> openly they all profess obedience and now, within all Northumberland, I cannot find one person that willfully will refuse to come to the church and communicate (a few women excepted). For I have driven out of that county the reconciling priests and massers whereof there was store. They are now gone into Lancashire and Yorkshire but we are rid of them.

It is true that Barnes noted a sharp contrast between the inhabitants of Northumberland and 'these stubborn, churlish people of the county of Durham and their neighbours of Richmondshire'. This, he claimed, was a 'savage people', 'as hard stubborn and rebellious as ever they were', but even there he had got many 'to haste to amend', with 'none extremity showed to any otherwise than by threatening'. The clergy, too, had proved reformable, those of 'the church of Durham excepted whose stink is grievous in the nose of God and of men'.

On this view, then, not only were there virtually no recusants in the whole of Northumberland, but the real threat to order in the notoriously conservative north-east emanated not from the papists but from the cathedral church of Durham with whose clergy, led by the notorious

---

[88] *The Correspondence of Dr. Matthew Hutton, Archbishop of York* (Surtees Society, 1844), 59, Huntingdon to Hutton, 20 May 1578.

'puritan' William Whittingham, Barnes was in open feud. This was decidedly not what Barnes was supposed to say and he compounded the offence by replying to the charge that he did not 'have a good mind to the archbishop of Canterbury in the time of his trouble', by repeating the official, anti-puritan case against Grindal.

> I detest his willfulness and contending with the regal majesty and obstinacy in not yielding to that which your honours sets down, the same being godly and expedient, for this time, the malapertness of brainbusy men considered, who nowadays, if but a proclamation, a decree, or commandment come forth from her majesty, and by your honours' advice, straightways, and first in their conventicles, will call the same into question and examine and determine whether, with safe conscience, they may or ought to obey the same, a thing so perilous as none can be more and savouring overmuch of the anabaptismeys [*sic*] who wish a popular government.

All the buzz words – 'conventicle', 'popular government', 'anabaptism' – of anti-puritanism were being invoked here, clustered around the figure of Grindal and the issue of prophesyings. As for the prophesyings themselves, Barnes opined, even well ordered, they tended only to the *bene esse* rather than to the *esse*, to the well being, rather than to the being or essence, of the church, and as such were 'not to be so urged of him as by the same to contend with her highness and her Council to the great hinderance of true religion'.

Not that Barnes had been free with these opinions; he had, he claimed, only made this case 'to some two or three persons at the utmost' whom he had heard maintain that Grindal was 'cruelly dealt withal and had not deserved to be straightened'. In reply to such 'slanders', 'I have been forward to affirm his own willfulness and undutifulnes toward his sovereign to be the just occasion of his trouble.' As for his failure to visit Grindal at Lambeth, on his last visit to London, Barnes had, he explained, intended to pay his respects, 'but I was warned by those whom I will obey not so to do, which ought to be my warrant'.[89]

This, of course, was to mute, almost to silence, the anti-papal register, that recent actions by the Council had been designed to excite in the bishops and others, and to replace it with an insistence on the persistence and seriousness of the puritan threat that echoed the queen's own values and rhetoric. This was the very opposite of what Sandys, in defending himself to Huntingdon, had at least claimed to be doing. Barnes, however, was having none of that; staring down the pressure exerted on him by individual councillors – in this case, it seems, by Burghley himself – he simply reiterated the official conciliar and royal line on the issue of the prophesyings, on Grindal's wilful disobedience and contempt of royal authority and on the pressing nature of the puritan threat. Whatever their private opinions and preferences, this was the view of the matter

---

[89] BL Lansdowne MSS, 25, no. 78, fos. 161–2, Barnes to Burghley, 11 Feb. 1578.

which even Grindal's conciliar allies – the likes of Sir Nicholas Bacon, Sir Walter Mildmay and even Burghley himself – had themselves been forced to articulate and endorse, often in public, in the queen's and their own names. Having thus been coopted to the anti-puritan consensus, they had given hostages to fortune that Barnes was now exploiting; even, in that slightly sinister reference to the 'warrant' provided him by 'those whom I will obey', daring to threaten Burghley, of all people, with the superior authority of the queen. And, of course, in the face of such an outstanding display of obedience and exemplary anti-puritan zeal not even Burghley could demur. There could scarcely be a more perfectly formed example of the enforced consensus which the well-timed recourse to the discourses either of anti-popery or of anti-puritanism could impose on even the most powerful of persons; nor of the often bitter, both ideological and personal, disagreements that could be not merely masked, but actively prosecuted by the skilful deployment of such talk.

But if these exchanges between Sandys and Huntingdon and Burghley and Barnes show us the game being played by the rules, the strange fates of Edmund Grindal and indeed of Cuthbert Mayne show us what happened when conscience got in the way of politics. For just as Sussex's attempt to save Tregian's career and Mayne's life had foundered on the former's conscientious refusal to at least go through the motions of outward conformity, so too were the Council's attempts to rehabilitate Grindal were broken on the archbishop's similarly intransigent refusal – despite all Burghley's careful coaching sessions[90] – to grovel before the queen in the approved manner. Put another way, Grindal was refusing to be co-opted (anymore) into supporting policies of which he disapproved by the playing of the anti-puritan card. In effect, he was refusing to accept the legitimacy, the widening ideological purchase, of anti-puritanism, as the functional equivalent, the counter balancing evil twin, of his own virulent anti-popery. The complete failure of that refusal which his sequestration from office represented renders his fall a major turning point in the history of the reign, indeed perhaps, as things turned out, in the whole post-Reformation period.

What we are seeing here is the emergence of something of a pattern – a pattern capable of more general application to the politics of the period as a whole; a politics which, at least in the high Elizabethan decades, might now be conceived not so much as factional, but rather as (emergently) ideological (and therefore as intermittently 'popular'), with the crucial issue being whether an anti-papal or an anti-puritan agenda predominated. The course of events from the late 1560s to the early

[90] *Ibid.*, 103, no. 8, fos.14r–15v, 'a missive to the Archbishop of Canterbury, sent by the dean of Westminster, containing the Lord Burghley's directions how to demean himself before the queen in respect of the offence he gave the queen by the exercises'.

1590s (if not beyond) might then be recast as a struggle between those two perspectives; as various groups and individuals, from the queen on down, struggled to change the subject from one to the other and back again. Thus was the marriage/succession issue of the 1560s displaced by the Vestiaran controversy; and then the anti-puritan focus of that event displaced, in turn, by the virulent anti-popery sparked by the revolt of the northern earls, the queen's excommunication and the Ridolfi conspiracy. Then again the Admonition Controversy sparked a renewed outbreak of a newly coherent and aggressive Whitgiftian anti-puritanism, with the two fighting it out through Grindal's rise and fall. Whitgift's elevation to Canterbury occasioned another outbreak of anti-puritanism, his anti-presbyterian push of 1583/4 coinciding with the outbreak of anti-popish fervour that, amongst other things, produced the Bond of Association. Finally, we might, with Glyn Parry, see Burghley's great anti-catholic proclamation of 1591 as another, final (?) attempt to change the subject from Whitgift's final push against the Elizabethan puritan movement back to the 'real' threat of popery.

What was at stake here was not a political style or scene created by a queen balancing factions or favourites, or, still less, by rival factions and favourites contending for royal favour and playing and manipulating the queen as they did so. What were being 'balanced' here were not 'factions' so much as the contradictory demands of anti-puritanism and anti-popery, as, in an increasingly threatening and confessionally polarised world, different elements within the regime (up to and including Elizabeth herself) sought to invoke and manipulate those two aspects of the royal view of the world in order to gloss events and push royal policy in directions that accorded with their view of their own, the queen's and of the state's interests.

And if, at times, the result of all this was an appearance of 'balance', of the pursuit of the sort of equipoise thought uniquely to repose in 'the middle way', that was in many ways an illusion; an effect produced by the evolving and mutating stalemate that pertained for much of the reign; a stalemate, of course, both framed and manipulated by the deployment of a rhetoric of moderation and consensus imposed by the queen and used by the various parties to push their preferred policies and priorities. (One thinks here of Alymer's advice to Walsingham that the queen be at least told that equal severity was being used towards the two extremes, 'or else you can guess what will follow' and of the Council's later invocation to Aylmer of the need to protect 'the common quietness of the realm' from the popish threat.) Thus, rather than the triumph of any one coherent vision of true order, or the realisation of any one version of a stable 'middle way' between those two inherently unstable and intensely glossable ideological quantities or categories, 'popery' and 'puritanism', it was this sort of stasis or stand off, this sort of repeated wrangle both over what the real threats were and over what might best be done about them, that produced the seeming stability of 'the Elizabethan compromise'.

Rather than pursue these increasingly abstract speculations further, however, I will end by returning to the anodyne historiographical observation with which I began. There have been and will continue to be, different, distinct narratives of this period – the complexity of the events involved, the volume of sources available, make that an inevitable, indeed a, in many ways, salutary division of scholarly labour – but there are moments which both demand and enable those different narratives to be reintegrated – and I have been dealing here with one such moment. The events discussed in this paper have been treated in distinct narratives; a political/protestant narrative, centred on Grindal; a diplomatic narrative, centred on the Low Countries; a catholic narrative, centred on the 1577 survey and on the death of Mayne; a set of local narratives which have been used to explain the course of the 1578 progress and the fate of Mayne largely in terms of gentry factions, and local religious tensions between catholics and protestants, puritans and conformists, bishops and JPs. All these narratives are true in their own way, and it has been no part of my purpose to criticise or disagree with any of them. But it is not until they have been correlated, put (back) into contact or conversation with one another, that we will see just what was happening and why.

So it is partly true that Cuthbert Mayne lost his guts to save Edmund Grindal's job, but stated baldly, such a claim would be both trivial and untrue. However, I have been concerned to argue here that how and why it both was, and was not, true, has a good deal to tell us about nature of Elizabethan politics and religion and the interplay between them.

Transactions of the RHS 18 (2008), pp. 165–86 © 2008 Royal Historical Society
doi:10.1017/S0080440108000698   Printed in the United Kingdom

THE LANGUAGE AND SYMBOLISM OF
CONQUEST IN IRELAND, *c.* 1790–1850*

By Jacqueline Hill

READ 27 APRIL 2007 AT THE UNIVERSITY OF WALES, BANGOR

ABSTRACT. The question of whether Ireland had been conquered by England
has received some attention from historians of eighteenth-century Ireland, mainly
because it preoccupied William Molyneux, author of the influential *The Case of
Ireland . . . Stated* (1698). Molyneux defended Irish parliamentary rights by denying
the reality of a medieval conquest of Ireland by English monarchs, but he did
allow for what could be called 'aristocratic conquest'. The seventeenth century, too,
had left a legacy of conquest, and this paper examines evidence of consciousness
among Irish Protestants of descent from ancestral conquerors. It considers how and
why this consciousness took a more pronounced sectarian turn during the 1790s.
Williamite anniversaries, increasingly associated with the Orange Order, became
identified in the Catholic mind as symbolic reminders of conquest. Thanks to the
protracted struggle for 'Catholic emancipation', this issue continued to feature in
political debate about Ireland well into the nineteenth century, while the passing of
the Act of Union (1800) revitalised the older debate about whether England could
be said to have conquered Ireland. Liberal Protestants and Catholics contended
that England had invariably intervened to prevent any possibility of reconciliation
between conquerors and conquered. Thus the language of conquest remained highly
adaptable.

The announcement yesterday that Northern Ireland's First Minister, Dr
Ian Paisley, is to visit the site of the battle of the Boyne (1690) in County
Meath, at the invitation of Republic of Ireland Taoiseach Mr Bertie
Ahern, has aroused much interest. The importance of that battle in
Irish history, and later in the anniversary tradition of the Orange Order,
suggests that the visit will be of particular significance. The event relates to
the theme of this paper because it was during the 1790s that seventeenth-
century events came to dominate talk of conquest in the public domain,
with lasting consequences for Irish history.

The subject of conquest has received considerable attention from
historians of medieval and early modern Ireland, but less so for later

* I am grateful to Allan Blackstock, John Gillingham and Cadoc Leighton for their
helpful comments on an earlier draft of this essay. Errors that remain are my own.

periods.[1] This paper focuses not on whether conquest did or did not occur in the past,[2] but on how it was perceived, and its wider significance in the public and political sphere. It examines why, during the 1790s, attention shifted from the invasion of Henry II to events in the 1690s, and the subsequent significance of that development. For the purposes of comparison, the language of conquest in the period from the Williamite wars down to the 1780s will first be considered.

I

Ideas about conquest in the eighteenth century have received some attention from historians because they featured in William Molyneux's influential *The Case of Ireland's Being Bound by Acts of Parliament in England, Stated* (Dublin, 1698). In the absence of a legislative union (which Molyneux commended briefly but thought unobtainable), *The Case* defended the integrity of Ireland's parliament. By passing laws purporting to bind Ireland, such as curbs on the woollen industry, the English parliament was allegedly acting beyond its powers. *The Case*, which went through nine reprintings during the eighteenth century,[3] had a bearing on conquest in two main ways. First, the question of whether the invasions of 1167–71 could be said to constitute conquest. In a much-cited passage, Molyneux argued that there had been no conquest by Henry II:

> [By contrast to the opposition given to William I in England] ... *Henry* the Second receiv'd not the least Opposition in *Ireland*, all came in Peaceably, and had large Concessions made them of the like Laws and Liberties with the People of *England*, which they gladly Accepted ... From what foregoes, I presume it Appears that *Ireland* cannot properly be said *so to be Conquer'd* by *Henry* the Second, as to give the Parliament of *England* any Jurisdiction over us.[4]

In arguing that Henry II's sovereignty had been accepted, freely, by the native Irish leaders, and that no conquest had occurred, Molyneux was attaching particular importance to one strand in the historiographical traditions surrounding the invasion. Giraldus Cambrensis, the first

---

[1] See, e.g., R. R. Davies, *Domination and Conquest. The Experience of Ireland, Scotland and Wales 1100–1300* (Cambridge, 1990); Nicholas Canny, *The Elizabethan Conquest of Ireland* (Hassocks, 1976); Colm Lennon, *Sixteenth-Century Ireland: The Incomplete Conquest* (Dublin, 1994); Hans Pawlisch, *Sir John Davies and the Conquest of Ireland* (Cambridge, 1985); Patrick Kelly, 'Conquest versus Consent as the Basis of the English Title to Ireland in William Molyneux's *Case of Ireland*', in *British Interventions in Early Modern Ireland*, ed. Ciaran Brady and Jane Ohlmeyer (Cambridge, 2005), 334–56.

[2] For which see Anthony Carty, *Was Ireland Conquered? International Law and the Irish Question* (1996).

[3] Patrick Kelly, 'William Molyneux and the Spirit of Liberty in Eighteenth-Century Ireland', *Eighteenth-Century Ireland*, 3 (1988), 136.

[4] William Molyneux, *The Case of Ireland Stated*, reprint of 1st edn (Dublin, 1977), 31, 33.

historian of those events, considered that at least a partial conquest had occurred.[5] His view had been endorsed by others who took conquest for granted, and this was widely accepted in Anglo-Irish circles in the early modern period.[6] Molyneux was, however, close to the position of another influential commentator, the Old English Catholic Geoffrey Keating, whose *Foras Feasa ar Éirinn* (written in the 1630s and published in English as *The General History of Ireland* in 1723) became a highly respected source for eighteenth-century ideas about Irish history. Keating contended that Henry II's authority, legitimated by Pope Adrian IV's bull *Laudabiliter* (1155), had been willingly accepted by most of the Irish clergy and nobility, and his account gave no grounds for supposing that Ireland had been conquered.[7] Molyneux – a Protestant and a friend of Locke – did not mention *Laudabiliter*, and gave what he called the 'Original Compact' between Henry II and the Irish leaders a more Lockian flavour than Keating had done, but his main deduction was that laws binding Ireland should receive the Irish parliament's assent.[8] A further attraction of the idea of a constitution obtained by consent, Patrick Kelly has recently argued, was its implication that the native Irish could claim no subsequent right of resistance to royal authority.[9]

The British government's verdict on Molyneux's arguments was enshrined in the Declaratory Act (1720), which affirmed the British parliament's right to legislate for Ireland. Although this right was used sparingly, *The Case* became an inspiration for those 'Patriots' who sought to defend what Colin Kidd has called 'the regnal privileges of the Irish kingdom'. The stakes were raised in the 1760s with Blackstone's *Commentaries on the Laws of England*, which asserted that Ireland had been conquered;[10] and as the campaign to defend Irish privileges neared its climax in the late 1770s, Patriots complained that it was in this spirit that Ireland was being governed.[11] Subsequently, the heat evaporated when, during the American revolutionary crisis of 1782–3, the British parliament

[5] *Expugnatio Hibernica: The Conquest of Ireland*, by Giraldus Cambrensis, ed. A. B. Scott and F. X. Martin (Dublin, 1978), 231–3.

[6] Ciaran Brady, 'The Decline of the Irish Kingdom', in *Conquest and Coalescence: The Shaping of the State in Early Modern Europe*, ed. Mark Greengrass (1991), 96–7; Kelly, 'Conquest versus Consent', 335–40.

[7] Bernadette Cunningham, *The World of Geoffrey Keating: History, Myth and Religion in Seventeenth-Century Ireland* (Dublin, 2000), 148–51.

[8] *Ibid.*, 111–12, 165–6; Molyneux, *Case of Ireland*, 40–7.

[9] Kelly, 'Conquest versus Consent', 354–5.

[10] Colin Kidd, *British Identities before Nationalism: Ethnicity and Nationhood in the Atlantic World, 1600–1800* (Cambridge, 1999), 254–5; Stephen Small, *Political Thought in Ireland 1776–1798* (Oxford, 2002), 62.

[11] R. B. McDowell, *Irish Public Opinion 1750–1800* (1944), 45–6; Small, *Political Thought*, 60–3, 78–80.

acknowledged the exclusive right of the Irish parliament to legislate for Ireland.

However, it has been shown that Molyneux's arguments about conquest were more complex than might at first appear. While the main thrust of *The Case* was that there had been no conquest of Ireland by Henry II, Molyneux did allow for what can be called 'aristocratic conquest' in Ireland.[12] Noting that Henry II's arrival had been preceded by 'some Conflicts between [the first Adventurers] and the *Irish*, in which the latter were constantly beaten', he argued that 'the Conquests obtain'd by those Adventurers, who came over only by the King's *License* and *Permission*, and not at all by his particular *Command* . . . can never be call'd the Conquest of *Henry* the Second'. And he continued:

> Supposing *Hen.* II had *Right* to Invade this Island, and that he had been opposed therein by the Inhabitants, it was only the *Ancient Race* of the *Irish*, that could suffer by this Subjugation; the *English* and *Britains* that came over and Conquered with him, retain'd all the Freedoms and Immunities of *Free-born* Subjects; they nor their Descendants could not in reason lose these, for being Successful and Victorious.

Molyneux softened the implications of this hypothetical conquest by proceeding, in a much-debated passage, to argue that 'the great Body of the present People of *Ireland*, are the progeny of the *English* and *Britains* that from time to time have come over into this Kingdom; and there remains but a meer handful of the Antient *Irish* at this day; I may say not one in a thousand'.[13] In making that statement, so apparently at odds with Irish realities, Molyneux has been variously interpreted as being disingenuous; as referring to the landed elite as the people of Ireland; or reflecting a belief that even the native Irish were originally of British extraction.[14] Whatever his meaning, the point was that conquest, and, more important, conquerors, were slipping in by the back door. For while Molyneux might seem to present such a conquest in purely hypothetical terms, the practical implications of the idea were too useful to remain hypothetical. By associating 'the present People of Ireland' with the descendants of those '*English* and *Britains*' who had conquered with Henry II, Molyneux was enhancing the importance to the crown of those free-born descendants of conquerors, and bolstering their claims to the full enjoyment of the rights associated with the kingdom of Ireland.

---

[12] C. D. A. Leighton, *Catholicism in a Protestant Kingdom: A Study of the Irish Ancien Régime* (Dublin, 1994), 31–7; Jacqueline Hill, 'Ireland without Union: Molyneux and his Legacy', in *A Union for Empire: Political Thought and the Union of 1707*, ed. John Robertson (Cambridge, 1995), 280–2; Kelly, 'Conquest versus Consent', 350–3.

[13] Molyneux, *Case of Ireland*, 32, 34–5.

[14] Jim Smyth, '"Like Amphibious Animals": Irish Protestants, Ancient Britons, 1691–1707', *Historical Journal*, 36 (1993), 789–91; Hill, 'Molyneux', 280–1; Kelly, 'Conquest versus Consent', 351.

It was, of course, the case that whereas Molyneux was speaking on behalf of an exclusively Protestant political elite, those conquering ancestors had been Old English Catholics, whose political rights in the 1690s were being eroded by those very Protestants. Molyneux was silent on this, but the point was made forcefully by the anonymous Jacobite author of 'A Light to the Blind' (*c.* 1711):

> The just interest of the crown of England is only preserved in Ireland by maintaining in a high state the true conquerors of that kingdom, who by their blood annexed the Irish crown to the English diadem . . . Those victors, being Catholics, landed from England . . . under Henry the Second . . . Their posterity have continued in the like . . . loyalty even to this day, propping the true kings of England . . . while the upstart Protestants have of late years endeavoured to cast down those crowned heads.[15]

But the Jacobite defeat, and subsequent introduction of new penal laws against Catholics, left political power in the hands of the Protestant minority, who for decades to come were able to concentrate on relations with Britain. Accordingly, as noted above, for the political elite the language of conquest in that period was mainly directed outwards, towards Anglo-Irish relations, and (inspired by Molyneux) denying the reality of conquest. Yet, as Cadoc Leighton has argued, the idea of descent from conquerors remained familiar to Irish Protestants.[16] Thus Archbishop King defended Irish constitutional rights by invoking conquests 'by the English that came into Ireland', while Jonathan Swift referred to 'the savage Irish, who our Ancestors conquered several hundred years ago'.[17]

The obvious inconsistency of Protestant Irishmen, most of whom had arrived in Ireland in the sixteenth and seventeenth centuries, assuming the mantle of medieval Old English Catholics does not appear to have troubled the political elite; and this phenomenon may be regarded as simply one facet of what Kidd has called 'the protean character' of Anglo-Irish identity. In any case, it should not be inferred that in appropriating the identity of Old English settlers Protestants placed exclusive or even primary emphasis on the 'conquering' element in that inheritance. More important was a commitment (derived from supposed 'Gothic' ancestry shared with the English) to free institutions, and a limited (and Protestant) constitution.[18] Moreover, such references sprang from resentment at Ireland's treatment at English hands, rather than a desire to emphasise internal differences. And such language could be used in relatively inclusive ways. In 1753, on the eve of the contentious 'money-bill

---

[15] Quoted in *A New History of Ireland*, III: *Early Modern Ireland, 1534–1691*, ed. T. W. Moody, F. X. Martin and F. J. Byrne (Oxford, 1976), lxii.

[16] Leighton, *Catholicism*, 78–9.

[17] Quoted in Hill, 'Molyneux', 292.

[18] Kidd, *British Identities*, 251–7.

dispute', the earl of Kildare, a Protestant of Old English descent, and Ireland's leading 'Patriot' peer, addressed the king, complaining of the conduct of the Irish administration. His memorial began by setting out:

> THAT your memorialist is the eldest peer of the realm, by descent, as lineally sprung from . . . the noble Earl of Kildare, who came over under the invincible banner of your august predecessor Henry the Second, when his arms conquered the kingdom of Ireland. That your memorialist, on this foundation, has the greater presumption to address your august majesty, as his ancestors have ever proved themselves steady adherents to the conquest of that kingdom, and were greatly instrumental in the reduction thereof . . . That though they were first sent over with letters patent, under Henry the Second's banner, to conquer that kingdom, yet by the inheritance of lands, by intermarriages with princesses of the kingdom, they became powerful, and might have conquered for themselves, notwithstanding which, their allegiance was such, as that, on that sovereign's mandate to stop the progress of war, we obeyed, and relinquished our title of conquest, laid down our arms, and received that monarch with due homage and allegiance, resigning our conquests as became subjects . . . That on this presumption, your memorialist has, in the most humble manner, at the request of the natives of Ireland, your majesty's true liege subjects, not only the aborigines thereof, but the English colonies [*sic*], sent over by Henry the Second, Richard the Second, . . . William the Third of glorious memory, and other kings, your majesty's predecessors, and the conquerors of Ireland, made bold to lay before your majesty, the true state of their several and respective grievances.[19]

Two points stand out about Kildare's references to conquest. In contrast to those made by Archbishop King and Swift, they were very self-conscious. Addressing the king in his own person, Kildare would have wished to mention all his credentials as a peer of the realm and loyal subject. Reference to the conquest of Henry II allowed him to mention that those 'who conquered with him' (to use Molyneux's phrase) included direct ancestors of his own.[20] He emphasised his ancestors' willingness to resign their own conquests in favour of royal claims. There was no sign of the usual Patriot insistence that no royal conquest had occurred, and which doubtless in other contexts Kildare would have endorsed.

Secondly, while Kildare distinguished between 'the aborigines [of Ireland]' and 'the English colonies sent over by Henry the Second', he stressed that he regarded himself as speaking on behalf of all 'the natives of Ireland' (those born in Ireland, as opposed to the English-born ministers about whom he was complaining). This representative character was reinforced by mention of the intermarriage of his ancestors with (Old Irish) 'princesses'. Thus, although in practice Kildare was speaking on behalf of Protestants, his talk of conquest, informed by aristocratic rather than religious values, owed nothing to sectarian divisions.

---

[19] Quoted in Francis Plowden, *A Historical Review of the State of Ireland, from the Invasion of that Country under Henry II to its Union with Great Britain* (5 vols., Philadelphia, 1805), II, Appendix LVIII, 8–10.

[20] See M. T. Flanagan, 'Fitzgerald, Maurice (d. 1176)', *Oxford Dictionary of National Biography* (Oxford, 2004).

It has been argued thus far that the language of conquest in the eighteenth century prioritised medieval events; focused on Anglo-Irish relations; and did not dwell unduly on internal divisions stemming from a consciousness of conquest. However, there were more recent events in Irish history that could be said to constitute conquest. The anniversary of the battle of the Boyne (1 July 1690 (OS)) had been celebrated by Protestants from the 1690s onwards (the equestrian statue of King William in Dublin was inaugurated on 1 July 1701). In the 1730s veterans of that battle paraded under arms, proclaiming 'We ... conquered [at?] the Boyne.'[21] Subsequently, while Dublin Castle and the political elite annually celebrated King William's birthday (4 November), Boyne and Aughrim societies were formed to commemorate Williamite military victories. These events featured processions of armed Protestants, drawn chiefly from the lesser gentry and middle classes.[22]

Moreover, seventeenth-century conquests had also involved Presbyterians, who invoked conquest in both agrarian and religious causes.[23] Writing in 1787, the Reverend Samuel Barber, Minister of Rathfriland (County Down), complained that Presbyterians as well as Catholics were obliged to pay tithes to the established church. Future readers, he suggested, would be astonished to discover

> that [Presbyterians] fought at their [the Church of Ireland] side and conquered with them; that they planted, civilised and improved the province of Ulster, and while they were doing so, forged their own chains ... they assisted in conquering the Roman Chatholicks [sic], and were reduced to the same servitude.[24]

That such a comment could be made, not by a rabid anti-Catholic, but by a reformer later accused of being a United Irishman,[25] is suggestive of how unexceptional was a sense of conquering status among eighteenth-century Protestants. Preaching to Volunteers at Strabane, County Tyrone, in 1779, the New Light Presbyterian minister Andrew Alexander defended Volunteering because 'gross mismanagement' of the empire had rendered 'the sons of conquerors ... dupes of a blundering adm[—]n'.[26] Such attitudes had political and social roots. Not until 1774 did it prove possible to frame an oath allowing Catholics to swear allegiance to the Hanoverians, and it was 1793 before Catholics were

[21] Quoted in James Kelly, '"The Glorious and Immortal Memory": Commemoration and Protestant Identity in Ireland 1660–1800', *Proceedings of the Royal Irish Academy*, 94, Sect. C (1994), 32, 37.

[22] *Ibid.*, 32, 41–4.

[23] Leighton, *Catholicism*, 68.

[24] Samuel Barber, *Remarks on a Pamphlet, Intitled [sic] The Present State of the Church of Ireland* (Dublin, 1787), 36.

[25] I. R. McBride, 'Barber, Samuel (1737/8–1811), *Oxford Dictionary of National Biography*.

[26] Quoted in Allan Blackstock, 'Armed Citizens and Christian Soldiers: Crisis Sermons and Ulster Presbyterians, 1715–1803', *Eighteenth-Century Ireland*, 22 (2007), 96–7.

legally entitled to bear arms. Surrounded by a Catholic (and putatively Jacobite) majority, Irish Protestants kept up a system of 'public banding' long after it had been abandoned in Great Britain; and Protestant tenants, including Presbyterians, were commonly called out under their landlords' leadership against a variety of foreign and domestic dangers.[27] Appeals to the spirit of the 'citizen soldier' might be couched in purely defensive terms, but could be more bellicose. Appealing for volunteers during the Jacobite scare of 1745, Reverend William Henry urged his mixed Presbyterian/Church of Ireland Ulster audience to defend the liberties of their country, but also invoked the spirit of 'our glorious Deliverer King WILLIAM, [who], when he marched through the *North* of *Ireland*, drew his Sword, and said, "it was a Country well worth the fighting for"'.[28]

II

The 1790s marked an irrevocable change in Irish politics, with the emergence of political rights for Catholics, which would dominate debate for nearly forty years. Although various civil rights, including the right to teach, and to buy and sell land, had been conceded by the early 1780s, the question of political rights was too sensitive (given Ireland's Catholic majority) to have encouraged much public discussion. But the French Revolution, and especially France's civil constitution of the clergy (1790), removed some inhibitions on discussion of this topic. As the prospect of war between Britain and France grew, ministers in London became readier to listen to those (including Edmund Burke) who recommended granting political rights to Irish Catholics to reinforce their supposed commitment to traditional institutions. Burke was not alone in commending this step – radicals in Belfast and Dublin hoped to win Catholic support for reform – but as someone standing outside Irish politics he could be blunter in his analysis of the political situation, and (as the author of the *Reflections on the Revolution in France*), far more influential. In his *Letter to Sir Hercules Langrishe* (February 1792), Burke distinguished between the Glorious Revolution in England and its Irish counterpart, describing the latter as 'not a revolution, but a conquest'. Alluding to Locke's contention that following conquest, conquerors and conquered usually became reconciled, Burke noted that this had not happened in Ireland. He blamed Irish Protestants, who had developed the principles of a 'master-cast' [*sic*], and a 'colonial garrison'. The penal laws were a manifestation of 'hatred and scorn towards a conquered people'. He was particularly critical of the Protestant monopoly of Irish political rights

---

[27] David W. Miller, *Queen's Rebels: Ulster Loyalism in Historical Perspective* (Dublin, 1978), 25.
[28] [Willam Henry], *A Philippic Oration, against the Pretender's Son, &* (Dublin, 1745), 14–15. I am grateful to Allan Blackstock for this reference.

because it extended beyond the landed class: 'a plebeian oligarchy is a monster'. And to compound Protestant discomfiture, Burke challenged the fixed Protestant nature of the Williamite settlement, noting that Irish Catholics had not been deprived of the vote until the 1720s.[29]

The idea of conquest – already the subject of Enlightenment critique – was coming under pressure from other sources at this time, notably Tom Paine's *Rights of Man* (1791–2), which sold in Ireland even more robustly than in Britain.[30] Paine's contention that aristocratic rights stemmed from conquest was hardly new, but it added to the pressures on Protestants in Ireland, where aristocratic and landed interests faced serious challenges in the 1790s. After the 1790s, it became less common for even hard-line or ultra-Protestants to articulate publicly their former, largely unselfconscious self-image as descendants of conquering ancestors. A new term was coming into use, one that had arisen in the 1780s as contemporaries sought to describe the realities of Protestant control, 'Protestant ascendancy'.[31] This term was deployed early on by Dublin Corporation, in its *Letter to the Protestants of Ireland* (September 1792), which, following repeal of the ban on Catholics practising law earlier in the year, sought to rally Protestants against further concessions. The Corporation – the very embodiment of that 'plebeian' element in the Protestant elite which Burke had deplored – defended 'Protestant ascendancy', defined as maintaining the exclusively Protestant character of the apparatus of government, established church, parliament and electorate.

However, the Corporation was not ready to surrender the idea of a Protestant constitution acquired by sword right. Positing a Lockian 'appeal to heaven' to describe the clash between William of Orange and James II, the Corporation contended that 'the great ruler of all things decided in favour of our ancestors, he gave them victory and Ireland became a Protestant nation enjoying a British constitution'.[32]

---

[29] Edmund Burke, *A Letter to Sir Hecules Langrishe, Bart. M.P., on the Subject of the Roman Catholics of Ireland*, in *The Works of Edmund Burke* (6 vols., 1884–99), III, 304–5, 312–15, 319–21; Hill, 'Molyneux', 293. Burke's views on conquest are further discussed by Sean Patrick Donlan, 'The "Genuine Voice of its Records and Monuments"? Edmund Burke's "Interior History of Ireland"', in *Edmund Burke's Irish Identities*, ed. Sean Patrick Donlan (Dublin, 2007), 69–101, and Richard Bourke, 'Edmund Burke and the Politics of Conquest', *Modern Intellectual History*, 4, 3 (2007), 403–32.

[30] Jacqueline Hill, 'Politics and the Writing of History: The Impact of the 1690s and 1790s on Irish Historiography', in *Political Discourse in Seventeenth- and Eighteenth-Century Ireland*, ed. D. George Boyce, R. Eccleshall and V. Geoghegan (Basingstoke, 2001), 231; David Dickson, 'Paine and Ireland', in *The United Irishmen: Republicanism, Radicalism and Rebellion*, ed. David Dickson, Dáire Keogh and Kevin Whelan (Dublin, 1993), 136–7.

[31] James Kelly, 'Eighteenth-Century Ascendancy: A Commentary', *Eighteenth-Century Ireland*, 5 (1990), 173–87.

[32] *Calendar of Ancient Records of Dublin*, ed. J. T. Gilbert and R. M. Gilbert (19 vols., Dublin, 1889–1944), XIV, 285–6.

A providential interpretation of the Williamite intervention had been aired by Protestants in the 1690s, but the Corporation's construction was consistent with recent interest being shown in Locke's views on government.[33] Catholics and liberal Protestants were outraged. The Catholic Society of Dublin counterattacked, using Patriot language: 'If conquest and the right of the sword could justify the stronger in retaining dominion, why did Great Britain abdicate her legislative supremacy over Ireland?' Henry Grattan argued that Catholics could plead the Corporation's 'law of conquest' to justify rebellion.[34]

The view that the Williamite revolution was a once-for-all transaction, stemming from providential conquest, and establishing an unalterable Protestant constitution securing civil and religious liberty, was endorsed by the first Orange societies, founded following clashes between (Protestant) Peep O'Day Boys and (Catholic) Defenders in County Armagh in 1795 ('We associate together . . . to defend the Protestant Ascendancy, for which our ancestors fought and conquered').[35] Orange lodges – exclusively Protestant, and with a strong demotic element – were soon caught up in the spread of counter-revolutionary loyalism in the mid-1790s, which was more militaristic and less open to accommodation with Catholics than the Irish loyalist associations of 1793–4. Orangemen commemorated primarily not William's birthday (still strongly associated with the elite) but, like the Boyne and Aughrim societies, his military victories. Down to 1795, the battle of the Boyne (1 July OS) was still being celebrated on 1 July (NS), despite the calendar change in 1752, which would have brought it to 12 July (NS); by adopting 12 July (NS) as the Boyne anniversary, the Orangemen were able to incorporate the anniversary of the battle of Aughrim (12 July (OS)). Gentry in mid-Ulster contributed to the reinvention of the Boyne tradition when in 1797 they actively encouraged plebeian Orangemen to see their clashes with Defenders (now allied with United Irishmen) as part of a military tradition stretching back to the Williamite era.[36]

From the outset, the new celebrations of the twelfth were controversial: those in 1796 followed serious disturbances in County Armagh, involving

<hr/>

[33] Ian McBride, *The Seige of Derry in Ulster Protestant Mythology* (Dublin, 1997), 20–1; Jacqueline Hill, *From Patriots to Unionists: Dublin Civic Politics and Irish Protestant Patriotism, 1660–1840* (Oxford, 1997), 224–5; Patrick Kelly, 'Perceptions of Locke in Eighteenth-Century Ireland', *Proceedings of the Royal Irish Academy*, 89, Sect. C (1989), 276–8.

[34] Both quoted in Dennis Taaffe, *An Impartial History of Ireland, from the Period of the English Invasion to the Present Time* (4 vols., Dublin, 1811), IV, 341, 393–4.

[35] Statement of General Principles, meeting of masters of Orange lodges, Armagh city, 1797, in *The Formation of the Orange Order 1795–1798: The Edited Papers of Colonel William Blacker and Colonel Robert Wallace*, ed. Cecil Kilpatrick and Brian Kennaway (Belfast, 1994), 109; Allan Blackstock, *Loyalism in Ireland 1789–1829* (Woodbridge, 2007), 57.

[36] Blackstock, *Loyalism*, 63–8, 72–5; and on choice of date, Niall Ó Ciosáin, *Print and Popular Culture in Ireland, 1750–1850* (Basingstoke, 1997), 111–17.

the expulsion of hundreds of Catholics from their homes.[37] But even before the Order's foundation, Williamite anniversaries – once (allegedly) accepted phlegmatically in Catholic circles[38] – were beginning to be deprecated as symbolic reminders of conquest. Thus the *Declaration of the Catholic Society of Dublin* (1791), which also expressed resentment at plebeian Protestant privilege, to which Burke would allude in 1792:

> The liberty of Ireland [the constitution of 1782] to those of our communion is a cala-mity . . . They may look with envy to the subjects of an arbitrary Monarch, and contrast that government in which one great tyrant ravages the land, with the thousand inferior despots whom at every instant they must encounter . . . [We complain particularly] of the celebration of festivals memorable only, as they denote the era, and the events, from which we date our bondage.[39]

Despite Protestant misgivings, Irish Catholics were granted many political rights in 1793, including the right to vote, and, crucially, to bear arms.[40] Only membership of parliament and some public service posts remained closed. However, exercising the new rights (frequently dependent on Protestant goodwill) often proved difficult, fuelling the demand for full political equality. During the 1790s that cause was beginning to be described in language like that of the anti-slave trade campaign, as involving Catholic 'emancipation'.[41] But powerful interests opposed further concessions, and meanwhile radicals of all three major denominations planned (with French help) to break the link with Britain. By 1798 Catholics were perceived to pose a special threat, and Dublin Castle reluctantly agreed to a partial arming of Orangemen. Incidents during the rebellion of 1798 prompted accusations that Catholics had aimed at extirpating Protestants,[42] and some Protestants became more amenable to legislative union with Britain. Since strategic considerations were leading the British government to think on unionist lines, an Act of Union was passed – not without opposition – in 1800.

III

During the first half of the nineteenth century, conquest continued to feature in political debate about Ireland because of its perceived connection with two great issues of the period – Catholic 'emancipation'

---

[37] Hereward Senior, *Orangeism in Ireland and Britain 1795–1836* (1996), 29–36.

[38] Jacqueline Hill, 'National Festivals, the State, and "Protestant Ascendancy" in Ireland, 1790–1829', *Irish Historical Studies*, 24 (1984), 34.

[39] *Transactions of the General Committee of the Roman Catholics of Ireland, during the Year 1791* (Dublin, 1792), 12.

[40] 33 Geo. III, c. 21.

[41] David Dickson, *New Foundations: Ireland 1660–1800*, 2nd edn (Dublin, 2000), 197.

[42] Blackstock, *Loyalism*, 90–3; Richard Musgrave, *Memoirs of the Different Rebellions in Ireland, from the Arrival of the English* (1801), 4th edn (Fort Wayne, 1995), 81, 115 n. 1.

and the Act of Union. Despite Catholic condemnation of Williamite anniversaries as symbolic of conquest, such events were acquiring new significance. This was principally owing to the Orange Order, but wartime considerations also applied. A string of victories over revolutionary France in 1795 invited comparisons with the 1690s, and Dublin Castle extended its countenance to the Boyne anniversary.[43]

It was not until 1806, when a new viceroy, the duke of Bedford, absented himself from the annual procession to mark King William's birthday that the state began to distance itself from the Williamite anniversary tradition – and even so, flags continued to be flown at the Castle on such occasions for some years to come, and popular celebrations continued.[44] Critics urged government to discountenance such events completely. William Parnell, a liberal Protestant, contended that they were 'notoriously intended by one party, and felt by the other, as a parade of insulting domination'.[45] According to Dennis Taaffe, a Catholic (and former United Irishman),

> party malevolence is kept alive and fomented, by annual commemorations of party success or calumny, invented by Machiavel [sic] statesmen for the ruin of some party in religion or politics. When . . . countenanced by public authority, they must be considered as annual manifestoes [sic], provoking civil war.[46]

Such comments reflected a sense that any official sanction for the reinvented Williamite tradition implied indefinite postponement of full 'emancipation'. There were certainly strong arguments in favour of emancipation – not least the growing reliance on Irish Catholics in the British armed forces. But various obstacles remained. The opposition of George III, and (more unexpectedly) of the prince regent, and English public opinion generally, were probably less important than the fact that before the establishment in 1822 of Robert Peel's county constabulary (recruited on non-sectarian lines), post-rebellion tranquillity in Ireland depended in practice on continued use of the yeomanry. Since the rebellion, the yeomanry had become almost entirely Protestant, much influenced by ultra-Protestant or Orange assumptions. Whereas loyalism in Great Britain had retained its original, inclusive character, in post-union Ireland the high profile of the yeomanry and the vitality of the Williamite anniversary tradition combined to suggest that post-rebellion loyalism was an exclusively Protestant preserve.[47] Thus requests by liberal Protestants and Catholics for restrictions on Williamite anniversaries had

---

[43] Hill, 'National Festivals', 37.

[44] *Ibid.*, 40–1.

[45] William Parnell, *An Historical Apology for the Irish Catholics* (Dublin, 1807), 139–40.

[46] Taaffe, *Impartial History*, II, 379–80.

[47] Blackstock, *Loyalism*, 129–30; idem, *An Ascendancy Army: The Irish Yeomanry, 1796–1834* (Dublin, 1998), 262–3, 278–91.

little effect. Those events, increasingly orchestrated by Orangemen, took place both in Ulster, with its Protestant majority, and in other areas with a significant Protestant presence. In Dublin, the decoration of King William's statue in Orange accoutrements was particularly contentious.

It was thus not until the 1820s that systematic attempts began to curb the displays on 12 July. George IV's visit to Ireland in 1821, and subsequent endorsement of 'conciliation', together with the appointment of a pro-Catholic viceroy, Lord Wellesley, culminated in 1822 in the first successful ban on the decoration of the Dublin statue. When Orangemen expressed their resentment during Wellesley's visit to the Theatre Royal, and a bottle was thrown at or near the viceregal box, the ringleaders were put on trial.[48] Speaking for the crown at the trial, the Irish attorney general, William Conyngham Plunket, reflected on the outcome of the Williamite wars in Ireland:

> No candid man can ... fairly say, that he thinks worse of the Roman Catholic, for having ... abided by his lawful Sovereign and his ancient faith. What was the result? They were conquered – conquered into freedom and happiness – a freedom and happiness to which the successful result of their ill-fated struggles would have been destructive. There is no rational Roman Catholic in Ireland who does not feel this to be the fact ... The memory of their unfortunate struggles is lost in the conviction of the reality of those blessings, which have been derived from their results equally to the conqueror and to the conquered. What wise or good man can feel a pleasure in recalling to a people so circumstanced, the fact that they have been conquered? ... He is a mischievous man, who for the gratification of his own whim, desires to celebrate, in the midst of that people, the anniversary of their conquest.[49]

The view that the Irish were fortunate to have been conquered was not new – variations on the theme stretched back to sixteenth-century commentators such as Edmund Campion.[50] But since the 1790s a generation of pro-Catholic spokesmen had highlighted the negative legacy for Catholics of Williamite conquest. Liberal Protestants, such as Plunket, faced a dilemma. Supporters of Catholic emancipation, they deplored what they regarded as the exclusive spirit of contemporary Williamite anniversaries. Yet no Protestant could afford to discountenance the Williamite revolution, with its connotations of civil and religious liberty, entirely. The best that could be done was to emphasise William's own tolerant values, and try to wrest his legacy from the more exclusive ultra-Protestants. But this did not necessarily satisfy Catholics, who had proud military traditions of their own. A palpable sense of indignation permeated Daniel O'Connell's post-emancipation history, *A Memoir on*

---

[48] Hill, *Patriots to Unionists*, 324–9; Christopher Morash, *A History of the Irish Theatre 1601–2000* (Cambridge, 2002), 94–102.

[49] *A Report of the Trial of James Forbes [et al.] for a Conspiracy to Create a Riot* (Dublin, 1823), 37–8.

[50] Hill, 'Politics and the Writing of History', 230.

Ireland Native and Saxon (1843). Inscribing the work to Queen Victoria, O'Connell was at pains to disabuse the sovereign of any misconceptions about the 1690s. Referring to the Treaty of Limerick (1691), which had ended the Williamite wars, he insisted: 'the Irish were not conquered, Lady, in the war. They had, in the year preceding the treaty, driven William the Third with defeat and disgrace from Limerick.' And O'Connell turned the issue of conquest on its head by presenting Catholics as the moral victors in the emancipation campaign:

> Wellington and Peel – blessed be heaven! We defeated you. Our peaceable combination ... was too strong for the military glory – bah! – of the one, and for all the little arts ... of the other ... Peel and Wellington, we defeated and drove you before us into coerced liberality, and you left every remnant of character behind you as the spoil of the victors.[51]

The passing of Catholic emancipation in 1829 afforded political equality to Catholics, but redressing the balance in public life would take much longer. Meanwhile bastions of Protestant privilege, including the established Church of Ireland, remained in place, its status guaranteed 'for ever' under the Act of Union. These realities, plus growing Catholic self-confidence, helped fuel demand for repeal of the Union in the 1830s and 1840s. Long before this, debates on the principle of legislative union had revitalised the Patriot tendency to use conquest to explain 'England's' cavalier attitude towards Irish institutions. Protestant critics of union spoke of despotism, slavery and tyranny. For Charles Kendal Bushe, Union represented 'a revival of the odious and absurd title of conquest'.[52] Admittedly, Francis Plowden, an English Catholic, writing when some optimism for speedy emancipation still remained, thought that the Union proved that England did not regard Ireland as a conquered country;[53] but as the emancipation campaign dragged on, and the economy deteriorated, others disagreed. One Protestant critic was George Ensor, of Armagh, whose *Addresses to the People of Ireland* (1822) urged readers to concentrate on opposing the Union rather than obtaining Catholic emancipation. Describing the Union as 'the ultimate act of conquest', Ensor claimed that Ireland had been 'seized as a conquered country, and ... ruled by the laws of war'. 'Remedial measures', he suggested, 'lie in disconquest. The primary measure is to conciliate the parties and factions which the conquerors have hitherto fomented, first as English and Irish, and afterwards as Protestant and Catholic, to continue their tyranny over the Irish nation.'[54] Thus conquest was being blamed both

[51] Daniel O'Connell, *A Memoir on Ireland Native and Saxon* (Dublin, 1843), 9, 33.

[52] W. J. Battersby, *The Fall and Rise of Ireland, or the Repealer's Manual*, 2nd edn (Dublin, 1834), 306, 310, 324, 349, 352, 370.

[53] Plowden, *Historical Review*, I, 28–9.

[54] George Ensor, *Addresses to the People of Ireland* (Dublin, [1822]), 9, 16, 21, 25–6.

for the loss of the Irish parliament, and for the enduring divisions in Ireland.

The years 1829–31 saw Irish politics transformed by the winning of Catholic emancipation, the advent of a Whig government under Lord Grey (an opponent of Union in 1800), the onset of the tithe war, which led to a brief reactivation of the yeomanry, and O'Connell's announcement that he would seek repeal of the Union. Few Protestants were willing to support repeal under Catholic leadership, though Sir Jonah Barrington argued that unless England was prepared to repeal the Union, Ireland could only be governed 'by physical force of arms, and the temporary right of conquest'.[55]

Such allegations sat awkwardly beside a sense of national identity in Britain that took for granted British constitutional superiority as against autocratic and militaristic continental regimes.[56] To the extent that conquest was perceived to have a role in Britain's 'empire of the sea', this was conquest in the interests of trade and the protection of British liberties at home and in the colonies of settlement – and the latter were in any case coming in for criticism as the age of mercantilism gave way to that of free trade. With Scottish and Irish legislative unions in place, there was little incentive to dwell on the historic military dimensions of creating a single government for the 'British Isles'. Defending the Union against O'Connellite attack in 1834, British statesmen avoided mentioning conquest. However, there was talk of the portentous consequences of repeal. Peel declared that it 'would involve a separation of the two countries, either immediate, or protracted only by a long, disastrous, and perhaps fatal conflict', while Prime Minister Lord Grey considered that repeal 'must inevitably prove fatal to the power and safety of the United Kingdom'.[57] Journalistic comment could be blunter. The *London Morning Post* contended:

> The necessity that Ireland shall be abandoned, or reconquered; abandoned to the unmitigated reign of a dark and brutal superstition, to degenerate into barbarism, to become the opprobrium of civilised Europe, ... certainly a thorn in the side of Great Britain; or reconquered through oceans of blood ... Such would be the fatal and inevitable consequences of giving to Ireland a separate Legislature.[58]

By the 1840s some British MPs were more sympathetic, not to repeal of the Union, but to the underlying grievances; and in condemning British policy towards Ireland they too spoke of conquest. The Radical J. A.

---

[55] Jonah Barrington, *The Rise and Fall of the Irish Nation* (Dublin, [1833]), vi.

[56] Kathleen Wilson, 'Empire of Virtue', in *An Imperial State at War*, ed. Lawrence Stone (1994), 128–64; J. P. Parry, 'The Impact of Napoleon III on British Politics, 1851–1880', *Transactions of the Royal Historical Society*, 11 (2001), 149–50.

[57] *Hansard*, 4 Feb. 1834, XXI, cols. 5, 99.

[58] Quoted in *Dublin Evening Mail*, 17 Jan. 1831.

Roebuck asked, rhetorically, 'are we to govern Ireland as a conquered country, by means of the garrison we have placed there in the Protestants of Ireland?' And the colonial reformer Charles Buller pronounced: 'The great evil of Ireland . . . has been originally the conquest of the country by the English invasion, and attempting to force the Church of the conqueror on the conquered people.'[59]

Not everyone was prepared to accept this verdict. In 1843 a Protestant Unionist, Robert Montgomery Martin, commenced his *Ireland Before and After the Union* by claiming: 'England stands charged before the civilised world with having conquered Ireland, and destroyed its independence as a kingdom; [and] with having practised the most cruel oppression towards Ireland for more than seven centuries.' On the contrary, argued Martin, 'poverty, degradation, and conquest' would have been Ireland's fate, 'had England not been truly generous'. Union, he asserted, had brought many benefits to Ireland, and would have brought more, had it not been for 'continuous agitation'.[60] Thus conquest was becoming a point of contention between Repealers and Unionists; and Molyneux's reputation in the post-Union period reflected this. During debates preceding the Act of Union, Molyneux continued to be mentioned with respect, but his brief commendation of Union in *The Case* meant that he was more often invoked by pro- than anti-Unionists.[61] As repealing the Union became an issue in the 1830s and 1840s both sides continued to enlist his authority.[62] However, much of the historical detail in *The Case* no longer seemed so compelling, and Thomas Moore chided Molyneux for suggesting that English rulers had ever accorded much significance to the Irish parliament.[63]

Mention of Molyneux is an indication that preoccupation with conquest affected perceptions of Ireland's past. The 1798 rebellion prompted contemporaries to return to the issue that Burke had raised. Why had there been no reconciliation in Ireland between conquerors and conquered? *Memoirs of the Different Rebellions in Ireland* by ultra-Protestant Sir Richard Musgrave was influential in Britain as well as Ireland. Although he spoke little of conquest directly, Musgrave characterised Protestants in seventeenth-century Ireland as 'conquerors', and (like Giraldus Cambrensis) defended English medieval settlers on the grounds

---

[59] *Hansard*, 11, 12 July 1843, LXX, cols. 963, 1057–8.

[60] R. M. Martin, *Ireland before and after the Union with Great Britain* (1843), 3rd edn (1848) Preface, ix, xxxvii.

[61] Kelly, 'William Molyneux', 144–7.

[62] Barrington, *Rise and Fall*, 1–2; Battersby, *Repealer's Manual*, 105–6; and on the pro-Union side see reference to Thomas Spring Rice by M[ichael] Staunton, 'Reasons for a Repeal of the Legislative Union between Great Britain and Ireland', in *Repeal Prize Essays: Essays on the Repeal of the Union* (Dublin, 1845), 82–6.

[63] Thomas Moore, *The History of Ireland* (4 vols., 1835–45), II, 333.

that they were more civilised and could make better use of the land than the 'barbarous' Irish. But the real issue, in his view, was religion. Under the tutelage of their priests and the Papacy, Irish Catholics were inherently intolerant and anti-Protestant, and therefore prone to rebellion and murder.[64] The idea that Catholics were in bondage to their priests and the pope was not new, but would be expressed more frequently in the nineteenth century, together with calls for the evangelisation of the Catholics. Ultra-Protestantism took on stronger religious overtones, tending to dilute its earlier militaristic and political character (although this could resurface at times of crisis, such as the late 1820s when the imminence of emancipation called forth the Brunswick club movement). The Dublin Protestant Association argued that the answer to Ireland's problems lay in 'Christian laws', to be obtained 'not by victory on the battlefield', but 'by the word of God'.[65]

On the pro-Catholic side, writers condemned a string of historians (including Musgrave) for depicting Irish Catholics in a false light. All this seemed to confirm the importance of religion as a cause of divisions in Ireland.[66] However, several of these critics stressed that problems had arisen long before the Reformation. Burke himself had suggested that 'the spirit of the Popery laws . . . as applied between Englishry and Irishry, had existed . . . before the words Protestant and Papist were heard of' and this cue was widely taken up.[67] Although Geoffrey Keating had regarded the first English invasion relatively benignly, there had always been Catholic historians who dissented,[68] and among pro-Catholic writers a negative view now became general. According to Dennis Taaffe, from the first English incursion, 'the Popish pale was as truly hostile to the national interest as the Orange confederation may be supposed now'. The real problem was 'clashing interests and national antipathies, necessarily subsisting between a conquering and an oppressed nation'. Liberal Protestant William Parnell set out to show from history that 'it is the principle of persecution adopted against the religion which makes the Catholics zealous and disaffected', and he traced persecution back to the

---

[64] Musgrave, *Memoirs*, 4–26, 582; see also James Kelly, *Sir Richard Musgrave 1746–1818: Ultra-Protestant Ideologue* (forthcoming).

[65] 'Address to the Protestant Young Men of Ireland', *The Warder*, 12 Sept. 1846; *Dublin Journal*, 24 Mar. 1804; *Reply of the Orangemen of Dublin to the Address of the Repealers* (Dublin, 1848), 6. See also Blackstock, *Loyalism*, 182–3, 214–16, 227–62.

[66] Taaffe, *Impartial History*, II, 377–80; *The Belfast Politics, Enlarged*, ed. John Lawless (Belfast, 1818), 1–2; Moore, *History*, II, 285–6, 342. See also Donal McCartney, 'The Writing of History in Ireland, 1800–50', *Irish Historical Studies*, 10 (1957), 353.

[67] Burke, *Langrishe*, 320.

[68] Abbé [James] MacGeoghegan, *Histoire de l'Irlande Ancienne et Moderne* (2 vols., Paris, 1758), I, xii–xiii.

medieval conquest, when the rights of native chieftains had been swept away by 'the English'.[69]

Not all critics agreed as to whether the twelfth-century invasion, or King William's victories, might properly be called conquests, but there was widespread agreement that the spirit emanating from both events was a conquering one, and that the English settlers, as well as the native Irish, had been victims of it. This helped explain why they in turn had oppressed the native Irish. According to Plowden, Henry II had behaved 'like a conquering despot to his Norman adventurers', making them 'feudatory princes' who had appropriated Irish land. This had laid 'the cornerstone of that rancorous animosity, which has withstood the revolutions of six centuries'. Thus 'the arrogance of conquest begat oppression [and] oppression engendered hatred and implacable revenge'. Taaffe noted that 'while the English colony ... so tyrannically ... persecuted the natives, their masters, in England, as arrogantly, deprived them of their legislative ... rights'.[70]

There was also a growing emphasis on racial differences: this was, after all, a period of early 'Celtic revival'.[71] Thomas Moore stressed the Celtic character of the Irish, denying that the first inhabitants of Ireland had originated in Britain, and praising Ireland's ancient Celtic laws and culture, which had only been finally subdued 'by the code of the conqueror' in the seventeenth century.[72] Moreover, by occasionally identifying the twelfth-century invaders as 'Normans', or 'Anglo-Normans' rather than 'English', as they had usually (and, it is argued, more correctly) been described, Moore was using a relatively new terminology, inspired in part by Sir Walter Scott's *Ivanhoe* (1819), and the French historian Augustin Thierry's *Histoire de la Conquête de l'Angleterre par les Normands* (Paris, 1825).[73] Both these works depicted the conquest of England as producing enmity between Normans and Saxons – 'animosity between conqueror and conquered' – which had endured until the 1190s, much longer than had been generally assumed.[74]

---

[69] Taaffe, *Impartial History*, I, 47; Parnell, *Historical Apology*, 3, 27–30.

[70] Plowden, *Historical Review*, I, 28–9; Taaffe, *Impartial History*, III, 571.

[71] Jeanne Sheehy, *The Rediscovery of Ireland's Past: The Celtic Revival 1830–1930* (1980), ch. 2; Damien Murray, *Romanticism, Nationalism and Irish Antiquarian Societies, 1840–80* (Maynooth, 2000), ch. 1.

[72] Moore, *History*, I, 1–2, ch. 2, 160.

[73] *Ibid.*, II, 213, 217, 222. For reasons for preferring 'English' to 'Normans' to describe the invaders, see 'Normans' in *The Oxford Companion to Irish History*, ed. S. J. Connolly (Oxford, 1998), 389–90, and John Gillingham, 'Normanizing the English Invaders of Ireland', in *Power and Identity in the Middle Ages: Essays in Memory of Rees Davies*, ed. Huw Price and John Watts (Oxford, 2007), 85–97. I am grateful to Professor Gillingham for allowing me to read his article before publication.

[74] Augustin Thierry, *History of the Conquest of England by the Normans; with its Causes, and Consequences to the Present Time* (1841), ix.

Thierry echoed Plowden and Taaffe in suggesting that a feature of the Irish conquest was that 'the conquerors of Ireland, justly classed as oppressors of the indigenous people, are to be considered as having been themselves equally oppressed by their countrymen who remained in England'. As for the native Irish, 'from the first day of the invasion the will of that race of men has been constantly opposed to the arbitrary will of its conquerors'. Hence, although 'the posterity of the Anglo-Normans has gradually become impoverished like that of the Irish', 'in our own days blood has flowed . . . for the old quarrel of the conquest'.[75] Thierry's concern for the fate of conquered peoples found a receptive audience among Irish Repealers, notably stimulating Thomas Davis's interest in conquest.[76] The Reverend James Godkin, a Presbyterian, produced a prize-winning Repeal Association essay in 1845, which discussed 'the Anglo-Norman conquest' of Ireland in the wider English and European context that Thierry had outlined, stressing the ill-treatment of Saxons by Normans in England as a precedent for the treatment of the Irish by Henry II, and (with a nod, too, to Lord Durham's report (1839) on the causes of conflict in Canada) highlighting 'the deadly antagonism of *races* between the English and the Irish'.[77]

Portraying internal Irish divisions in racial terms did not signify a desire to copper-fasten those divisions. The point was not to highlight biological difference between Celts and Saxons (or Normans), but to condemn conquest for fostering a slavish mentality on the one side, and arrogance on the other.[78] For these historians, racial conflict, however severe, could be overcome – as illustrated by Normans and Saxons in England. It was argued that in Ireland conquerors and conquered had occasionally been close to reconciliation, but England's influence had invariably blocked this.[79] According to Godkin, 'a *master*-nation will inevitably oppress' and therefore 'Ireland never can be one with England': the only solution lay in repeal of the Union.[80] When Thomas Davis observed that five-sixths of the Irish people were Celts, he merely intended non-Celts to recognise the value of cultural difference as a defence against English

---

[75] *Ibid.*, 233–4, 273.

[76] Helen F. Mulvey, *Thomas Davis and Ireland: A Biographical Study* (Washington, 2003), 218–21.

[77] James Godkin, 'The Rights of Ireland', in *Repeal Prize Essays*, ch. 2, 33. Cf. 'I found a struggle, not of principles, but of races; . . . the deadly animosity that now separates the inhabitants of Lower Canada into the hostile divisions of French and English', in *The Report of the Earl of Durham* (new edn, 1902), x.

[78] Moore, *History*, III, 74–5; Godkin, 'Rights', 53.

[79] Thierry, *Conquest*, vii, 273–80; Godkin, 'Rights', 2, 24–5, 62.

[80] Godkin, 'Rights', 67, 144, 159.

misrule: 'Had Ireland used Irish in 1782, would it not have impeded England's re-conquest of us?'[81]

One work that brought together some of these themes was Macaulay's *History of England*. Published in 1848, and an immediate bestseller, it was a characteristically Whiggish history of gradual improvement, except where it touched on Ireland. Macaulay's account of English history down to the Normans treated prominently of race and conquest, but emphasised that by the early 1200s Norman and Saxon conflicts had been largely overcome. Any ambitions for continental conquest were abandoned after the Hundred Years War, and England had become celebrated as the best governed country in Europe. Medieval Ireland, however, was ruled 'as a dependency won by the sword'. 'The English colonists submitted to the dictation of the mother country ... and indemnified themselves by trampling on the people among whom they had settled.' As for 'the vanquished race', 'the new feud of Protestant and Papist inflamed the old feud of Saxon and Celt', and in 1641 'the smothered rage of the Irish broke forth into acts of fearful violence'. An admirer of the Glorious Revolution, Macaulay's ambivalence about its Irish counterpart was apparent in his account of 'the Saxon defenders of Londonderry' and 'the Celtic defenders of Limerick': 'to this day a more than Spartan haughtiness alloys the many noble qualities which characterise the children of the victors, while a Helot feeling, compounded of awe and hatred, is but too often discernible in the children of the vanquished'.[82]

And in Ireland, divisions continued. The Orange Order was dissolved under parliamentary pressure in 1825, and again in 1836, but anniversary commemorations were only temporarily interrupted. By the mid-1840s the Order was being reconstituted and experiencing one of several revivals. Orangemen associated the Repeal campaign's mass mobilisation of Catholics with the disturbances of the 1790s, and insisted that 'the blessings purchased by the brave blood of their fore-fathers' would not be handed over to 'rebel hands'.[83] Such attitudes posed problems for Repealers seeking electoral support from Protestants as well as Catholics. Addressing Protestant freemen (mostly artisans and tradesmen) in Dublin at the general election of 1847, the Irish Confederation (the political voice of Young Ireland) urged: 'You need not forget your fathers' victories, nor let their anniversaries pass by unhonoured, but honour them in a larger,

---

[81] Thomas Davis, *Literary and Historical Essays*, ed. Charles Gavan Duffy (Dublin, 1845), 176–8; see also Murray, *Romanticism*, 102–3.

[82] T. B. Macaulay, *The History of England from the Accession of James II* (4 vols., I and II, 1849, III and IV, 1855), I, 3–18, 67–8, 105, II, 127–9.

[83] Report of Enniskillen meeting, *The Warder*, 8 Aug. 1846.

more generous, and national spirit . . . Only in Ireland is memory of civil war perpetuated in the animosities of faction.'[84]

In conclusion, it has been argued that after a century in which the language of conquest mainly concerned Anglo-Irish relations, during the 1790s the focus shifted from external to internal conquest, and from medieval to seventeenth-century events. The main reason for this was the granting of extensive political rights to Catholics. Undertaken for essentially conservative reasons, this nevertheless had a destabilising effect because under the penal laws even plebeian Protestants had belonged to a privileged minority. One privilege had been the exclusive right to bear arms. During the eighteenth century, a culture of commemoration of Williamite victories had taken root outside the elite, marked by parades under arms. That tradition was resented by Catholics, as symbolising a spirit of conquest, even before the foundation of the Orange Order, which would reinvent the anniversary tradition and carry it forward into the 1800s and beyond.

Of course the proposition that Orangeism could be reduced to a single component was untenable. Those who paraded on 12 July were celebrating many things, including civil and religious liberty, loyalty to the dynasty and the link with Britain. They were also bidding defiance to 'Popery', perceived as inimical to those values and a threat to the very existence of Protestantism in Ireland. But given the exclusion of Catholics from membership,[85] and the significance accorded to Williamite victories, defenders of the Order could not be surprised if such anniversaries continued to rankle as symbolising Protestant conquest.

After 1798, the absence of reconciliation in Ireland between conquerors and conquered seemed more serious than ever. No agreed diagnosis was forthcoming. Ultra-Protestants highlighted Catholic bondage to Rome; evangelicals contended that little had been done to convert Catholics; Catholics and liberal Protestants blamed government. All sides paid lip service to the need to overcome divisions, and one attraction of redirecting the language of conquest outwards once more, against the Union, was the possibility of rekindling Protestant resentment against England's hegemony. Irish history was reinterpreted by liberal Protestants and Repealers, to emphasise the enduring effects of conquest by England from the twelfth century onwards in perpetuating internal divisions and damaging Anglo-Irish relations. (England was even accused of a general 'tendency to war' and a 'thirst of conquest'; which must have perplexed any English readers, more accustomed to associate such sentiments with

---

[84] Address of Irish Confederation to the Protestants of Ireland, *Freeman's Journal*, 8 July 1847.

[85] 'Rules of the Orange Society, 1798', in Senior, *Orangeism*, App. A, 299, 301.

the French.)[86] However, political realities at this period did not favour reconciliation. Even before Catholics finally obtained emancipation, Protestant support for reform and repeal of the Union was coming to be regarded by some Catholic leaders as merely auxiliary.[87] Meanwhile, Protestants increasingly saw their own interests as bound up with the Union, which the governing classes in Britain had come to consider, for the time being, as fundamental to British security. All this helped ensure that the various forms of conquest rhetoric remained highly adaptable.

Postscript: Speaking at his meeting with Mr Ahern at the battle of the Boyne site on 11 May 2007, Dr Paisley said:

For Protestants and Unionists the Boyne carries with it a powerful significance for our culture, our history and our pride. It represents liberty, triumph and determination, features that have too often been forgotten because of more recent troubles. [The Boyne has a wider European importance] but it is here in Ireland that the Boyne is most significant. I welcome that at last we can embrace this battle site as part of our shared history.

Presenting Mr Ahern with a Jacobite musket carried away from the battlefield, Dr Paisley concluded:

This musket was used by a soldier in King James's army, I need not remind you that was the losing side. But you can declare to this weapon, 'welcome home'.[88]

---

[86] Godkin, 'Rights', p. 144.

[87] Daniel O'Connell to Lord Cloncurry, 24 Sept. 1828, in *The Correspondence of Daniel O'Connell*, ed. M. R. O'Connell (8 vols., Dublin, 1972–80), III, letter 1489.

[88] *Irish Times*, 12 May 2007.

Transactions of the RHS 18 (2008), pp. 187–210 © 2008 Royal Historical Society
doi:10.1017/S0080440108000704   Printed in the United Kingdom

WRITING WAR: AUTOBIOGRAPHY, MODERNITY AND WARTIME NARRATIVE IN NATIONALIST CHINA, 1937–1946*

By Rana Mitter

READ 21 SEPTEMBER 2007

ABSTRACT. The Sino-Japanese War of 1937–45 was perhaps the single most destructive event in twentieth-century Chinese history. However, there has been relatively little attention paid to how war was experienced in the Nationalist-controlled area ('Free China') under Chiang Kaishek. Two autobiographical texts are examined here, one a sequence of reportage from the early war years by the journalist Du Zhongyuan, and one a *biji* (notebook) written immediately after the war's end by the social scientist Xu Wancheng. By choosing particular modern or anti-modern genres and styles to write in, the authors expressed a wider sentiment about the war's ambiguous role in modernising China. Du's work hopes to create modernity from destruction; Xu's suggests that modern warfare has created chaos.

When it comes to politics, those who have modern thoughts, and are uncorrupt and deal in facts, have come into this war without trauma, and developed their political strength. But those who in normal times have corrupt bureaucratic minds, who specialise in entertaining and socialising, and who carry out their tasks perfunctorily, have already become agitated and panicked, and are at their wits' end...But why must we despair? Why must we be pessimistic?...The Republic of China will inevitably have her great bright future, but we must go through a very painful course, and must work hard to overcome this pain.[1]

Du Zhongyuan, 1937

In Chongqing, there is male/female mixed bathing. In the tearoom of the bathhouse, you can bring in a woman to clean your back...Chongqing's bathhouses are very dirty. There's a stench of urine.[2]

Xu Wancheng, 1946

* I wish to thank the many friends and colleagues who commented on this paper, including the audience at the meeting of the Royal Historical Society where it was presented in September 2007. Other colleagues, including Glen Dudbridge, Akira Iriye, Chloe Starr and Hilde de Weerdt were of invaluable assistance in the revision of earlier versions. I am particularly grateful for a Philip Leverhulme Prize which enabled me to visit China and the USA and obtain materials for this paper which are unavailable in the UK.
  [1] Originally in *Dikang* (Resistance) (6 Oct. 1937), in *Huan wo heshan: Du Zhongyuan wenji* (Return Our Rivers and Mountains: Collected Essays of Du Zhongyuan), ed. Du Yi and Du Ying (Shanghai, 1998) [hereafter DZY], 270.
  [2] Xu Wancheng, *Chongqing huaxu* (Chongqing gossip) (Shanghai, 1946), 36.

On 7 July 1937, a military incident broke out at the village of Wanping near Beijing when soldiers of the Japanese north China garrison clashed with local Chinese troops. The incident ended quickly, but the Japanese nonetheless demanded major concessions from the Chinese authorities, which would have allowed the Imperial Army even greater influence in north China, building on Tokyo's expansion into the region since 1931. However, the Chinese reaction was unexpected. Up to that point, the leader of the ruling Nationalist (*Kuomintang* or *Guomindang*) party, Chiang Kaishek, had generally not resisted incursions in north China, knowing that the Chinese army was not yet sufficiently well trained to cope with the technologically superior Japanese armed forces. However, by early 1937, Chiang was more confident of the Chinese army's capabilities, and public opinion was no longer favourable to conciliation of the Japanese.[3] This time, Chiang refused the demands and escalated the conflict. Within weeks, he had opened up two fronts, one in the north of China near Beijing, and one in central China around Shanghai. The Sino-Japanese War had begun. Before it ended, some 15 million Chinese (a low estimate) would be killed, some 80 million would become refugees and a significant proportion of the country's hard-won modern infrastructure would be destroyed. In the words of Lloyd Eastman, the war was 'the most momentous event in the history of the Republican era in China'.[4]

In many countries, the events of the Second World War became central to the shaping of the post-1945 social fabric and cultural life, whether it was Britain's attempts to cope with a post-imperial role, the American rise to superpower status or Japan's and Germany's desire to reshape their roles as peaceful post-war democracies. However, in China, there was relatively little such opportunity to reflect on wartime experience and absorb it into nation-building myths. Political imperatives imposed by the Cold War meant that in Mao's China, very few aspects of the wartime experience could be discussed, and that the history of the war became important primarily as a means of explaining the Chinese Communist Party's (CCP) rise to power. Only in the past decade or two has it been feasible to explore aspects of China's wider wartime experience, and, in doing so, understand much more fully the significance of that experience in shaping China's path for the six decades and more that have followed the war itself.

This paper takes advantage of the new arena for the discussion of wartime in China to argue for a reinterpretation of that experience as a struggle for a new narrative of Chinese modernity and identity.

---

[3] See Parks Coble, *Facing Japan: Chinese Politics and Japanese Imperialism, 1931–1937* (Cambridge, MA, 1991), ch. 9 ; Marjorie Dryburgh, *North China and Japanese Expansion, 1933–1937: Regional Power and the National Interest* (Richmond, Surrey, 2000), ch. 5.

[4] Lloyd E. Eastman, 'Nationalist China during the Sino-Japanese War', in L. Eastman *et al.*, *The Nationalist Era in China, 1927–1949* (Cambridge, 1991), 115.

Using the autobiographical writings of two figures who reflected on the experience of war, I suggest that there was a conscious attempt from the very earliest days of the war to create a positive narrative of progress from the war's events, and to portray it as a force for the renewal of a recently formed but already deeply flawed Chinese modernity. However, that narrative became subverted from within by an increasing realisation that the modernising narrative itself had failed. In particular, it did not capture the non-teleological absurdity of the wartime experience as well as a widespread, almost postmodern, anti-narrative perception of what had happened in wartime China.

The story of the Second World War in China has always been a battle between narratives, and it remains one today. At one level, this is an obvious statement; but it is worth noting that until very recent years, the understandings that we have of the events and significance of wartime in China have been the products of very *specific* narrative strategies, and ones that have become so ingrained in historical consciousness that historians have tended to frame their debates within their parameters, consciously or otherwise. The following few lines give a thumbnail sketch of a common understanding both in the west and the People's Republic of China (PRC) (Taiwan has its own rather different historiographical trajectory with regard to the war against Japan): that during the Sino-Japanese War, a Nationalist government under Chiang Kaishek failed to offer much resistance to the invasion of China, instead retreating to the interior, and that in contrast the Communists carried the greatest burden of the fighting in resistance to Japan. Each of these understandings is now subject to significant revision by specialists in the field, and was in fact disputed by many knowledgeable figures at the time. However, during the Cold War, the Sino-Japanese War was interpreted in the west and in China itself primarily as a staging-post in a teleological narrative of Communist victory. Immediately after the war ended in 1945, political considerations in the west also reinforced an existing preconception that the China Theatre had been of secondary value in the overall war effort; that it had been under the control of an incompetent and now irrelevant figure (Chiang Kaishek); and that study of its complexities, already difficult because of the closing of China to the west, was not worth a great deal of effort. The restrictions of the Cold War also meant that the PRC was unwilling to open up discussion of a conflict in which the Nationalists had played their part in opposing Japan, and the west was equally unwilling to give much thought to the wartime efforts and suffering of a country which had moved from the allied to the enemy camp after the Communist victory in 1949.[5]

---

[5] The classic popular history statement of this viewpoint remains Barbara Tuchman, *Sand against the Wind: Stilwell and the American Experience in China* (New York, 1972). Tang Tsou's *America's Failure in China* (Chicago, 1963) remains a standard scholarly account of the

This began to change in the 1980s, as the War of Resistance to Japan (as the Sino-Japanese War of 1937–45 is still known in China itself) has begun to emerge in the historiography of modern China as a traumatic event to rival the other, more prominent, catastrophes in recent history: the Civil War of 1946–9, the Cultural Revolution and the Great Leap Forward. The reexamination of the narratives that underpinned wartime China depended on a variety of historiographical changes that emerged in the 1980s and 1990s. The most important overall change in focus is the move away from concentration on the role of the CCP. From the 1960s to the 1980s, much of the scholarship in the west and the vast majority of scholarship within the People's Republic of China concentrated on the problematique of war as a catalyst to peasant revolution under the CCP.[6] Yet most of China in 1937–45 was under the control of either the Nationalist government ('Free China') or else collaborationist governments dealing with the Japanese. This has led to a more complex historiography which takes account of the differing nature of experience and ideology during the war years across all of China.[7] For instance, much Cold War historiography was underpinned by an interpretation of the decline of the Nationalists and rise of the Communists that owed something to melodrama: a need for heroes and villains. Examination of archival evidence has suggested that the wartime Nationalist record, while marked by corruption, inefficiency and human rights abuses, needs to be understood in the context of the massive social crisis that was engendered by the arrival of some millions of refugees in the woefully under-equipped region of Sichuan where the government in exile retreated.[8] These interpretations are not intended to rehabilitate the Nationalists or denigrate the Communists, in a rerun of Cold War-era arguments about 'who lost China': rather, they subject China's wartime experience to the same powerful mixture of social and political analysis that has long been standard for societies such as Britain, the USA and

---

aftermath of the war, and a powerful revisionist view of the 'Stilwell myth' is Hans van de Ven, *War and Nationalism in China, 1925–1945* (2003), ch. 1.

[6] A very useful review essay is S. Pepper, 'The Political Odyssey of an Intellectual Construct: Peasant Nationalism and the Study of China's Revolutionary History – A Review Essay', *Journal of Asian Studies*, 63, 1 (2004), 63.

[7] See, for instance, Timothy Brook, *Collaboration: Japanese Agents and Chinese Elites in Wartime China* (Cambridge, MA, 2005), and van de Ven, *War and Nationalism in China*. The most important Chinese outlet for the new scholarship is *Kang-Ri zhanzheng yanjiu* (Research on the War of Resistance), published by the Chinese Academy of Social Sciences (1991–).

[8] Stephen MacKinnon points out that the numbers of refugees are still highly disputed, and cites numbers from 3 to 90 million ('Refugee Flight at the Outset of the Anti-Japanese War', in *Scars of War: The Impact of Warfare on Modern China*, ed. Diana Lary and Stephen MacKinnon (Vancouver, 2001), 119). However, the majority of estimates place the number at the much higher end of this scale.

even the USSR.[9] The Nationalists have been partially rehabilitated as sincere, if often ineffective and corrupt, patriots whose contribution was an important part of the wider struggle against Japan.

Yet in some respects, the *nature* of the discourse within China has not altered greatly. Previously, the War of Resistance made up part of a narrative of heroic struggle against Japanese imperialism, led by the CCP. Since the 1980s, it has instead been the story of Chinese nationalism, with CCP and Nationalists both in prominent roles, in opposition to Japan as part of a world anti-fascist war. However, the war remains trapped in a different sort of teleological narrative in which the end-point, now located in the victory over Japan in 1945 rather than the CCP's victory in 1949, leads to an ultimately beneficial result, the establishment of an independent China (the unfortunate fratricide of the Civil War is now swiftly passed over in this account). However, this new teleology fails to capture the way in which, for many Chinese, the War of Resistance was not experienced at the time as part of a series of linear developments within the trajectory of Chinese nationalism, but rather was responsible for a culture of disorientation shaped by fear of the unknown. The most characteristic events of everyday experience for Chinese all across the country were bombings and refugee flight: in other words, events that shattered the stability of everyday life, and particularly of the sense of place which underpinned Chinese society. It was a very non-teleological event. The fact that at the time, and for the generations that followed, it has been possible to trace the changing but clear narratives that have defined the war's meaning in China is a tribute to the resilience of the narrative strategies that quickly arose to underpin the wartime experience.

War in the first person

In 2000, the collector Fan Jianchuan published his book *One Person's War of Resistance* (*Yi ge ren de kangzhan*). Despite the title, it is not a memoir but rather an intriguing set of reflections by a collector of memorabilia from the wartime years, who discusses his understanding of contemporary Chinese identity in the context of rediscovering wartime history.[10] The

---

[9] Among recent articles on China's changing attitude toward its own wartime history are A. Waldron, 'China's New Remembering of World War II: The Case of Zhang Zizhong', *Modern Asian Studies*, 30, 4 (1996), 945–78; R. Mitter, 'Old Ghosts, New Memories: Changing China's History in the Era of Post-Mao Politics', *Journal of Contemporary History*, 38, 1 (2003), 117–31; and P. Coble, 'China's "New Remembering" of the Anti-Japanese War of Resistance 1937–1945', *China Quarterly*, 190 (June 2007), 394–410.

[10] Fan Jianchuan, *Yi ge ren de kangzhan: cong yi ge ren de cangpin kan yi chang quan minzu de zhanzheng* (Beijing, 2000). This and other first-person contemporary texts are discussed in Rana Mitter, 'China's "Good War": Voices, Locations, and Generations in the Interpretation of the War of Resistance to Japan', in *Ruptured Histories: War and Memory in Post-Cold War Asia*, ed. Sheila Jager and Rana Mitter (Cambridge, MA, 2007).

interpretation of first-person accounts of wartime in China is still at an early stage, and the field has not yet thoroughly developed the type of complex reading of traumatic experience that marks the interpretation of western warfare, and in particular, the Holocaust.[11] Arguments have begun to circulate about the Chinese twentieth-century experience as shaped by 'survivor guilt', but this interpretation is still in a preliminary phase, and much of this discussion is primarily concerned with the Cultural Revolution or Great Leap Forward, and is often the province of anthropologists and literary critics rather than historians.[12] Of course, it is important to stress that the War of Resistance is not equivalent to the Holocaust: most of the arguments that are made about the comparability of one set of atrocities to another are emotional and political, not historical, in their concerns.[13] However, Andrea Reiter has usefully reflected on the variety of interpretative techniques that have been used in analysing the Holocaust, particularly creative use of autobiography:

> Which linguistic devices, which genres, do the survivors rely upon to communicate their experiences? How does literature in the broadest sense, and language and genre more narrowly, become a means of coming to terms with life?. . .From its mystical antecedents onwards, the autobiographical genre has changed time and time again to take account of the most recent experience of life.[14]

Autobiography is particularly valuable in that it allows analysis of self-presentation and subjectivity, and in twentieth-century China, allows us to assess the ways in which modernity, and its sudden disruption by war, was experienced and expressed. There is a lively debate about the point of origin of the modern self in China. Nonetheless, the impact of a western-derived, imperialist modernity in China from the late nineteenth century onward demanded a profound rethinking of how the individual should be defined in relation to the wider society.[15]

Du and Xu were both clearly shaped by that modernity and the way in which it forced a new assessment of the role of the individual in society. However, each of them expressed that reshaping in a very distinct sort of autobiographical writing. Du Zhongyuan (1895–1944) wrote reportage from the battle front and from cities that were major targets for the Japanese in 1937–8. Xu Wancheng (1905– ?) wrote an account

[11] But see *Scars of War*, ed. Lary and MacKinnon.
[12] See for instance Charles Laughlin, *Chinese Reportage: The Aesthetics of Historical Experience* (Durham, NC, 2002).
[13] On this question, see the essays in *The Nanking Atrocity: Complicating the Picture*, ed. Bob T. Wakabayashi (Oxford, 2007).
[14] Andrea Reiter, *Narrating the Holocaust*, trans. Patrick Camiller (2000), 2.
[15] One point of entry into this debate by a prominent Chinese political philosopher is Wang Hui, 'Zhang Taiyan's Concept of the Individual and Modern Chinese Identity', in *Becoming Chinese: Passages to Modernity and Beyond*, ed. Wen-hsin Yeh (Berkeley, 2000).

of Chongqing's wartime experience in the immediate aftermath of the Japanese surrender in 1945; yet he himself had not been in Chongqing, but in occupied Shanghai, during the war. Who were these two writers, and what makes their writing relevant for a wider understanding of the times they lived through?

Du Zhongyuan was born in the Chinese north-east (then widely known as Manchuria). He studied in Japan, and in the 1920s, became a prominent entrepreneur in Shenyang (Mukden), first running a brick factory, then moving on to his real love, the manufacture of porcelain. He also became an adviser to Zhang Xueliang ('The Young Marshal') (1901–2001), the militarist ruler of the region from 1928 to 1931. Zhang was the son of a classic warlord, the regional ruler Zhang Zuolin, who was primarily concerned with conquest, and was eventually assassinated by the Japanese in 1928. His son was no less interested in power, but, unlike his father, was convinced that nationalism was the best ideological solution for China, and allied Manchuria with Chiang's Nationalist government in 1928 on the understanding that Chiang would have little practical influence within the north-east. Zhang also sponsored spending on education and infrastructure in the region, earning a reputation as one of the more progressive militarist leaders within the precarious Chinese republican structure. As a prominent local business leader, Du became close to Zhang because the latter was interested in commercial development as a means of strengthening the region against foreign influence, particularly Japanese and Soviet. At the same time, Du also became friendly with Zou Taofen, the editor of *Life* (*Shenghuo*), the single most successful weekly publication in Republican China, which may have had up to 2 million readers at its peak. The sudden invasion of Manchuria by the Japanese on 18 September 1931 saw prominent political figures including Du Zhongyuan forced to flee the region. Over the next few years, a substantial Manchurian Chinese exile community kept up pressure on Chiang Kaishek, trying to persuade him to recapture Manchuria. Chiang did not fall in with their wishes; he felt, with some justification, that China's forces were simply too weak and until 1937, opted instead for a policy of diplomatic protest rather than military resistance to Japan, while at the same time using a German adviser to revitalise the Chinese army and also encouraging secret economic planning for a war against Japan via the government's National Resources Commission.[16]

Du wrote regular columns in *Life* supporting the recapture of Manchuria, and when Zou Taofen was forced to leave the country in 1933, under Nationalist government pressure, Du took over and wrote weekly columns in a successor journal, *New Life* (*Xinsheng*). Eventually,

[16] On the NRC, see Xie Yi, *Guomin zhengfu ziyuan weiyuanhui yanjiu* (Research on the Nationalist Government's National Resources Commission) (Shanghai, 2005).

the Japanese threatened to create a diplomatic incident because of a column in Du's journal that insulted the emperor of Japan, and Du was imprisoned for fourteen months in 1935–6. During the 1930s, his frustration with Chiang's policies meant that he began to sympathise with the CCP, although he never joined the party. The outbreak of war with Japan meant that his anti-Japanese sentiments were no longer politically problematic, and he became a frontline reporter for the journal *Resistance (Dikang)* in 1937–8, from which many of the writings considered here are taken. Shortly afterward, he accepted a position as head of the Xinjiang Academy, the major higher education institute in China's most westerly province, but in 1941, the local militarist ruler, Sheng Shicai, turned against Du and other CCP fellow-travellers, and he was arrested and imprisoned. He died in still-mysterious circumstances in prison in Urumqi in 1944.[17]

Xu Wancheng followed a profession which owed something to the old Confucian tradition of 'rectification of names' (*zhengming*) and a great deal to the emergence of social sciences in China. He was a 'social investigator', a compiler of information which he then published and sold on a commercial basis. His major work in this area was a listing of Shanghai's major schools, which he divided up into 38 colleges, 199 middle schools and 1,275 primary schools. The success of this work enabled him to give up his own job as a teacher and set up his own bookshop and publishing enterprise. In 1935, he and a team of colleagues produced a guide to libraries throughout China, with detailed information about their classification systems and visitor numbers. However, his interests were not just quantitative. He also investigated social change by sponsoring questionnaires that asked newspaper readers about a variety of social issues including marriage, education, employment and love. His motivation was shaped by an assumption that individual problems ('atoms', in the social scientific phrasing of the time) were reflected in wider crises within society.[18]

The politics of style

In some respects, Du Zhongyuan and Xu Wancheng would appear to be similar in their political positions. Both were Chinese patriots opposed to the Japanese invasion, and both condemned collaboration with the enemy, even though they expressed nuanced views on this question,

[17] On Du Zhongyuan, see R. Mitter, 'Manchuria in Mind: Press, Propaganda, and Northeast China in the Age of Empire, 1930–37', in *Crossed Histories: Manchuria in the Age of Empire*, ed. Mariko Asano Tamanoi (Honolulu, 2005), and Rana Mitter, *A Bitter Revolution: China's Struggle with the Modern World* (Oxford, 2004).

[18] Zheng Zu'an, '"Diaochajia" Xu Wancheng' (The 'investigator' Xu Wancheng), *Dang'an yu shixue* (2001/3), 58–60.

understanding if not excusing acts of collaboration under desperate circumstances. They were also both products of the May Fourth era, the period of relative freethinking in the 1910s and 1920s, when the idea of 'science and democracy' as the recipe for 'saving China' had great currency: 'science', with the wider implication of empirical rationality or *Wissenschaft*, and 'democracy' suggesting popular participation rather than specifically the mechanics of elections. Xu's interests in social scientific method and Du's in widening political participation clearly speak to both sets of concerns and mark them out as exponents of a modernity that defined itself in terms of a rational, dynamic forward progression for both the individual and society. Crucially, both were also public figures who had commercial success. Du was a 'brand-name' weekly columnist who was read by hundreds of thousands (perhaps more), and Xu had also been successful enough to live off his publications. The two of them, therefore, were not simply writing for themselves, but had a recognisable public: for that reason, their attitudes toward the war are significant in that they relate to self-presentation to an identifiable readership, primarily the emergent urban lower middle class (*xiao shimin*) that had been torn apart by the impact of war in 1937.[19] Despite these similarities, however, the contrasts between the two were greater.

Both Du and Xu write about wartime experience in the first person and use the *baihua* ('plain language') vernacular style to do so. However, the contrast in the style in which they write, and the genre within which they express themselves, not only shows the different possibilities that existed as part of the first-person narrative, but also the way in which the choice of style and genre could *in themselves* express attitudes toward the war. Reiter addresses the question of how choice of genre was used by Holocaust survivors to tell their stories: the contrasting genres of the Hasidic folktale and the travel report were adapted as frameworks to narrate events which corresponded to nothing in the experience or collective memory of those who lived through them.[20]

Stylistically, Du revealed himself as influenced by the new, reportage style of journalism that had emerged in the 1920s. This type of writing reflected an American-influenced interest in objectivity and clear reporting, with events set down in a modern, unadorned style.[21] Du was a friend of Fan Changjiang, one of the most prominent members of the New Journalism school, although by the late 1930s, Du had his own, very

[19] The concept of *xiao shimin* is detailed in Hanchao Lu, *Beyond the Neon Lights: Everyday Shanghai in the Early Twentieth Century* (Berkeley, 2000), 61–3.

[20] Reiter, *Narrating the Holocaust*, ch. 2.

[21] On reportage as journalism, see Chang-tai Hung, *War and Popular Culture: Resistance in Modern China, 1937–1945* (Berkeley, 1994), 39–48; on reportage as literature, see Laughlin, *Chinese Reportage*, 1–36.

distinct, journalistic reputation. His war reportage was written in plain, colloquial language, with numerous conversations set on the page as if taken down in the heat of the moment, and plenty of reflection on events with the reader as confidant. Conversational asides within the reports such as 'We were meant to set off from Shanghai at 6 p.m., but we Chinese don't stick to agreed times, so when we set off it was already getting toward 7 p.m.' are common and reflect the intimacy created with the reader (who as a regular magazine purchaser was likely to have known of Du's writings for some seven years or so).[22] To western readers, Du's style reads very naturally, but the very fact of this seeming naturalism shows how skilful the construct was, since the use of the vernacular in an explicitly first-person pronoun (*wo*) was a relatively new literary device, a product of the *baihua* movement that sought to make written Chinese more similar to the language as it was spoken, superseding the classical forms that still dominated 'respectable' writings such as newspapers or textbooks.[23] Du's seeming spontaneity was the product of very careful construction. He wrote in a first person that stressed the individuated self and its activities, and embraced a narrative of the war as a positive, modern force that had the potential to change China for good into a country that was centralised, industrialised and technologically empowered. Between his asides and homely anecdotes, he promoted a political agenda that was quite clear, encouraging the incorporation of north-west China (Xinjiang province) within a much stronger centralised economic and political framework, and setting up agencies to make it easier to transmit news around the country; in other words, the sinews of the Andersonian 'imagined community' of the nation, a political formation that was still highly contested in the China of the 1930s.[24]

Xu Wancheng's self-presentation was significantly different from Du's. His 1946 work *Chongqing huaxu* ('Chongqing gossip') was in stark contrast to Du's war reportage, both in his self-portrayal and his depiction of the war. This is not just a matter of chronology, although Xu was of course able to see the troubled aftermath of the war in a way that Du was not; nonetheless, even though by 1946 Xu could see the destruction that the war had wrought on the Nationalist state, the reality that surrounded Du in 1937 was highly destructive and chaotic. Rather, the genre in which Xu presents his thoughts on the war is in itself important in understanding his attitude toward it. Instead of the modern reportage style which Du

[22] Orig. *Dikang* (23 Sept. 1937), in DZY, 257.

[23] But for the persistence of the classical tradition in twentieth-century bureaucratic examinations, see J. Strauss, 'Symbol and Reflection of the Reconstituting State: The Examination Yuan in the 1930s', *Modern China*, 20/2 (Apr. 1994), 211–38.

[24] Benedict Anderson, *Imagined Communities: Reflections on the Origins and Spread of Nationalism* (1983).

favoured, Xu consciously styled his work as a *biji*. The term was used in the late imperial era to refer to the private writings of literati, often in a scholarly jotter or notebook in which short comments would follow on one from another, often in seemingly random order. The *biji* was not one of the canonical forms in traditional Chinese literature, but it was a recognised form, and in its heyday, used for a variety of strategies: it could be an exploration into the Confucian self, it could be a means of showing the cultural level or power of the writer and it could be used to record the pleasures of everyday random living. Yet while the use of the genre was not unknown in the twentieth century, to adopt it in 1946 suggests a rather conscious archaism and a desire to contrast oneself from the now-common modernity of linear narrative.[25]

Xu's use of the *biji* form suggests his own ambiguity about China's wartime experience. Crucially, Xu chose not to write about his own wartime experience, but instead to reconstruct the experience of a part of China where he had *not* been during the war. During the war, Xu had lived in Shanghai under Japanese occupation. His trip to Sichuan to visit the wartime capital took place over several months from December 1945 to September 1946, and his impressions and anecdotes were gathered during that time. While Du wrote in a continuous first-person narrative, a story developing in real time, Xu, as in the traditional *biji*, moves from topic to topic without any necessary link.

The impression given is of a disjointed narrative without a clear teleology. Yet this impression has its own significance, since it becomes increasingly clear that Xu sees the post-war settlement as suffering from the same problem of how the state that had won the war could now progress politically. Du Zhongyuan's genre is teleological and narrative. Xu Wancheng's is non-linear and non-teleological; Du invites metanarrative, Xu defies it.

Xu engages directly with the legendary status of Chongqing as a key site of resistance during the war, noting that

> Chongqing was China's heart during wartime, the base area that led the whole country in the war of resistance, the place where the government and leadership were. Military, political, and legal edicts came from there, and it was the political centre. This was the base for economic construction in the Interior (*da houfang*).[26]

---

[25] There is very little scholarly work on the *biji* as such, although there is plenty on specific *biji*; this may be because it was not a canonical literary genre in traditional China. For an explanation of the genre, see Endymion Wilkinson, *Chinese History: A Manual* (Cambridge, MA, 2000), ch. 32 ('Biji'). For a stimulating discussion of limitations of the traditional genres of Chinese literary writing, see 'A thousand years of literary narrative in China', in Glen Dudbridge, *Books, Tales, and Vernacular Culture: Selected Papers on China* (Leiden, 2005).

[26] Xu, *Chongqing huaxu*, 1.

This narrative of Chongqing as 'China's heart' was not a purely Chinese construction: the journalist Theodore White, sent by Time-Life Publications to wartime Chongqing, described the defence of the city in *Thunder out of China* as 'an episode shared by hundreds of thousands of people who had gathered in the shadow of its walls out of a faith in China's greatness and an overwhelming passion to hold the land against the Japanese'.[27] Du Zhongyuan visited the city in his role as a director of the Sichuan Minsheng company shortly after it had taken up its role as wartime capital, in April 1938, and reflected on how it had changed since even the early 1930s:

> I had been to Chongqing seven years before. It was an utterly feudal place full of opium and gambling. This time, it was not the same as before. The roads had been newly repaired, the face of the city had changed, and government agencies filled up the whole city. There were lots of new advances on the cultural and industrial fronts. . .These new features made me harbour limitless hope about the future of the resistance war.[28]

Xu acknowledges the legend of Chongqing but also undermines it swiftly. Shanghai, where he himself spent the war, offered few legends, either heroic or horrific. After the initial, brutal bombings of the city in 1937–8, life became calm if hardly normal until the war ended.[29] Nor was Shanghai subjected to mass killings like those in Nanjing in 1937–8 (the notorious 'Rape of Nanking'). In contrast, Chongqing had been one of the most heavily bombed cities on earth from 1938 to 1943. Chongqing's suffering became part of a new, immediately post-war metanarrative. One example of this is a pictorial history of the war produced in Shanghai in 1947, which portrays the great raids on Chongqing of 3–4 May 1939 as a crucial event: yet this new reading of the war's meaning was to be superseded within a few years with Mao's victory in 1949.[30] And even during the period 1945–9 itself, an alternative to the grand narrative would emerge which portrayed wartime life as lived in the interstices rather than the grand sweep of history. Paul Pickowicz has skilfully analysed the disillusionment that characterised the immediate post-war period by examining the highly ambiguous films about the wartime experience that were produced and attracted large audiences in China in the years 1945–9. He cites the director Shi Dongtian, who in 1946 declared that for him,

---

[27] Theodore White and Annalee Jacoby, *Thunder out of China* (New York, 1946), 1.

[28] Orig. *Kangzhan* (24 Apr. 1938), in DZY, 276.

[29] See 'Introduction' by the editors in *In the Shadow of the Rising Sun: Shanghai under Japanese Occupation*, ed. Christian Henriot and Wen-hsin Yeh (Cambridge, 2004).

[30] *Zhongguo kangzhan huashi* (Pictorial History of the Chinese War of Resistance', ed. Shu Songqiao (Shanghai: Zhongguo shudian, 1947), 236. I am very grateful to Graham Hutchings for the loan of this rare item.

the task of filmmaking was to help himself and his friends 'understand why, in the months after victory, we felt defeated'.[31]

Xu's Chongqing *biji* is both premodern and postmodern in its form: a succession of matters great and small with little discrimination between them, and little desire to draw a larger lesson or framework in the way that had underpinned Du's seeming naturalism and conversational tone. Xu had, of course, had a role as an important and commercially successful compiler of social information in the years before 1937; this makes his abandonment of taxonomy and social scientific method in his *biji* particularly poignant, suggesting that the experience of war had disillusioned him with the promise of modernity to build a rational and ordered society.

The modern and the Confucian self

Both Du and Xu employed a self-presentation that combined elements of the premodern Confucian public persona with a very modern subjectivity. One sign of this is the apologia that both authors make for their intrusion in the public world of letters, the implication being that a truly public-minded figure keeps himself discreetly at a distance from any form of self-publicity. Du Zhongyuan did not make such an apologia in his war reporting. But he had had the opportunity to do so some three years earlier, at the start of one of the many troublemaking episodes in his life. In 1934, his journalistic colleague and mentor, Zou Taofen, had hastily left China after the Nationalist government had shut down his bestselling *Life* weekly magazine because of its strong pro-resistance line on the Japanese occupation of the north-east. Du took up the baton, launching a successor title waggishly named *New Life* (*Xinsheng*), subtitled on the masthead in English as 'The Renaissance Weekly'. He published a long opening letter in its first issue, showing both premodern and modern conventions of self-presentation:

> I am not a cultured man (*wenxuejia*), and I am not a news reporter, nor am I a famous or great character. Formerly, I was an entrepreneur in Shenyang. I set up a ceramics works with over 1,000 workers. Although the factory is still running, because I was not willing to fall in with Japanese imperialism, I became what I am now, a man with no home to return to, and with no trade to turn to.
>
> I don't know what country I am from. Can I say I am Chinese? My home village clearly is no longer part of China's territory. Can I say I'm not Chinese? But I was nurtured and raised in the same environment with 450 million compatriots; only because it is the cause of the Chinese people do I feel the pain and shame...There are people who are stray curs, like the slaves of a lost country, and now I have become a stray cur.

[31] P. Pickowicz, 'Victory as Defeat: Postwar Visualizations of China's War of Resistance', in *Becoming Chinese*, ed. Yeh, 396.

...But as I have experienced the pain of a lost country (*wangguo*), I therefore have the authority and the necessity to call out a war-cry to the masses of the whole country.[32]

While much of Du's language and political analysis is modern in origin, informed in particular by nationalism and Marxism, it is also implicitly, and on occasion, explicitly informed by a desire to adapt Confucian norms within a modern context. Du's self-declared modesty was part of that strategy. 'I am not a cultured man [or] a news reporter', Du had started by declaring, and a little further in the initial issue, another contributor started his open letter by declaring: 'Why don't I write essays [i.e. more formal literary prose] but instead write "letters"?...I could never write essays. Even when I was little and at school, I couldn't write essays well.'[33]

The *moral* imperatives of national salvation are also embedded everywhere in Du's writings, along with his exhortations to his readership to turn away from their own apathy and resist Japan. Yet the 'new' modern self is clearly visible in Du and his associates' self-presentation as well. The conventions of premodern autobiography mean that

> the disinclination to use the first person, perhaps a virtue in a historian, has rendered many an autobiography indistinguishable from biography; they share the same impersonality of tone, the same suppression of an individual voice with its own whims and quirks, the same opacity as to the yearnings of a heart or the inward workings of a mind.[34]

This is not true of Du Zhongyuan. For the traditional autobiographer, credibility rested on distance from subjectivity: for Du's purposes, credibility rested rather in exactly that subjectivity and a very strong personal voice.

Xu Wancheng starts *Chongqing huaxu* by noting:

> This book reports the secret story of the political stage of Chongqing...so that even people who had not fled to the Interior also should know the things that happened in the Interior during the War. I will only record facts, and will not add empty talk (relating the facts is the basis of human happiness).[35]

He elaborated:

> (1) I won't record anything that is not factual or is not pretty close to being factual...

---

[32] *Xinsheng* 1/1, 10 Feb. 1934, 1. There is a further discussion on Du's use of Confucian norms in public writing in R. Mitter, '"Life" as They Knew It: Du Zhongyuan's editorial strategies for the *Xinsheng* (New Life) Weekly, 1934–35', in *Reading China: Fiction, History and the Dynamics of Discourse*, ed. Daria Berg (Leiden, 2007); and in the contemporary context in Mitter, 'China's "Good War"'.

[33] *Xinsheng* 1/1, 10 Feb. 1934, 11.

[34] Pei-yi Wu, *The Confucian's Progress: Autobiographical Writings in Traditional China* (Princeton, NJ, 1990), 6–7.

[35] Xu, *Chongqing huaxu*, 2.

(2) Reading this book is like eating [snacks] – the flavours are not all the same! They are all varied.

(3) . . . I have no party, and no prejudice. . .just recording the facts.[36]

Much of Xu's self-presentation is Confucian in tone: it is self-deprecating and sceptical of much of the nature of modern politics. A true Confucian gentleman would be reluctant to join a party or a faction, and Xu's book ends with a round condemnation of all of China's major political parties as corrupt, brutal or irrelevant. Neither Du nor Xu were crude enough writers to demand that readers made a specific inference from their writings. Yet it is clear that there is a clear divide, in that Du's narrative strategy is one of creating a linear, teleological 'meaning' to the war, and Xu's is, if not hostile to meaning, at least indifferent toward it, or, at least, toward imposing a linear narrative on the recently concluded war. Reiter analyses this tension in the context of the Holocaust, in which experience that is beyond words in its destructiveness has to be placed somehow within the context of language and narrative.[37] At a time of clashing grand narratives (the Civil War breaking out around Xu as he wrote was such a narrative no less than the War of Resistance), he chose a consciously non-modern and diffuse genre in which to record the meaning of the war. Xu's take on the war is dry and unexplicit. He records Chiang Kaishek's defiant statements of resistance against the Japanese, but also discusses the corruption which marked the wartime capital. In doing so, he casts doubt on Du's 'limitless hope about the future of the resistance war' and suggests that it has been dissipated.

The war writings of Du Zhongyuan: modernity from chaos

It is not that Du was naïve and Xu was worldly-wise or cynical. Instead, they both used the experience of war to interrogate a newly formed and highly protean grand narrative: modernity and its Chinese inflection. Du's vision, perhaps precisely because of the desperation of his country's position at the time he was writing, was a very positive one about the potential for China to use the war as a vehicle for modernity. Xu's more elliptical observations suggest a more cautious view of the war's effects. Take, for instance, an observation from the streets of the capital just after

---

[36] *Ibid.*

[37] Reiter, *Narrating the Holocaust*, chs. 3 and 4. See also Imre Kertesz's novel *Fateless* ('Sorstalanság') (New York, 1975); the protagonist, Gyuri, repeatedly seeks to make rational explanations for the increasingly irrational events around him that eventually lead to him being sent to Auschwitz. On Holocaust fiction, also see Inga Clendinnen, *Reading the Holocaust* (Cambridge, 1999).

the war's end:

> At the headquarters of the Dazhong steamer company in Baixiang street in Chongqing, there are two advertisements. One says: This company's boat XX [*sic* – this indicates a generic name] is safe and swift from Nanjing to Shanghai. The second says: Travelling by boat is pretty dangerous, be quick to get insurance from this company.[38]

In this short anecdote, Xu shows the disruption of an only recently created modernity, with its fragility and contradictions. The juxtaposed pair of posters that Xu noted indicated the absurdity that could arise from the contradictory messages of two modern phenomena: one, the arrival of high-technology transport, and the other, an abandonment of Confucian ideas of 'fate' for the security of life insurance.

Much recent writing on Chinese modernity has concentrated on the performative aspects of a model that derives from Enlightenment assumptions about rationality, the shaping of an epistemology that stressed progress and the creation of a new, non-hierarchical mass identity.[39] Other work has also contributed to the idea that aspects of modernity, such as the creation of a 'public', were encouraged through the growth of mass-produced narrative prose.[40] Du Zhongyuan's old mentor Zou Taofen also contributed strongly to this tendency, using his widely read magazine to tell the life-stories of figures such as Curie, Edison and Pasteur, who seemed to him to embody the spirit of the age, the 'science and democracy' of the May Fourth era that were supposed to build a modern China.[41] Du's war reporting had to follow in this tradition by reconciling a difficult combination of factors: taking the reality of disorientation and disruption, finding points of continuity with the pre-war narrative of progress, and concluding that, counterintuitively, the chaos of war could in fact be the crucible of modernity.

In Du's writings, the most obvious indicator of disrupted modernity is the delayed train. The train had been a powerful symbol of modernity in China since the late Qing, albeit not always an entirely positive one: Zhang Henshui's popular novel *Pinghu tongche* (1930) portrayed the characters who rode the eponymous train as glamorous, but also potentially sinister, and

---

[38] Xu, *Chongqing huaxu*, 6.

[39] Chinese modernity is a huge topic and only a few indicative works can be named here; on literary performativity, see Leo Ou-fan Lee, *Shanghai Modern: The Flowering of a New Urban Culture in China, 1930–1945* (Cambridge, MA, 1999); on the links between modern consumerism and the 'exhibitionary complex', see Karl Gerth, *China Made: Consumer Culture and the Creation of the Nation* (Cambridge, MA, 2003); on the creation of modern citizenship, see Henrietta Harrison, *The Making of the Republican Citizen: Political Ceremonies and Symbols in China, 1911–1929* (Oxford, 2000).

[40] See, for instance, Eugenia Lean, *Public Passions: The Trial of Shi Jianqiao and the Rise of Popular Sympathy in Republican China* (Berkeley, 2007).

[41] Mitter, *A Bitter Revolution*, ch. 4.

out to rook the naïve and foolish.[42] Nonetheless, the train was crucial in providing cheap transport that could move very large numbers of people over long distances. Railways had just a few decades of existence in China by the time war broke out in 1937, and they had hardly had enough time to settle in the popular imagination as a symbol of technological progress before the war brought them under attack.

Trains (and his problems travelling on them) are central to Du's writing from the battlefront, and he uses them to illustrate two wider themes, both of which had changed significantly with the Sino-Japanese conflict: time and distance. These two concepts were useful to Du in that they linked literal and metaphorical disorientation, and enabled him to give a new interpretation to disasters which had been understood for centuries. Refugee flows, after all, had been known for years, with Jurchen and Xiongnu invasions from the north regularly causing Chinese imperial capitals to be emptied so that people could flee to safety. However, the refugee flight that took place during the War of Resistance was on a scale that simply could not have been imagined before new technology enabled the conflict to become 'total'. While the civil wars that had convulsed China in the 1910s and 1920s were large scale and had also been highly disruptive, they were still not on the scale of the post-1937 conflict.[43] Du's reporting was therefore able to take advantage of the unprecedented nature of the war to express the disruption of modernity.

One sign of that disruption appears in Du's obsession with time, and, in particular, time counted according to the western calendar. Naturally, timetelling had also been a longstanding Chinese institution, not least since China invented the water clock, but the late Qing and Republic meant that new methods of timing were necessary along with technological innovation: it would not have been easy, for instance, to run a railway without a timetable. Yet it is the disruption of this still-new temporal modernity that one sees in Du's writing overall:

> Our train ought to have got to Xuzhou at 1 a.m., and we would then have connected with the Longhai train, but because of the delays, we didn't get there till 5 a.m., and we had no choice but to get off the train and stay at the Huayuan hotel. At 6.30 p.m., the train starting moving west again. Although Xuzhou used to be a tourist spot, everyone was now tearing around in a hurry, and not looking properly at anything.[44]

Du repeatedly recounts train times and delays to his readers; on a journey to Taiyuan in September, he notes: 'I talked with Shao till 6, then got on the train to go west. When we got to Zhengzhou, it was 2 a.m.,

---

[42] Zhang Henshui, *Shanghai Express*, trans. William Lyell (Honolulu, 1997).

[43] On these wars, see Arthur Waldron, *From War to Nationalism: China's Turning Point, 1924–5* (Cambridge, 1995).

[44] Orig. *Dikang* (26 Sept. 1937), in DZY, 260.

and I changed to the Ping-Han train, to go north, and when we got to Shijiazhuang, it was already 6 p.m.'[45] Or else, on the way to Fengzhen,

> Fengzhen isn't more than a couple of hundred li from Datong, and I would get there in normal times in an hour or two, but this time, because the stations had all been raided by enemy planes, they were repairing them at the same time as running the trains. I got on the train at Taiyuan at 10 p.m., and we didn't arrive until 5 a.m.[46]

As Du had become one of the most prominent travel writers in the mid-1930s, with his weekly column from round the country published in *Life*, this type of reporting also drew on the world he had previously created for his readers: having written in a way that was supposed to let those readers associate a wider idea of China with new cultural and geographical insights and pleasures, the same journey was now being undertaken in circumstances of necessity and fear; Du makes the link between the China of pre- and post-1937 explicit in his frequent references to his earlier visits in his reportage.

Du's conversational style does not prevent him using highly literary images in his writing; for instance, descriptions of bad weather become a defining environmental determinant as Du's battlefront is caked in mud; when he and his companions get out of the car driving from Datong back to Taiyuan, they have to wade through the mud, and having climbed back into the vehicle, they are delayed by fog so that they get into the city at 1 a.m.[47] Then there are floods: in October, he 'went on to Ci county, and then I heard that the Zhang river had risen and submerged the bridge, and we had no choice but to return with the car to Shijiazhuang'.[48] Descriptions in detail now totally displace the old, formulaic tropes that Du had used to describe war in Manchuria ('suffering beneath the iron hooves of the Japanese'): a real change in the language of explaining war.

Casual language also helped to shape Du's style: in a piece about a businessman who thinks he knows it all, but predicts the war's progress in highly pessimistic terms, Du reports his conversation as:

> According to him, Chiang absolutely couldn't fight a war of resistance, the reason being that Japan's imperial army was so blah blah [*zenyang zenyang*] powerful, and China's troops were blah blah no good, and Japan's aircraft were blah blah just terrific, and China's aircraft were blah blah backward.[49]

One other linguistic trope, which would have previously been avoided in this sort of writing intended to inspire and elevate, was swearing. In the

---

[45] *Ibid.*

[46] Orig. *Kangzhan* (29 Sept. 1937), in DZY, 264.

[47] Orig. *Dikang* (3 Oct. 1937), in DZY, 267.

[48] Orig. *Kangzhan* (6 Oct. 1937), in DZY, 269.

[49] *Ibid.* (21 Aug. 1937), in DZY, 271. 'Blah blah' is not a literal translation: I have tried to bring over in the translation the way that Du's Chinese seems to express dismissiveness of the businessman's words.

1930s, Du's weekly column was notable for its earthy language, and he used this authentic-seeming form of speech to flavour his war reporting, as in a report on the breakdown of a car (again, the trope of dysfunction is important here):

> At 3 p.m., there was a car from the Sixth cavalry division returning to Taiyuan, and via the introduction of friends, I got a seat in it. There was a lot of rain for days on end, and the highway got even muddier; the car went 60 li, and suddenly there was a breakdown. The driver got down and spent ages doing repairs, and then we got on our way again. When it got dark, it broke down again. The driver angrily said: 'Today we're getting shitty [ma de] stuff we never usually get.' (Two cars breaking down at the same time, that's pretty rare.)[50]

This kind of writing in effect sets down conversations on the page. While the conversation itself may well have been constructed, the style is still innovative, because, however well disguised, Du's purpose is not literary experimentation, but political education. However, his approach to political education is very different from either the traditional exhortations from government during the Qing, or indeed from the parallel types of political writings, many supposedly aimed at the masses, which emerged in the early twentieth century. The writings of the Nationalist government, for example, via its exhortatory New Life campaign, were hardly designed to engender complicity with their readers. Nor, indeed, was much of Mao's writing, which is punchy enough, but generally wears its ideology very openly; it educates, to be sure, but is not intended to place the reader at the same level as the author. In the writings of political leaders and the ideological apparatus that they maintained, terms such as 'imperialism' and 'nation' come up frequently, but they are usually isolated within a rarefied, somewhat theoretical discussion, and rarely embedded in an account of lived experience.

Du's writings create a world whose flavour is clear and pungent even when read today. In the early 1930s, Du had written about the occupation of Manchuria by the Japanese, but he was hobbled in his ability to bring over the reality of occupation to his readers for two reasons: first, they were not themselves living under Japanese rule and had little way to understand that experience personally, and, second, Du himself was in exile and therefore writing at second hand about the situation in Manchuria. But in 1937, Du's readership were experiencing exactly the same disorientation that he was describing. What Du did was to reinterpret the chaos of wartime in terms that had some meaning. His writing is among the few places that ordinary readers could have related their everyday experience to a wider narrative that accounted for the sudden disruption in their lives. At the end of the homely anecdote in which the travellers had been forced to abandon their car after it broke down (hence the swearing), Du and

---

[50] Orig. *Dikang* (29 Sept. 1937), in DZY, 266.

his companions ended up walking to a village and breaking into the local bathhouse to sleep, being surprised by early morning bathers the next day. But Du follows up the bathhouse anecdote by asking: 'The country hasn't yet been defeated, and already people are suffering disaster – and who does everybody think gave us this distress?'[51] The relationship of everyday disaster to a wider narrative of anti-Japanese nationalism was crucial to Du's strategy. Furthermore, Du led his readers into an understanding of why war has changed. In another piece, he recalls a story well known to his readers about the single-handed defence of a Chinese city by the ancient Chinese general Zhuge Liang, but then subverts the connection he has made to premodern Chinese culture by noting: 'I often think about [what Zhuge Liang did], but in reality it wouldn't be possible...today's communications and today's weaponry cannot be compared with those of ancient times.'[52]

The ideological agenda is never hidden in Du's writing, and, after all, he had had years of previous experience as a propagandist that had made his public reputation in the first place. However, Du's talent was to present his propaganda to his readers in the guise of being the counsel of a friend. The style is not always attractive to the contemporary reader; one tends to see similarities with the sorts of kitschy false bonhomie identified by Paul Fussell in his analysis of the sort of sentimental writings in unofficial but popular writings about US involvement in the Second World War. Du Zhongyuan, having met the prominent general Li Zongren, came away from the meeting feeling that Li was 'not only worthy of respect, but also very lovable'.[53] Fussell, too, noted that patriotic writers in the wartime USA would use sentimentality to appeal to their readers, as in the piece by Carl Sandburg describing a modest tailgunner whose quiet demeanour apparently led an officer present to ask: 'Didn't you just want to reach out your arms and put them around him?'[54] But one should not ignore the power of this type of writing: Du knew what he was doing.

Xu Wancheng: chaos from victory

Xu Wancheng, in contrast, uses an elliptical and astringent style for his observations, relying on the readers to make inferences rather than presenting them with a direct statement. Early on, he observes that people came to Sichuan province (where Chongqing is situated) for a variety of different reasons.

[51] Orig. *Kangzhan* (29 Sept. 1937), in DZY, 266.
[52] *Ibid.* (6 Apr. 1938), in DZY, 274.
[53] *Ibid.* (6 Apr. 1938), in DZY, 275.
[54] Paul Fussell, *Wartime: Understanding and Behavior in the Second World War* (New York, 1989), 174.

> During this last seven or eight years, people from other provinces have been coming to Sichuan. Some people say that they 'came to Sichuan for resistance and reconstruction'. Others say they 'fled to Sichuan'. I praise the sentence that we 'fled to Sichuan' as honest talk (*laoshihua*).[55]

This deflating of the official narrative line sets the tone for much of the rest of Xu's reflections on the recently ended war. It is intriguing to think (though impossible to prove) that this opening statement may well be a deliberate dig against Du Zhongyuan, whose weekly column in *New Life* was called 'Honest Talk' (*Laoshihua*), as Xu's Shanghai readers would have known. Du had died two years earlier, but it was still only a decade or so since Du's column had been a talking-point among Shanghai's readers, and his progressive and modernising certainties of the 1930s would have seemed hollow to many in the months after the Japanese defeat. Ironically, by 1946, one of Du's most important anti-imperialist aims had been achieved; as a result of the Second World War, the old international concessions within Shanghai (and elsewhere in China) had been abolished permanently, and Shanghai was at last a unified city in an independent China. Yet the city did not seem a place of celebration for many living there at the time that Xu was writing.

Repeatedly, Xu uses short, seemingly pointless observations to hint at something wider about the war's effects on Chongqing and China more widely:

> Chongqing doesn't have any newsstands. It has a lot of tobacco kiosks, teahouses, and snack shops.[56]

Or:

> There are a lot of mice in Sichuan. There are a lot of sparrows too. If somebody could invent a trap for mice and sparrows, then they would be on sale everywhere. But Sichuan people couldn't catch sparrows. They didn't find out whether the flavour of sparrow was good enough to eat.[57]

The tone is not merely nihilistic. Xu does respect the role of Chiang Kaishek in resisting the Japanese:

> When Dushan was lost, Chongqing was in crisis. The heads of departments and ministries variously asked the Zongcai [Chiang Kaishek] where the government would move to. The Zongcai...replied, 'Even if the National Government has been bombed so that there is only one stone left, I'm still going to set up office on that one stone.'[58]

However, much more of the document makes it clear that the heroic myth of Chongqing resisting even if 'there is only stone left' has given

[55] Xu, *Chongqing huaxu*, 1.
[56] *Ibid.*, 4.
[57] *Ibid.*, 5.
[58] *Ibid.*, 6.

way to a much harsher reality:

> The big officials curse the middle officials, the middle officials curse the lower officials, the lower officials curse the *Jiwubing*, the *Jiwubing* go home and curse their wives, the wives curse the kids, the kids beat the little dogs and cats, and the little dogs and cats cry out tearfully.[59]

Another anecdote suggests a creeping cynicism that has infected the whole bureaucracy:

> Some bureaucrat developed a technique. . .When his superior swore at him strongly, he just stood to attention, and with a smile on his face, said: 'Yes. Yes. You're cursing me correctly.' After he went home, his wife would ask him why he didn't want face [i.e. personal dignity]. He replied: 'You really don't understand. The Head curses me. I then go and curse my subordinates. I've made no business loss. What need to get angry?'[60]

Furthermore, Du's vision of disrupted modernity, which was used in 1937 to project the idea that progress might come out of chaos, is made much less hopeful in Xu's vision, expressed in a little jingle that rhymes in Chinese:

> In Chongqing, the phone doesn't connect.
> The light doesn't light up.
> The roads are not flat. (*Chongqing dianhua bu ling, diandeng bu ming, malu bu ping.*)
> These are the three 'Nots'
> A big headache.[61]

Xu's *biji* is notable for its concentration on Chongqing, the location from which he was absent during the war years, and he makes only an occasional reference to his own experience in occupied Shanghai. When he does make the comparison, it is in the context of naming, something with which his pre-1937 role as a 'social investigator' gave him a great familiarity. He also makes a link between conditions in Chongqing and Japanese-occupied Shanghai that is politically daring by hinting at the ambiguous zone between resistance and collaboration during wartime:

> During the period of enemy occupation of Shanghai, names of roads changed a great deal. . .Changing the road name is the most silly and confused thing to do. If you only change the road name, and don't mend the road, then this is confused.
> Chongqing's road names also changed a lot.
> In Chongqing, it was difficult being unfamiliar with the street and having to go and ask the way. It wasn't that people were unwilling to tell you. The streets had old and new names, and they kept changing so it was no longer clear. When I returned to Shanghai, the names had changed yet again a lot. The names that had been changed during the enemy puppet period had changed again, but there were still some that had not been changed. Alas! China is a nation that changes names and yells out slogans![62]

---

[59] *Ibid.*, 8.
[60] *Ibid.*, 30.
[61] *Ibid.*, 34.
[62] *Ibid.*

But perhaps most pointed is one short anecdote that carries no explicit commentary at all:

In the winter of 1944, near the crossroads at Zhangjia gardens, two people were carrying a jar. They stopped for a rest. Suddenly you couldn't see the two people any more. You could see the inside of the jar: there were a human head, and human hands and feet, and various pieces of human flesh. The blood and the flesh were all mixed up.[63]

Conclusion

The experience of Chongqing and the surrounding areas forced the emergence of a narrative of war that was tinged with uncertainty. For this was not the war as seen in the Rape of Nanking, with a clear and obvious enemy; nor did it have the sullen certainty of life under occupation, nor even the ideological underpinnings of the base areas controlled by the Communists. Rather, it was the unease and uncertainty of a 'Free China' which was always under threat from the air, and the end point of whose narrative remained uncertain up to, and in many ways, even beyond 1945.

Yet it is also worth noting that attitudes toward the wartime experience under the Nationalists were not wholly negative; or, rather, that the negativity was nonetheless informed by realisation that the myth of resistance had been fuelled by something more than mere propaganda. Du and Xu each drew his authority to speak from a very different source. Du used his presence on the front to give himself *authenticity* as a reporter, whereas Xu used his absence from wartime Chongqing to give himself *objectivity* as a later observer. For Du, it was important to say 'I was there'; for Xu, it became a source of strength rather than weakness to say 'I was not there.' Yet Xu's writing is also tinged by a melancholy at having been absent and having lived through less heroic times. The young Israeli novelist Ron Leshem caused controversy with his 2005 novel *Beaufort*, which describes a group of soldiers involved in the final Israeli withdrawal from Lebanon in 2000. The novel makes it clear that the fictional protagonist, who stays in Lebanon until the last moment of withdrawal, thinks that 'it was all for nothing'. Yet the author, in an afterword, is at pains to point out that as a young Israeli, he felt compelled to write about Lebanon as a traumatic moment in his country's history precisely because he himself had *not* been there: 'the deep, personal feeling of having missed something by not having been there and experienced it. . .are what brought me to write this book'.[64]

Xu's work is not partisan, and his *biji* ends with a despairing account of the inadequacy of all political actors in the China of 1946. Some of its complaints, for instance about corruption within the Nationalist

[63] *Ibid.*, 23.
[64] Ron Leshem, *Beaufort* (2008), 304, 310.

government, echo those of the CCP, and the western observers who became increasingly disillusioned at the degeneration of the Nationalist regime in Chongqing. He observes of the Nationalists:

> Once the revolution had succeeded, the Revolutionary Party (the Nationalists)...took national power, but then a lot of politicos and grafters flooded in...who depended on the party to eat, and had no idea what the Three People's Principles [of Sun Yatsen] were, or the National Revolution. Everywhere appeared the so-called 'Party old gents' or 'Party thugs'.

But the solution is not, for Xu, the CCP:

> But the Chinese, when we talk about communism, are talking about a tiger's face and skin! Why? Because the CCP sets fires and kills people, and in everything its talents are for destruction. When they get to a place, 'they reach the place and take the resources'. They carry out the Three Alls policy. ['Burn all, kill all, destroy all': a reference to the Japanese Army policy of the same name.] Whoever in a place has money or power...they kill them all, not asking the right or wrongs of it.

Xu's linking of the CCP's tactics to those of the marauding Japanese (the 'Three Alls') is just as inflammatory as his earlier comparison of street name changes under the Nationalists and the occupation government in Shanghai, and just as dismissive of pious myths of resistance. He concludes bleakly: 'As the blood flows between Guomindang and CCP, the ordinary people are suffering!'[65] For Xu, the final legacy of an ambiguous war was a political aporia, a tragedy with no catharsis.

Du Zhongyuan was lucky, albeit only in a very limited sense. He died in 1944 before it became clear that the narrative of modernisation through war that he had helped to propagate was deeply flawed. Of course, just five years later, the arrival of the Chinese Communist Party in power substituted a new modernising ideology upon the people of the country, this time penetrating and moulding society in a way that none of its predecessors – the late imperial governments, the militarists of the early Republic, and the Nationalists – had managed to do. But this was done at the price of huge distortion of the narratives of wartime experience. The ambiguities and disappointments felt by millions, and articulated by Xu Wancheng, were simply swept away by a new party-state that had no time or interest in recalling any aspects of the war against Japan except those that helped to cement a new narrative of Communist victory. In this version of history, there would be no positive contributions of any sort by the Nationalists toward victory, and collaboration with the Japanese would be condemned simply as anomalous treachery. It would be nearly half a century before Chongqing would be allowed to remember the full scale of its wartime experience; and even now, the space to remember and to grieve is constrained by the demands of contemporary ideology, looser than in the days of Mao, but still visibly present.

[65] Xu, *Chongqing huaxu* (appendix), 8.

Transactions of the RHS 18 (2008), pp. 211–36 © 2008 Royal Historical Society
doi:10.1017/S0080440108000716   Printed in the United Kingdom

THE DEATH OF A CONSUMER SOCIETY

By Matthew Hilton

READ 11 MAY 2007

ABSTRACT. This paper argues that the meaning of consumer society has changed
over the last half century, principally through the prioritisation of choice over
access. It does this through an examination of the global consumer movement
and a consideration of its successes and failures. It demonstrates that through the
movement's own tactics, and the defeats it suffered by opponents of regulation, its
earlier emphasis on the right of consumers to enjoy basic needs has given way to a
greater focus on choice. Consequently, the changing fortunes of consumer activism
around the world both reflect and explain the reorientation of global consumer
society over the last few decades.

The study of consumption has expanded exponentially in recent years.
Indeed, it is now twenty-five years since consumer society was arguably
born as a subject. In their hugely pioneering work, Neil McKendrick,
John Brewer and J. H. Plumb proclaimed *The Birth of a Consumer Society*.
McKendrick in particular was keen to be the father, mother and midwife
to his new bouncing baby boy. It is worth recalling his opening words
in the book and to explore what he meant by 'the birth of a consumer
society':

> There was a consumer revolution in eighteenth-century England. More men and
> women than ever before in human history enjoyed the experience of acquiring material
> possessions. Objects which for centuries had been the privileged possessions of the rich
> came . . . to be within the reach of a larger part of society than ever before, and, for the
> first time, to be within the legitimate aspirations of almost all of it.[1]

McKendrick's metaphor of birth was extended such that his baby
was not only rooted in his period and chosen case study – eighteenth-
century England – but that its parentage was clearly wrested away from
previous analysts of early modern commerce.[2] McKendrick wrote of
embryos, false pregnancies and premature births prior to the eighteenth

---

[1] Neil McKendrick, John Brewer and J. H. Plumb, *The Birth of a Consumer Society: The
Commercialisation of Eighteenth-Century England* (1982), 1.

[2] Principally, Joan Thirsk, *Economic Policy and Projects: The Development of a Consumer Society
in Early Modern England* (Oxford, 1978).

century, and of growth and maturity thereafter. He attempted to set the tone such that other historians would be forced to write of consumer society's adolescence in the nineteenth-century retailing revolution, its full flourishing into adulthood during the twentieth-century's world of mass consumption and its decadent old age in the post-1960s society of the spectacle when our eyesight has deteriorated so badly that we can no longer see beyond the image, the brand and the bright neon lights of our post-modern, late capitalist hyperreality.

How far can we run with this metaphor of birth so beloved by these three men and their baby? Having reached old age, can we now then proclaim its death as a reality for our twenty-first-century lives and perhaps even as a subject for scholarly attention? To do so would seem particularly ridiculous as we live in a world where it seems every need, pleasure and desire is packaged and sold to us, and where the freedom to choose – but never, be warned, the freedom not to choose – is heralded as the philosophy to guide us through the world and the few decades we are given on this planet to truck, barter and exchange. By death, then, its meaning cannot be taken too literally, just as with McKendrick's birth we cannot dismiss the centuries of interactions with the world of goods prior to his consumer revolution.[3] But death perhaps highlights the end of a particular type of consumer society and to understand this we need to appreciate just what McKendrick believed was being born in the eighteenth century. By consumer society, McKendrick meant a world defined not so much by *choice* – the watchword of our supposed consumer society today – but *access*. It was not more choice that is the phenomenon to emphasise in eighteenth-century England, but the fact that there was simply more stuff, for more people, for more of the time: 'In fact, the later eighteenth century saw such a convulsion of getting and spending, such an eruption of new prosperity, and such an explosion of new production and marketing techniques, that a greater proportion of the population than in any previous society in human history was able to enjoy the pleasures of buying consumer goods.'[4]

It is this birth – about standards of living, about higher rates of consumption, about participation, about more stuff – that will be explored below. Have we witnessed the death of this defining element of consumer society and its replacement with one that emphasises choice, and choice alone?

Certainly, a case can be made that consumer society is not just about the individual's right to choice but about the access society as a whole

---

[3] See, for instance, Evelyn Welch, *Shopping in the Renaissance: Consumer Cultures in Italy 1400–1600* (New Haven, CT, 2005); Craig Clunas, *Superfluous Things: Material Culture and Social Status in Early Modern China* (Cambridge, 1991).

[4] McKendrick *et al.*, *Birth of a Consumer Society*, 1.

has to the world of goods. Orthodox economic theory itself speaks of hidden hands and trickle-down effects, such that wealth will ultimately be enjoyed by all. Such optimism about consumption can be detected from a variety of political perspectives. There is a rich tradition of leftwing, radical, progressive, liberal and mainstream thinking which has envisioned consumer society as a benefit for all. Early socialist writers distinguished between necessities and luxuries arguing that unproductive attention to luxurious consumption degraded workers as they were engaged in the production of goods which did not alleviate their own condition: better would it be if the rich spent their money on higher wages as this would increase the demand for food and manufactured goods and bring the benefits of greater trade to all.[5] Cooperative theorists especially wrote of the consumers' 'cooperative commonwealth', where, in the words of the French political economist, Charles Gide, the mutual aid principles of the organic and familial institution of the cooperative society would establish a 'reign of truth and justice'.[6] And by the end of the nineteenth century and into the twentieth, consumer-oriented economists in the United States were advocating the gearing of market structures around the basic needs of consumers.[7]

Activists were concerned with the rights of all to participate in consumer society, be these concerned consumers connected to the National Consumers Leagues of continental Europe and North America, the anti-sweating campaigns in Britain or the living wage campaigners of the US labour movement.[8] By the twentieth century it could be argued

---

[5] N. Thompson, 'Social Opulence, Private Asceticism: Ideas of Consumption in Early Socialist Thought', in *The Politics of Consumption: Material Culture and Citizenship in Europe and America*, ed. M. Daunton and M. Hilton (Oxford, 2001), 51–68.

[6] C. Gide, *Principles of Political Economy* (1903), 680; A. Bonner, *British Co-operation: The History, Principles and Organisation of the British Co-operative Movement* (Manchester, 1961).

[7] Kathleen G. Donohue, *Freedom from Want: American Liberalism and the Idea of the Consumer* (Baltimore, 2003); Frank Ackerman, 'Foundations of Economic Theories of Consumption: Overview Essay', in *The Consumer Society*, ed. Neva R. Goodwin, Frank Ackerman and David Kiron (Washington, DC, 1997), 149–58.

[8] Lawrence B. Glickman, *A Living Wage: American Workers and the Making of Consumer Society* (Ithaca, NY, 1997); Lawrence Glickman, 'Workers of the World, Consume: Ira Steward and the Origins of Labour Consumerism', *International Labour and Working Class History*, 52 (1997), 72–86; Julien Vincent, 'The Moral Expertise of the British Consumer, c. 1900: A Debate between the Christian Social Union and the Webbs', in *The Expert Consumer: Associations and Professionals in Consumer Society*, ed. Alain Chatriot, Marie-Emmanuelle Chessel and Matthew Hilton (Aldershot, 2006), 37–51; Maud Nathan, *The Story of an Epoch-Making Movement* (1926), 23–4; Kathryn Kish Sklar, 'The Consumer's White Label Campaign of the National Consumer's League, 1898–1918', in *Getting and Spending: European and American Consumer Societies in the Twentieth Century*, ed. Susan Strasser, Charles McGovern and Matthias Judt (Cambridge, 1998), 17–35; Warren Breckman, 'Disciplining Consumption: The Debate on Luxury in Wilhelmine Germany, 1890–1914', *Journal of Social History*, 24 (1991), 485–505; Kathryn Kish Sklar, *Florence Kelley and the Nation's Work: The Rise of Women's Political Culture*,

that consumerism had become a state project, the protection and defence of consumers' interests having become a legitimate and central aspect of a government's responsibilities to its citizens during an era of expanding democracy. Consumption, or the right to enjoy its pleasures, had become an entitlement to citizens who had made sacrifices in two world wars and expected a share in the societies being reconstructed in their name in the late 1940s and 1950s. The affluent society had to promise more choice for those who could afford it, but also more stuff for those who so far could not. In the United States, the 'consumer democracy' has been argued to have been at the heart of post-war planning, whereby consumers were able to exercise their citizenship not only at the ballot box but on a daily basis through their participation in the marketplace.[9] Consumer democracy might not capture the full range of consumer regimes which emerged in the latter half of the twentieth century, but there was clearly a widely expressed desire to improve standards of living and to ensure that all could participate in the good life. In Germany, Erhard declared a 'social market' economy; in Scandinavia, social democracy took account of workers' desires to share in the good life, and even amidst the apparent asceticism of 1950s Britain, there existed a sense of universal entitlement to affluence which surely emerged out of the 'fair shares' policies associated with the foundations of the welfare state.[10]

Most dramatically, at the heart of the Cold War was an argument as to which political ideology best provided more goods to more people more of the time. While consumption arguably brought down many of the command economies of eastern Europe, in the affluent post-war decades even the communist party-state paid lip service to the needs of the consumer. Famously, in 1959, at the American Trade Fair in Moscow, Nikita Khrushchev and Richard Nixon got into a schoolboy spat about living standards, trading verbal blows as to which system, communism or capitalism, brought the greatest stuff to the greatest number for the greatest amount of the time. In the consumer societies built after the war – and in the protection regimes established to look over them – there existed a broad-ranging consumer politics which aimed to bring

---

1830–1900 (New Haven, CT, 1995); Marie-Emmanuelle Chessel, 'Consommation et réforme sociale à la Belle Époque: la conference internationale des ligues socials d'acheteurs en 1908', *Sciences de la Société*, 62 (2004), 45–67.

[9] Lizabeth Cohen, *A Consumers' Republic: The Politics of Mass Consumption in Postwar America* (New York, 2003).

[10] Gunnar Trumbull, *Consumer Capitalism: Politics, Product Markets and Firm Strategy in France and Germany* (Ithaca, NY, 2006); Iselin Theien, 'Shopping for the "People's Home": Consumer Planning in Norway and Sweden after the Second World War', and Katherine Pence, 'Shopping for an "Economic Miracle": Gendered Politics of Consumer Citizenship in Divided Germany', in Chatriot *et al.*, *Expert Consumer*, 105–20, 137–50; Lawrence Black, *The Political Culture of the Left in Britain, 1951–1964* (Basingstoke, 2003).

everybody within its grasp. This might have been challenged, coopted and even only half-heartedly followed through in practice, but in the diversity of voices seeking to speak for the consumer, consumption became an activity that was potentially democratic, universal and open to all.[11]

In what follows, it will be argued that the meaning of consumer society has shifted such that the emphasis is no longer on participation for all but on more choice for the individual (that is, for those who can already afford it). This will be demonstrated through a focus on the activities of organised consumers since 1945. Organised consumerism enables the discussion of consumer society, consumer politics and consumer activism to take place at the global level, something which is so far missing from a literature largely dominated by national – and overwhelmingly western – case studies. Today, of course, it is easy and natural for us to consider the politics of consumption to be a global concern. But in the comparative testing consumer movement – that is, of the organisations which have produced *Which?* in the UK, *Que Choisir* in France, *Test* in Germany, *Consumer Reports* in the US – there has also been a global form of consumer activism. What will become apparent is that the consumer movement spread throughout the developed and the developing world. As it did so, consumer activists became leading players in global civil society, pioneering transnational advocacy networks on issues such as the inappropriate marketing of breastmilk substitutes, the dumping of dangerous and useless pharmaceuticals in the developing world and the use and ingestion of pesticides by farmers in the south and consumers in the north.

Consumer activism therefore has had much to say about needs and affluence, and as a case study it serves a useful purpose in exploring the meaning of consumer society more generally. What the second half of the essay will therefore focus on is the decline of the consumer movement's global, needs-based agenda, a trend which parallels the changing dominant definition of consumption such that it is not inappropriate to speak of the death of a consumer society. Two issues are particularly pertinent to this narrative. First, a brief section will examine the contradictions inherent to the consumer movement's advocacy of a rights-based policy. This opened it up to appropriation as others could pick and choose from the consumer movement's shopping list of rights:

---

[11] Victoria de Grazia, *Irresistible Empire: America's Advance through Twentieth-Century Europe* (Cambridge, MA, 2005); Sheryl Kroen, 'La magie des objets, le Plan Marshall et l'instauration d'une démocratie de consommateurs', in *Au nom du consommateur: consommation et politique en Europe et aux États-Unis au xxe siècle*, ed., Alain Chatriot, Marie-Emmanuelle Chessel and Matthew Hilton (Paris, 2005), 80–97; Sheryl Kroen, 'Negotiations with the American Way: The Consumer and the Social Contract in Post-War Europe', in *Consuming Cultures, Global Perspective: Historical Trajectories, Transnational Exchanges*, ed. John Brewer and Frank Trentmann (Oxford, 2006), 251–77.

and here the right to choice could have very different implications from the right to basic needs. Related to this, a second section will then explore how the consumer movement lost a number of symbolic campaigns to a resurgent anti-regulatory movement increasingly prominent at global fora from the late 1970s. The implications here, it will be argued, have been profound, not least in the promotion of choice as the foremost defining element of consumer society. Basic needs, access and participation have therefore been sidelined as, arguably, have entire nations and consumers in the modern global marketplace. At one level, a glib conclusion could be that the death of consumer society is the death resulting from the oft-quoted figures of the hundreds of millions who live on less than a dollar a day and die from the resulting poverty. But the death for our purposes is really the death of one particular meaning of consumer society, the death of a participatory vision of consumption which McKendrick so eloquently claimed was born in the eighteenth century.

I

The origins of the modern comparative-testing consumer movement lie in interwar America. In 1929, Consumers Research began publishing its *Bulletin* in order to help consumers overcome their relative ignorance in the marketplace. It rode the wave of a developing consumer consciousness in 1930s America which saw the establishment of a consumer infrastructure within the New Deal bodies and the flourishing of several other consumer organisations.[12] Following a strike in 1936, Consumers Research was split as several disgruntled staff went off to form Consumers Union. Unsurprisingly for an organisation founded amidst a labour dispute, Consumers Union would pay close attention to the labour conditions of those who made the products featured in its reports, though for the many millions of shoppers who would read *Consumer Reports* over the course of the twentieth century, it was the quality tests themselves that explain the organisation's tremendous growth and popularity. By the turn of the millennium, the circulation figures of *Consumer Reports* topped 5 million.[13]

---

[12] Cohen, *A Consumers' Republic*; Meg Jacobs, *Pocketbook Politics: Economic Citizenship in Twentieth-Century America* (Princeton, NJ, 2005); Gary Cross, *An All-Consuming Century: Why Commercialism Won in Modern America* (New York, 2000); Donohue, *Freedom from Want*.

[13] Lawrence B. Glickman, 'The Strike in the Temple of Consumption: Consumer Activism and Twentieth-Century American Political Culture', *Journal of American History*, 88 (2001), 99–128; Robert N. Mayer, *The Consumer Movement: Guardians of the Marketplace* (Boston, MA, 1989); Norman Isaac Silber, *Test and Protest: The Influence of Consumers Union* (New York, 1983); Michael Pertschuk, *Revolt against Regulation: The Rise and Pause of the Consumer Movement* (Berkeley, CA, 1982); Charles McGovern, *Sold American: Consumption and Citizenship, 1890–1945* (Chapel Hill, NC, 2006).

The appeal of comparative testing consumerism was not confined
to the United States. After the Second World War, consumer groups
began to appear across western Europe as post-war economies shifted
into a prolonged period of affluence. First, in France, the Union
Fédéral des Consommateurs was formed in 1951. It was followed
by Consumentenbond in the Netherlands in 1953, and then the
Consumers' Association of the United Kingdom in 1956 and the
Association des Consommateurs of Belgium in 1957. These private-
testing bodies were joined by a range of state-assisted agencies such
as the Arbeitsgemeinschaft der Verbraucherverbände in Germany
(1953), the Norwegian Forbrukerrådet (1953) and the Swedish Statens
Konsumentråd (1957).[14]

By 1969 the comparative testing magazine had become a feature
of most advanced capitalist economies. *Consumer Reports* led the way
with sales of over $1\frac{1}{2}$ million, though by this time sales of *Which?*
by the UK Consumers' Association had topped $\frac{1}{2}$ million also. In
Belgium, there were 190,000 members of the two competing consumer
groups (Association des Consommateurs and the Union Féminine pour
l'Information et la Défense du Consommateur), over a quarter of a
million subscribers to *Consumentengids* in the Netherlands (representing
one in ten households), and while the number of actual subscribers
to *Test* in Germany reached only 67,000, total sales of the magazine
from the newsstands brought that figure to 190,000. Most impressive
were the Scandinavian countries: although their consumer magazines
were published by the state rather than by private testing organisations,
subscriptions ran into six figures such that Norway could claim the greatest
number of sales relative to households in the world.[15] While a comparative
testing magazine had failed to establish itself in the mainstream in France,
sales of *Que Choisir* took off in the early 1970s, such that there were 300,000
subscribers in 1975.[16] By 1969, there were twenty-two organisations
engaged in comparative testing in all of the principal countries of the
North Atlantic community. Collectively, they operated on a budget of
$20 million (rising to $30 million just three years later), could claim a
subscriber base of 3 million and a readership of many millions more.[17]

For affluent consumers, enjoying the world of goods but nevertheless
living in an age of post-war dislocation and insecurity, comparative testing
offered a means by which they could escape from the alienation of the

---

[14] *Encyclopaedia of the Consumer Movement*, ed. S. Brobeck, R. N. Mayer and R. O. Herrmann
(Santa Barbara, CA, 1997), various entries.

[15] Hans B. Thorelli and Sarah V. Thorelli, *Consumer Information Systems and Consumer Policy*
(Cambridge, MA, 1977), 234.

[16] *Ibid.*, 340.

[17] Hans B. Thorelli and Sarah V. Thorelli, *Consumer Information Handbook: Europe and North
America* (New York, 1974), xxiv.

modern technocracy. It offered the opportunity to establish themselves as an elite who would be able to reconnect with the world of goods, leaving behind the massed ranks of consumers who continued to be uninformed and systematically duped on a daily basis. Marx argued that modern capitalism creates a fetish of the commodity, the product becoming a hieroglyphic which we seek to decode to understand the labour relations behind it.[18] The publication of endless statistics in comparable tables was precisely an attempt to break that code, though rarely to understand the labour theory of value. Rather, comparative testing consumerism enrolled the skills of the scientist and the engineer to help consumers to reconnect with goods. Testing stood in defiance of the promotional devices of advertising and literally stripped a product down to its constituent parts to render it knowable, understandable and meaningful. It was an attempt to establish consumer sovereignty, but it was a sovereignty never fully appreciated in these terms. Sovereignty meant control and participation in the forms of power that gave meaning to goods. It was always more than being free to choose and it is for these reasons that consumerism can be said to have provided an ideology of far wider significance than just assisting the acquisitive shopper.

There are important points to be made about the consumer movement. It should not be assumed that we are only concerned with the growth of a movement associated with disgruntled middle-class shoppers. What is clear is that the organised testing movement represented the vanguard of a heightened consumer consciousness after the Second World War. In the reconstruction of the post-war economies, politicians had to offer shoppers some protection in this unknown age of affluence. If consumers were to behave with confidence, providing the impetus for economic growth and making all the improvements in technology and productivity worthwhile, then they required assistance and support. They needed to know that in borrowing heavily to purchase a car, a house and all the furniture to arrange inside it, they would not lose everything if the house was found to be shoddily built, that the car broke down on every trip and that the appliances bought for the home harmed those who switched them on. Citizens needed to know that constraints and curbs would be placed on businessmen's behaviour, that capitalism would be kept in check and that, somehow, if not through the authority of choice but the authority of government, the market would still serve the interests of those for whom it claimed to exist.

There are important differences to be noted in the consumer protection regimes built in the 1960s and 1970s. Important work has been conducted comparing the different models of consumer protection pursued by

---

[18] Marx, *Capital*, I, in *The Portable Karl Marx*, ed. E. Kamenka (Harmondsworth, 1930), 446–50.

various governments across the affluent capitalist world. For instance, in Germany and Austria a more corporatist set of consumer-producer mechanisms were adopted. In Japan the consumer had to fit in with a strong state and the existence of great producer political power at the centre. While France and the United States have regarded the consumer as a political entity, the US has sought, as with Britain, market-based solutions to their grievances, while France, though sporadically and through much experimentation, has mobilised statist mechanisms to protect the consumer.[19]

But the overall point to emphasise is that states did respond: it is with good reason that many consumer activists look back on these decades as the time when they achieved many of their greatest successes. The growth in consumer protection measures was simply incredible. In Germany, there were just 25 new laws relating to consumer protection from 1945 to 1970, but there were a further 338 adopted by 1978. In France there were similarly just 37 laws and ministerial decrees before 1970, a total which had grown to 94 by 1978.[20] In Britain, major laws relating to consumer safety, hire purchase, resale price maintenance and trade descriptions appeared in the 1960s, followed by wider regulations on fair trading, credit and unsolicited goods and services in the first half of the 1970s.[21] In the United States, a flurry of consumer protection laws appeared in the late 1960s relating to the automobile industry, drug safety, meat quality, package labelling, credit reporting, product safety and a whole host of other trade practices.[22]

What was witnessed in the post-war years was a global social movement of consumers that played a large part in the establishment of consumer protection internationally. Indeed, one can even go so far as to suggest that consumer protection straddled the iron curtain. Advocates of consumer protection emerged within economic planning departments of the communist bloc. In East Germany, leaders had to contend with the Soviet emphasis on production goods while acknowledging that many of their citizens looked favourably upon the new prosperity being enjoyed in the west. A distinct consumer lobby emerged in the 1950s in the

---

[19] Trumbull, *Consumer Capitalism*; Alain Chatriot, 'Qui defend le consommateur? Associations, institutions et politiques publiques en France, 1972–2003', in Chatriot *et al.*, *Au nom du consommateur*, 165–81; Gunnar Trumbull, 'National Varieties of Consumerism', *Jahrbuch für Wirtschaftsgeschichte*, 1 (2006), 77–93; Patricia L. Maclachlan, *Consumer Politics in Postwar Japan: The Institutional Boundaries of Citizen Activism* (New York, 2002).

[20] Trumbull, *Consumer Capitalism*, 8–9.

[21] Matthew Hilton, *Consumerism in Twentieth-Century Britain: The Search for a Historical Movement* (Cambridge, 2003).

[22] Mayer, *The Consumer Movement*, 29, 101; James E. Finch, 'A History of the Consumer Movement in the United States: Its Literature and Legislation', *Journal of Consumer Studies and Home Economics*, 9 (1985), 23–33.

Ministry for Trade and Provisioning, to be followed with similar lobbies in Poland, Hungary and Yugoslavia.[23] Indeed, such was the pressure for consumer protection in Poland, that once Solidarity took off, a grassroots consumer movement emerged in 1981, with tens of thousands of members and dozens of consumer clubs around the country.[24] Even today, for all that consumer protection institutes have been cynically exploited by authoritarian regimes to contain political opposition, consumer protection bodies have proved tremendously popular. In China for instance, one estimate has suggested that the total number of institutional and supervisory contact points for consumers from the village upwards amounts to over 150,000. By 2000, the number of complaints the China Consumer Association was receiving was approaching 1 million a year (by the end of 2001, it had dealt with a total of over 6 million). Because of such discontent, the State Administration for Industry and Commerce set up the '12135' consumer complaints hotline. Within five years, this had managed to intervene on behalf of $2\frac{1}{4}$ million complaints and is today, after the emergency services, one of the most popular phone numbers in the country.[25]

Following on from these examples, it must also be acknowledged that consumer activism was not just a western phenomenon. In 1960, the leaders of the main European and US groups came together to found the International Organisation of Consumers Unions (IOCU). Originally conceived as an institute to foster cross-national testing procedures for private, subscriber-based consumer organisations, the international body soon grew beyond this limited role.[26] In the 1960s, it first took on board

[23] Mark Landsman, *Dictatorship and Demand: The Politics of Consumerism in East Germany* (Cambridge, MA, 2005).

[24] Malgorzata Mazurek and Matthew Hilton, 'Consumerism, Solidarity and Communism: Consumer Protection and the Consumer Movement in Poland', *Journal of Contemporary History*, 42 (2007), 315–43.

[25] Beverley Hooper, 'The consumer citizen in contemporary China', Working Paper No. 12, Centre for East and South-East Asian Studies, Lund University, available at: www.ace.lu.se/images/Syd_och_sydostasienstudier/working_papers/Hooper.pdf (accessed Apr. 2007); 'Complaint Hotline Saves 4.4 Billion Yuan for Consumers during Five Years', *People's Daily*, 26 Mar. 2004, available at: http://english.peopledaily.com.cn/200403/26/eng20040326_138603.shtml (accessed Apr. 2007); Jing Jian Xiao, 'Chinese consumer movement', in Brobeck *et al.*, *Encyclopaedia of the Consumer Movement*, 104–8; Donald B. King and Tong Gao, *Consumer Protection in China: Development and Recommendations* (Littleton, CO, 1991); Tong Gao, 'Chinese Consumer Protection Philosophy', *Journal of Consumer Policy*, 14 (1992), 337–50.

[26] International Organisation of Consumers Unions (IOCU), *The Consumer and the World of Tomorrow: Report of the Second Conference of the International Organisation of Consumers Union* (The Hague, 1962); Eirlys Roberts, *International Organisation of Consumers Unions, 1960–1981* (The Hague, 1981); Foo Gaik Sim, *IOCU on Record: A Documentary History of the International Organization of Consumers Unions, 1960–1990* (Yonkers, NY, 1991); IOCU, *Programme of First International Meeting on Consumer Testing* (The Hague, 1960).

the agendas of the state-sponsored consumer organisations of Scandinavia and northern Europe and then spread around the world. This growth was initially achieved in relatively prosperous post-colonial societies – New Zealand, South Africa, Hong Kong – but then more dramatically in the developing world.[27] By 1990, IOCU had extended well beyond the affluent west. The Council consisted of representatives of most western European states, but also of consumer organisations in Argentina, Hong Kong, India, Indonesia, Jamaica, Japan, Mauritius, Mexico, Poland and South Korea. An Executive had been formed which showed the domination of the founding members (excluding Belgium) though even here South Korea and Mauritius were represented and the Presidency was held by Erna Witoelar of the Yayasan Lembaga Konsumen, Indonesia.[28]

Today, IOCU is called Consumers International, and in November of 2003 it held its Seventeenth World Congress in Lisbon, Portugal. Its headquarters are in London, but there are thriving regional offices in Africa, Asia and Latin America. At the turn of the millennium, it had 253 members from 115 different countries which ranged from all the states of the western world to post-communist eastern Europe and a whole collection of developing states (China, Chad, Guatemala, El Salvador, Gabon, Nigeria, Malawi and Burkina Faso) which, on first instinct, one might suppose had other interests that needed defending than those of consumers.[29]

It is perhaps of no surprise that the consumer movement first took off outside the capitalist west in Asia. In the first part of the twentieth century, consumption was a central tactic of Chinese and Korean nationalists in their struggle against the Japanese, while the *swadeshi* movement politicised homespun cloth for generations of Indian nationalists inspired, in particular, by Mahatma Gandhi.[30] In 1956, the Indian Association of Consumers was created, predating many equivalent organisations in Europe. It was followed by equivalent organisations across Southeast Asia. The first was set up in 1963 as the Consumers Federated Groups of the Philippines which emerged out of the women's movement and, around the same time, several other consumer movements appeared in

---

[27] IOCU, *Knowledge Is Power: Consumer Goals in the 1970s. Proceedings of the 6th Biennial World Conference of the International Organisation of Consumers Unions* (1970), 115–17.

[28] IOCU, *Consumer Power in the Nineties: Proceedings of the Thirteenth IOCU World Congress* (1991), 113.

[29] Consumers International, *Annual Report, 1999* (1999), 37–41.

[30] Karl Gerth, *China Made: Consumer Culture and the Creation of the Nation* (Cambridge, MA, 2003); Michael Edson Robinson, *Cultural Nationalism in Colonial Korea, 1920–1925* (Seattle, 1988); Laura C. Nelson, *Status, Gender and Consumer Nationalism in South Korea* (New York, 2000); C. A. Bayly, 'The Origins of *Swadeshi* (Home Industry): Cloth and Indian Society, 1700–1930', in *The Social Life of Things: Commodities in Cultural Perspective*, ed. Arjun Appadurai (Cambridge, 1986).

the region, most notably the Consumer Association of Singapore and the Philippine Consumers Movement in 1971, and the Indonesian Consumers Organisation in 1973.[31]

In order to understand this growth of organised consumerism across the developing world it is illustrative to focus on a specific country and on one organisation in particular, the Consumers' Association of Penang. Undoubtedly, consumer activists in Malaysia have been instrumental in promoting an alternative type of consumer politics and pushing for the inclusion of basic needs as a fundamental consumer right. From the 1960s, Malaysian consumer activists have been some of the most prominent in the global south and many of its leaders have gone on to play key roles in IOCU, not least because IOCU's first regional office was based in Penang. However, although there is much that is specific about Malaysian consumer history its attention to questions of poverty make it also representative of policy shifts inspired by consumer movements across Asia, especially India, Indonesia and the Philippines and, subsequent to that, to developments in Latin America and Africa.

The Consumers' Association of Penang (CAP), was set up immediately after the ethnic-based riots of the 1969 general election. CAP soon turned its attention to basic consumer goods and to the issues of adulteration, fraudulent sales, pesticide use and inappropriate marketing, all of which were rife in a country missing the same consumer protection mechanisms enjoyed by western consumers. But as a civil society organisation tolerated by an at times oppressive regime for its supposedly non-radical nature, it soon found itself entering upon questions of social and economic injustice as few other NGOs were in existence to tackle them. Thus by the end of the 1970s, CAP had extended its definition of consumerism to include women's rights, the plight of fishing and farming communities threatened by development projects, the land rights of the Orang Asli (indigenous) community, environmental destruction (CAP has gone on to set up Friends of the Earth Malaysia), and the appropriate direction to take for an expanding economy which at times has seemed more concerned with prestige projects than promoting the standard of living of the majority poor.[32]

---

[31] Josie Fernandez, 'Consumer Protection in Asia: The Challenges Ahead', *Journal of Development Communication*, 12 (2001), 42–52; Josie Fernandez, 'Asian-Pacific Consumer Movement', in Brobeck *et al.*, *Encyclopaedia of the Consumer Movement*, 38–42; John T. D. Wood, 'Consumer Protection in the Asian-Pacific Region', *Journal of Consumer Policy*, 14 (1991), 99–106.

[32] What follows is a summary of my work on Malaysia. Further details can be found in Matthew Hilton, 'Social Activism in an Age of Consumption: The Organised Consumer Movement', *Social History*, 32 (2007), 121–43, and 'The Consumer Movement and Civil Society in Malaysia', *International Review of Social History*, 52 (2007), 373–406.

By the mid-1980s, CAP had developed a consumerism which posited consumers as the expert commentators on the whole nature of economic development. CAP has gone on to outline a general critique of global economic policy which champions the rights of developing nations to enjoy the profits of their own resources. Indeed, to this end, CAP has established Third World Network, now a leading player in global civil society and whose economist, Martin Khor, still an officer with CAP, has achieved a prominence at events organised by the European and World Social Forums. At the heart of this politics is an assumption that development projects should be focused on providing the majority of the population with access to a basic standard of living, rather than assuming a trickle-down effect from the high profits granted to a few well-positioned rent-seekers.

Here then lies a wider critique of economic globalisation which offers the chance for the consumer to fight for the right to basic needs as the main platform of a human rights manifesto which places as much importance on economic and social rights as political and civil rights. Indeed, this is precisely what has occurred, especially through individuals such as Anwar Fazal, one of the founders of CAP, who went on to become the regional director for IOCU from 1974 to 1990 and who, from 1978 to 1984, also served as the international movement's president. During this time, when he served as both figurehead and employee, IOCU's centre of gravity shifted firmly from its supposed headquarters in The Hague to the regional office in Penang, and IOCU came to be articulating an agenda more in line with other development agencies than with the concerns of affluent shoppers who purchased the testing magazines of *Que Choisir*, *Which?*, *Test* and *Consumer Reports*.

By the late 1970s, then, the consumer movement had been revitalised by its developing world initiatives. This, in turn, meant it had come to adopt a far wider social and economic agenda at the global level than is usually assumed, and it resulted in the consumer movement becoming something of a leader among the global community of international non-governmental organisations by the 1980s. Most importantly, for the argument of this essay, it meant that consumer activists themselves were articulating a vision of consumer society far removed from one that emphasised the satisfaction of individual acquisitiveness.

This is seen no more clearly than in the campaigning tactics adopted by the global movement. IOCU brought a number of issues to international prominence through the creation of networks; that is collections of pre-existing organisations prepared to work together on a specific issue. Although campaigning networks had clearly existed at the national level for some time, and more general networks – or federations – existed within the labour and women's movements, the creation of single-issue, international campaign networks in the late 1970s was an important precedent which in many ways still has a fundamental influence on the nature of global civil society today.[33] Most prominently, IOCU initiated the International Baby Food Action Network (IBFAN) in 1979, Health Action International (HAI) in 1981 and the Pesticide Action Network (PAN) in 1982. Led and administered by IOCU, the networks brought together a variety of NGOs and enabled many smaller groups to have a say in which issues should be brought to the attention of the UN. They overrode any more fundamental and political differences that might have existed within the different branches of the international NGO community and constituted an agreement by diverse entities to set aside their more general agendas in order to focus specifically on one particular problem.[34]

Moreover, the networks emerged out of the direct experience of developing world consumer activists. Recognising the limited resources of consumer groups in various national contexts, leaders such as Anwar Fazal urged greater collaboration among diverse civil society groups: 'the value of such partnerships is that while you are sharing costs and manpower you are also obtaining *entré* into other elite and important groups in the community and enlarging their consumer consciousness'.[35] As president of IOCU, he was aware of the mutual benefits to consumer and non-consumer groups alike in coming together in networks. Following his establishment of IBFAN he realised he had created a model for other international campaigns that would be copied not only by the consumer movement but global civil society as a whole: today, networks are generally recognised as a key campaign tactic of global activism.[36] According to Fazal, IBFAN had 'brought together a variety of social and development action groups, each independent and yet acting in complete empathy and

[33] Harold K. Jacobson, *Networks of Interdependence: International Organisations and the Global Political System* (New York, 1984).

[34] G. Goldenman and S. Rengam, *Problem Pesticides, Pesticide Problems: A Citizens' Action Guide to the International Code of Conduct on the Distribution and Use of Pesticides* (Penang, 1988); K. Balasubramaniam, *Health and Pharmaceuticals in Developing Countries: Towards Social Justice and Equity* (Penang, 1996); Foo Gaik Sim, *The Pesticide Poisoning Report: A Survey of Some Asian Countries* (Penang, 1985); Michael Hansen, *Escape from the Pesticide Treadmill: Alternatives to Pesticides in Developing Countries* (Penang, 1987); IOCU and IBFAN, *Protecting Infant Health: A Health Workers' Guide to the International Code of Marketing of Breastmilk Substitutes* (Penang, 1985); IBFAN, *Breaking the Rules 1991: A Worldwide Report on Violations of the WHO/UNICEF International Code of Marketing of Breastmilk Substitutes* (Penang, 1991); Charles Medawar, *Drugs and World Health: An International Consumer Perspective* (1984).

[35] IOCU Archive, Kuala Lumpur, Box 61a, File G5a.6, Anwar Fazal, 'An Outline Strategy for the Promotion and Financing of Consumers' Organisations in Developing Countries', paper presented to IOCU World Congress, 23–7 Mar. 1975, Sydney, 3.

[36] Margaret E. Keck and Kathryn Sikkink, *Activists beyond Borders: Advocacy Networks in International Politics* (Ithaca, NY, 1998).

concert'.[37] It connected the consumer movement to a number of NGOs, while these in turn were able to unite beneath the outwardly respectable umbrella of organised consumerism.

By the 1980s, therefore, the consumer movement had achieved a global prominence not generally recognised in existing accounts of the history of consumer society. Through the logic of networking, the consumer movement presented itself as a neutral entity, to which other NGOs could attach themselves without invoking wider divisions based on broader value frameworks. As such, networks would enable socialists and Christians and conservatives and radicals to come together on specific subjects, just as the global consumer movement contained elements from across the political spectrum within its own national organisations. In addition, it enabled consumer politics to become directed by the concerns of the world's poor rather than those of the world's rich. Pesticides, breastmilk substitutes and pharmaceuticals were products far removed from those that filled the pages of western consumer testing magazines, yet they – and other such basic necessities – came to dominate the global consumer movement's agendas, creating a politics of consumption as much attuned to the interests of those excluded from consumer society as those already benefiting from its packaged pleasures.

II

So far, then, we have a story of relative success, global expansion and even political influence, at least within the internal dynamics of a global civil society of non-governmental organisations. Consumer activism had spread all around the world, creating an international body with a reach many other more prominent NGOs could only admire at the time. Through its networks, it had begun to take a lead in global civil society, combining the respectability it enjoyed in the global north – which gave it a foothold at the United Nations – with the radicalism that drove its campaigns from the global south. In addition, it could claim for itself some notable successes. Not only had consumer protection been established as a mainstream political principle and a reality for many millions of consumers, but it could claim some victories on the global stage. It had helped develop in 1982 a UN 'Consolidated List of Products whose Consumption and/or Sale have been Banned, Withdrawn, Severely Restricted or Not Approved by Governments.'[38] It enjoyed constant representation at various UN agencies and it had long been an active

[37] IOCU Archive, Box 61a, File G5a.32, Anwar Fazal, 'Brave and Angry: The International Consumer Movement's Response to MNCs', paper presented to ASEAN Consumer Protection Seminar, 1–4 Oct. 1980, Quezon City, Philippines, 8.

[38] IOCU, *Annual Report, 1986*, 10; Michael J. Vernon, *Evaluation of the Consumer Interpol: A Report to IOCU* (Penang: IOCU-ROAP, 1984); IOCU Archive, Box 17, File B3em, Martin

discussant on the Codex Alimentarius Commission which dealt with food standards. At ECOSOC it was asked to provide written statements on a number of issues, from science and technology, to disability rights, to education programmes and the legal aspects of consumer protection.[39] Finally, in 1985, it achieved one of its greatest successes with the passing of the UN Guidelines on Consumer Protection which have become the model law for countless consumer protection regimes subsequently implemented in countries all over the world.[40]

The question that therefore remains is what happened? Today, the influence of the consumer movement has been eclipsed by many other activist groups and by huge gatherings such as at the World and European Social Forums. IOCU does not enjoy the same name recognition as NGOs such as Amnesty International, and nor has it been able to attract the same level of media attention and public fascination in its campaigns as those initiated by Greenpeace, Médecins sans Frontières or Oxfam. In addition, its attention to basic needs and standards of living represents a form of consumer politics which has arguably been eclipsed by other visions of consumer society. Indeed, it has been some time since 'consumerism' itself was generally understood to refer to its original meaning of organised political action: nowadays, it has become a cultural term used to describe the symptoms rather than the cures for consumer society's ills.[41]

In order to understand the relative decline of the consumer movement and the attendant shift in the meaning of consumer society, it is necessary to pay attention to two particular issues. First, we can detect a retreat of the consumer movement from some of its more radical undercurrents and a consolidation of its core philosophy. On 15 March 1962, President John F. Kennedy made a speech to the US Congress in which he acknowledged the responsibility of government to respond to the key concerns of consumer activists. Most crucially, he listed four consumer rights which he took to be the heart of the political philosophy of the consumer. These were the right to safety, the right to be informed, the right to choose

---

Abrahams, 'Consumer Interpol: A Citizen's Action Approach to Police Corporate Dumping of Hazardous Products', *Project Appraisal*, 3 (1988), 155–8.

[39] IOCU, *Report for 1975–1978*, 32–43; IOCU, *Annual Report, 1979*, 21–36; IOCU, *Report for 1972–1974*, 28–30, 40–5; IOCU, *Biennial Report, 1970–1972*, 27.

[40] David Harland, 'The United Nations Guidelines for Consumer Protection', *Journal of Consumer Policy*, 10 (1987), 245–66; Esther Peterson and Jean M. Halloran, 'United Nations Consumer Protections', in Brobeck *et al.*, *Encyclopaedia of the Consumer Movement*, 581–3.

[41] Quoted in R. Swagler, 'Evolution and Applications of the Term Consumerism: Themes and Variations', *Journal of Consumer Affairs*, 28 (1994), 350. For other definitions see the *Oxford English Dictionary*; *Consumerism: Search for the Consumer Interest*, ed. D. A. Aaker and G. S. Day, 3rd edn (Basingstoke, 1978), 2; Y. Gabriel and T. Lang, *The Unmanageable Consumer: Contemporary Consumption and its Fragmentation* (1995), 7–9.

and the right to be heard.[42] These four consumer rights were adopted as the central pillars of IOCU policy and the date chosen for the World Consumer Rights Day was the anniversary of Kennedy's coming out into the consumerist fold. Moreover, this rights-based perspective became the basis for political consumerism as a whole. They can be found at the heart of national consumer protection systems the world over. They form the basis of European Union consumer policy and they have been replicated in the UN Guidelines on Consumer Protection.[43]

However, over the decades the consumer movement has also added incrementally to these four rights. Particularly as it has embraced the concerns and interests of developing world consumers – attuned to the needs of the poor as much as the affluent – it has incorporated other consumer rights into its operating rationale such that by the end of the 1970s IOCU had begun to campaign for a list of eight. In addition to Kennedy's original four, IOCU added the right of redress and the right to consumer education. More challengingly, it had also added the right to a healthy environment; and the right to basic needs. The emphasis placed on needs reflected the agendas of figures such as Fazal. Symbolically, in a publicity poster from the 1980s, the Penang office deliberately excluded the right to choice from its published list of eight rights. Few people at the time noticed, but nothing could have more clearly expressed the reorientation of the world's consumer movement to the needs of the poor rather than to the desires of the affluent.[44] For those consumer activists in the developing world this message was that choice was the privilege of the affluent. They did not deny that choice in itself was a good thing and that it was intimately bound up with notions of freedom, it was just that, for them, it was simply not a priority. Fazal and others believed that the rights to basic needs were far more important concerns for the majority of the world's consumers.

Yet by the end of the 1980s there was a retreat from this prioritisation of the right to basic needs over the right to choice. The consumer movement had always been made up of those committed liberal internationalists of the post-war decades who remained optimistic about the potential

[42] IOCU Archive, Box 71, File H3.1, John F. Kennedy, 'Special Message to the Congress on Protecting the Consumer Interest', 15 Mar. 1962.

[43] Stephen Weatherill, *EC Consumer Law and Policy* (1997); Commission of the European Communities, *Consumer Protection and Information Policy: Third Report* (Luxembourg, 1981); Commission of the European Communities, *Consumer Representation in the European Communities* (Luxembourg, 1983); Commission of the European Communities, *Ten Years of Community Consumer Policy: A Contribution to a People's Europe* (Luxembourg, 1986); Economic and Social Consultative Assembly, *The Consumer and the Internal Market* (Brussels, 1993); Consumers in the Europe Group, *EU Consumer Protection Policy: A Review of European Union Consumer Programmes, EU Consumer Protection Legislation and European Commission Consumer Initiatives* (1999).

[44] Interview with Anwar Fazal, 13 Apr. 2004.

of such intergovernmental organisations as the United Nations. They embraced the basic needs approach of the developing world activists and allowed these agendas to dominate their international body, particularly as the UN launched its development decades and the New International Economic Order seemed to give a priority to developing world nations. But by the 1980s, many of these early activists were reaching retirement and many of the western private testing bodies had suffered under the economic recession of the 1980s. This meant more commercially oriented management structures were set in place to help ensure the testing magazines continued to thrive. This resulted in a retreat into testing which, at the international level, meant there existed a renewed pressure to cater to the interests of magazine subscribers, rather than the needs of the world's poor consumers.

Moreover, for many moderates in the global north, many of the core aims of the consumer movement had been achieved, especially through the consumer protection regimes that had been put in place in various national contexts across the capitalist west. These activists shunned the radicalism emanating from the developing world and, since they held the trump card of providing most of the finance for the international organisation, they began to reign in the consumer movement from its more aggressive tactics. It meant, at the national level, that prominent consumer leaders such as Ralph Nader would no longer ally themselves with bodies such as Consumers Union and, at the global level, that radicals such as Malaysia's Anwar Fazal would be ousted from the movement. Alongside this, IOCU also disassociated itself from the networks thereby cutting off its links with broader sectors of global civil society. Instead, the concerns of the affluent began to predominate once more and here the notion of rights becomes crucial. The consumer movement has not given up on basic needs and environmental activism – it still does incredibly interesting work in these fields. But what a list of rights does is create essentially a shopping list upon which different emphases can be placed on each item. So, while basic needs topped the list in the 1970s and 1980s, the right to choice has slowly crept back up the agenda. In 1981 Anwar Fazal had deliberately excluded choice. After he left the movement, choice would return with renewed energy and importance.

The danger is, though, that anyone can be in favour of choice, and this has enabled other spokesgroups for the consumer to emerge: they too can pick from the shopping list of consumer rights and be seen to be promoting the consumer cause. This brings us on to a second and perhaps more important reason for the decline of the consumer movement and the attendant redefinition of the dominant meaning of consumer society. This is a narrative not so much of decline or retreat, but of defeat.

To understand this defeat, our narrative must return to the United States. In the 1960s, organised consumerism had been revived by the ascendancy of Ralph Nader's public interest movement. This had resulted in a whole raft of legislation introduced by Presidents Johnson and Nixon which substantially altered the regulatory character of American politics and American business. In just a few years after the publication of *Unsafe at Any Speed*, a flurry of legislation was introduced on behalf of consumers, including the Fair Packaging and Labelling Act 1966, the National Traffic and Motor Vehicle Safety Act 1966 and the Wholesome Meat Act 1967. It was bolstered by the strengthening of existing regulatory agencies, such as the Food and Drug Administration, and the establishment of new federal bodies such as the Environmental Protection Agency and the National Highway Traffic Safety Administration.[45]

It was precisely because of these successes that public interest activism, organised consumerism and Naderism were soon matched by an anti-regulatory backlash that would seek to rein in the perceived encroachment of the state upon the free market. By the early 1970s, the downturn in the global economy meant far fewer US corporations were prepared to tolerate the perceived luxury of government regulation. Beginning with attacks on Nader himself, business groups, journalists, politicians and intellectuals began to react against the consumer protection measures introduced by Johnson and Nixon. Within a few years, an assertive, well-financed and well coordinated assault on regulation as a whole had been launched.[46]

This anti-regulatory movement was strongly associated with the organisations of American big business such as the Business Roundtable and those rightwing think-tanks which would later be described as 'neo-conservative' (for example, the American Enterprise Institute and the Heritage Foundation).[47] In the 1970s, they engaged in a symbolic battle with Nader and the organised consumer movement over a proposed Consumer Protection Agency which would have meant America's model of consumer protection would have more closely resembled the social democratic principles implemented by European governments. The Consumer Protection Agency Bill was ultimately defeated but it is the

[45] Finch, 'A History of the Consumer Movement'; Kansas State University Archive, Dorothy Willner papers, Box 11, Virginia H. Knauer, *President's Committee on Consumer Interests and Office of Consumer Affairs: The Years 1969–1977* (Washington, DC, 1977).

[46] Capital Legal Foundation, *Abuse of Trust: A Report on Ralph Nader's Network* (Chicago, 1982); Melvin J. Grayson and Thomas R Shepard, *The Disaster Lobby: Prophets of Ecological Doom and Other Absurdities* (Chicago, 1973); Mary Bennett Peterson, *The Regulated Consumer* (Los Angeles, CA, 1971).

[47] Sidney Blumenthal, *The Rise of the Counter-Establishment: From Conservative Ideology to Political Power* (New York, 1986); *The Essential Neoconservative Reader*, ed. Mark Green (Reading, MA, 1996); Peter Steinfels, *The Neoconservatives: The Men Who Are Changing America's Politics* (New York, 1979); James Allen Smith, *The Idea Brokers: Think Tanks and the Rise of the New Policy Elite* (New York, 1991); Derk Arend Wilcox, *The Right Guide: A Guide to Conservative and Right-of-Centre Organisations* (Ann Arbor, MI, 1997).

nature of the defeat that was most impressive. It involved a massive mobilisation of corporate interests against the consumer movement, the influx of corporate lawyers into Washington, the establishment of numerous political action committees and sustained assaults on the media, public opinion and Capitol Hill legislators. Tip O'Neill, Speaker of the House from 1977, claimed that in twenty-five years he had 'never seen such extensive lobbying' and subsequent studies by political scientists have concluded that, along with the Labour Law Reform Bill and the Economic Recovery Tax Act, the Consumer Protection Agency Bill assumed a symbolic importance for both the consumer and the anti-regulatory movements.[48]

The implications of the 'corporatisation' of US politics did not end in Washington. It constituted a more general victory of free market principles which would result in the export of an anti-regulatory and pro-big business agenda on to the world stage. Ronald Reagan came into power on the back of a resurgent right and supported by a number of key neoconservative think-tanks which capitalised on the anti-regulatory mood they had helped foster among the US public. The American Enterprise Instititute turned its attention to the perceived problems of regulation at the international level. It attacked the 'global straitjacket' imposed on business by bodies such as UNCTAD while it accused WHO and the NGOs which lobbied it of 'biting the hand that cures them'.[49] In the attempts to impose codes of conduct on the marketing of pharmaceuticals and baby foods, the American Enterprise Institute accused bodies supporting the consumer movement's campaigns of an implicit 'colonialism' since they assumed that indigenous peoples – now operating as independent states – were 'incapable of governing themselves'.[50]

The Heritage Foundation likewise launched a comprehensive critique against the institutions of global governance. From 1982, it systematically monitored the work of the UN, seemingly seeking to undermine the entire

---

[48] Schlesinger Library, Harvard University, Esther Peterson Papers, Box 89, Folder 1746: Cohen and Tremaine, *Consumer Agency History*, 66; David Vogel, *Kindred Strangers: The Uneasy Relationship between Politics and Business in America* (Princeton, NJ, 1996); Graham Wilson, 'American Business and Politics', in *Interest Group Politics*, ed. Allan J. Cigler and Burdett A. Loomis (Washington, DC, 1986), 221–35; Patrick J. Ackard, 'Corporate Mobilisation and Political Power: The Transformation of US Economic Policy in the 1970s', *American Sociological Review*, 57 (1992), 597–615; Dan Clawson and Mary Ann Clawson, 'Reagan or Business? Foundations of the New Conservatism', in *The Structure of Power in America: The Corporate Elite as a Ruling Class*, ed. Michael Schwartz (New York, 1987), 201–17.

[49] Richard Berryman and Richard Schifter, 'A Global Straitjacket', *Regulation*, Sept./Oct. 1981, 19–28; Kenneth L. Adelman, 'Biting the Hand that Cures Them', *Regulation*, July/Aug. 1982, 16–18.

[50] Adelman, 'Biting', 18; Harry Schwartz, 'The UN System's War on the Drug Industry', *Regulation*, July/Aug. 1982, 19–24.

infrastructure.[51] It published a series of reports attacking the policies of the World Bank, UNESCO, the World Health Organisation and UNCTAD as well as the intellectual underpinnings of regulation as a whole. They claimed the UN was persistently 'anti-West, anti-American, and anti-free market'.[52] It too turned its attention to the consumer movement. It argued that multinational corporations were becoming 'the first victim of the UN war on free enterprise'. This was being directed behind the scenes by 'an assault from a growing and potentially dangerous, internationally based, and self-styled "consumerist" movement that already is helping set the agenda at various UN agencies'. Specifically, IOCU was identified as the source of an 'anti-capitalist and anti-free enterprise bias, which in the past decade has grown to alarming proportions within UN documents and literature'.[53] IOCU had developed a campaigning style based around networks which placed consumers in alliance with trade unions, church-based groups and less developed countries in order to promote codes of conduct which attacked specific industries. The pamphlet amounted to a broad-ranging swipe against the UN, the New International Economic Order and the Commission on Transnational Corporations but which eventually homed in on 'the extremist wing of the interational consumerist movement', especially IOCU.[54] Heritage identified Anwar Fazal as the main cause of the problem, due to his spawning of a new wave of consumer organisations such as IBFAN, PAN, HAI and Consumer Interpol and his supposed 'distortions designed to undermine the MNCs and private sector approach to development'.[55] It concluded by urging the Reagan administration to 'become more aware of the dangers posed to US-based multinational firms by the internationalist consumerist movement' and to oppose all efforts to implement codes of conduct.[56] This should be achieved, it was argued, by increasing industry participation in UN negotiations and within the US Mission, proposing weak counter-proposals and by forging international alliances with other states even if this meant making it 'abundantly clear to those countries that the US does not look favourably upon their support for the anti-free enterprise, restrictive initiatives'.[57]

[51] Lee Edwards, *The Power of Ideas: The Heritage Foundation at 25 Years* (Ottowa, 1997), 77.

[52] Burton Yale Pines, 'Introduction', in *A World without a U.N.: What would Happen If the U.N. Shut Down*, ed. Burton Yale Pines (Washington, DC, 1984), x.

[53] Roger A. Brooks, *Multinationals: First Victim of the UN War on Free Enterprise* (Washington, DC, 1982), 1–3; Anon., 'Heritage Foundation Slams "Extremist" Consumer Organisations', *Multinational Monitor*, 4 (Jan. 1983), 8.

[54] Brooks, *Multinationals*, 19.

[55] *Ibid.*, 21.

[56] *Ibid.*, 23.

[57] *Ibid.*, 24.

The consequences of this new international anti-regulatory agenda were soon apparent. American government opposition to the codes of conduct proposed by IOCU at the UN was both consistent and out of line with majority opinion. Often, only a handful of countries opposed consumer measures: the United States was always one of these and frequently the sole dissenting voice. In the early 1980s, the consumer movement was still able to mobilise global civil society and government missions at the UN around its key demands and it achieved notable successes: the UN Guidelines on Consumer Protection were perhaps the culmination of a series of codes of conduct (e.g., on the marketing of breastmilk substitutes) which had been drawn up in the years previously. However, the new international agenda meant that the consumer movement's next campaign, a Code of Conduct on Transnational Corporations, was doomed to fail. This initiative had its origins in the early 1970s following the investigation by the UN's Group of Eminent Persons into the role of multinational corporations in the Chilean political process. By the 1980s, the consumer movement was leading the campaign to restrict the activities of these companies and the Code of Conduct, although voluntary, was to be the first stage in achieving this. However, the opposition the consumer movement faced from both US diplomats and advisors, many of whom had direct links with the exact same business and neoconservative groups that had defeated the Consumer Protection Agency Bill in the 1970s, meant that the Code of Conduct never stood a chance. The campaigns persisted, eventually petering out in the early 1990s when the US State Department was able to claim, in a telex to all US embassies, that the Code was 'a relic of another era', supported only by those countries that held to outmoded notions of foreign investment.[58]

The consumer movement was clearly defeated on this matter, but the nature of the defeat needs to be emphasised. Because just as the consumer movement was seeking a regulatory system through the UN Economic and Social Council, the entire structure of global trade was being renegotiated through the Uruguay Round, which would ultimately culminate in the creation of the World Trade Organisation and the renewed emphasis placed on the World Bank and the IMF in determining the rules and consequences of trade and opened markets. If we are to insist, therefore, that the consumer movement was defeated by big business in negotiations over a Code of Conduct, then this was not simply a defeat on a level playing field. But neither was it a defeat because the goal posts had been moved, as they repeatedly were, during the various stages of the Code's progress. Rather it was a defeat in which the consumer movement

[58] IOCU Archive, Box 102, File H88.6, telex from US State Department to US Embassies, 26 Mar. 1991.

looked to be playing alone on the field provided by the UN, unaware that there was no longer an opposition. Multinational enterprise and advocates of de-regulation, meanwhile, had joined a game being played in another stadium. For them, and for governments supporting the system of trade liberalisation being promoted by the US, the real action would come to take place at the World Trade Organisation and not the UN. Here was a new arena for governing world trade in which the consumer movement would have some considerable difficulty in both understanding the rules and finding either a role to play or a seat from which to spectate.

The comparison of the influence of NGOs at the UN with their influence at the WTO is quite spectacular. NGO influence at the UN was ruled by a complex system of category status recognition which determined how much of a say NGOs could have in intergovernmental debates. Many hundreds of NGOs, often spearheaded by the consumer movement, had access to the seats of power. At the WTO, however, that access was reduced to nothing. Over the years, NGOs have managed to negotiate some sort of relationship with the WTO, but it still remains minimal and much was perhaps lost for NGOs in the meantime. For instance, it became clear in 1996 that the WTO was not going to allow NGO participation and would restrict publication of most of its documents for six months.[59] Indeed, it would take until May 1997 for the WTO to actually listen to NGOs: a year earlier, at a symposium on trade and the environment, government ministers at the WTO meeting simply failed to turn up. The contrast with the 1980s, when IOCU had a prominent impact on global institutions, could not have been more stark.

III

It is these two aspects of the organised consumer movement's recent history – retreat and defeat – that enables us to reflect more broadly on the changing meaning of consumer society. I began this essay with birth. The death I therefore conclude with is the growing irrelevance of the consumer movement to the global regulation of the marketplace. At the same time, its earlier vision of the meaning of consumer society – based as much upon necessity as affluence – has become increasingly sidelined for reasons as much to do with its own operating logic as the criticisms made from it by outside forces. Nevertheless, it has meant that other aspects of consumer society – and especially individual choice – have assumed a greater prominence which has eclipsed the older social welfare aspects of living in an age of consumption and mass affluence. The decline of the

[59] IOCU Archive, Box 'Council Meetings, 1996–2003', File CM47/3(v), Global Policy and Campaigns Unit, 'Summary Progress Report, November 1995–September 1996'.

global consumer movement therefore parallels and partially explains the death of this older meaning of consumer society.

Death, of course, is a common pessimistic trope of critiques of consumer society. It lurks in the supposed emptiness of our souls, in the decay of our sensibilities, in the 'malaise' of our values that President Carter even castigated his fellow Americans for in his famous 'crisis of confidence' speech of 1979 when he warned that 'We've learned that piling up material goods cannot fill the emptiness of lives which have no confidence or purpose.'[60]

It is tempting to conclude on a similar pessimistic note, as so many other historians have found themselves doing. But in the decline of the organised consumer movement it is better not to see in its changing fortunes a shift towards an inevitable consumerist dystopian end point marked by individual acquisitiveness and the collapse of the social fabric, but further evidence of the constant re-politicisation of consumption that has taken place whenever people have identified themselves as consumers. Prior to the movement studied in this article were the millions of free traders, cooperators, cost-of-living campaigners and fair wage advocates. Subsequent to the events examined here have been the growth of ethical and green consumer movements, the explosion of fair trade and the widespread politics of consumption emerging out of the latest trends within anti-globalisation protest. The point is that although individual choice may well have replaced the standard of living as the benchmark for measuring the success of consumer society, this is just one phase in the evolving history of consumer society which will continue for many decades to come.

It therefore seems pertinent to finish by returning to another classic text on consumer society, the fiftieth anniversary of which occurs this year, the same year as the hundredth anniversary of the author's birth. In *The Affluent Society*, published in 1958, John Kenneth Galbraith left us in no doubt as to the real choices facing us as consumers. In a famous passage he pointed to the problems lurking behind America's newfound prosperity in its new affluent age. He described a family out for a picnic in the countryside supposedly living the American dream, but 'Just before dozing off on an air mattress, beneath a nylon tent, amid the stench of decaying refuse, they may reflect vaguely on the curious unevenness of their blessings. Is this, indeed,' Galbraith asked, 'the American genius?'[61]

Galbraith's commentary seems as pertinent today as it did in 1958. His point is not that we should criticise or condemn consumer society as a whole. Indeed, it has actually done much to improve people's lives and

[60] Daniel Horowitz, *The Anxieties of Affluence: Critiques of American Consumer Culture, 1939–1979* (Amherst, MA, 2004).

[61] John Kenneth Galbraith, *The Affluent Society* (1958; Penguin edn, 1999), 188.

is undoubtedly a good thing, especially for those consumer activists who flocked to the comparative testing organisations in the 1950s. Rather, the point is that we should question its meaning and remember that there is more than one consumer society. So Galbraith's passage actually reminds us of one of the real choices facing consumer society: between more private or more public goods. The choices that we are confronted with today are not actually choices: they are preferences, they are not the choices which we must face when trading off climate change against higher rates of consumption; when balancing the needs of the world's poor with the needs of the world's rich. Instead, we are faced with an impoverished set of choices: and there is evidence that these are choices which we do not actually want.

The choice is not between equally attractive pre-packaged commodities and services: remember, Buridan's ass starved to death when confronted with two equally attractive piles of hay. The choice is between the competing demands of affluence and necessity. These two competing aspects of consumer society are embodied in the problems faced by affluence by rapidly expanding economies such as China's, and the problems faced by those who cannot even achieve a most basic quality of life, as in so many countries in Africa. But in the death throes of consumption, where will the consumer voice be heard? As the global economy rushes headlong to embrace the consumer society of China, what of Africa and the problems its consumers face which, for so long, had been the central concern of both consumer activists and those planners and bureaucrats who helped shape the post-war international consumer society?

To return to our opening text, there was an optimism about *The Birth of a Consumer Society*. McKendrick's consumers might have been concerned with status and conspicuous consumption. But like Mandeville's bees in *The Grumbling Hive*, there was the expectation that greed and self-interest – our private vices – would lead to the greater public benefits of economic growth and greater prosperity for all. For many consumer activists over the next three centuries, this has simply not been the case. Too many consumers have been left behind in the long-run perspectives provided by the invisible hand. This is why basic needs have been so central to the creation and the politics of consumer societies around the world. Standards of living and meeting basic consumer interests do not quite face the challenge of the environmental concerns of many of today's ethical shoppers, but if they are left behind then what we are witnessing is the deletion of a basic goal of consumer society, shared by consumer activists such as America's Ralph Nader and Malaysia's Anwar Fazal, but also by politicians such as Nixon and Krushchev who, by arguing in the kitchen, demonstrated the very real links between the politics of the housewife and the politics of the entire world's development more generally. The deletion, now, though is not like Fazal's deletion of the right to choice, but it is the deletion of the right to basic needs. Of course, to proclaim the death of consumer society is absurd. But if we allow the insertion an indefinite article such as in McKendrick's *Birth of a Consumer Society*, then perhaps it is valid to conclude now with a *Death of a Consumer Society*. There is a degree of pessimism here, but it is by no means the end of the story.

ROYAL HISTORICAL SOCIETY
REPORT OF COUNCIL
SESSION 2007–2008

Officers and Council

- At the Anniversary Meeting on 25 November 2007 the Officers of the Society were re-elected.
- The Vice-Presidents retiring under By-law XVII were Professor J E Burton and Dr P Seaward. Mr R Fisher, MA and Professor D M Palliser, MA, DPhil, were elected to replace them.
- The Members of Council retiring under By-law XX were Professor J Ohlmeyer, Professor M E Rubin and Dr EM C van Houts. Professor C Given-Wilson, MA, PhD, Professor M Ormrod, BA, DPhil and Dr D Thomas, PhD were elected in their place.
- The Society's administrative staff consists of Sue Carr, Executive Secretary and Melanie Batt, Administrative Assistant.
- Kingston Smith were appointed auditors for the year 2007–2008 under By-law XXXIX.
- Brewin Dolphin Securities were appointed to manage the Society's investment funds.

Activities of the Society during the Year

The Annual Report contains individual reports of the activities of the seven Committees which support the work of Council – Research Policy, Teaching Policy, General Purposes, Publications, Finance, Membership and Research Support – and the remarks which now follow are a preface to these more detailed reports.

Throughout the year the Society has maintained its prominent role in defending and advancing the interests of the discipline and the profession.

Following last year's useful meeting with Natalie Ceeney, CEO of The National Archives, David Thomas and James Strachan, Dr David Thomas was proposed, and subsequently elected, as a member of Council. Collaboration with The National Archives continues, in the form of the Gerald Aylmer seminar and the visit to TNA organized for candidates for the Royal Historical Society/*History Today* prize for the best undergraduate dissertation.

The President, President-Elect, and Honorary Secretary have maintained contact with the AHRC. Issues of continuing concern include the implications of changing committee structures at AHRC, and the sense that AHRC needs to listen more to the views of subject associations and learned societies. The Society has expressed concern at the reduction in postgraduate funding and the cancellation of the Autumn 2008 round of AHRC bi-annual Research Leave Award Scheme. We will monitor the operation of the new institutional block grant scheme for postgraduate research grants. The President is in contact with other learned societies about the co-ordination of responses to developments at AHRC and in the field of Humanities research more generally. The Honorary Secretary also attended an informal meeting with representatives of ESRC, organized by the Economic History Society, along with representatives of economic, social and business history.

Council has continued to monitor, largely through reports from the President, the future of RAE/REF, including the extent to which metrics will form part of the future assessment of research, and the ranking or journals.

As usual, the Society made two very successful visits outside London, the first to the University of Essex on 19 October 2007, and the second to Sheffield Hallam University on 25 April 2008, as reported in the Spring 2008 Newsletter. Council has greatly valued these visits as a means of getting to know individuals and departments, hearing their concerns and their views on the Society's role and activities. The visits are combined with a paper reading by an invited speaker. The next visit is to the University of Dundee on 17 October 2008.

Council and the Officers record their gratitude to the Society's administrative staff: the Executive Secretary Sue Carr and the Administrative Secretary Melanie (Batt) Ransom. We thank them for their expert and dedicated work on the Society's many activities.

RESEARCH POLICY COMMITTEE, 2007–8

The G.E Aylmer Seminar, co-organized by the committee, on behalf of the Society, together with The National Archives, was held at the British Library on October 23rd 2007 on the subject of *Digital Horizons: How the Digital Revolution Changes the Relationship between Historians and their Archival Sources*. It was very successful, well attended and stimulated a lively debate. A full report can be accessed via the Society's website.

The Committee continues to monitor the Bologna Process. Dr Elisabeth van Houts has taken responsibility for this. There was no apparent progress in 2007–8.

The Committee monitors the activities of AHRC informed by comments from Fellows and Council and the Society's representatives on its panels and committees. Aspects of AHRC activity in which it has taken a close interest include: 1) the decision to devolve selection for postgraduate awards to HEIs. It was decided to monitor the system as it unfolds, taking account of the experience of Fellows and Council Members; 2) concern was expressed at the closure of the Arts and Humanities Data Service without adequate replacement provision being available. There were suggestions that the needs of historians would be provided for by the Data Archive at the University of Essex. It was agreed to monitor the outcome. Concern was also expressed at the substantial cut in postgraduate awards in 2008 which, it was felt had not been adequately justified. The President agreed to seek a meeting with the newly appointed AHRC Director of Research, Professor Shearer West. She will be attending a future meeting of the committee to discuss aspects of AHRC policy.

The Committee carefully follows RAE arrangements, actual and proposed, present and future, including the contentious issue of the use of metrics. It was agreed to await further policy announcements and also the outcome of the British Academy study of the uses of metrics in the humanities and social sciences

Developments in research support in Wales, Scotland and Northern Ireland are also closely watched and helpfully reported upon by members of the committee. The committee noted, with pleasure, the forthcoming AHRC/IRCHSS agreement facilitating collaborative research across the border. It expressed concern about the continuing exclusion of Scottish universities from JISC funding. It expressed still greater concern at a report in cuts in university funding by the Scottish Executive

The committee continued to monitor the issue of preservation and management of modern records in the IT age. It is in constant touch with TNA on this matter.

The committee endorsed concerns expressed by the President about the organization and costs of the forthcoming International Congress of Historical Sciences, to be held in Beijing in 2009.

The committee considered a proposal for the formation an All-Party Parliamentary Group on Archives. It expressed some dissatisfaction at a lack of clarity in its objectives and the absence from the proposed group of any MPs/peers who are historians and of representatives of the Houses of Parliament's own archives service. It was agreed that the Society would recommend names of suitable members and request inclusion of an RHS representative in the group. The historian Lord (Paul) Bew has now become secretary of the group.

It was agreed that the Society would make a submission to the committee established by the Prime Minister to review the 30-Year Rule governing the release of government records.

TEACHING POLICY COMMITTEE, 2007–8

The role of the Teaching Policy Committee of the Royal Historical Society is essentially to investigate matters relating to the teaching of History from A levels to postgraduate qualifications, to keep the society informed of developments and concerns, and to seek to influence policy within university departments and at government level. We have also been concerned to report on matters relating to the wider 'infrastructure' supporting History teaching, namely the work of colleagues in archives, museums, art galleries and heritage sites.

Much, alas, has been on hold this year. The flurry of activity over A- level reforms has died down and we have been holding our breath to find out how the new Humanities Diploma will be developed. The examination boards have switched their attention to changes at GCSE level, where our colleagues in the Historical Association are better qualified to offer advice. We have been represented at meetings of QCA, but that body has now informed us that its resources to fund valuable meetings with interested parties from time to time has been cut; indeed, they are now looking to the RHS to fill the gap.

We have maintained a watching brief elsewhere with the continued unfolding of the Bologna Agreement and its possible impact on taught Masters provision in the UK and discussions of the shape of the doctorate. Likewise, we have monitored meetings held by QAA and HEFCE, the latter in relation to proposals for the Research Excellence Framework designed to replace the RAE.

There has been a hiatus alas, regarding the occasional meetings held between our President, colleagues from the IHR, History UK (HE) and the HA and senior government advisors; we hope such meetings will resume before too long. While we have drawn closer to our colleagues in the HA – and recently backed their campaigns to raise the profile of History in schools and to champion CPD for teachers – the year has witnessed changes in the leadership of all our close allies in related professional bodies. The IHR, scene of another important conference this year, has seen the departure of David Bates – to whom we owe a great debt of thanks for his sterling work in recent years – to be replaced by Professor Miles Taylor whom we welcome. Professor Barry Coward has retired from his tour of duty as President at the Historical Association to be replaced by – dare we say 'one of our own' – Professor Anne Curry, for she is a Vice-President of the RHS! The problems of the leaderless element of the History, Archaeology and Classics Subject Centre have been resolved by the appointment in the summer of Dr Sarah Richardson to lead on History. The RHS continues to be represented on its advisory panel and we contributed to the annual conference held at Oxford at Easter. History UK (HE) has also moved into a new phase with Professors Jackie Eales and Ann Hughes taking over the role of co-convenors of its activities, with an important meeting planned for November.

Our remit is large and seems to be growing ever larger, hence we shall continue to explore opportunities to collaborate with our colleagues in related bodies, seek funding for projects of importance, and share the load of auditing developments that raise concerns. We lobbied about further dramatic cuts to the number of students being trained on PGCE courses to become History teachers in secondary schools; we have concerns about the plight of History in primary schools; we have anxieties about what might happen in our public archive offices, museums and galleries. 'Public History' is more popular than ever, but the infrastructure which supports it all requires our close attention.

GENERAL PURPOSES COMMITTEE, 2007–8

As its title suggests, the remit of this committee ranges widely across the activities of the Society. It receives suggestions from Fellows and Council for paper-givers and makes recommendations to Council on the card of session, taking into account the need for a balanced programme in terms of chronological and geographical spread. In addition to the regular sessions held at UCL, it is also responsible for the Prothero Lecture, the Colin Matthew Lecture and the Gerald Aylmer Seminar.

In the past, the Society had arranged for two of its regular lectures each year to be given at other universities, but it had continued to choose the speakers. Last year it was decided to continue the visits outside London but to link them to symposia organised by institutions themselves. Information was sent to all heads of history. We were particularly keen to encourage university departments to join together with libraries, archives and museums, as well as with other higher education institutions, in putting forward bids. The Committee was pleased to receive excellent proposals for two symposia: 'Victorian Cities Re-visited', to be held at the University of Leeds in spring 2009; 'Poverty and Welfare in Ireland c. 1833–1922', to be held at Queens University Belfast on 26 June 2009.

The Committee is also responsible for the appointment of assessors for the Society's prizes, and receives their report and proposals for award winners. It also reviews regularly the terms and conditions of the awards. This year it has reviewed the arrangements for the Gladstone and Whitfield Prizes, and revised the remit of the David Berry Prize for Scottish History, opening up the criteria to include chapters from doctoral dissertations, complete Masters dissertations, and articles up to

10,000 words in length. From 2008 there will be both an essay prize, and a book prize, to be awarded if the runner-up to either the Whitfield or the Gladstone prize is on a Scottish historical subject. The Committee is delighted to report that the Historiographer Royal of Scotland has agreed to act as one of the judges for the David Berry prizes.

Meetings of the Society

5 papers were given in London this year and 2 papers were read at locations outside London. Welcome invitations were extended to the Society to visit the History Departments at the University of Essex and Sheffield Hallam University.

At the ordinary meetings of the Society the following papers were read:

- ○ 'A tale of two (episcopal) surveys: the strange fates of Edmund Grindal and Cuthbert Mayne revisited' Professor Peter Lake (4 July 2007: Prothero Lecture)
- ○ 'War stories: disaster and narrative in wartime China, 1937–46' Dr Rana Mitter (21 September 2007)
- ○ 'Centre and periphery in the dynamic of the early modern European book trade' Professor Andrew Pettegree (19 October 2007 at the University of Essex)
- ○ 'Humanism and Reform in Pre-Reformation English Monasteries' Dr James Clark (8 February 2008)
- ○ 'Cultures of Exchange: Atlantic Africa in the Era of the Slave Trade' Professor David Richardson (25 April at Sheffield Hallam University)
- ○ 'Representation, c.800: Arab, Byzantine, Carolingian' Professor Leslie Brubaker (9 May 2008)

At the Anniversary Meeting on 23 November 2007, the President, Professor Martin Daunton delivered his third address on 'Britain and globalization since 1850: III. The world of Bretton Woods, 1939–1974'

The Colin Matthew Memorial Lecture for the Public Understanding of History was given on Wednesday 31 October by Dr Simon Thurley on 'The Fabrication of Medieval History: Archaeology and Artifice at the Office of Works'. These lectures continue to be given in memory of the late Professor Colin Matthew, a former Literary Director and Vice-President of the Society.

Prizes

The Society's annual prizes were awarded as follows:

- The Alexander prize was awarded in 2008 to Mary Partridge for her article 'Thomas Hoby's translation of Castiglione's *Book of the Courtier*' in *Historical Journal*, vol. 50, No. 4 (December 2007).

- The David Berry Prize for an essay on Scottish history for 2007 was awarded to Mark Towsey for his essay "An Infant Son to Truth Engage". Virtue, responsibility and self-improvement in the reading of Elizabeth Rose of Kilvarock, 1747–1815' in *Journal of the Edinburgh Bibliographical Society*, 2 (2007).
- The Whitfield Book Prize for a first book on British history attracted 32 entries.

The Prize for 2007 was jointly awarded to:

Duncan Bell, *The Idea of Greater Britain: Empire and the Future of World Order, 1860–1900* (Princeton University Press)

The judges' citation read:

An earlier generation of historians studied and researched the highly charged political debate which took place in mid and late Victorian Britain concerning Britain's place in the world as a great imperial power in the face of mounting challenges from other great power rivals, future as well present, most notably the United States. In recent times historians have shown little interest in engaging with this debate. In his *The Idea of Greater Britain: Empire and the Future of World Order, 1860–1900* (Princeton and Oxford: Princeton University Press, 2007) Duncan Bell has breathed new and vigorous life into this subject. In a masterly and penetrating examination of this debate he demonstrates with great clarity and insight the concerns, anxieties, hopes and expectations of a generation of Victorian political thinkers with regard to the British present and future. This book is based on a very impressive range of primary and secondary sources and is exceptionally well written. It is a pioneering work of research which makes a major contribution to modern intellectual history, most notably to the emerging field of the history of international thought.

and

Stephen Baxter, *The Earls of Mercia: Lordship and Power in Late Anglo-Saxon England* (Oxford University Press)

The judges' citation read:

Stephen Baxter's *The Earls of Mercia: Lordship and Power in Late Anglo-Saxon England* (Oxford: Oxford University Press, 2007) takes as its starting point the idea that the power of the great earldoms of late Anglo-Saxon England was not as secure as has generally been supposed. Working outwards from the house of Mercia (or 'Leofwinesons', to counterbalance the 'Godwinesons'), this book presents a novel, nuanced and above all convincing interpretation of the interaction of local and national power structures in England during the last century or so before the Norman Conquest. For a first book, *The Earls of Mercia* is remarkably confident and mature in its judgements and exposition, and is written with clarity and precision. Based on intimate knowledge of a relatively small but thoroughly problematic range of sources (including Domesday Book, which is used to excellent effect to chart the extent and nature of Leofwineson lordship), it provides an interpretation of this period which will change significantly the way in which future historians view the late Anglo-Saxon polity and its destruction at the hands of the Normans.

The Gladstone Book Prize for a first book on non-British history attracted 14 entries.

The Prize for 2007 was awarded to:

Yasmin Khan, *The Great Partition: the Making of India and Pakistan* (Yale University Press)

The judges' citation read:

A powerful and evocative study, Yasmin Khan's, *The Great Partition: the Making of India and Pakistan*, provides a compelling and highly original insight into the aftermath of the partition of 1947 by setting accounts of its impact on ordinary people against a wider political backdrop. This is a study of memory and the multiple ways in which the past is reconfigured in the present. The obliviousness of all parties to what the realities of Partition would bring, and especially its impact on the general population is powerfully shown, the consequences of the ensuing displacement and death shockingly evoked. Khan's is indubitably a scholarly study, drawing on a huge range of sources and employing a large historiography with sensitivity and skill, but the extent of the scholarship is not overtly advertised. She deploys her footnotes modestly and discretely at the end of the volume, so that the apparatus does not get in the way of the importance of the message she articulates. Her narrative has a dignity and brevity that cannot but impress. The judges were persuaded of the importance of the narrative Khan tells; this is a largely untold and ill-understood tragedy of the twentieth century, which deserves a wide hearing. Khan has produced a well-written and accessible book that has a regrettable modern resonance as well as a profound historical significance. It is a work all Members and Fellows of the Society will want to read.

The judges nominated a proxime accesit:

Filippo De Vivo, *Information and Community in Venice* (Oxford University Press)

The Society's Rees Davies Essay Prize was not awarded in 2007.

In order to recognise the high quality of work now being produced at undergraduate level in the form of third-year dissertations, the Society continued, in association with *History Today* magazine, to award an annual prize for the best undergraduate dissertation. Departments are asked to nominate annually their best dissertation and a joint committee of the Society and *History Today* select in the autumn the national prizewinner from among these nominations. The prize also recognizes the Society's close relations with *History Today* and the important role the magazine has played in disseminating scholarly research to a wider audience. 33 submissions were made.

The Prize for 2007 was awarded to:

Morgan Daniels for his dissertation 'Scarcely seen or felt. British Government and the 1960s satire boom'.

The article by the prize-winner presenting his research will appear in *History Today* in 2008. Twelve prize entrants and five of their respective tutors accepted the invitation to visit the National Archives on 9 January 2008, where they were welcomed by Dr David

Thomas (Director of Government and Archive Services, and given a guided tour of the Archives facilities.

The German History Society, in association with the Society, agreed to award a prize to the winner of an essay competition. The essay, on any aspect of German history, including the history of German-speaking people both within and beyond Europe, was open to any postgraduate registered for a degree in a university in either the United Kingdom or the Republic of Ireland.

The Prize for the winning essay in 2007 was awarded to:

David Motadel for his essay 'Intercultural Royal Visits. State Visits of Persian Shahs to Germany, 1873–1905)

The Frampton and Beazley Prizes for A-level performances in 2007 were awarded following nominations from the examining bodies:

Frampton Prize

OCR: Clare Walker-Gore, Wakefield Girls' High School, Leeds

Beazley Prize:

SQA: Kyle Lawson, Stewart's Melville College, Edinburgh

- The Director of the Institute of Historical Research announced the winner and runners-up of the Pollard Prize, at the Annual Reception on 2 July 2008. The prize is awarded annually to the best postgraduate student paper presented in a seminar at the IHR.

The Pollard Prize winner for 2008 was awarded jointly to:

- Mark Towsey for his essay 'Philosophically playing the devil': readers' responses to David Hume and the Scottish Enlightenment'

  and

- Alice Taylor for her essay 'Historical Writing in 12th and 13th- century Scotland: the Dunfermline Compilation'.

Publications

PUBLICATIONS COMMITTEE, 2007–8

Last year we reported the arrival of *Transactions* on JSTOR. It was very pleasing to see the first year of user statistics, which showed a very high level usage: virtually every article has been downloaded at least once. An average 1,155 downloads per volume were recorded for the years

1976–2001; what we could not have predicted was the level of interest in the earliest years, for the first 25 years of *Transactions* an average of 218 downloads per volume were recorded. The most 'popular' article was Roy Foster's paper 'History and the Irish Question' published in 1983 and accessed 1,329 times. The Society now draws a modest revenue from its participation in JSTOR. We are still keen to licence the digitisation of the back list of Camden Society volumes. Several are already available through British History On-Line; others will become available through the Electronic Enlightenment project based in Oxford; others still through Google books. But we would like to see a more comprehensive approach adopted.

It has been another year of solid achievement for the Society's bibliography. Another 18,600 records have been added to the database since the last report; 4,932 of these have been added by our sister project Irish History On-Line. The overall size of the database is now 446,000 records, of which 65,500 relate to Irish history. It is striking that when the Bibliography went live as on line resource in 2002 there were 300,000 records. Remarkably, since then it has grown by nearly 50%, in large part a tribute to the collaborations with London's Past On-Line and Irish History On-Line, but also due to the extraordinary (and, it is to be feared, sometimes under-appreciated) industry of the core project staff, Peter Salt and Simon Baker. In addition to the basic but essential tasks of adding records, much effort has been expended on improving the searching facilities (e.g. increasing speeds, allowing the marking of records between individual pages of results) and the linkages to other resources. Work on developing the links to Google's digital books is at the testing stage, and although progress on on-line tutorials is slower than we would have hoped, it is hoped to launch them early in 2009. The General Editor attended the second conference on historical bibliographies hosted by the Berlin Brandenburg Academy of Social Sciences on 15–16 September 2008; although we have much to learn from our continental colleagues, it was reassuring to see that the RHS remains at the cutting edge in terms of its connectivity to other resources and on-line text (intriguingly most of the Library based bibliographies were encountering internal resistance to the notion of linkage to Google books); it is also apparent that it offers good value for money in terms of numbers of records generated per unit of staff employed. The meeting took further the discussions about possible cross-searching of the various European databases, and it is hoped that a bid for funding to bring this about will be made in the near future. A user survey conducted in the summer of 2008 revealed very high levels of satisfaction with the service offered by the RHS Bibliography, while also providing helpful feedback on possible improvements.

It is unfortunate that all these achievements are now at risk. By the end of 2009 we will have benefited from nine years continuous funding by the AHRC (and its predecessor the AHRB), but it has been made clear that further funding from this source is highly unlikely, and the financial difficulties of the IHR which continues to host the resource, call into question its continued viability. The Society has established a working group which is exploring a variety of scenarios, which include the possibility of moving to a subscription model. If this happens, it will only be with the greatest reluctance on the part of the Society, but it needs to be understood that the charity sector also increasingly takes the view that while it will provide seed corn funding for resources such as ours, it does not expect to enter open-ended commitments, and that resources should earn their keep. Whether that is actually realistic for a resource such as ours (initial work suggests that the subscription opportunities are constrained, and the Society and partners would still need to provide a subsidy) is a moot point.

The General Editor has written a piece about the history of the Society's commitment to bibliographies for the IHR's new facility on 'Making History'. It was Sir George Prothero who pushed the Society into involvement, and his enthusiasm was echoed on the other side of the Atlantic. It was in 1909 that the Society took the key decision to develop bibliographies of British history in collaboration with colleagues in the USA. It would be a pity if the centenary year of the Society's involvement were to become a wake! Suffice it to say, that Council is working hard to avert that possibility.

The profit-sharing agreement between the Society and Cambridge University Press to publish both the *Transactions* and the accompanying Camden volumes continues to work smoothly to mutual advantage, and the Society is grateful for the support and professionalism of the staff at CUP, especially Ella Colvin and Daniel Pearce from the Periodicals Group. The Society is also pleased to report that, since his election to a Vice Presidency, Richard Fisher, a fellow since 2001, and Executive Director of Academic Publishing at CUP, has agreed to act as chair of its Publications Committee.

Transactions, Sixth Series, Volume 17 was published during the session, and *Transactions*, Sixth Series, Volume 18 went to press, to be published in November 2008.

In the Camden, Fifth Series, *The Affairs of Others': The Diaries of Francis Place, 1825*–1836, ed. James Jaffe (vol. 30) and *The Correspondence of Henry Cromwell, 1655*–1659, ed. Peter Gaunt (vol. 31) were published and *Marital Litigation in the Court of Requests, 1542*–1642, ed. Tim Stretton (vol. 32) and *Dublin Castle and the First Home Rule Crisis: The Political Journal of Sir George Fotrell, 1884*–1887, ed. Stephen Ball went to press for publication in 2008–9.

The *Studies in History* Editorial Board continued to meet throughout the year. The second series continued to produce exciting volumes. The following volumes were published, or went to press, during the session:

- *Popular Conservatism in Imperial London, 1868–1906*, Alex Windscheffel
- *Protesting about Pauperism. Poverty, Politics and Poor Relief in late-Victorian England*, Elizabeth Hurren
- *Robert Southey and Romantic Apostasy. Political Argument in Britain, 1780–1840*, David Craig
- *Imagining Roman Britain. Victorian Responses to a Roman Past*, Virginia Hoselitz
- *George Canning and Liberal Toryism. C. 1801–27*, Stephen Lee
- *Radicalism, Reform and National Identity in Scotland, 1820–1833*, Gordon Pentland

As in previous subscription years, volumes in *Studies in History* series were offered to the membership at a favourably discounted price. Many Fellows, Associates and Members accepted the offer for volumes published during the year, and the advance orders for further copies of the volumes to be published in the year 2008–2009 were encouraging.

The Society acknowledges its gratitude for the continuing subventions from the Economic History Society and the Past and Present Society to the *Studies in History* series.

Finance

FINANCE COMMITTEE, 2007–8

The Finance Committee approves the Society's accounts each financial year and its estimates for the following year. This year we changed auditors and Kingston Smith acted very professionally and thoroughly. They audit a number of charities of a similar size, and their team's head had previous experience of dealing with the Society's accounts several years ago. The accounts are presented elsewhere in *Transactions*, together with the Trustees' Annual Report. Since that Report discusses the main financial developments of the year, there is very little more to say here.

This was the year when our increase in subscriptions took effect, and at this stage in the subscription cycle one would naturally expect a profit. This profit was enhanced by a cash inflow from the sale of part of the Society's library, together with efficiency savings in administration, several of which are due to the good sense and rigour of the Executive Secretary.

At the same time, however, we have to report a significant, if unsurprising, fall in the value of the Society's investments, owing to stock market conditions. However this has not affected the high income yield of the funds, on which the Society has traditionally relied. As explained in last year's *Transactions*, the Society changed its broker at the end of September 2007. The new brokers, Brewin Dolphin, inherited the portfolio, and have made relatively few changes, which the Committee agreed to be prudent given the state of the markets. There has been a minor increase in the proportion of the portfolio in commodities and in alternative investments, and some rationalisation of smaller holdings as a result of the pooling of the Society's four investment funds in one portfolio. Nonetheless, the Robinson, Whitfield and Berry Funds will continue to be accounted for separately from the Main Fund.

One new external member joined the Committee this year, Mr Paul ffolkes Davis, the Bursar of Trinity Hall, Cambridge, who has extensive historical interests as well as many years' experience in the City.

- Council records with gratitude the benefactions made to the Society by:
  - Mr. L.C. Alexander
  - Dr. D.J. Appleby
  - The Reverend David Berry
  - Professor Andrew Browning
  - Professor J.E. Burton
  - Professor Sir Geoffrey Elton
  - Mr. P.J.C. Firth
  - Dr. J.C. Gardner
  - Dr F. Goodall
  - Miss B.F. Harvey
  - Professor S.P. Hong
  - Miss V.C.M. London
  - Dr Martin Lynn
  - Professor P.J. Marshall
  - Professor B.R. O'Brien
  - Reverend N.R. Paxton
  - Dr. S. Petrow
  - Sir George Prothero
  - Dr. L. Rausing
  - Professor H.G. Roseveare
  - Miss E.M. Robinson
  - Professor Lord Smith of Clifton
  - Mr A.T.P Suchcitz
  - Dr A.F. Sutton
  - Professor N.P. Tanner
  - Dr. E.G. Thomas
  - Dr. E.A. Wasson

Membership

MEMBERSHIP COMMITTEE, 2007–8

The Committee reviews all the applications received by the Society for Fellowship and Membership, and makes recommendations to Council. We are always pleased to receive new applications for either category, and we hope that Fellows will encourage others known to them to apply. Full details are available on the Society's website, and the published criteria for eligibility can also be found in last year's report (*Transactions* 6th Series, 17, p. 199). Please encourage applicants to fill in the necessary forms carefully – we still receive some applications not properly completed, which can take longer to process – and also remind them that they will need a reference from a current Fellow.

In recent years the total membership of the Society has risen considerably, a trend which continues. Though we look for contributions to the study of history, we encourage a broad rather than a narrow definition of the subject in assessing applications.

The following were elected to the Fellowship:

Charlotte L R ALSTON, BA, MLitt, PhD
Roberta J ANDERSON, BA, MA, PhD
David J APPLEBY, BA, MA, PhD
Matthias R ASSUNCAO, MA, PhD
Andrew C ATHERSTONE, MA, MSt, DPhil
David AUSTIN, BA, Dip Arch
Cordelia BEATTIE, BA, MA, DPhil
Tito M BENADY, MA
Troy O BICKHAM, BA, MPhil, DPhil
Eugene P BRODERICK, BA, MA, PhD
Sue BRULEY, BSc, MSc, PhD
Robert O BUCHOLZ, AB, DPhil
Edward J BUJAK, PhD
Marcus G BULL, BA, PhD
Fernando CERVANTES, MA, PhD
Elaine H CHALUS, Bed, MA, DPhil
James G CLARK, BA, MA, DPhil
Peter A COATES, MA, PhD
Tim COLE, BA, PhD
Timothy D COOPER, BA, PhD
Rory T CORNISH, BA, PhD
David J COX, BA, MA, PhD
Howard T COX, BA, MSc, PhD
David M CRAIG, BA, MPhil, PhD
Jack CUNNINGHAM, BA, MA, PhD
Robert DASSANOWSKY, BA, MA, PhD
James R T DAYBELL, BA, MA, PhD
Anne DEIGHTON, BA Dip Ed, MA, PhD
Enda DELANEY, BA, MA, PhD
James DELBOURGO, BA, MPhil, PhD
Thomas DIXON, BA, MSc, PhD
Dejan DJOKIC, BA, PhD
Abd al-Fattah EL-AWAISI, BA, PhD

Tanya EVANS, MA, MA, PhD
Elizabeth EWAN, BA, PhD
Kirsten A FENTON, MA, MPhil, PhD
Serena FERENTE, PhD
Lars FISCHER, BA, PhD
John N FISHER, MA, PhD
Stella R FLETCHER, BA, PhD
Peter S FORSAITH, PhD
Murray FRAME, MA, MLitt, PhD
Margret FRENZ, MA, PhD
Nikolas GARDNER, BA, MA, PhD
Christian GOESCHEL, BA, MPhil, PhD
Michael S GOODMAN, BA, MA, PhD
Adrian G GREEN, BA, MA, PhD
Ian D GROSVENOR, BA, PhD
Maura HAMETZ, PhD
Beth HARTLAND, BA, MA, PhD
Colin M HEYWOOD, BA, PhD
Edward J HIGGS, BA, DPhil
Victor M HOUSDEN, BA, MA, MSc, PhD
Stephen J HOWE, BA, MA, DPhil
Michael J HUGGINS, BA, MA, PhD
Iain C HUTCHISON, BA, PhD
William D IRVINE, BA, PhD
J Clare L JACKSON, BA, MPhil, PhD
Christopher N JONES, BA, MA, PhD
David C JONES, BA, PhD
Elizabeth P KEANE, BA, MA, PhD
Julie E KERR, MA, MLitt, PhD
Anne-Marie KILDAY, MA, DPhil
Toby LEADBETTER, MA, BD, AKC
Robert J LEE, BA, MA, PhD
Kate J P LOWE, BA, PhD
Julian M LUXFORD, BA, PhD
Kenneth R MACMILLAN, BA, BA, MA, PhD
John W MARSHALL, BA, MA, PhD
John S MATTHEWS, BA
Christopher D MCKENNA, BA, MA, MA, PhD
John S MCNEILL, BA, MA
Catherine MERRIDALE, BA, PhD
Julia MERRITT, BA, MA, CPhil, PhD
Stephen MILLER, BA, MA, PhD
Jane A MILLS, MinstLM, LCGI, ACMI
Hilary S MORRIS, BA, MA
Stana S NENADIC, BA, PhD

John A NULL, BA, MDiv, STM, PhD
Barry J O'TOOLE, BA, MSc, PhD
Deirdre E P PALK, BA, MA, PhD
Stephen G PARKER, Bed, MA, PhD
David R PARRATT, LLB, PhD
Nicola PIZZOLATO, BA, MA, PhD
Linda A POLLOCK, MA, PhD
Charles A PRIOR, BA, MA, PhD
Yossef RAPOPORT, BA, PhD
Sara E ROBERTS, BA, MSt, DPhil
George S ROUSSEAU, BA, MA, PhD
Paul W SANDERS, MA, DEA, PhD
Michael W SCHAICH, MA, MLS, PhD
Antonio SENNIS, BA, PhD
James SHAW, MA, PhD
Karen STOBER, MA, MPhil, PhD
Grant P TAPSELL, MA, MPhil, PhD
Frederick L TAYLOR, BA
Emlyn G THOMAS, BA, MA, PhD
David THOMSON, MA, DPhil, MA
Frank TRENTMANN, BA, MA, PhD
Georgios VAROUXAKIS, BA, MA, PhD
Christina VON HODENBERG, MA, DPhil
Kerstin VON LINGEN, MA, DPhil
Christopher C WEBB, BA, DAA, MA
Evelyn WELCH, BA, PhD
Mark J WHITE, BA, MA, PhD
Jane WINTERS, MA, PhD
Richard M WOODMAN

The following were announced in the Queen's Honours' Lists during the year:

Dr Clive Field – Fellow – O.B.E for services to History
Professor James Walvin – Fellow – O.B.E for services to History

Council was advised of and recorded with regret the deaths of 5 Fellows, 12 Retired Fellows, 1 Life Fellow and 1 Member.

These included
Dr L W Ackroyd – Member
Reverend F Azzopardi – Retired Fellow
Mrs M Cheney – Retired Fellow
Sir Howard Colvin – Retired Fellow
Dr N E Edmunds – Fellow
Mr G A J Hodgett – Life Fellow
Professor L A J Hughes – Fellow

Mr D J Johnson – Retired Fellow
Professor G H Jones – Fellow
Professor M A Jones – Retired Fellow
Dr J D Marshall – Retired Fellow
Professor G H Martin – Fellow
Professor J L McCracken – Retired Fellow
Mr D H Pennington – Retired Fellow
Professor D G Pritchard – Retired Fellow
Professor A F C Ryder – Retired Fellow
Professor K R Short – Retired Fellow
Professor F C Spooner – Retired Fellow
Dr P T M Woodland – Fellow

Over the year ending on 30 June 2008, 79 Fellows and 16 members were elected, and the total membership of the Society on that date was 2960 (including 1968 Fellows, 612 Retired Fellows, 14 Honorary Vice-Presidents, 91 Corresponding and Honorary Fellows, 64 Associates and 211 Members. This reflects the very welcome growth in our total membership, from for instance 1811 in 1990 and 2588 in 2002.

The Society exchanged publications with 15 Societies, British and Foreign.

Representatives of the Society

• The representation of the Society upon other various bodies was as follows:
  ○ Professor David Ganz on the Anthony Panizzi Foundation;
  ○ Dr. Julia Crick on the Joint Committee of the Society and the British Academy established to prepare an edition of Anglo-Saxon charters;
  ○ Professor Nicholas Brooks on a committee to promote the publication of photographic records of the more significant collections of British Coins;
  ○ Dr Christopher Kitching on the Council of the British Records Association;
  ○ Mr. Phillip Bell on the Editorial Advisory Board of the *Annual Register*;
  ○ Professor Christopher Holdsworth on the Court of the University of Exeter;
  ○ Professor Claire Cross on the Council of the British Association for Local History; and on the British Sub-Commission of the Commission Internationale d' Histoire Ecclesiastique Comparée;
  ○ Professor Miri Rubin on the Advisory Council of the reviewing committee on the Export of Works of Art;
  ○ Professor Margot Finn on the Court of the University of Birmingham;

- ○ Professor Janet Burton on the Court of Governors of the University of Cardiff;
- ○ Professor Rosamund McKitterick on a committee to regulate British co-operation in the preparation of a new repertory of medieval sources to replace Potthast's *Bibliotheca Historica Medii Aevi*;
- ○ Dr. Jane Winters on the History Data Service Advisory Committee;
- ○ Professor Arthur Burns on the user panel of the RSLP Revelation project 'Unlocking research sources for 19th and 20th century church history and Christian theology';
- ○ Professor Richard Rathbone on the Court of Governors of the University of Wales, Swansea;
- ○ Dr. Christopher Kitching on the National Council on Archives;
- ○ Professor John Breuilly on the Steering Committee of the British Centre for Historical Research in Germany.

- Council received reports from its representatives.

Grants

RESEARCH SUPPORT COMMITTEE, 2007–8

The Committee met 5 times in the course of the year. Its pleasant task, the granting of financial assistance to young scholars and to those assisting young scholars to attend valuable conferences, has been even more enjoyable following Council's imaginative and very welcome decision to increase considerably its grant to the Research Support Committee. This additional funding has enabled us to increase the size of grants in some cases to go somewhere towards meeting the mounting costs of travel both in the United Kingdom and abroad. It has also enabled us to extend our eligibility criteria to post-doctoral students in the first year after their examination.

In the course of the year the Committee has emphasised the importance of the accountability of those to whom it has made grants, insisting upon the submission of full details of expenditure and of reports on the ways in which grant money has been spent. These reports are not only a donor's reasonable expectation of any scholar who has received a discretionary award; they also allow the Committee to learn about the varied experiences of young scholars researching in the United Kingdom and abroad and consequently affect our understanding of new opportunities and problems which in turn inform our decision-making.

An expanded budget has allowed us to make more awards to organisers seeking to encourage young scholars to attend future conferences. The number of such applications has risen in recent years although some of them are opportunistic and have little to do with historical studies; this suggests that some disciplines do not have access to comparable funding.

The Committee remains eager to support the convening of scholarly conferences and workshops about history which are committed to the involvement of younger scholars.

The Committee has been concerned about the relatively limited number of HEIs whose students have applied for financial support. Predictably we read many applications from "the usual suspects" and there is no doubt that they show an under-representation of the numbers of research students in history we know to be working in many universities and especially newer universities. It is obvious that many students and, as worryingly, too many of their teachers are unaware of this important aspect of the Society's role. We have consequently distributed posters alerting staff and students to all departments known to be involved in historical studies to the availability of our awards. We hope that these will be prominently displayed. Additionally the Committee would appreciate it if the entire Fellowship were to ensure that all their colleagues and students were aware that the Society can make a significant financial contribution to the work of young historians.

The Royal Historical Society Centenary Fellowship was not awarded in the academic year 2007–2008.

The Society's P.J. Marshall Fellowship was awarded in the academic year 2007–2008 to Jan Lemnitzer (LSE) for work on 'The Declaration of Paris and the Abolition of Privateering – An International History'.

- Grants during the year were made to the following:

Travel to Conferences (Training Bursaries)

o Emily BANNISTER, PhD, Keele University
The Annual Meeting of the Medieval Academy of America
Vancouver, 3rd–5th April 2008.
o Alex BARBER, PhD, Royal Holloway, University of London
NACBS Conference 2007
San Francisco, 9th–11th November 2007.
o Michael COLLINS, DPhil, University of Oxford
Heidelberg Kolloquium on South Asian Studies
Heidelberg, 30th October 2007.
o Val DUFEU, PhD, University of Stirling
Maritime Societies of the Viking and Medieval World
Orkney, 31st May–4th June 2008.
o Chiara FORMICHI, PhD, School of Oriental and African Studies,
University of London AseasUK Annual Conference
Liverpool, 21st–22nd June 2008.
o Miguel GARCIA-SANCHO, PhD, Imperial College, University of
London

International Society for the History, Philosophy and Social Studies of Biology (ISHPSSB) 2007 Meeting
University of Exeter, 25th–29th July 2007.

o Emily GRAHAM, PhD, University of St Andrews
The New College Conference on Renaissance and Medieval Studies
Florida, 6th–8th March 2008; and
"Power and Patronage in the Middle Ages," the Annual Conference of the Centre for Medieval Studies
Toronto, 14th–15th March 2008.

o David HARRISON, PhD, University of Liverpool
British Society of Eighteenth Century Studies Annual Conference
Oxford, 3rd–5th January 2008.

o Graciela IGLESIAS ROGERS, DPhil, University of Oxford
The Napoleonic Empire and the New European Political Culture
Madrid, 2nd–6th April 2008; and
International Congress of the Bicentenary of the Spanish War of Independence
Madrid, 8th–11th April 2008.

o Miranda KAUFMANN, DPhil, University of Oxford
A Bicentenary Conference on Discourses of Resistance: Culture, Identity, Freedom & Reconciliation
Montego Bay, 5th–8th December 2007.

o Deborah LEA, PhD, University of Liverpool
Societas Magica Conference, Magic: Frontiers and Boundaries
Ontario, 11th–15th June 2008.

o Yu Ping LUK, DPhil, University of Oxford
Eleventh Annual Harvard East Asia Society Graduate Student Conference
Harvard, 29th February–2nd March 2008.

o Melanie MADDOX, PhD, University of St Andrews
43rd International Congress on Medieval Studies
Kalamazoo, 8th–11th May 2008.

o Joe MERTON, DPhil, University of Oxford
American Politics Group 2008 Conference
London, 3rd–5th January 2008.

o Zsuzsanna PAPP, PhD, University of Leeds
43rd International Congress on Medieval Studies
Kalamazoo, 8th–11th May 2008.

o Gabriela PETKOVA-CAMPBELL, PhD, Newcastle University
De l'imitation dans les musées: la diffusion des modèles de musées, XIXe-XXIe siècles
Paris, 5th–7th December 2007.

o Marija PETROVIC, DPhil, University of Oxford

13th Annual World Convention of the Association for the Study of Nationalities
New York, 10th–12th April 2008.
o Hilary POWELL, DPhil, University of Oxford
43rd International Congress on Medieval Studies
Kalamazoo, 8th–11th May 2008.
o John SHERRY, PhD, University of Ulster
58th Conference of the International Commission for the History of Representative and Parliamentary Institutions
University of Edinburgh, University of St Andrews and the Scottish Parliament, 4th–7th September 2007.
o Stephanie SOLYWODA, DPhil, University of Oxford
Philosophical Heritage of Semion Frank in the Context of European Culture
Moscow, 19th–23rd September 2007.
o Piotr STOLARSKI, PhD, University of Aberdeen
American Association for the Advancement of Slavic Studies Conference
Philadelphia, 20th–23rd November 2008.
o Claire SWAN, PhD, University of Dundee
4th European Business History Association Postgraduate Summer School
Terni, 5th–12th September 2007.
o Dr Peter TURNER, University of Oxford
American Philological Association 139th Annual Meeting
Chicago, 3rd–6th January 2008.
o Maki UMEMURA, PhD, London School of Economics, University of London
38th International Congress for the History of Pharmacy
Seville, 19th–22nd September 2007.
o Martina VIARENGO, PhD, London School of Economics, University of London
Social Science History Association Annual Conference 2007
Chicago, 15th–18th November 2007.
o Dr Charlotte WILDMAN, University of Manchester
Social History Society Annual Conference 2008
Rotterdam, 27th–29th March 2008.
o Sara WOLFSON, PhD, Durham University
The New College Conference on Medieval and Renaissance Studies
Florida, 5th–9th March 2008.
o Jonathan YEAGER, PhD, University of Stirling
Eighteenth-Century Scottish Studies Society Conference
Halifax, 26th–29th June 2008.

Research Expenses Within the United Kingdom:

- o Stavroula ANDRIOPOULOU, PhD, University of Birmingham
  Bodleian Library, Oxford, 9th February–30th April 2008.
- o Luke BLAXILL, PhD, King's College London
  Archives in East Anglia and London, December 2007–July 2008.
- o Fiona BOWLER, PhD, University of Birmingham
  Archives in London, July–August 2008.
- o George DOUKAS, PhD, University of Birmingham
  Archives in London, Oxford and Glasgow, June–July 2008.
- o Nathan FISHER, DPhil, University of Oxford
  Archives in London, Durham, Hull, Newcastle-upon-Tyne, December 2007–October 2008.
- o Jameel HAMPTON, PhD, University of Bristol
  Archives in Kew and Essex, November 2007–March 2008.
- o Benjamin HELLER, DPhil, University of Oxford
  Archives in London, January–December 2008.
- o Nara IMPROTA FRANCA, PhD, University of Stirling
  Archives in Birmingham, 21st October–17th November 2007.
- o Peiling LI, MPhil, University of Oxford
  Archives in Winchester, 8th October–1st December 2007.
- o Weichong ONG, PhD, University of Exeter
  National Archives, 1st–30th April 2008.
- o Shinsuke SATSUMA, PhD, University of Exeter
  Archives in London and Cambridge, April–June 2008.
- o Tommy SWEENEY, PhD, University of Dundee
  British Library, 20th–27th August 2007.
- o Maria VALENCIA-SUAREZ, PhD, University of Cambridge
  Archives in London, February–March 2008.

Research Expenses Outside the United Kingdom:

- o Robert BARNES, PhD, London School of Economics, University of London
  Archives in USA and Canada, 1st September–1st December 2008.
- o Georgina BREWIS, PhD, University of East London
  Archives in Philadelphia and Northampton, USA, November 2007.
- o Michela COLETTA, PhD, UCL, University of London
  Archives in Buenos Aires and Montevideo, July-August 2008.
- o James COOPER, PhD, Aberystwyth University
  Archives in USA, 3rd June–1st July 2008.
- o Anthony CROSS, PhD, University of Reading
  Archives in Geneva, 10th–24th June 2008.
- o Matthew D'AURIA, PhD, University of London
  Archives in Paris, France, 1st February–1st March 2008.

- o Francesca DI MARCO, PhD, SOAS
  Archives in Tokyo and Tsukuba, Japan, March–April 2008.
- o Dawn DODDS, PhD, University of Cambridge
  Archives in France, 6th July–3rd August 2008.
- o Elaine DOYLE, PhD, Queen's University Belfast
  Archives in Nigeria, 1st December–16th December 2007.
- o Xavier DURAN, PhD, London School of Economics, University of London
  Archives in California, Iowa and Illinois, USA, 1st–30th April 2008.
- o Chiara FORMICHI, PhD, SOAS
  Archives in Kuala Lumpur, Singapore and Jakarta, 15th October 2007–15th July 2008.
- o Priyali GHOSH, PhD, Canterbury Christ Church University
  Archives in India, July 2007–January 2008.
- o Katherine HILL, DPhil, University of Oxford
  Archives in Germany, 2nd–13th December 2007.
- o Andrew HOLT, PhD, University of Nottingham
  Archives in Texas, USA, 2nd–11th April 2008.
- o Graciela IGLESIAS ROGERS, DPhil, University of Oxford
  Archives in Spain, 21st October–2nd December 2007.
- o Catherine KINCHIN, PhD, Bangor University
  Archives in Canada, 15th July–28th August 2008.
- o Karoly KONECSNY, PhD, University of Exeter
  Archives in Germany, January -July 2008.
- o Karoly KONECSNY, PhD, University of Exeter
  Archives in Germany, July–September 2008.
- o Mark LAWRENCE, PhD, University of Liverpool
  Archives in Madrid and Zaragoza, Spain, 5th–17th August 2007.
- o James LEES, PhD, King's College London
  Archives in Bangladesh, 1st-14th September 2008.
- o Yi LI, PhD, School of Oriental and African Studies, University of London
  Rangoon and Mandalay, Burma, September–December 2008.
- o Alois MADERSPACHER, PhD, University of Cambridge
  Archives in Germany and Switzerland, 1st July–18th August 2007.
- o Erin-Lee McGUIRE, PhD, University of Glasgow
  Archives in Iceland, 12th–19th September 2008.
- o Weichong ONG, PhD, University of Exeter
  Archives in Australia, 10th–30th July 2007.
- o Sebastian PRANGHOFER, PhD, University of Durham
  Archives in The Netherlands, August–September 2007.
- o Lucas RICHERT, PhD, Institute for the Study of the Americas, University of London
  Archives in the USA, August–September 2007.

- John RICHMOND, PhD, Royal Holloway, University of London
  Central Zionist Archives, Jerusalem, 7th–21st October 2007.
- Thomas RODGERS, PhD, University of Warwick
  Archives in North Carolina, South Carolina and Georgia, USA,
  5th January–10th March 2008.
- Jonathan SHEA, PhD, University of Birmingham
  Thessaloniki, Monemvasia, Mistra, Aristotle University Thessaloniki
  and the Centre for Balkan Studies, Autumn 2008.
- Eva STAMOULOU, PhD, University of Manchester
  Archives in Venice, Italy, March–June 2008.
- Iain STEWART, PhD, University of Manchester
  Bibliothèque Nationale, Paris, 14th March–3rd April 2008.
- John STEWART, PhD, University of Dundee
  Archives in Pennsylvania, USA, 2nd–23rd August 2007.
- omas

  Dagmar WERNITZNIG, DPhil, University of Oxford

  Archives in Amsterdam, 28th January–15th February 2008.
- Harun YILMAZ, DPhil, University of Oxford
  Archives in Azerbaijan, Georgia and the Ukraine, August 2008–
  September 2009.

Conference Organisation (Workshop):

- Nathan ABRAMS
  "Religion, Faith, Spirituality: An Interdisciplinary and International
  Postgraduate Conference on the Past and Present"
  Bangor University, 25th–26th June 2008.
- Karen ADLER
  "Homes and Homecomings"
  University of Nottingham, 26th–28th March 2008.
- Alexandra BAMJI
  "Gender and generations: women and the life cycle in historical
  perspective"
  University of Glasgow, 5th–7th September 2008.
- Debby BANHAM
  "The 'missing link': medicine in late antiquity and the early middle
  ages"
  University of Cambridge, March 2008.
- Nadia BISHAI and Astrid STILMA
  "Truth Will Out: Crime, Criminals and Criminality, 1500–1700"
  Canterbury Christ Church University, 22nd–24th August 2007.
- Caroline BOWDEN
  "Women Religious and the Political World"
  National University of Ireland, Galway, 22nd–23rd August 2008.

○ Katharine BRADLEY
"The Children's Act 1908: Centennial reflections, contemporary perspectives"
University of Kent at Medway, 30th June–1st July 2008.

○ Janet BURTON and Karen STOBER
"The Regular Canons in the British Isles in the Middle Ages"
University of Wales Conference Centre, 6th–9th March 2008.

○ Fiona CLARK
"Ireland and medicine in the 17th and 18th centuries"
Queen's University Belfast, 25th–26th April 2008.

○ Martin DAUNTON
"Social policy across borders: commonalities, convergence and paradoxes in connectivity, 1850–1975"
University of Cambridge, 12th–13th September 2008.

○ James DAYBELL
"Material readings in early modern culture, 1550–1700"
University of Plymouth, 11th–12th April 2008.

○ Daniel DEGROFF
"Joseph de Maistre: Reappraisals/reconsiderations"
University of Cambridge, 5th–6th December 2008.

○ Kirsten FENTON
"Gender and difference in the Middle Ages"
Edinburgh, 11th–13th January 2008.

○ Tudor GEORGESCU
"Greater Romania's interwar nation (re-)building project"
Oxford Brookes University, 11th–12th April 2008.

○ George GOSLING
"History of Medicine Research Student Conference"
Wellcome Trust Centre for the History of Medicine at UCL, 19th–20th June 2008.

○ Clare GRIFFIN
"Perpetual Motion? Transition and Transformation in Central and Eastern Europe"
UCL School of Slavonic and East European Studies, 18th–20th February 2009.

○ Adam GRYDEHOJ
"Taking Shetland out of the box: Island cultures and Shetland identity"
Lerwick, Shetland, 7th–10th May 2009.

○ Rachel JOHNSON
"Writing African Histories"
University of Sheffield, 9th June 2008.

○ Jennifer JORDAN
"Men's Dilemma? Sources and Methodologies in the History of Masculinity"
University of Exeter, 22nd–23rd July 2008.

○ Catriona KENNEDY
"Books on the Battlefield: The reception, use and appropriation of texts in warfare, 1450 to the present"
University of York, 2nd–3rd November 2007.

○ Jennifer KORST
"4th Annual Medievalism Transformed Conference: medieval education in perspective"
Bangor University, 13th June 2008.

○ Sergio LUSSANA and Lydia PLATH
"Masculinity in the American South History Postgraduate Symposium"
University of Warwick, 7th June 2008.

○ Matthew McCORMACK
"Men at Arms: New histories of soldiering in Britain and Ireland, c.1750–1850"
University of Northampton, 4th–5th September 2008.

○ Gabriel PAQUETTE
"Enlightened Reform in Southern Europe and its Atlantic Colonies, 1750–1830"
Cambridge, 12th–14th December 2007.

○ Jason PEACEY
"Collecting revolution: the history and importance of the Thomason Tracts"
British Library and UCL, 30th June–1st July 2008.

○ Sara PENNELL
"Reading and writing recipe books, c.1600–1800"
University of Warwick, 8th–9th August 2008.

○ Valentina PUGLIANO
"On the Fringes of Science? Natural Knowledge and its Practitioners in Early Modern Europe, 1450–1650"
University of Oxford, 27th June 2008.

○ James RAVEN
"Connected by books: transatlantic literary communities"
University of Essex, 2nd December 2007.

○ Katharina RIETZLER
"Interwar internationalism: conceptualising transnational thought and action, 1919–1939"
UCL, 25th–26th April 2008.

○ John ROBERTSON
"The intellectual consequences of religious heterodoxy in Europe, 1650–1750"
University of Oxford, 14th–15th March 2008.

○ Sarah ROSE and Marcus MORRIS
"HISTFEST"
Lancaster University, May 2008.

- ○ Hannah SMITH and Erica CHARTERS
  "The Armed Forces and British Society, c.1650-c.1790"
  University of Oxford, 7th July 2008.
- ○ Shafquat TOWHEED
  "Evidence of Reading, Reading the Evidence"
  School of Advanced Study, University of London, 21st–23rd July 2008.

Martin Lynn Scholarship:

No award was made this year.

Royal Historical Society Postgraduate Speakers Series (RHSPSS):

Centre for Reformation and Early Modern Studies, University of Birmingham.

26 September 2008

THE ROYAL HISTORICAL SOCIETY
FINANCIAL STATEMENTS
FOR THE YEAR ENDED 30 JUNE 2008

THE ROYAL HISTORICAL SOCIETY REFERENCE AND ADMINISTRATIVE INFORMATION

Members of Council:

Professor M J Daunton, MA, PhD, FBA	President – Officer
Professor C M D Jones, BA, DPhil	President-Elect – Officer (from November 2007)
V A Harding, MA, PhD	Honorary Secretary – Officer
I W Archer, MA, DPhil	Literary Director – Officer
J M Lawrence, BA, PhD	Literary Director – Officer
J P Parry, MA, PhD	Honorary Treasurer – Officer
Professor M Cragoe, MA, DPhil	Honorary Director of Communications – Officer
Professor J E Burton, DPhil	Vice-President (to November 2007)
Professor A Curry, MA, PhD	Vice-President
Mr R Fisher, MA	Vice-President (from November 2007)
A W Foster, BA, DPhil	Vice-President
Professor D M Palliser, MA, DPhil	Vice-President (from November 2007)
Professor R J A R Rathbone, PhD	Vice-President
P Seaward, MA, DPhil	Vice-President (to November 2007)
Professor P M Thane, MA, PhD	Vice-President
Professor G W Bernard, MA, DPhil	Councillor
Professor P G Burgess, MA, PhD	Councillor
Professor S Connolly, DPhil	Councillor
Professor S R I Foot, MA, PhD	Councillor
Professor R I Frost, MA, PhD	Councillor
Professor C Given-Wilson, MA, PhD	Councillor (from November 2007)
Professor T Hitchcock, AB, DPhil	Councillor
C A Holmes, MA, PhD	Councillor
Professor J.H. Ohlmeyer, MA, PhD	Councillor (to November 2007)
Professor M Ormrod, BA, DPhil	Councillor (from November 2007)
Professor M E Rubin, MA, PhD	Councillor (to November 2007)
Professor S Smith, MSocSci, PhD	Councillor
Professor G A Stone, MA, PhD	Councillor
D Thomas, PhD	Councillor (from November 2007)
E M C van Houts, MA, LittD, PhD	Councillor (to November 2007)

Executive Secretary:	S E Carr, MA
Administrative Assistant	M FN Batt, BA
Registered Office:	University College London Gower Street London WC1E 6BT
Charity registration number:	206888
Auditors:	Kingston Smith LLP Chartered Accountants Devonshire House 60 Goswell Road London EC1M 7AD
Investment managers:	Brewin Dolphin 12 Smithfield Street London EC1A 9BD
Bankers:	Barclays Bank Plc 27 Soho Square London W1A 4WA

THE ROYAL HISTORICAL SOCIETY
REPORT OF THE COUNCIL OF TRUSTEES'
FOR THE YEAR ENDED 30 JUNE 2008

The members of Council present their report and audited accounts for the year ended 30 June 2008.

STRUCTURE, GOVERNANCE AND MANAGEMENT

The Society was founded on 23 November 1868 and received its Royal Charter in 1889. It is governed by the document 'The By-Laws of the Royal Historical Society', which was last amended in November 2006. The elected Officers of the Society are the President, six Vice-Presidents, the Treasurer, the Secretary, the Director of Communications and not more than two Literary Directors. These officers, together with twelve Councillors constitute the governing body of the Society, and therefore its Trustees. The Society also has two executive officers: an Executive Secretary and an Administrative Secretary.

Appointment of Trustees

The names of the trustees are shown above. The President shall be *ex-officio* a member of all Committees appointed by the Council; and the Treasurer, the Secretary, the Director of Communications and the Literary Directors shall, unless the Council otherwise determine, also be *ex-officio* members of all such Committees.

In accordance with By-law XVII, the Vice-Presidents shall hold office normally for a term of three years. Two of them shall retire by rotation, in order of seniority in office, at each Anniversary Meeting and shall not be eligible for re-election before the Anniversary Meeting of the next year. In accordance with By-law XX, the Councillors shall hold office normally for a term of four years. Three of them shall retire by rotation, in order of seniority in office, at each Anniversary Meeting and shall not be eligible for re-election before the Anniversary Meeting of the next year.

All Fellows and Members of the Society are able to nominate Councillors; they are elected by a ballot of Fellows. Other Trustees are elected by Council.

At the Anniversary Meeting on November 2007, the Officers of the Society were re-elected. The Vice-Presidents retiring under By-law XVII were Professor J Burton and Dr P Seaward. Mr R Fisher and Professor D Palliser were elected to replace them. The Members of Council retiring under By-law XX were Professor J Ohlmeyer, Professor M Rubin and Dr E van Houts. In accordance with By-law XXI, Professor C Given-Wilson, Professor M Ormrod and Dr D Thomas were elected in their place.

Trustee training and induction process

New Trustees are welcomed in writing before their initial meeting, and sent details of the coming year's meeting schedule. They are advised of Committee structure and receive papers in advance of the appropriate Committee and Council meetings, including minutes of the previous meetings. Trustees are already Fellows of the Society and have received regular information including the annual volume of *Transactions of the Royal Historical Society* which includes the annual report and accounts. They have therefore been kept apprised of any changes in the Society's business. Trustees may have previously served on Council, in which case their knowledge of procedures will assist their understanding of current issues. Details of a Review on the restructuring of the Society in 1993 are available to all Members of Council.

Standing Committees

The Society has operated through the following Committees during the year ended 30 June 2008:

MEMBERSHIP COMMITTEE: Dr P Seaward – Chair (to November 2007)
                            Professor D Palliser – Chair (from November 2007)
                            Professor R I Frost (to November 2007)
                            Professor T Hitchcock
                            Dr C Holmes (from November 2007)

Risk assessment

The trustees are satisfied that they have considered the major risks to which the charity is exposed, that they have taken action to mitigate or manage those risks and that they have systems in place to monitor any change to those risks.

OBJECTS, OBJECTIVES AND ACTIVITIES

The Society remains the foremost society in Great Britain promoting and defending the scholarly study of the past. The Society promotes discussion of history by means of a full programme of public lectures and conferences, and disseminates the results of historical research and debate through its many publications. It also speaks for the interests of history and historians.

The Society offers grants to support research training, and annual prizes for historical essays and publications. It produces the Bibliography of British and Irish History, a database of over 400,000 records, by far the most complete online bibliographical resource on British and Irish history, including relations with the empire and the Commonwealth. The Bibliography is updated annually, and includes near-comprehensive coverage of works since 1901 and selected earlier works.

The Society's specific new objectives for the year are set out in 'Plans for Future Periods' below.

The Society relies on volunteers from among its Fellows to act as its elected Officers, Councillors and Vice-Presidents. In many of its activities it also relies on the goodwill of Fellows and others interested in the study of the past. It has two salaried staff, and also pays a stipend to the Series Editor of *Studies in History* and to certain individuals for work on the Society's Bibliography.

ACHIEVEMENTS AND PERFORMANCE

Grants, Fellowships and Prizes

The Society awards funds to assist advanced historical research by distributing grants to individuals, mostly research students and other junior scholars. It operates five separate schemes, for each of which there is an application form. The Society's Research Support Committee considers applications at meetings held regularly throughout the year. In turn the Research Support Committee reports to Council. The Royal Historical Society Postgraduate Speakers' Series was continued this year, after a successful first year. This year the grants budget was increased from £20,000 to £30,000, but in the event the quantity and quality of applications did not justify an increase in expenditure beyond last year's level and £19,110 was spent. The Society was able to award its Marshall Fellowship this year and took the decision that with effect from October 2008 it would be able to award both a Centenary Fellowship and a Marshall Fellowship each year until further notice. Full details and a list of awards made are provided in the Society's Annual Report.

Lectures and other meetings

During the year the Society holds meetings in London and at universities outside London at which papers are delivered. It continues to sponsor the joint lecture for a wider public with Gresham College. It meets with other bodies to consider teaching and research policy issues of national importance. It re-commenced the annual Gerald Aylmer seminar, between historians and archivists, which had not been held in 2005 or 2006. Full details are provided in the Annual Report.

Publications

This year, as in previous years, it has delivered an ambitious programme of publications – a volume of *Transactions*, two volumes of edited texts in the *Camden* Series and further volumes in the *Studies in History* Series have appeared. Exceptionally, eight were published in 2007 and it was agreed to increase the number to be published in a normal year from six to seven.

Library

The Society sold a second tranche of its library holdings, which are held in the Council Room. This raised just over £10,000, making £28,000 in all so far. Once the third and final tranche has been sold, the Society will be in a position to make a final decision on the best use of the money raised. It also continues to subscribe to a range of record series publications housed in the room immediately across the corridor from the Council room, in the UCL History Library.

Membership services

In accordance with the Society's 'By-laws', the membership is entitled to receive, after payment of subscription, a copy of the Society's *Transactions*, and to buy at a preferential rate copies of volumes published in the *Camden* series, and the *Studies in History* series. Society Newsletters continue to be circulated to the membership twice annually, and in 2008 a new editorial policy has been adopted. The membership benefits from many other activities of the Society including the frequent representations to various official bodies where the interests of historical scholarship are involved.

Investment performance

The Society holds an investment portfolio with a market value of about £2.36 million (2007: £2.64 million). It has adopted a "total return" approach to its investment policy. This means that the funds are invested solely on the basis of seeking to secure the best total level of economic return compatible with the duty to make safe investments, but regardless of the form the return takes.

The Society has adopted this approach to ensure even-handedness between current and future beneficiaries, as the focus of many investments moves away from producing income to maximising capital values. The total return strategy does not make distinctions between income and capital returns. It lumps together all forms of return on investment – dividends, interest, and capital gains etc, to produce a "total return". Some of the total return is then used to meet the needs of present beneficiaries, while the remainder is added to the existing investment portfolios to help meet the needs of future beneficiaries.

During the year the Society changed its investment managers, from Heartwood Wealth Management to Brewin Dolphin plc. The costs incurred in the change were negligible. Brewin, like Heartwood, report all transactions to the Honorary Treasurer and provide three-monthly reports on the portfolios, which are considered by the Society's Finance Committee which meets three times a year. In turn the Finance Committee reports to Council. A manager from Brewin attends two Finance Committee meetings a year.

The change of investment manager, at the end of September 2007, coincided with the Society's decision to pool the investments in its various funds. From that point, the Robinson and Whitfield Funds were no longer managed as separate funds, but they retain their former weighting in the amalgamated portfolio. The David Berry Fund, which had been invested separately with COIF, was also amalgamated in the Brewin portfolio on the same basis.

The Society assesses its portfolio against the FTSE APCIMS balanced benchmark. During the year the portfolio generated a negative return, owing to the state of world markets. In the first nine months of Brewin's stewardship of the funds (but with a largely unchanged portfolio), their value fell by 13% as against 10.6% for the benchmark and 18% for the FTSE 100 index.

The estimated yield on current values is 4.78%. Fees are now less than 0.5% of the value of the portfolio. The Society has a policy of not drawing down more than 4% of the market value of the portfolio in any one year. Thus, though the investments are run on a total return basis, it is in fact currently possible to meet our draw down policy without touching capital. The Finance Committee will be reviewing investment strategy and its total return policy during the current financial year.

FINANCIAL REVIEW

Results

The Society generated a surplus this year of £65,511 (2007: £53,964) before investment losses, which have been discussed above. This surplus was anticipated and exceptional; it was primarily due to an increase in subscription income from £75,980 to £102,834, as a result of the increase in subscriptions in July 2007. £10,698 was also generated from the sale of part of the Society's Library. Other income was broadly in line with the previous year's.

There was a small and probably temporary decline in expenditure on grants, and savings were made on the investment manager's fees, the cost of photocopying and insurance, and Council travel costs.

As a consequence, very unusually, the Society did not draw down any of its investment income during the year. However, in the future it is anticipated that a draw down will be required of nearly 4% of the value of the investment portfolio.

Fixed assets

Information relating to changes in fixed assets is given in notes 5 and 6 to the accounts.

Reserves policy

Council has reviewed the reserves of the Society. To safeguard the core activities in excess of the members' subscription income, Council has determined to establish unrestricted, general, free reserves to cover three years' operational costs (approximately £650,000). Unrestricted, general, free reserves at 30 June 2008 were £2,190,270 (after adjusting for fixed assets). Council is satisfied with this level.

The Society's restricted funds consist of a number of different funds where the donor has imposed restrictions on the use of the funds which are legally binding. The purposes of these funds are set out in Notes 11 – 13.

PLANS FOR FUTURE PERIODS

Council plans to use its new website, unveiled during the year, to improve communication and interaction with Fellows and Members. It also plans to continue its extensive involvement in public discussions about teaching and research issues. It will inaugurate a new model for its meetings outside London, by offering support for two wide-ranging seminar/lecture events in Leeds and Belfast. During the coming year it will consider the future of the RHS Bibliography project, in view of the threats to the future of its external funding; it is aware that the Society may need to increase significantly the level of its support for the project. It plans an increase in the financial support that it gives to postgraduate and other young historians, and to improve the publicity given to its grants policy so as to raise the number and quality of applications for support. As part of this initiative, it will implement revised criteria for the David Berry Prize.

STATEMENT OF COUNCIL'S RESPONSIBILITIES

The Council is responsible for preparing the Annual Report and the financial statements in accordance with applicable law and regulations.

Charity law requires the Council to prepare financial statements for each financial year in accordance with United Kingdom Generally Accepted Accounting Practice (United Kingdom Accounting Standards and applicable law). The financial statements are required by law to give a true and fair view of the state of affairs of the charity and of the income and expenditure of the charity for that period. In preparing these financial statements, the Council is required to:

- select suitable accounting policies and apply them consistently;
- make judgments and estimates that are reasonable and prudent;
- state whether applicable UK Accounting Standards have been followed, subject to any material departures disclosed and explained in the financial statements;
- prepare the accounts on the going concern basis unless it is inappropriate to presume that the Society will continue in operation.

The Council is responsible for keeping proper accounting records that disclose with reasonable accuracy at any time the financial position of the charity and enable it to ensure that the financial statements comply with the Charities Act 1993. It is also responsible for safeguarding the assets of the charity and hence for taking reasonable steps for the prevention and detection of fraud and other irregularities.

In determining how amounts are presented within items in the statement of financial activities and balance sheet, the Council has had regard to the substance of the reported transaction or arrangement, in accordance with generally accepted accounting policies or practice.

AUDITORS

Kingston Smith LLP were appointed auditors in the year. They have indicated their willingness to continue in office and a proposal for their re-appointment will be presented at the Anniversary meeting.

By Order of the Board

Honorary Secretary

Dr V Harding

26 September 2008

THE ROYAL HISTORICAL SOCIETY
INDEPENDENT AUDITORS' REPORT TO THE TRUSTEES
OF THE ROYAL HISTORICAL SOCIETY

We have audited the financial statements of The Royal Historical Society for the year ended 30 June 2008 which comprise the Statement of Financial Activities, the Balance Sheet and the related notes. These financial statements have been prepared in accordance with the accounting policies set out therein and the requirements of the Financial Reporting Standard for Smaller Entities (effective January 2007).

This report is made solely to the charity's trustees, as a body, in accordance with regulations made under section 43 of the Charities Act 1993. Our audit work has been undertaken for no purpose other than to draw to the attention of the charity's trustees those matters which we are required to include in an auditor's report addressed to them. To the fullest extent permitted by law, we do not accept or assume responsibility to any party other than the charity and charity's trustees as a body, for our audit work, for this report, or for the opinion we have formed.

Respective Responsibilities of Trustees and Auditors

The trustees' responsibilities for preparing the Trustees' Annual Report and the financial statements in accordance with applicable law and United Kingdom Accounting Standards (United Kingdom Generally Accepted Accounting Practice) are set out in the Statement of Trustees' Responsibilities.

We have been appointed as auditors under section 43 of the Charities Act 1993 and report in accordance with regulations made under section 44 of that Act. Our responsibility is to audit the financial statements in accordance with relevant legal and regulatory requirements and International Standards on Auditing (UK and Ireland).

We report to you our opinion as to whether the financial statements give a true and fair view and are properly prepared in accordance with the Charities Act 1993. We also report to you if, in our opinion, the Trustees' Report is not consistent with the financial statements, if the charity has not kept proper accounting records, or if we have not received all the information and explanations we require for our audit, or if information specified by law in respect of trustees' remuneration and other transactions is not disclosed.

We read the Trustees' Annual Report and consider the implications for our report if we become aware of any apparent misstatements within it.

Basis of audit opinion

We conducted our audit in accordance with International Standards on Auditing (UK and Ireland) issued by the Auditing Practices Board. An audit includes examination, on a test basis, of evidence relevant to the amounts and disclosures in the financial statements. It also includes an assessment of the significant estimates and judgements made by the trustees in the preparation of the financial statements, and of whether the accounting policies are appropriate to the charity's circumstances, consistently applied and adequately disclosed.

We planned and performed our audit so as to obtain all the information and explanations which we considered necessary in order to provide us with sufficient evidence to give reasonable assurance that the financial statements are free from material misstatement, whether caused by fraud or other irregularity or error. In forming our opinion we also evaluated the overall adequacy of the presentation of information in the financial statements.

Opinion

In our opinion the financial statements:

- give a true and fair view, in accordance with the United Kingdom Generally Accepted Accounting Practice applicable to Smaller Entities, of the state of the charity's affairs as at 30 June 2008 and of its incoming resources and application of resources of the charity for the year then ended; and
- have been properly prepared in accordance with the Charities Act 1993.

Devonshire~House
60 Goswell Road
London EC1M 7AD

Kingston Smith LLP
Chartered Accountants
and Registered Auditors

Date:

THE ROYAL HISTORICAL SOCIETY

STATEMENT OF FINANCIAL ACTIVITIES
FOR THE YEAR ENDED 30 JUNE 2008

	Notes	Unrestricted Funds £	Endowment Funds £	Restricted Funds £	Total Funds 2008 £	Total Funds 2007 £
INCOMING RESOURCES						
Incoming resources from generated funds						
Donations, legacies and similar incoming resources	2	6,200	–	–	6,200	21,958
Investment income	6	99,522	–	1,191	100,713	103,562
Incoming resources from charitable activities						
Grants for awards		–	–	10,000	10,000	12,000
Grants for publications		4,000	–	–	4,000	6,000
Lectures and meetings		–	–	–	–	399
Subscriptions		102,834	–	–	102,834	75,980
Royalties		34,481	–	–	34,481	35,460
Other incoming resources		21,056	–	–	21,056	18,996
TOTAL INCOMING RESOURCES		268,094	–	11,191	279,285	274,355
RESOURCES EXPENDED						
Cost of generating funds						
Investment manager's fee		13,742	–	298	14,040	15,987
Charitable activities						
Grants for awards	3	33,484	–	12,250	45,734	53,367
Lectures and other meetings		9,936	–	–	9,936	12,004
Publications		70,559	–	–	70,559	67,918
Library		4,859	–	–	4,859	4,716
Membership services		48,025	–	–	48,025	45,209
Governance		20,620	–	–	20,620	21,190
TOTAL RESOURCES EXPENDED	4a	201,226	–	12,548	213,774	220,391
NET INCOMING/(OUTGOING) RESOURCES BEFORE TRANSFERS		66,868	–	(1,357)	65,511	53,964
Gross transfers between funds						
NET INCOMING / (OUTGOING) RESOURCES BEFORE GAINS		66,868	–	(1,357)	65,511	53,964
Other recognised gains and losses						
Net gain on investments	6	(349,265)	(5,730)	–	(354,995)	195,408
NET MOVEMENT IN FUNDS		(282,397)	(5,730)	(1,357)	(289,484)	249,372
Balance at 1 July 2007		2,592,254	73,789	4,157	2,670,200	2,420,828
Balance at 30 June 2008	15	2,309,857	68,059	2,800	2,380,716	2,670,200

The notes on pages 11 to 17 form part of these financial statements.

THE ROYAL HISTORICAL SOCIETY

BALANCE SHEET AT 30 JUNE 2008

	Notes	2008 £	2008 £	2007 £	2007 £
FIXED ASSETS					
Tangible assets	5		1,489		1,187
Investments	6		2,361,968		2,638,551
			2,363,458		2,639,738
CURRENT ASSETS					
Stocks	7	–		2,925	
Debtors	8	5,484		6,598	
Cash at bank and in hand		35,464		46,140	
		40,948		55,663	
LESS: CREDITORS					
Amounts due within one year	9	(23,689)		(25,201)	
NET CURRENT ASSETS					
			17,258		30,462
NET ASSETS			2,380,716		2,670,200
REPRESENTED BY:					
Endowment Funds	11				
A S Whitfield Prize Fund			45,552		49,833
The David Berry Essay Trust			22,507		23,956
Restricted Funds	12				
A S Whitfield Prize Fund			1,687		1,983
P J Marshall Fellowship			–		–
The David Berry Essay Trust			1,113		1,174
The Martin Lynn Bequest			–		1,000
Unrestricted Funds					
Designated – E M Robinson Bequest	13		118,098		150,210
General Fund	14		2,191,759		2,442,044
			2,380,716		2,670,200

The accounts have been prepared in accordance with the Financial Reporting Standard for Smaller Entities (effective January 2007).

The notes on pages 11 to 17 form part of these financial statements.

The financial statements were approved and authorised for issue by the Council on . . . .
and were signed below on its behalf by:

. . . .
Professor M Daunton – **President**

. . . .
Dr J Parry – **Honorary Treasurer**

THE ROYAL HISTORICAL SOCIETY

Notes to the Financial Statements for the Year Ended 30 June 2008

1. ACCOUNTING POLICIES

Basis of accounting

The financial statements have been prepared under the historical cost convention, as modified to include the revaluation of fixed assets including investments which are carried at market value, in accordance with the Statement of Recommended Practice (SORP 2005) "Accounting and Reporting by Charities", published in March 2005, with applicable accounting standards and the Financial Reporting Standard for Smaller Entities (effective January 2007).

Depreciation

Depreciation is calculated by reference to the cost of fixed assets using a straight line basis at rates considered appropriate having regard to the expected lives of the fixed assets. The annual rates of depreciation in use are:

Furniture and equipment   10%
Computer equipment   25%

Stock

Stock is valued at the lower of cost and net realisable value.

Library and Archives

The cost of additions to the library and archives is written off in the year of purchase.

Subscription Income

Subscription income is recognised in the year it became receivable with a provision against any subscription not received.

Investments

Investments are stated at market value. Any surplus/deficit arising on revaluation is included in the Statement of Financial Activities. Dividend income is accounted for when the Society becomes entitled to such monies.

Donations and Other Voluntary Income

Donations and other voluntary income are recognised when the Society becomes legally entitled to such monies.

Grants Payable

Grants payable are recognised in the year in which they are approved and notified to recipients.

Funds

Unrestricted: these are funds which can be used in accordance with the charitable objects at the discretion of the trustees.

Designated: these are unrestricted funds which have been set aside by the trustees for specific purposes.

Restricted: these are funds that can only be used for particular restricted purposes defined by the benefactor and within the objects of the charity.

Endowment: permanent endowment funds must be held permanently by the trustees and income arising is separately included in restricted funds for specific use as defined by the donors.

The purpose and use of endowment, restricted and designated funds are disclosed in the notes to the accounts.

Allocations

Wages, salary costs and office expenditure are allocated on the basis of the work done by the Executive Secretary and the Administrative Assistant.

Pensions

Pension costs are charged to the SOFA when payments fall due. The Society contributed 12.5% of gross salary to the personal pension plan of two of the employees.

2. DONATIONS AND LEGACIES	2008 £	2007 £
G R Elton Bequest	1,308	438
Donations via membership	709	1,007
Gladstone Memorial Trust	600	600
Browning Bequest	63	1,263
Vera London Bequest	–	14,450
Sundry income	500	530
Gift Aid reclaimed	3,021	3,670
	6,200	21,958

3. GRANTS FOR AWARDS	Unrestricted Funds £	Restricted Funds £	Total 2008 £	Total 2007 £
RHS Centenary Fellowship	2,500	–	2,500	10,622
Alexander Prize	–	–	–	250
Sundry grants	–	–	–	300
Research support grants (see below)	18,110	1,000	19,110	20,615
A-Level prizes	200	–	200	300
AS Whitfield prize	–	1,000	1,000	1,144
E M Robinson Bequest			–	
Grant to Dulwich Picture Library	4,000	–	4,000	
Gladstone history book prize	1,000	–	1,000	1,690
P J Marshall Fellowship	–	10,000	10,000	10,790
Britishg History Bibliography project grant	–	–	–	
David Berry Prize	–	250	250	22
History Today Prize	–	–	–	–
Staff and support costs (Note 4a)	7,674	–	7,674	7,634
	33,484	12,250	45,734	53,367

During the year Society awarded grants to a value of £19,110 (2007 – £20,615) to 85 (2007 – 85) individuals.

GRANTS PAYABLE	2008 £	2007 £
Commitments at 1 July 2007	–	2,500
Commitments made in the year	38,060	45,733
Grants paid during the year	(38,060)	(48,233)
Commitments at 30 June 2008	–	–

Commitments at 30 June 2008 and 2007 are included in creditors.

4a. TOTAL RESOURCES EXPENDED	Staff costs £	Support costs £	Direct costs £	Total £
Cost of generating funds				
Investment manager's fee	–	–	14,040	14,040
Charitable activities				
Grants for awards (Note 3)	5,350	2,324	38,060	45,734
Lectures and meetings	5,350	1,162	3,424	9,936
Publications	9,511	4,648	56,400	70,559
Library	2,378	1,162	1,319	4,859
Membership services	29,722	11,621	6,682	48,025
Governance	7,133	2,324	11,163	20,620
Total Resources Expended	59,444	23,241	131,089	213,774
	(Note 4a)	**(Note 4c)**		

4b. STAFF COSTS	2008 £	2007 £
Wages and salaries	48,642	43,958
Social security costs	4,705	7,895
Other pension costs	6,097	3,990
	59,444	55,843

4c. SUPPORT COSTS	2008 £	2007 £
Stationery, photocopying and postage	10,161	13,065
Computer support	684	559
Insurance	923	1,520
Telephone	181	119
Depreciation	831	716
Bad debts	4,113	8,324
Other	6,347	2,900
	23,241	27,203

The average number of employees in the year was 2 (2007 – 2). There were no employees whose emoluments exceeded £60,000 in the year.

During the year travel expenses were reimbursed to 20 (2007: 20) Councillors attending Council meetings at a cost of £1,531 (2007 – £3,536). No Councillor received any remuneration during the year (2007 – £Nil).

Included in governance is the following:

	2008 £	2007 £
Audit fees – current year	6,974	8,031
– in respect of prior years	1,369	–

5. TANGIBLE FIXED ASSETS

	Computer Equipment £	Furniture And Equipment £	Total £
COST			
At 1 July 2007	33,224	1,173	34,397
Additions	–	1,134	1,134
At 30 June 2008	33,224	2,307	35,531
DEPRECIATION			
At 1 July 2007	32,037	1,173	33,210
Charge for the year	718	113	831
At 30 June 2008	32,755	1,286	34,041
NET BOOK VALUE			
At 30 June 2008	469	1,020	1,489
At 30 June 2007	1,187	–	1,187

All tangible fixed assets are used in the furtherance of the Society's objects.

6. INVESTMENTS

	General Fund £	Designated Robinson Bequest £	Whitfield Prize Fund £	David Berry Essay Trust £	Total £
Market value at 1 July 2007	2,418,165	140,793	52,636	26,957	2,638,551
Additions	307,589	16,789	34,915	–	359,293
Disposals	(237,452)	(5,510)	(36,031)	(1,888)	(280,881)
Net gain on investments	(315,291)	(33,974)	(4,281)	(1,449)	(354,995)
Market value at 30 June 2008	2,173,011	118,098	47,239	23,620	2,361,968
Cost at 30 June 2008	2,131,659	83,399	16,777	12,872	2,244,707

	2008 £	2007 £
UK Equities	1,399,452	1,675,378
UK Government Stock and Bonds	467,151	472,181
Overseas Equities	267,424	212,897
Uninvested Cash	227,941	278,096
	2,361,968	2,638,552
Dividends and interest on listed investments	100,524	102,873
Interest on cash deposits	189	689
	100,713	103,562

7. STOCK	2008 £	2007 £
Stock	–	2,925

8. DEBTORS	2008 £	2007 £
Other debtors	3,710	4,820
Prepayments	1,774	1,778
	5,484	6,598

9. CREDITORS: Amounts due within one year	2008 £	2007 £
Sundry creditors	7,608	2,786
Taxes and social security	1,444	1,268
Subscriptions received in advance	3,494	3,128
Accruals and deferred income	11,143	18,019
	23,689	25,201

Included within Sundry creditors is an amount of £358 (2007: £Nil) relating to pension liabilities.

10. LEASE COMMITMENTS

The Society has the following annual commitments under non-cancellable operating leases which expire:

	2008 £	2007 £
Within 1 – 2 years	9,846	25,140

11. ENDOWMENT FUNDS	Balance at 1 July 2007 £	Investment Loss £	Balance at 30 June 2008 £
A S Whitfield Prize Fund	49,833	(4,281)	45,552
The David Berry Essay Trust	23,956	(1,449)	22,507
	73,789	(5,730)	68,059

A S Whitfield Prize Fund

The A S Whitfield Prize Fund is an endowment used to provide income for an annual prize for the best first monograph for British history published in the calendar year.

The David Berry Essay Trust

The David Berry Essay Trust is an endowment to provide income for annual prizes for essays on subjects dealing with Scottish history.

12. RESTRICTED FUNDS	Balance at 1 July 2007 £	Incoming Resources £	Outgoing Resources £	Transfers £	Balance at 30 June 2008 £
A S Whitfield Prize Fund	1,983	1,002	(1,298)		1,687
P J Marshall Fellowship	–	10,000	(10,000)	–	–
The David Berry Essay Trust	1,174	189	(250)		1,113
Martin Lynn Bequest	1,000	–	(1,000)	–	–
	4,157	11,191	(12,548)	–	2,800

A S Whitfield Prize Fund Income

Income from the A S Whitfield Prize Fund is used to provide an annual prize for the best first monograph for British history published in the calendar year.

P J Marshall Fellowship

The P J Marshall Fellowship is used to provide a sum sufficient to cover the stipend for a one-year doctoral research fellowship alongside the existing Royal Historical Society Centenary Fellowship at the Institute of Historical Research.

The David Berry Essay Trust Income

Income from the David Berry Trust is to provide annual prizes for essays on subjects dealing with Scottish history.

The Martin Lynn Bequest

This annual bequest is used by the Society to give financial assistance to postgraduates researching topics in African history.

13. DESIGNATED FUND	Balance at 1 July 2007 £	Incoming Resources £	Outgoing Resources £	Investment Loss £	Transfers £	Balance at 30 June 2008 £
E M Robinson Bequest	150,210	5,026	(4,702)	(33,974)	1,538	118,098

E. M. Robinson Bequest

Income from the E M Robinson Bequest is to further the study of history and to date has been used to provide grants to the Dulwich Picture Gallery.

14. GENERAL FUND	Balance at 1 July 2007 £	Incoming Resources £	Outgoing Resources £	Investment Loss £	Transfers £	Balance at 30 June 2008 £
	2,442,044	263,068	(196,524)	(315,291)	(1,538)	2,191,759

15. ANALYSIS OF NET ASSETS BETWEEN FUNDS

	General Fund £	Designated Fund £	Restricted Funds £	Endowment Funds £	Total £
Fixed assets	1,489	–	–	–	1,489
Investments	2,173,011	118,098	2,800	68,059	2,361,968
	2,174,500	118,098	2,800	68,059	2,363,458
Current assets	40,948	–	–	–	40,948
Less: Creditors	(23,689)	–	–	–	(23,689)
Net current assets/(liabilities)	17,258	–	–	–	17,258
Net Assets	2,191,759	118,098	2,800	68,059	2,380,716